Arata
THE LEGEND

3

We are Man, born of Heaven and Earth,
Moon and Sun and everything under them.

Eyes, Ears, Nose, Tongue, Body, Mind...

Purity will pierce evil and
open up the world of darkness.

All life will be reborn and invigorated.

Appear now.

STORY & ART BY
Yuu Watase

Arata
THE LEGEND

CHARACTERS

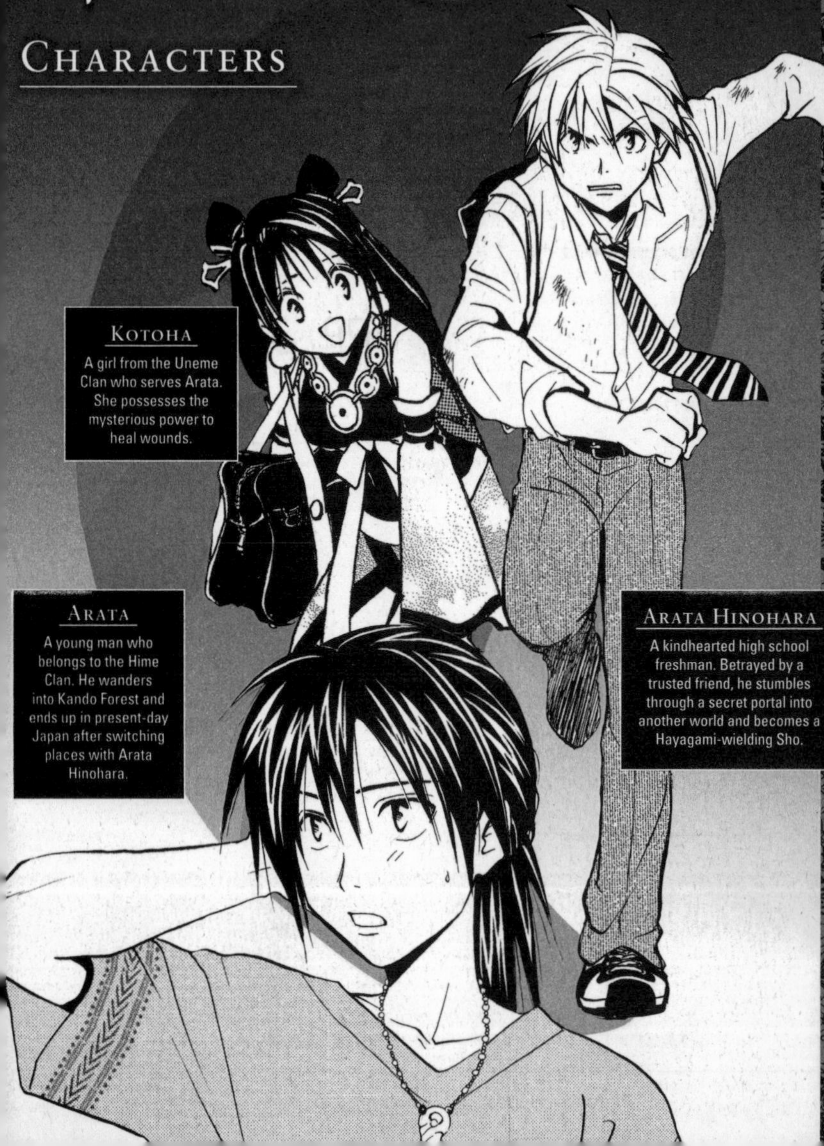

KOTOHA

A girl from the Uneme Clan who serves Arata. She possesses the mysterious power to heal wounds.

ARATA HINOHARA

A kindhearted high school freshman. Betrayed by a trusted friend, he stumbles through a secret portal into another world and becomes a Hayagami-wielding Sho.

ARATA

A young man who belongs to the Hime Clan. He wanders into Kando Forest and ends up in present-day Japan after switching places with Arata Hinohara.

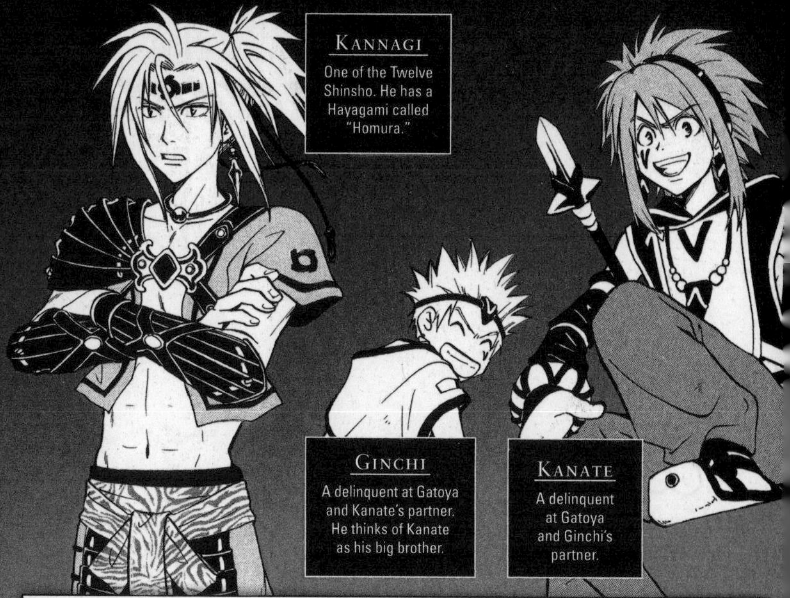

Kannagi

One of the Twelve Shinsho. He has a Hayagami called "Homura."

Ginchi

A delinquent at Gatoya and Kanate's partner. He thinks of Kanate as his big brother.

Kanate

A delinquent at Gatoya and Ginchi's partner.

Present Day

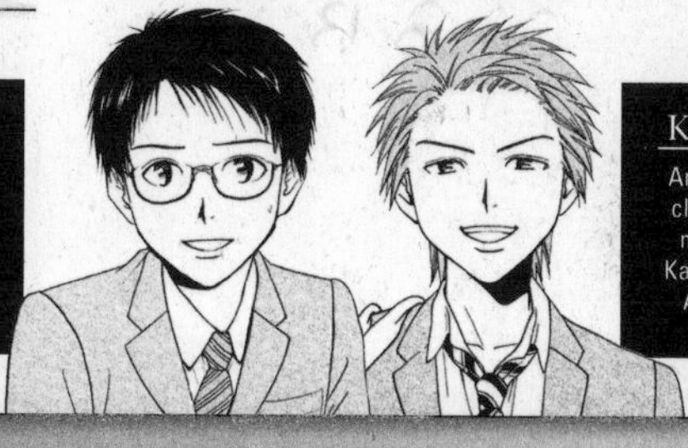

Suguru Nishijima

The first friend Arata makes in high school. Suguru betrays Arata at Kadowaki's request.

Kadowaki

Arata Hinohara's classmate since middle school. Kadowaki targets Arata to bully.

The Story Thus Far

Betrayed by his best friend, Arata Hinohara, a high school student of present-day Japan, wanders into another world where he is framed for the murder of Princess Kikuri and exiled to the prison island of Gatoya.

Gatoya is ruled by a cruel Sho called Tsutsuga who uses the powers of his Hayagami blade to punish and terrorize his prisoners. In order to save Kanate and Ginchi, Arata battles with Tsutsuga only to find that he is no match for Tsutsuga's enormous strength.

However, Arata's determination in the face of defeat awakens his Hayagami from its long slumber. In the end, Tsutsuga has a change of heart because of Arata, and he finds peace after shouldering the pain of betrayal from his past...

3

Arata
THE LEGEND

CONTENTS

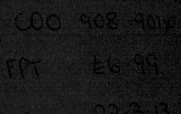

COO 908 901x

FPT   £6-99

22-3-13

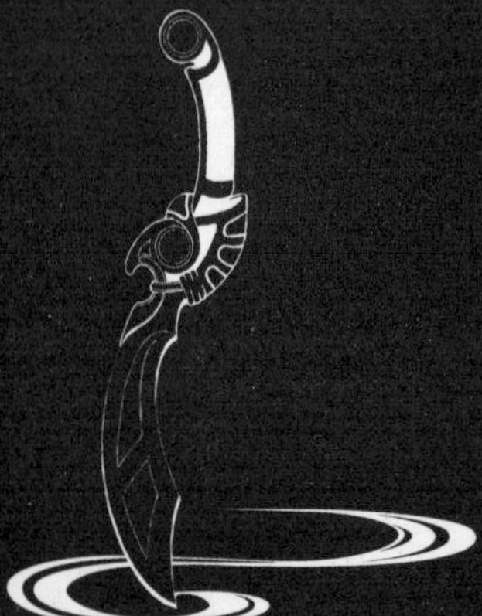

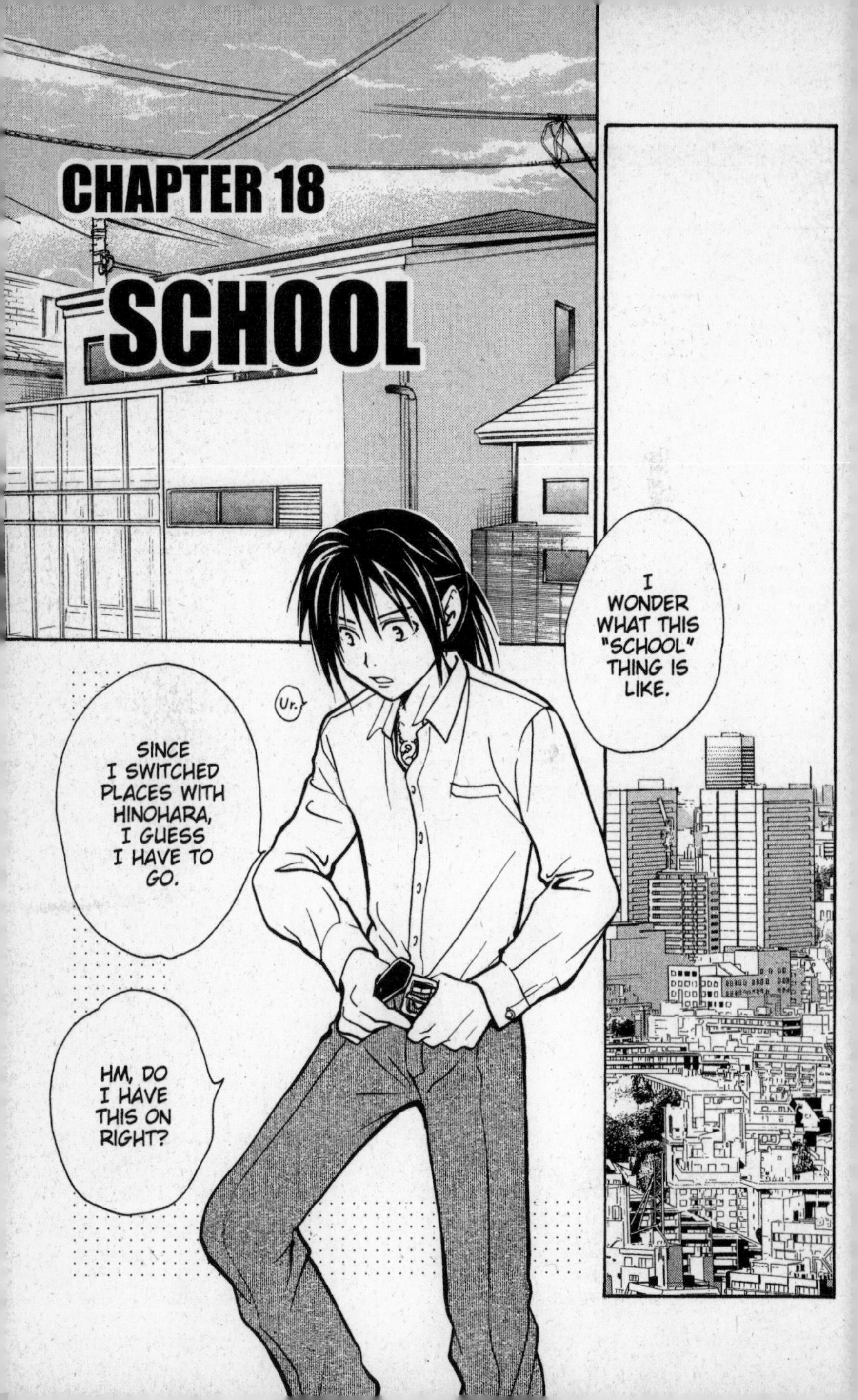
CHAPTER 18
SCHOOL
I WONDER WHAT THIS "SCHOOL" THING IS LIKE.
Ur.
SINCE I SWITCHED PLACES WITH HINOHARA, I GUESS I HAVE TO GO.
HM, DO I HAVE THIS ON RIGHT?

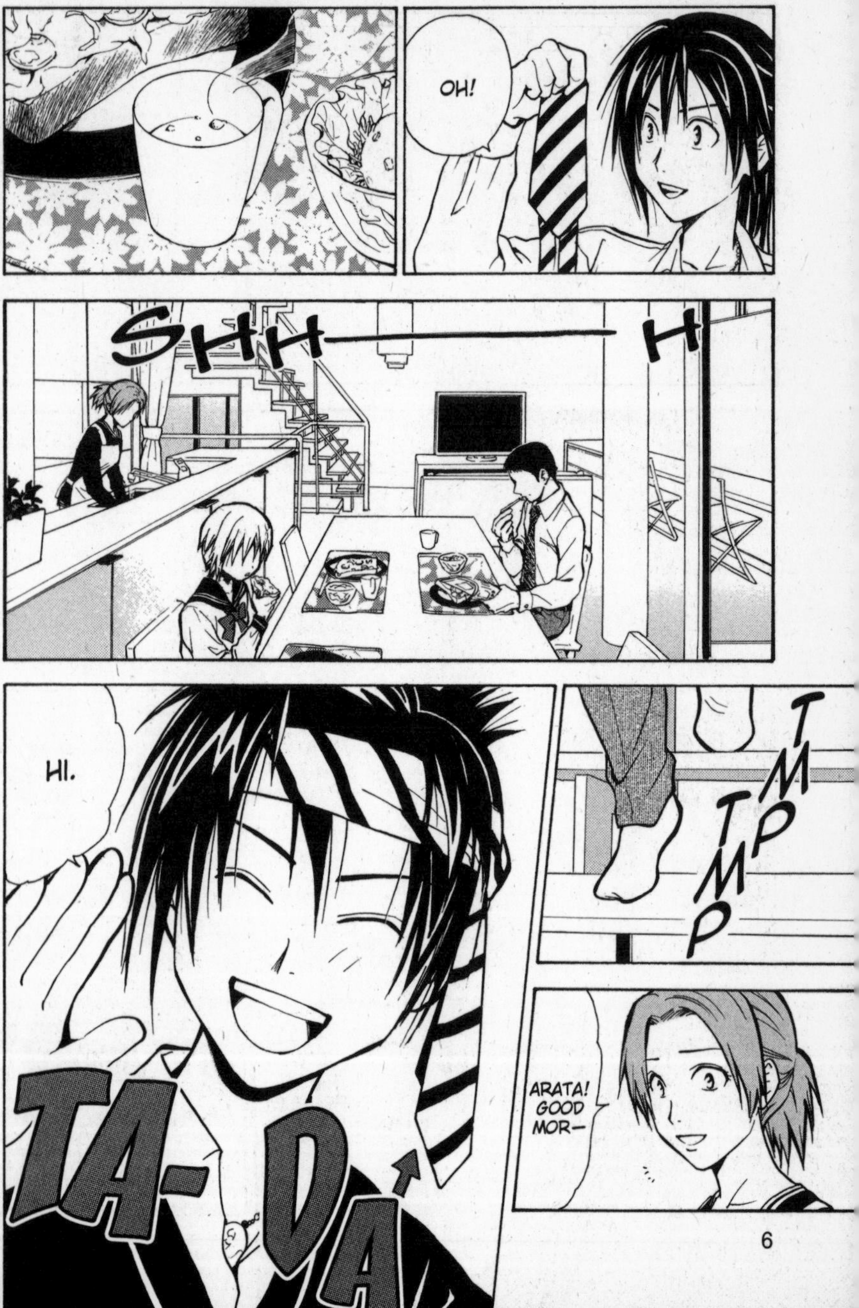
OH!
SHH——H
TMP TMP
ARATA! GOOD MOR—
HI.
TA-DA

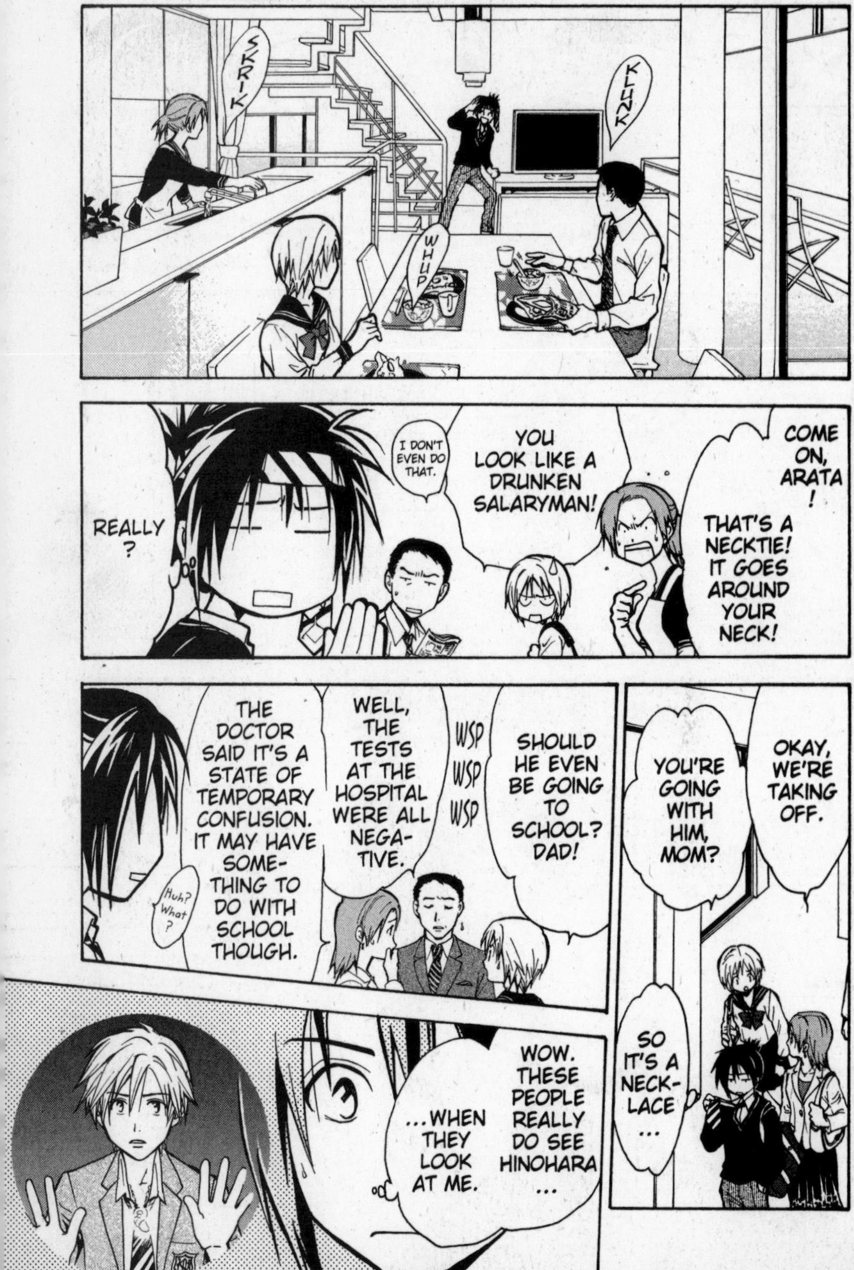
KLUNK
SKRIK
WHUP
COME ON, ARATA!
THAT'S A NECKTIE! IT GOES AROUND YOUR NECK!
YOU LOOK LIKE A DRUNKEN SALARYMAN!
I DON'T EVEN DO THAT.
REALLY?
OKAY, WE'RE TAKING OFF.
YOU'RE GOING WITH HIM, MOM?
SO IT'S A NECK-LACE...
SHOULD HE EVEN BE GOING TO SCHOOL? DAD!
WSP WSP WSP
WELL, THE TESTS AT THE HOSPITAL WERE ALL NEGA-TIVE.
THE DOCTOR SAID IT'S A STATE OF TEMPORARY CONFUSION. IT MAY HAVE SOME-THING TO DO WITH SCHOOL THOUGH.
Huh? What?
WOW. THESE PEOPLE REALLY DO SEE HINOHARA...
...WHEN THEY LOOK AT ME.

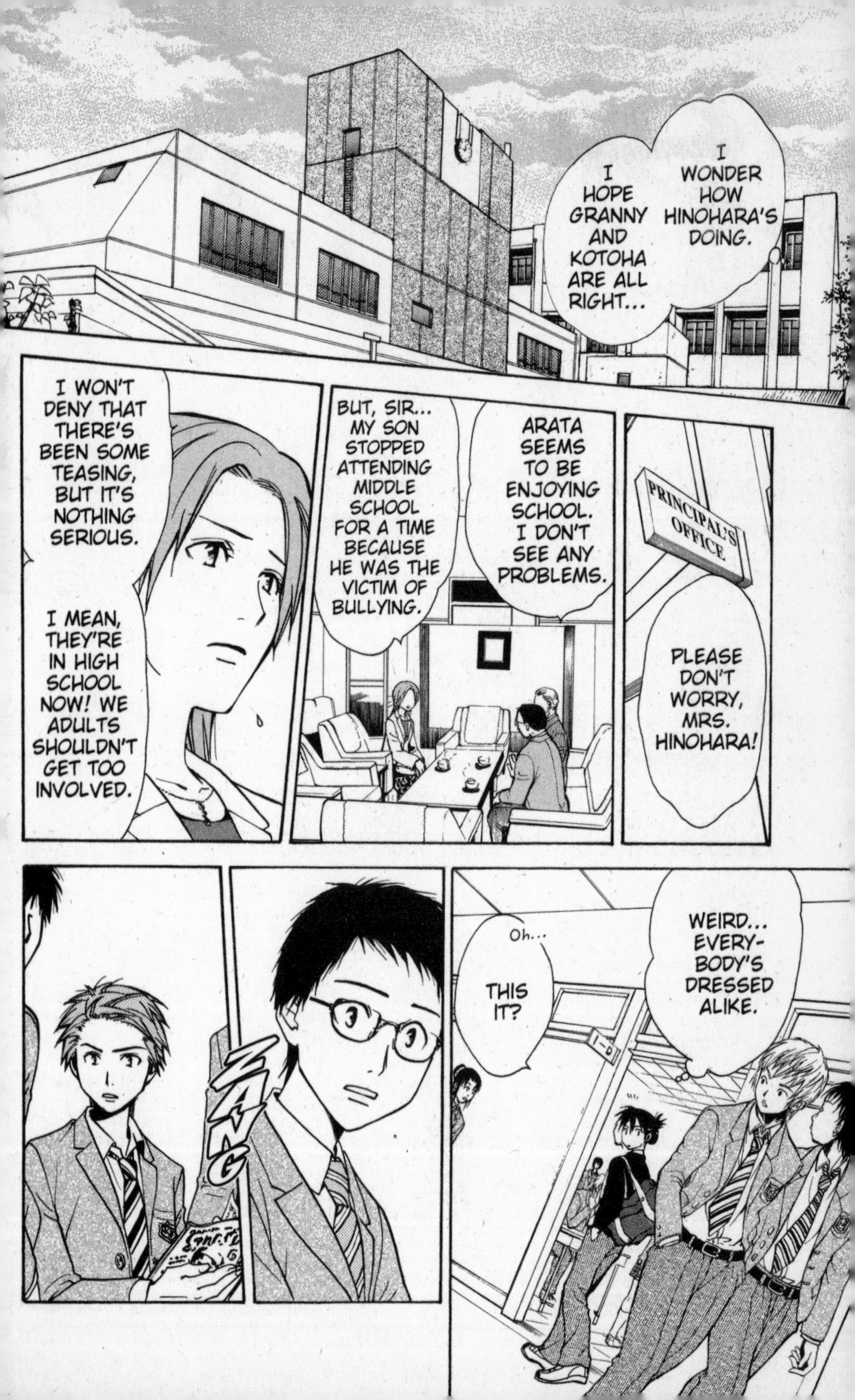
I WONDER HOW HINOHARA'S DOING.
I HOPE GRANNY AND KOTOHA ARE ALL RIGHT...
PRINCIPAL'S OFFICE
PLEASE DON'T WORRY, MRS. HINOHARA!
ARATA SEEMS TO BE ENJOYING SCHOOL. I DON'T SEE ANY PROBLEMS.
BUT, SIR... MY SON STOPPED ATTENDING MIDDLE SCHOOL FOR A TIME BECAUSE HE WAS THE VICTIM OF BULLYING.
I WON'T DENY THAT THERE'S BEEN SOME TEASING, BUT IT'S NOTHING SERIOUS.
I MEAN, THEY'RE IN HIGH SCHOOL NOW! WE ADULTS SHOULDN'T GET TOO INVOLVED.
WEIRD... EVERYBODY'S DRESSED ALIKE.
Oh...
THIS IT?
WANG

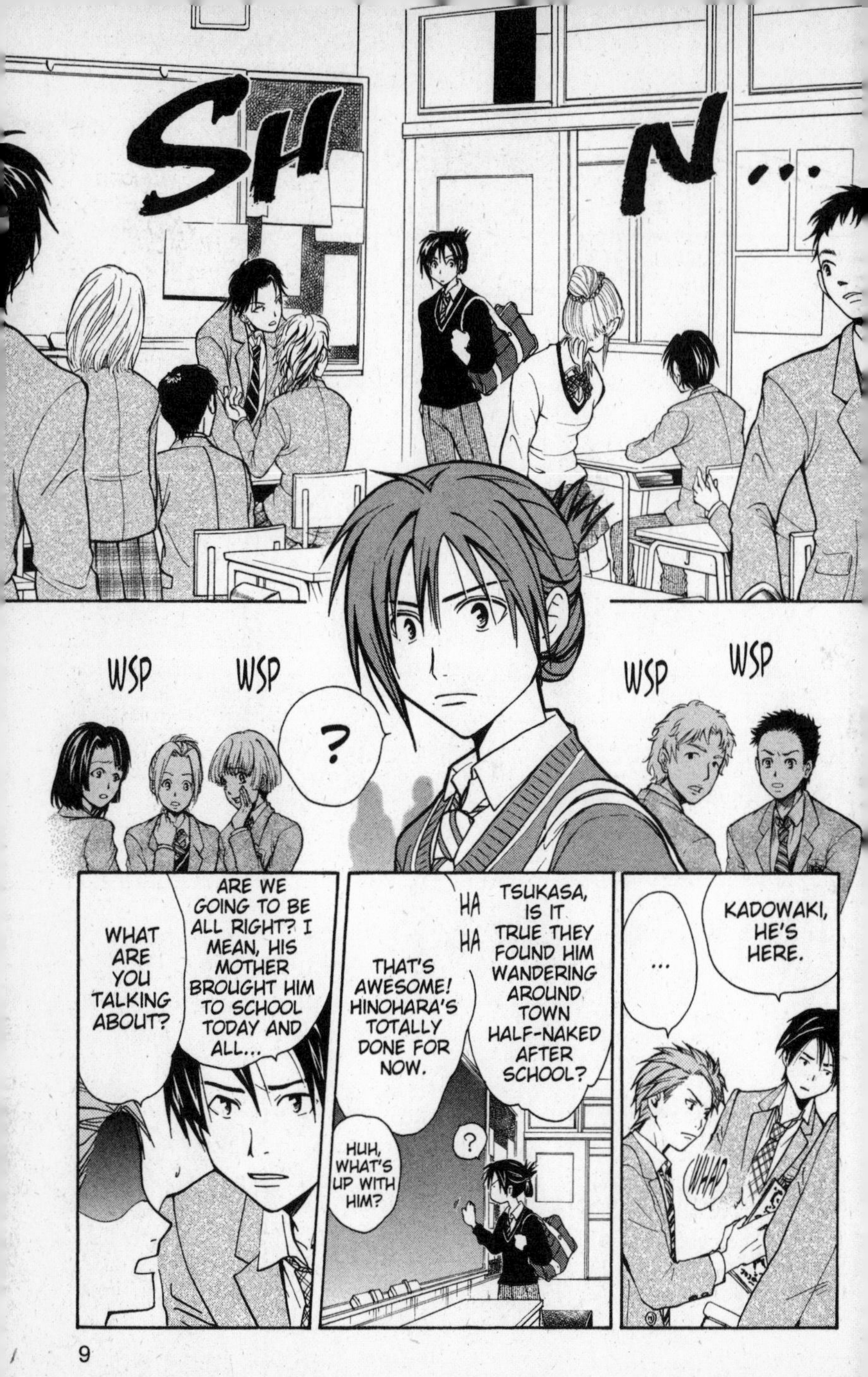
SHIN...
WSP WSP
WSP WSP
?
KADOWAKI, HE'S HERE.
...
WHAP
TSUKASA, IS IT TRUE THEY FOUND HIM WANDERING AROUND TOWN HALF-NAKED AFTER SCHOOL?
HA HA
THAT'S AWESOME! HINOHARA'S TOTALLY DONE FOR NOW.
?
HUH, WHAT'S UP WITH HIM?
ARE WE GOING TO BE ALL RIGHT? I MEAN, HIS MOTHER BROUGHT HIM TO SCHOOL TODAY AND ALL...
WHAT ARE YOU TALKING ABOUT?

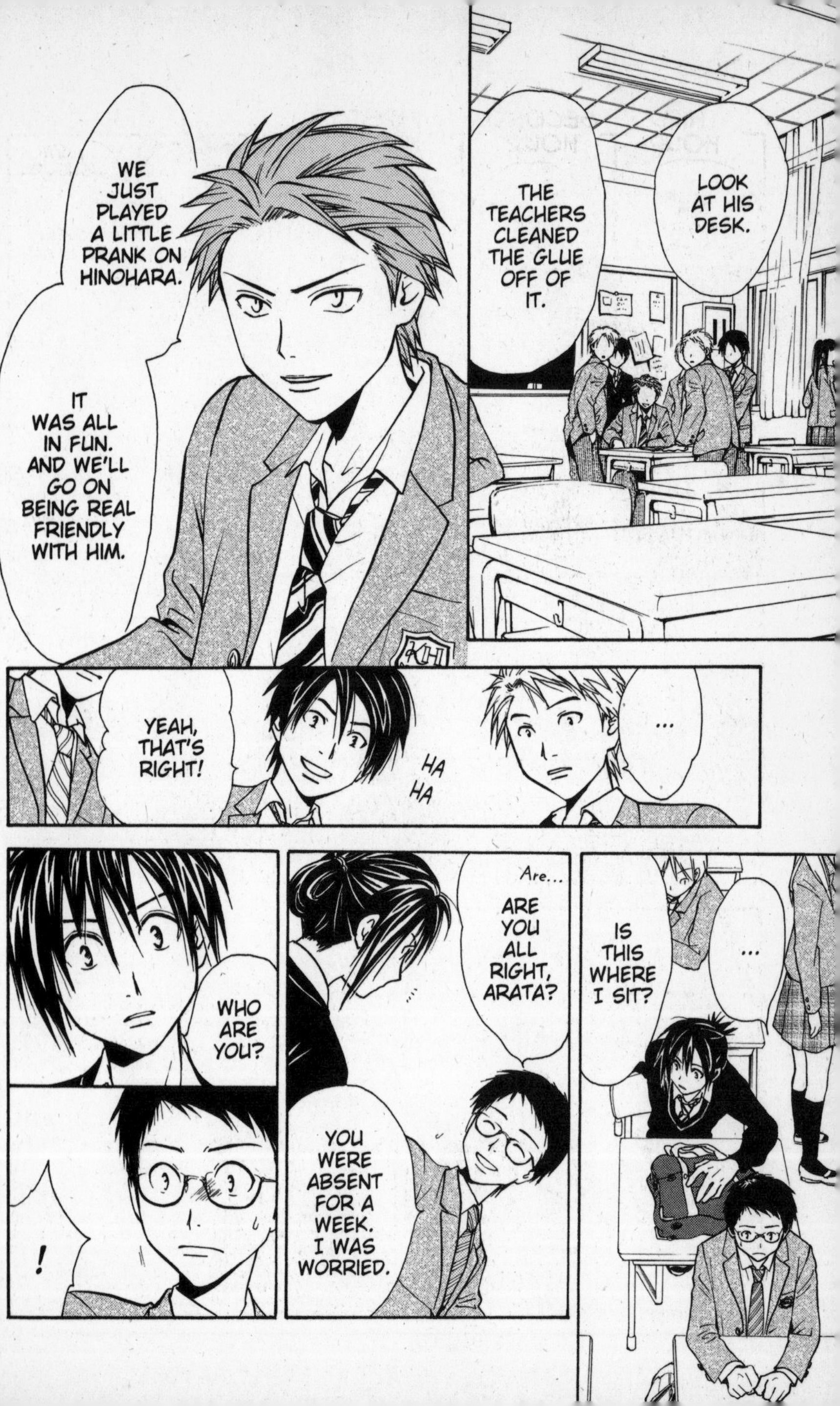
LOOK AT HIS DESK.
THE TEACHERS CLEANED THE GLUE OFF OF IT.
WE JUST PLAYED A LITTLE PRANK ON HINOHARA.
IT WAS ALL IN FUN. AND WE'LL GO ON BEING REAL FRIENDLY WITH HIM.
...
HA HA
YEAH, THAT'S RIGHT!
...
IS THIS WHERE I SIT?
Are...
ARE YOU ALL RIGHT, ARATA?
YOU WERE ABSENT FOR A WEEK. I WAS WORRIED.
WHO ARE YOU?
!

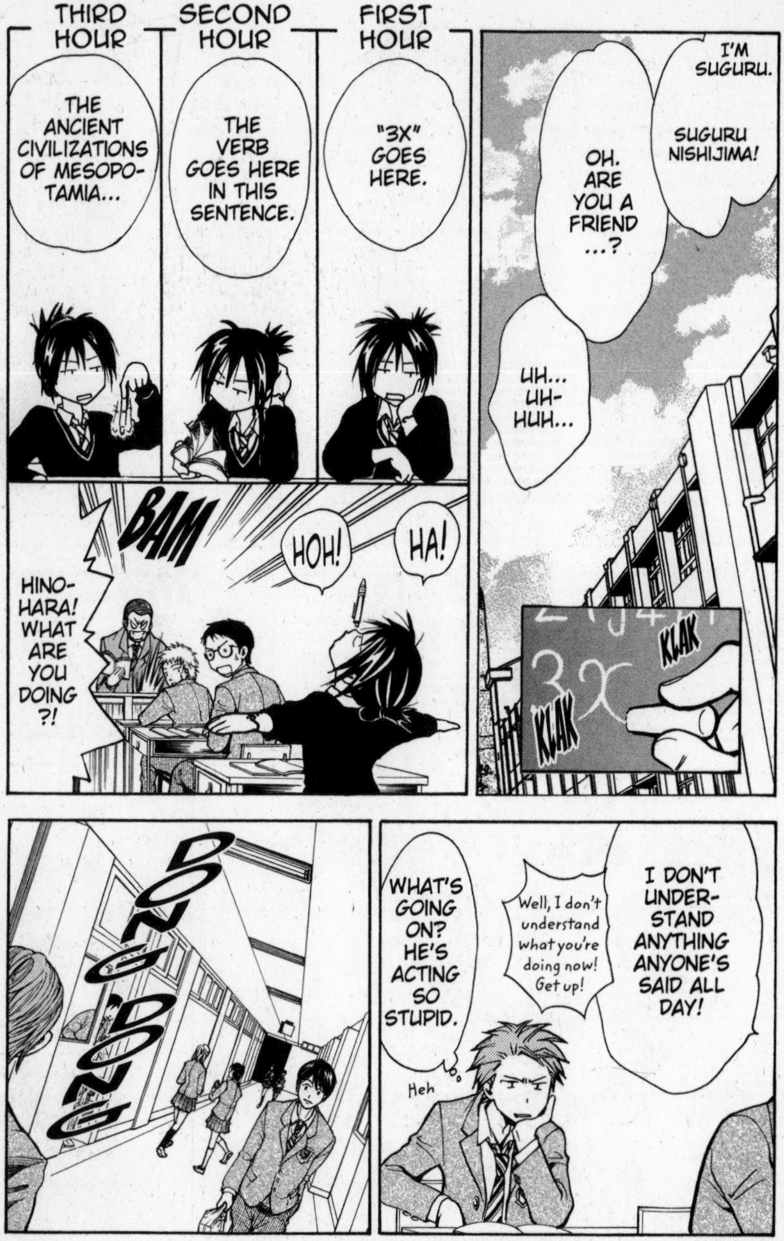
I'M SUGURU.
SUGURU NISHIJIMA!
OH. ARE YOU A FRIEND ...?
UH... UH-HUH...
KLAK
KLAK
FIRST HOUR
"3X" GOES HERE.
SECOND HOUR
THE VERB GOES HERE IN THIS SENTENCE.
THIRD HOUR
THE ANCIENT CIVILIZATIONS OF MESOPO-TAMIA...
HA!
HOH!
BAM
HINO-HARA! WHAT ARE YOU DOING?!
I DON'T UNDER-STAND ANYTHING ANYONE'S SAID ALL DAY!
Well, I don't understand what you're doing now! Get up!
WHAT'S GOING ON? HE'S ACTING SO STUPID.
Heh
DONG DONG

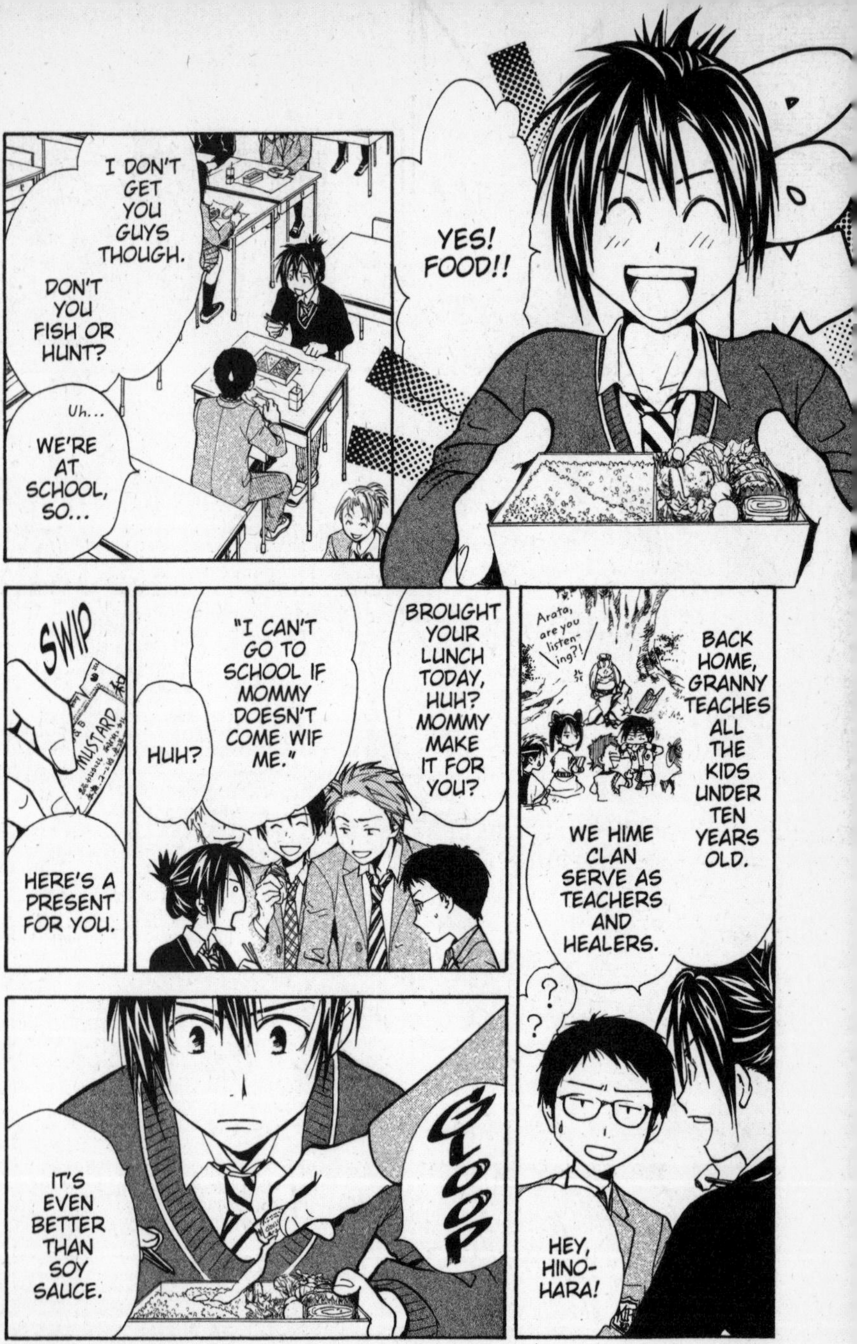
YES! FOOD!!
I DON'T GET YOU GUYS THOUGH.
DON'T YOU FISH OR HUNT?
Uh...
WE'RE AT SCHOOL, SO...
BACK HOME, GRANNY TEACHES ALL THE KIDS UNDER TEN YEARS OLD.
Arata, are you listen-ing?!
WE HIME CLAN SERVE AS TEACHERS AND HEALERS.
?
?
HEY, HINO-HARA!
BROUGHT YOUR LUNCH TODAY, HUH? MOMMY MAKE IT FOR YOU?
"I CAN'T GO TO SCHOOL IF MOMMY DOESN'T COME WIF ME."
HUH?
SWIP
MUSTARD
HERE'S A PRESENT FOR YOU.
GLOOP
IT'S EVEN BETTER THAN SOY SAUCE.

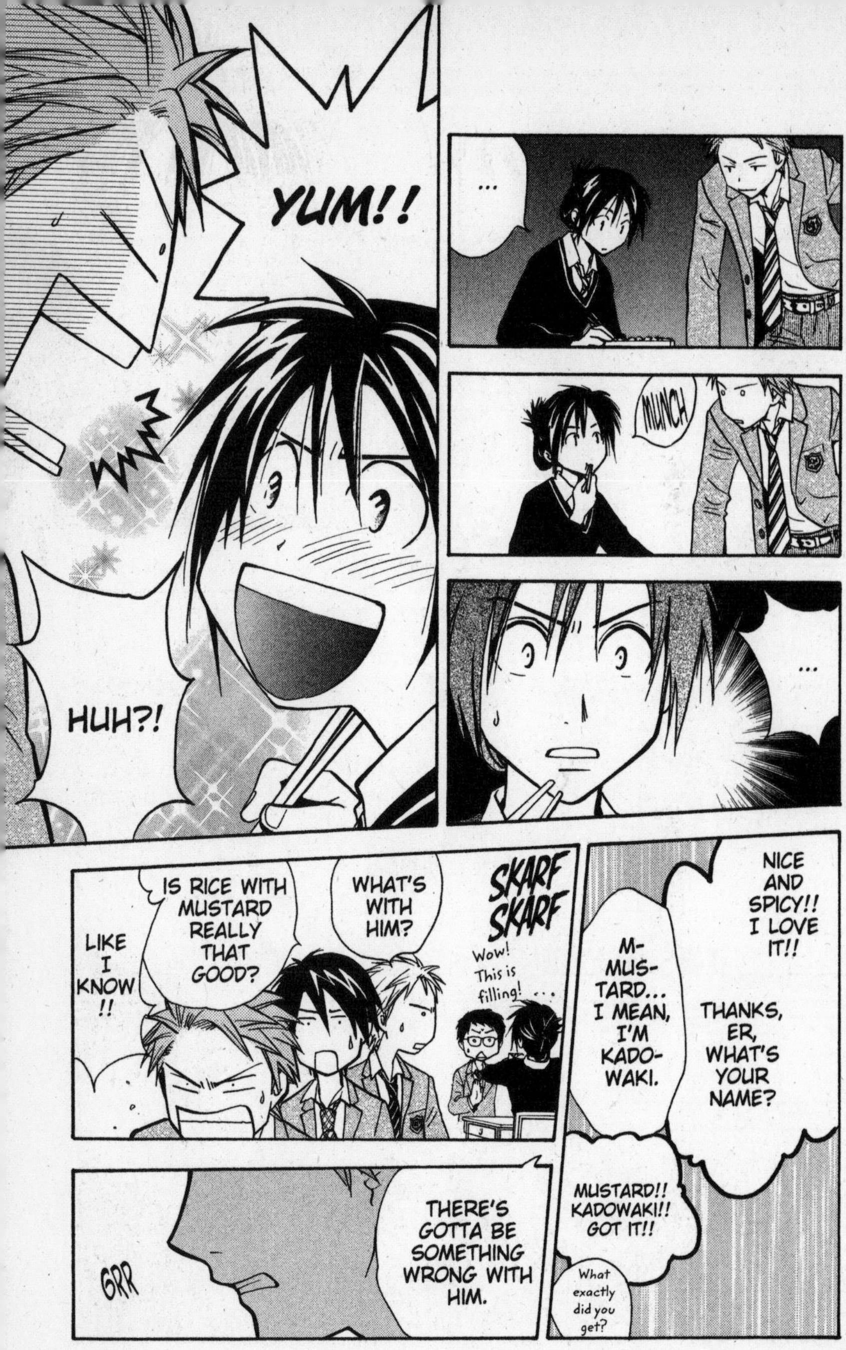
...
MUNCH
...
YUM!!
HUH?!
NICE AND SPICY!! I LOVE IT!!
THANKS, ER, WHAT'S YOUR NAME?
M-MUSTARD... I MEAN, I'M KADOWAKI.
MUSTARD!! KADOWAKI!! GOT IT!!
What exactly did you get?
SKARF SKARF
Wow! This is filling!
...
WHAT'S WITH HIM?
IS RICE WITH MUSTARD REALLY THAT GOOD?
LIKE I KNOW!!
THERE'S GOTTA BE SOMETHING WRONG WITH HIM.
GRR

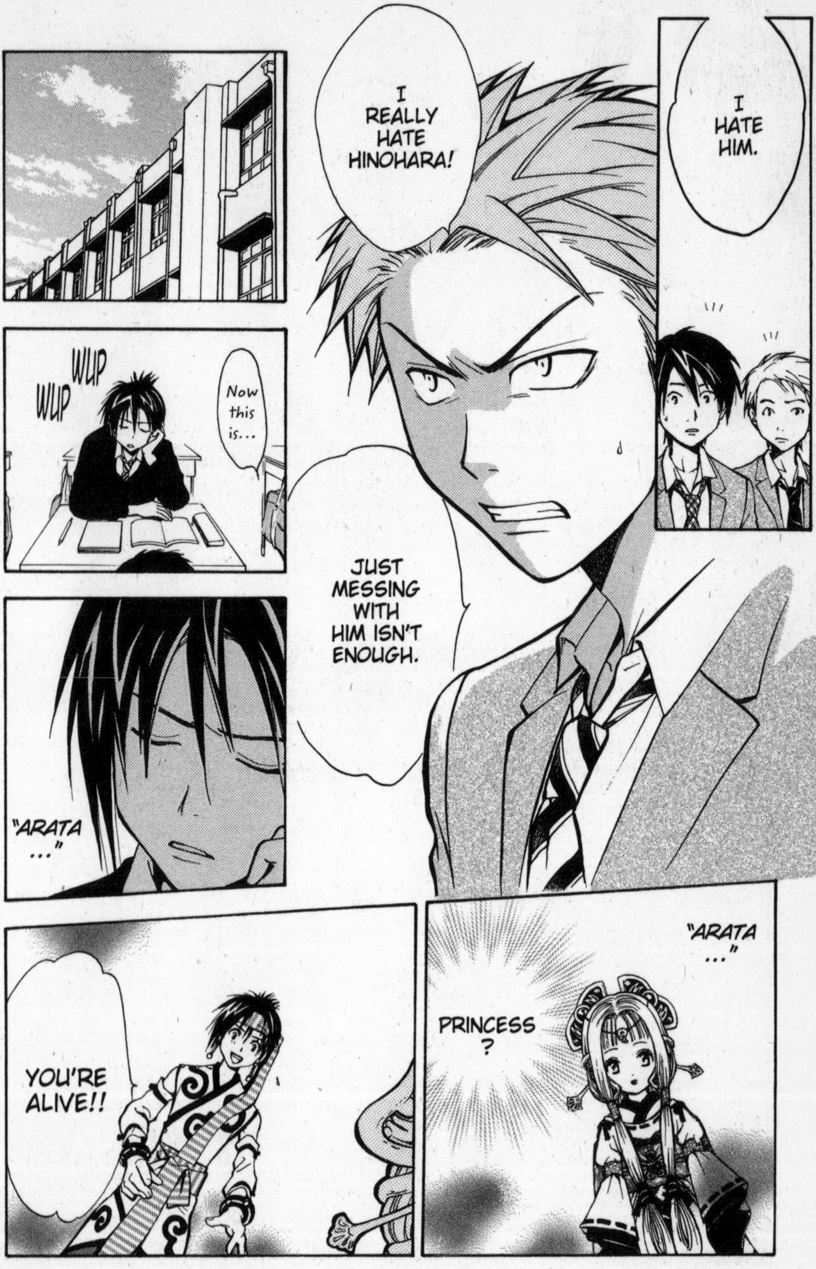
I HATE HIM.
I REALLY HATE HINOHARA!
JUST MESSING WITH HIM ISN'T ENOUGH.
WUP WUP
Now this is...
"ARATA ..."
"ARATA ..."
PRINCESS ?
YOU'RE ALIVE!!

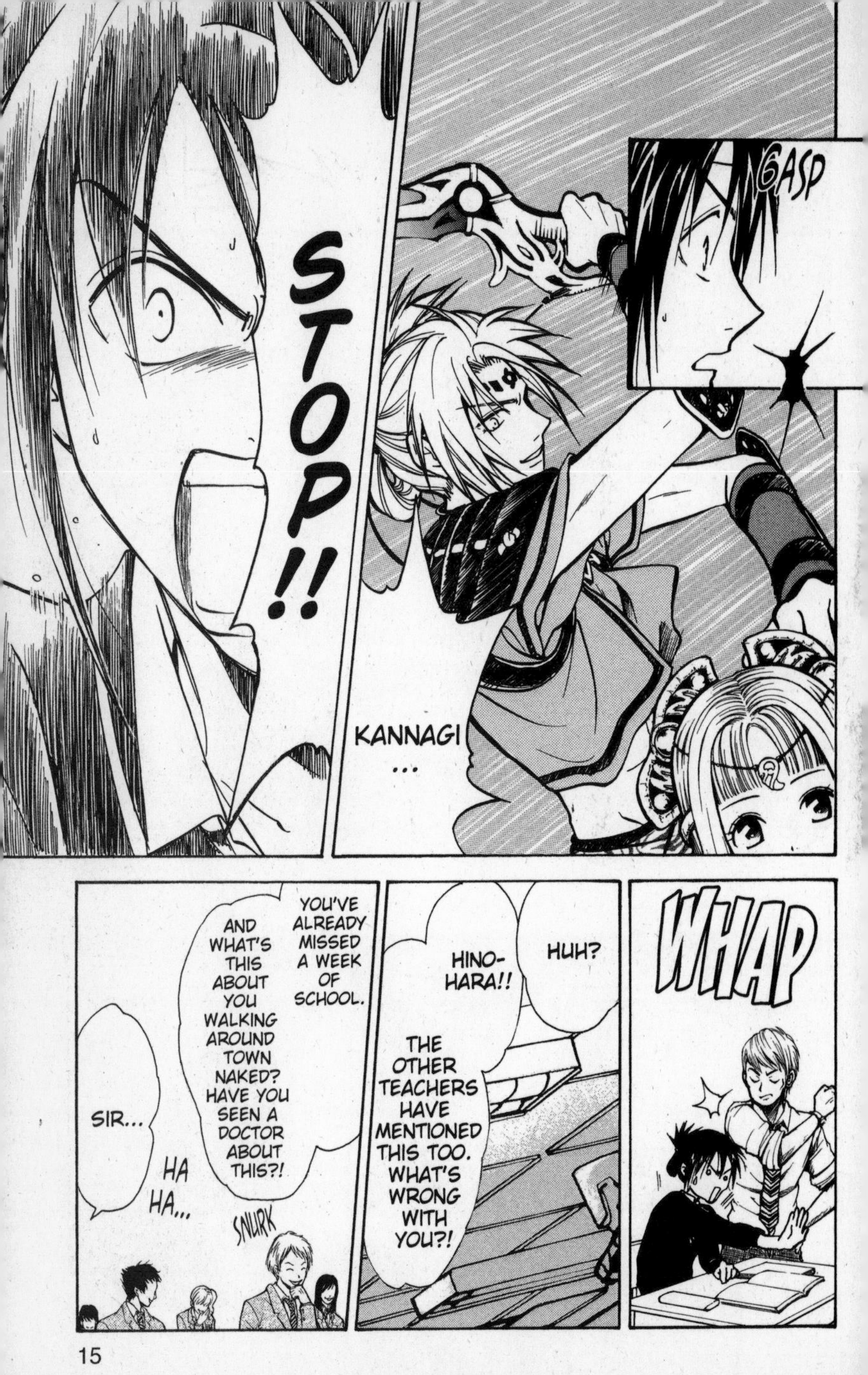
GASP
KANNAGI ...
STOP!!
WHAP
HUH?
HINO-HARA!!
THE OTHER TEACHERS HAVE MENTIONED THIS TOO. WHAT'S WRONG WITH YOU?!
YOU'VE ALREADY MISSED A WEEK OF SCHOOL.
AND WHAT'S THIS ABOUT YOU WALKING AROUND TOWN NAKED? HAVE YOU SEEN A DOCTOR ABOUT THIS?!
SIR...
HA HA...
SNURK

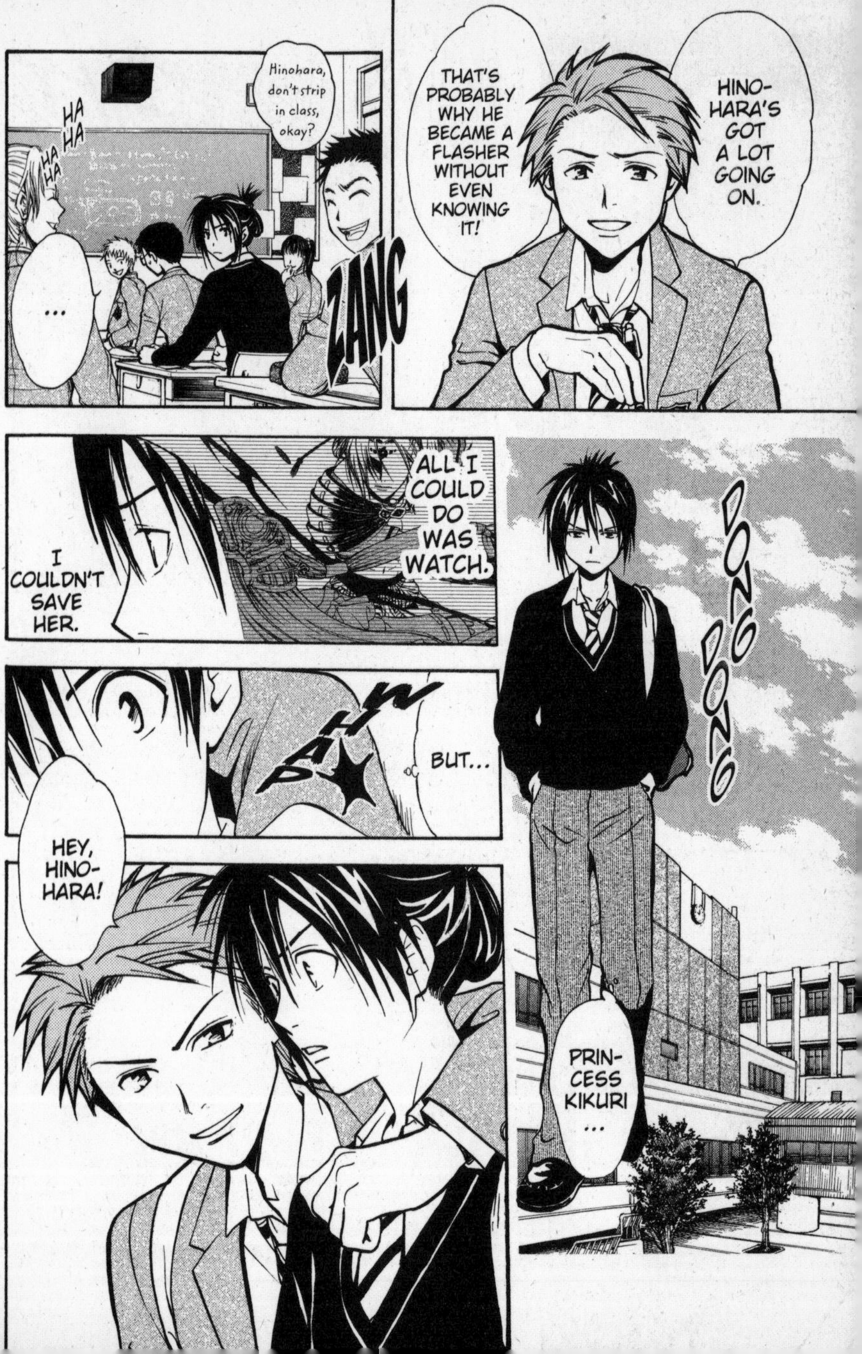
HINO-HARA'S GOT A LOT GOING ON.
THAT'S PROBABLY WHY HE BECAME A FLASHER WITHOUT EVEN KNOWING IT!
Hinohara, don't strip in class, okay?
ZANG
HA HA
HA HA
...
DONG DONG DONG
PRIN-CESS KIKURI ...
ALL I COULD DO WAS WATCH.
I COULDN'T SAVE HER.
WHAP
BUT...
HEY, HINO-HARA!

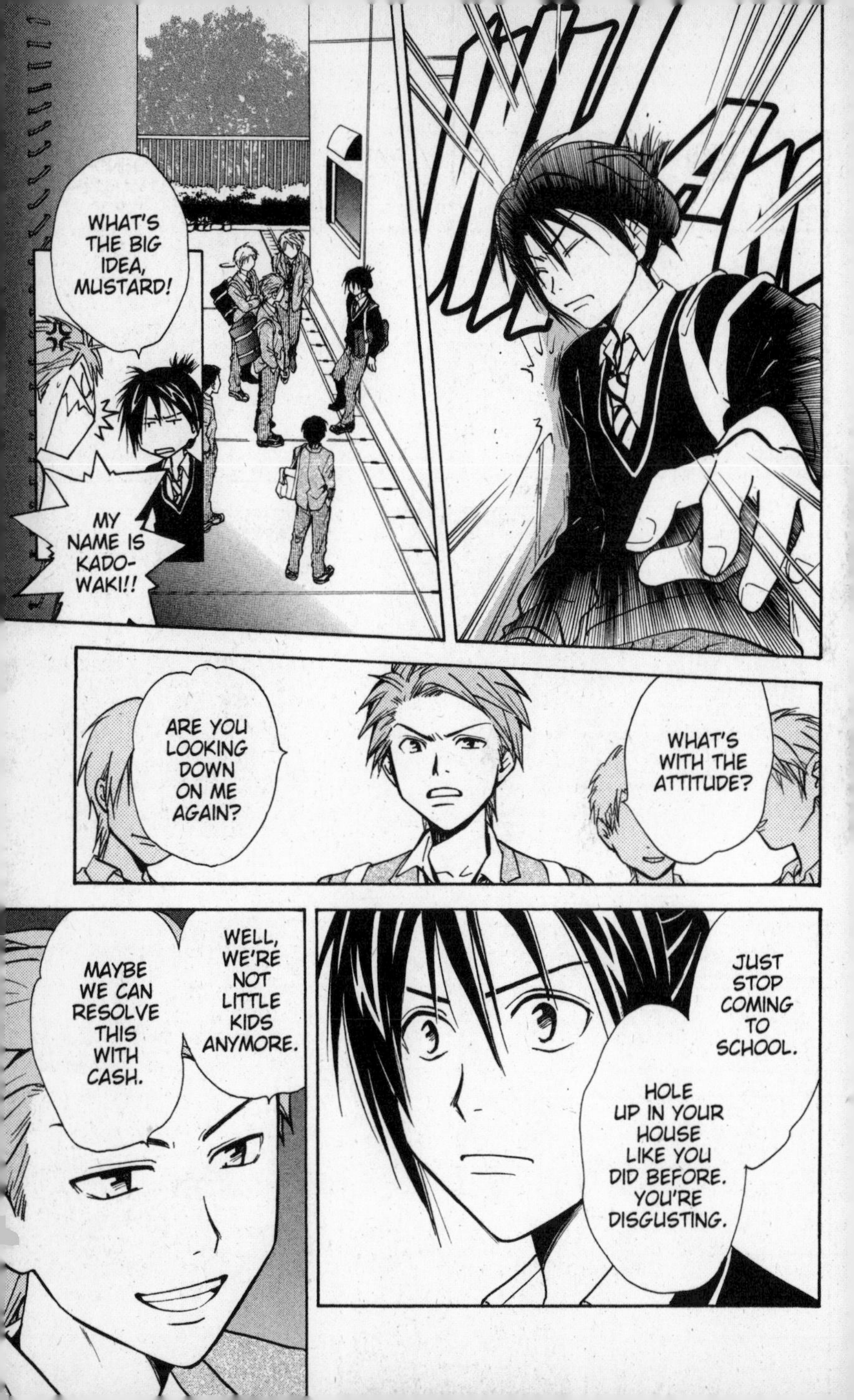
WHAT'S THE BIG IDEA, MUSTARD!
MY NAME IS KADO-WAKI!!
WHAT'S WITH THE ATTITUDE?
ARE YOU LOOKING DOWN ON ME AGAIN?
JUST STOP COMING TO SCHOOL.
HOLE UP IN YOUR HOUSE LIKE YOU DID BEFORE. YOU'RE DISGUSTING.
WELL, WE'RE NOT LITTLE KIDS ANYMORE.
MAYBE WE CAN RESOLVE THIS WITH CASH.

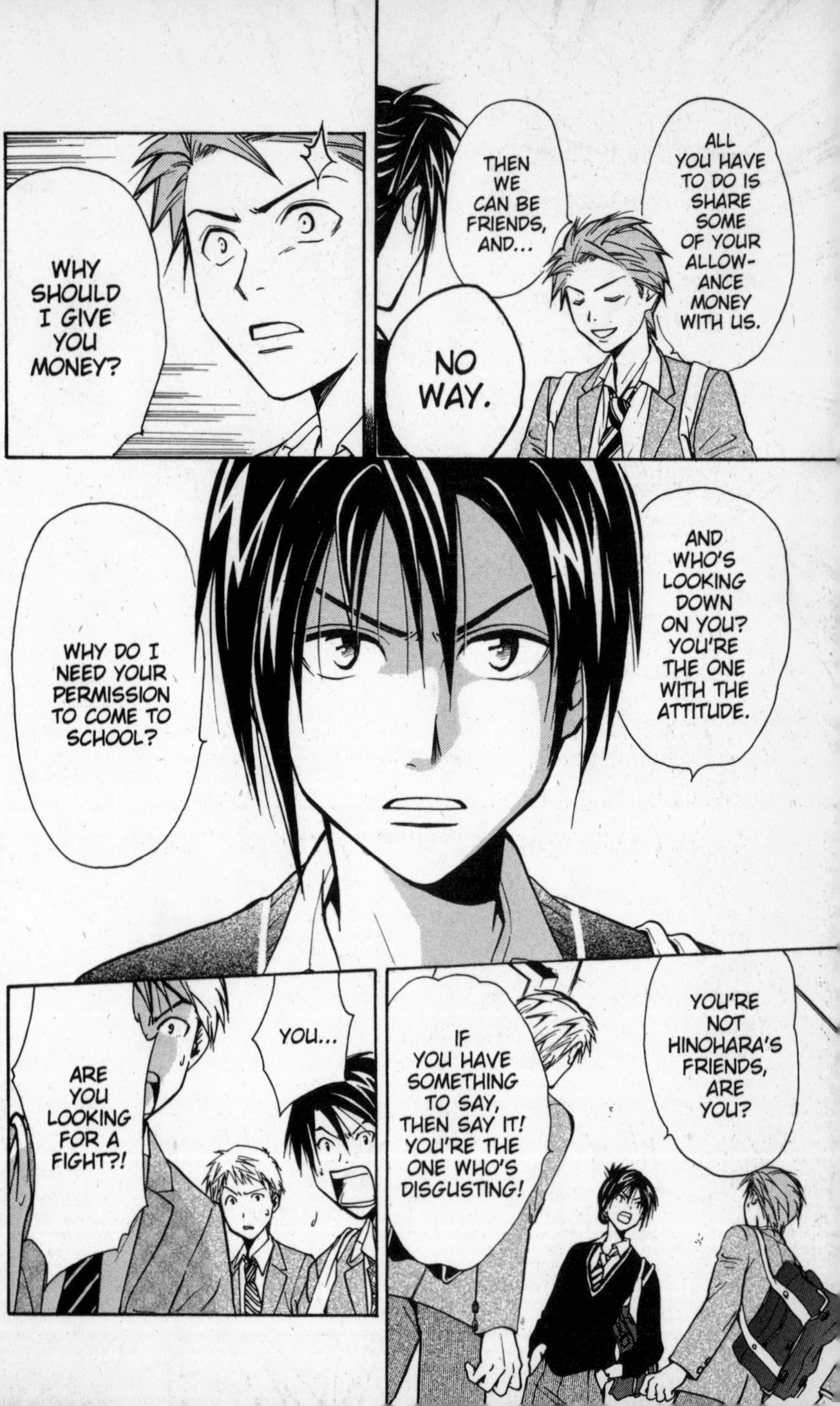
ALL YOU HAVE TO DO IS SHARE SOME OF YOUR ALLOW-ANCE MONEY WITH US.
THEN WE CAN BE FRIENDS, AND...
NO WAY.
WHY SHOULD I GIVE YOU MONEY?
AND WHO'S LOOKING DOWN ON YOU? YOU'RE THE ONE WITH THE ATTITUDE.
WHY DO I NEED YOUR PERMISSION TO COME TO SCHOOL?
YOU'RE NOT HINOHARA'S FRIENDS, ARE YOU?
IF YOU HAVE SOMETHING TO SAY, THEN SAY IT! YOU'RE THE ONE WHO'S DISGUSTING!
YOU...
ARE YOU LOOKING FOR A FIGHT?!

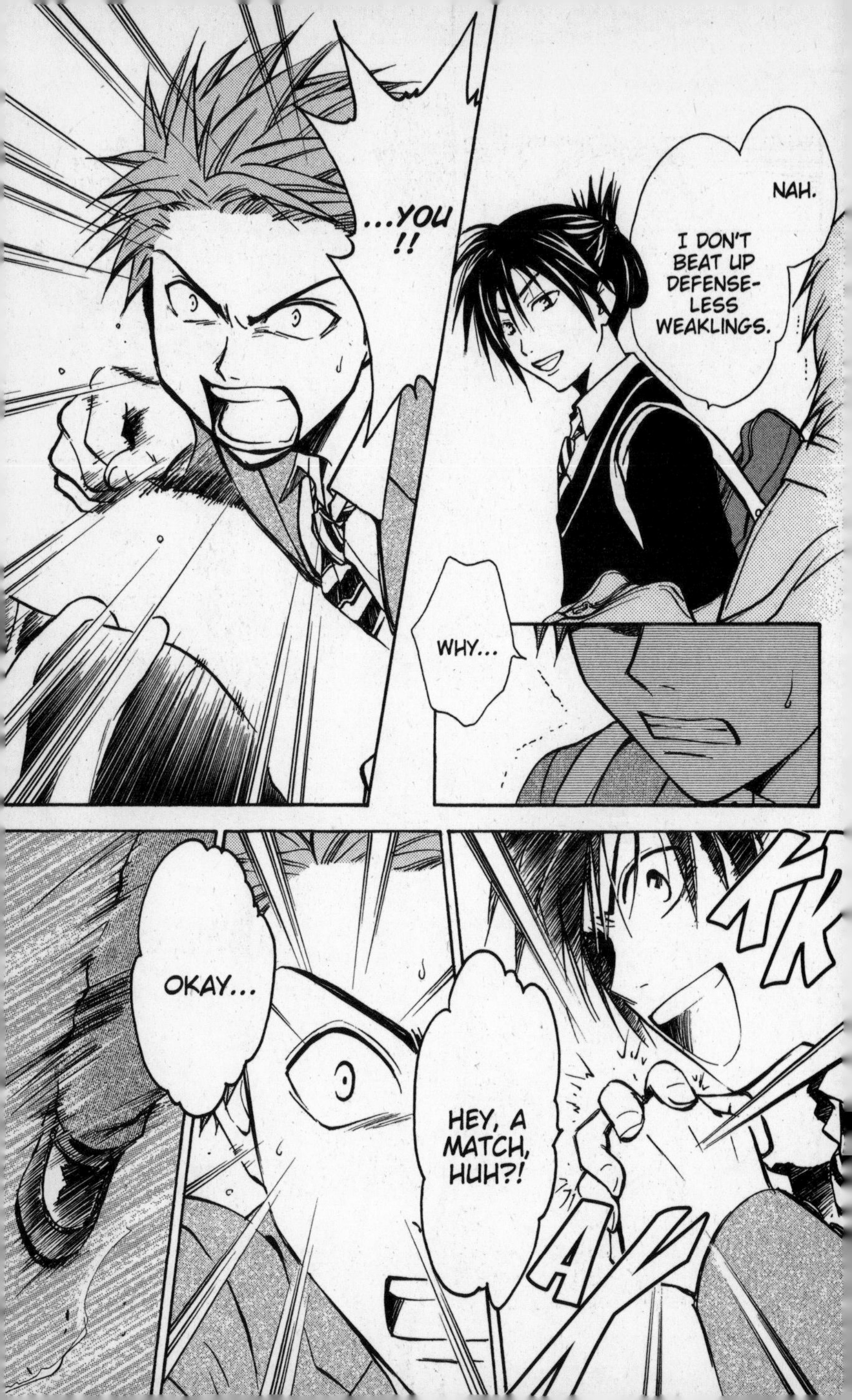
NAH.
I DON'T BEAT UP DEFENSE-LESS WEAKLINGS.
WHY...
...YOU!!
HEY, A MATCH, HUH?!
OKAY...

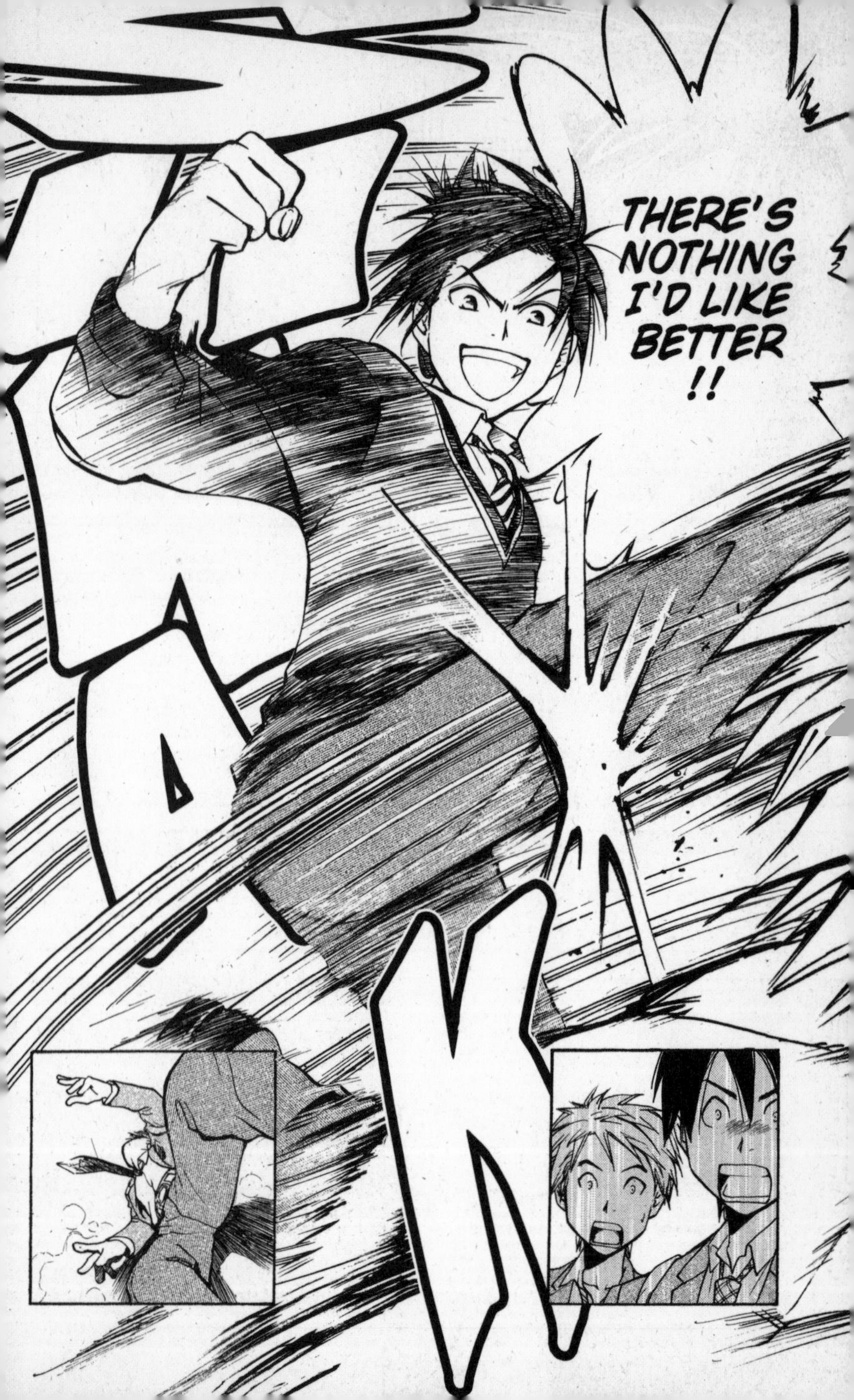
THERE'S NOTHING I'D LIKE BETTER !!

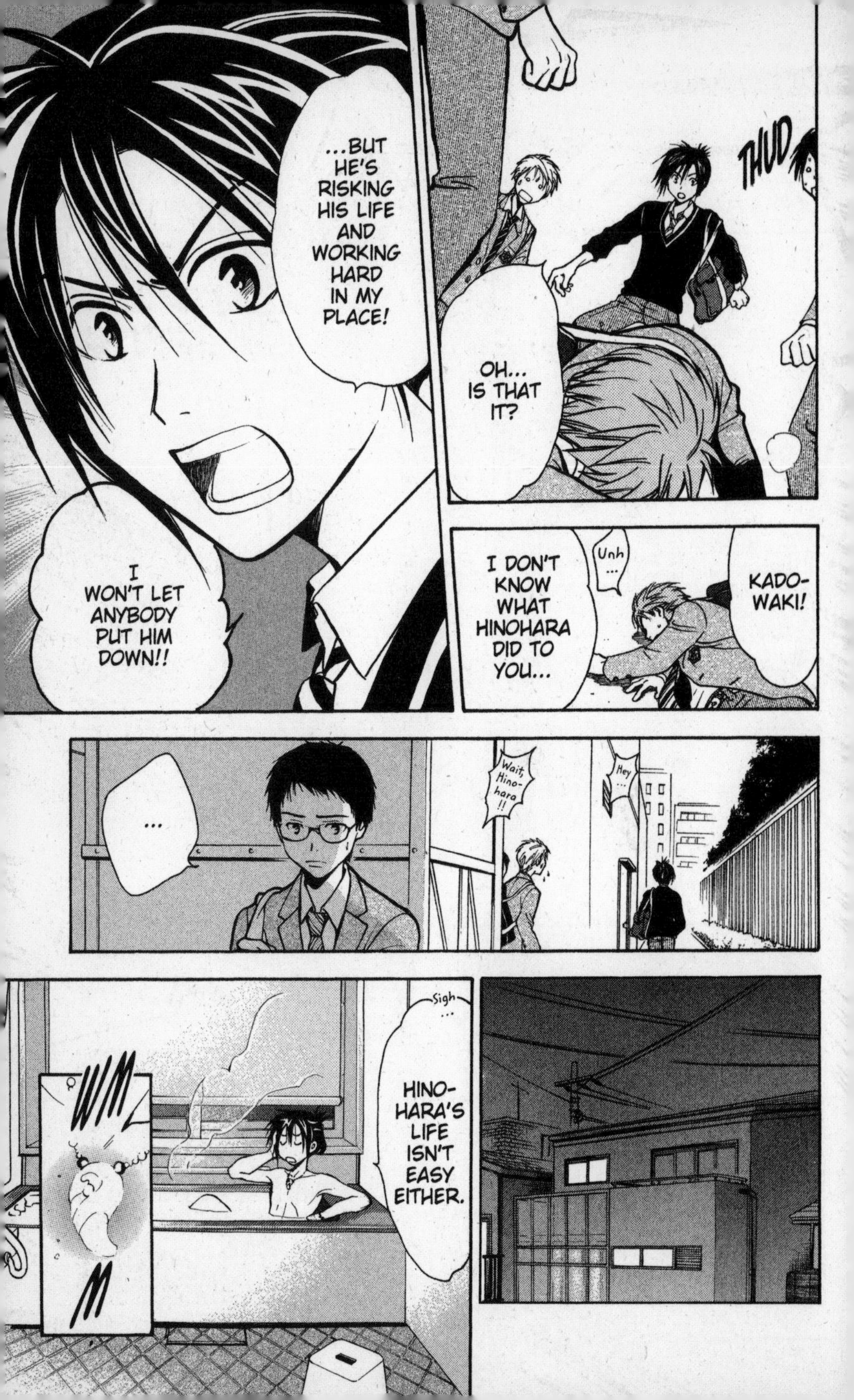
THUD
OH... IS THAT IT?
KADO-WAKI!
Unh...
I DON'T KNOW WHAT HINOHARA DID TO YOU...
...BUT HE'S RISKING HIS LIFE AND WORKING HARD IN MY PLACE!
I WON'T LET ANYBODY PUT HIM DOWN!!
Hey...
Wait, Hinohara!!
...
Sigh...
HINOHARA'S LIFE ISN'T EASY EITHER.

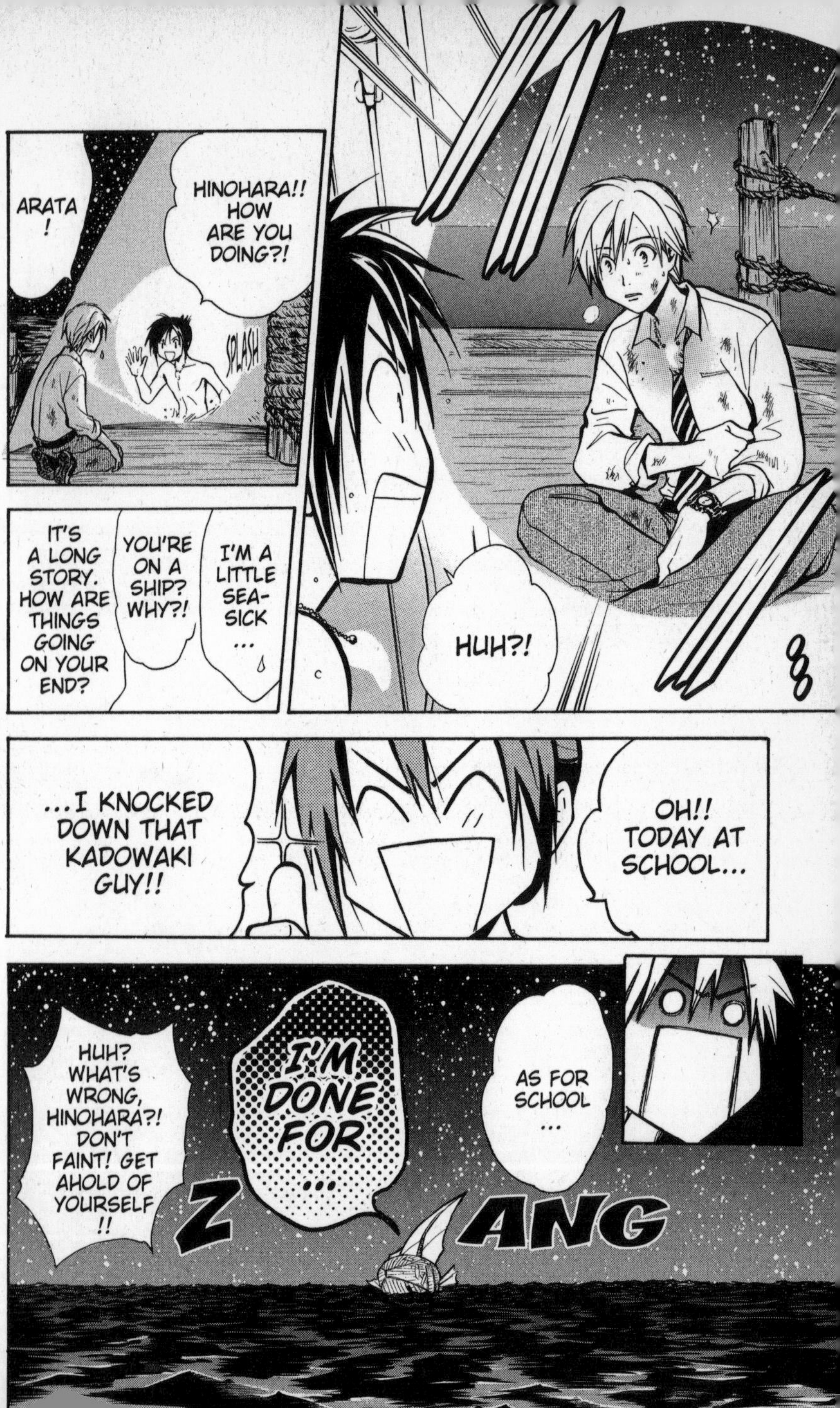
HUH?!
HINOHARA!! HOW ARE YOU DOING?!
ARATA!
SPLASH
I'M A LITTLE SEA-SICK...
YOU'RE ON A SHIP? WHY?!
IT'S A LONG STORY. HOW ARE THINGS GOING ON YOUR END?
OH!! TODAY AT SCHOOL...
...I KNOCKED DOWN THAT KADOWAKI GUY!!
AS FOR SCHOOL...
I'M DONE FOR...
HUH? WHAT'S WRONG, HINOHARA?! DON'T FAINT! GET AHOLD OF YOURSELF!!
Z ANG

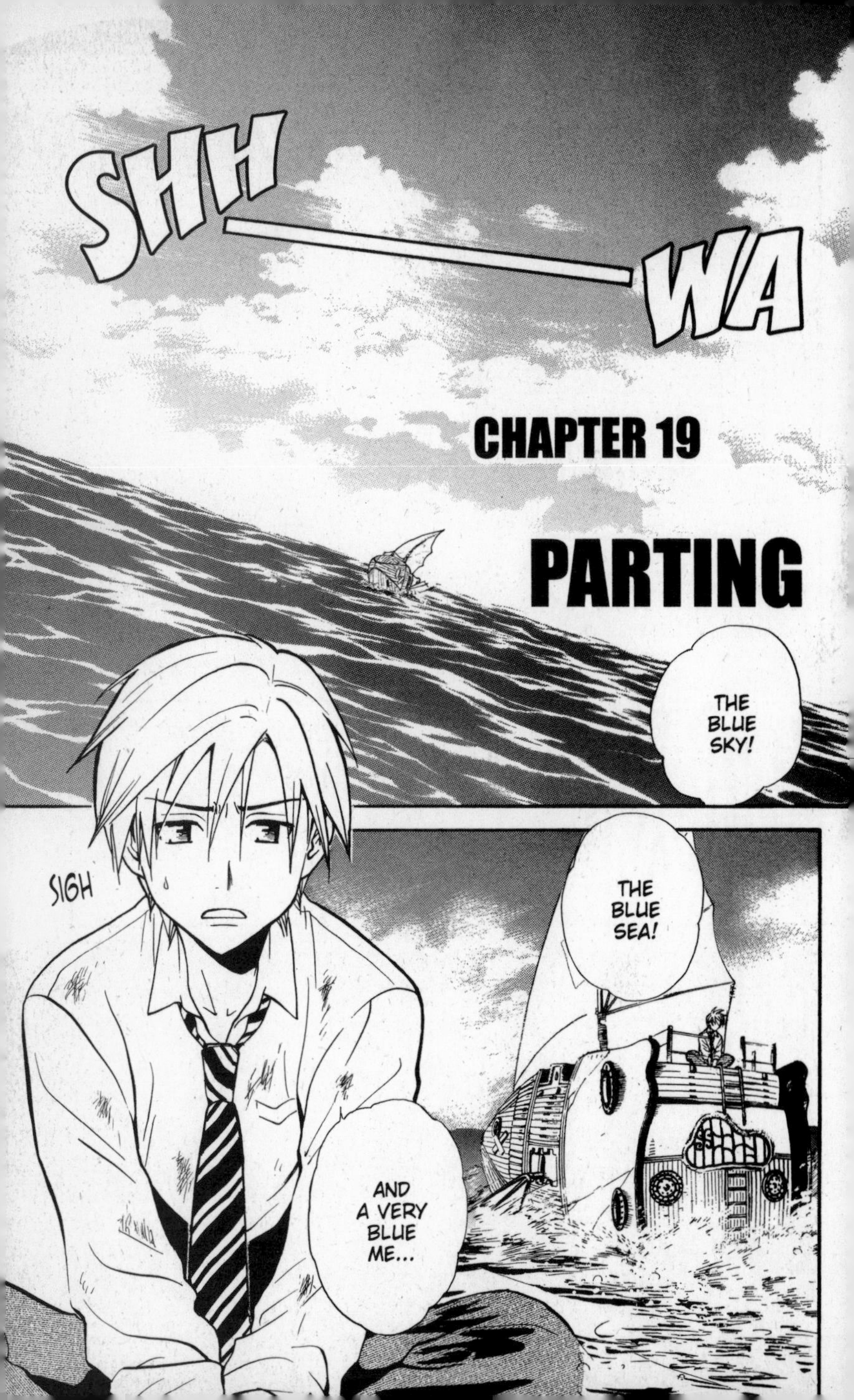
SHH—WA
CHAPTER 19
PARTING
THE BLUE SKY!
THE BLUE SEA!
AND A VERY BLUE ME...
SIGH

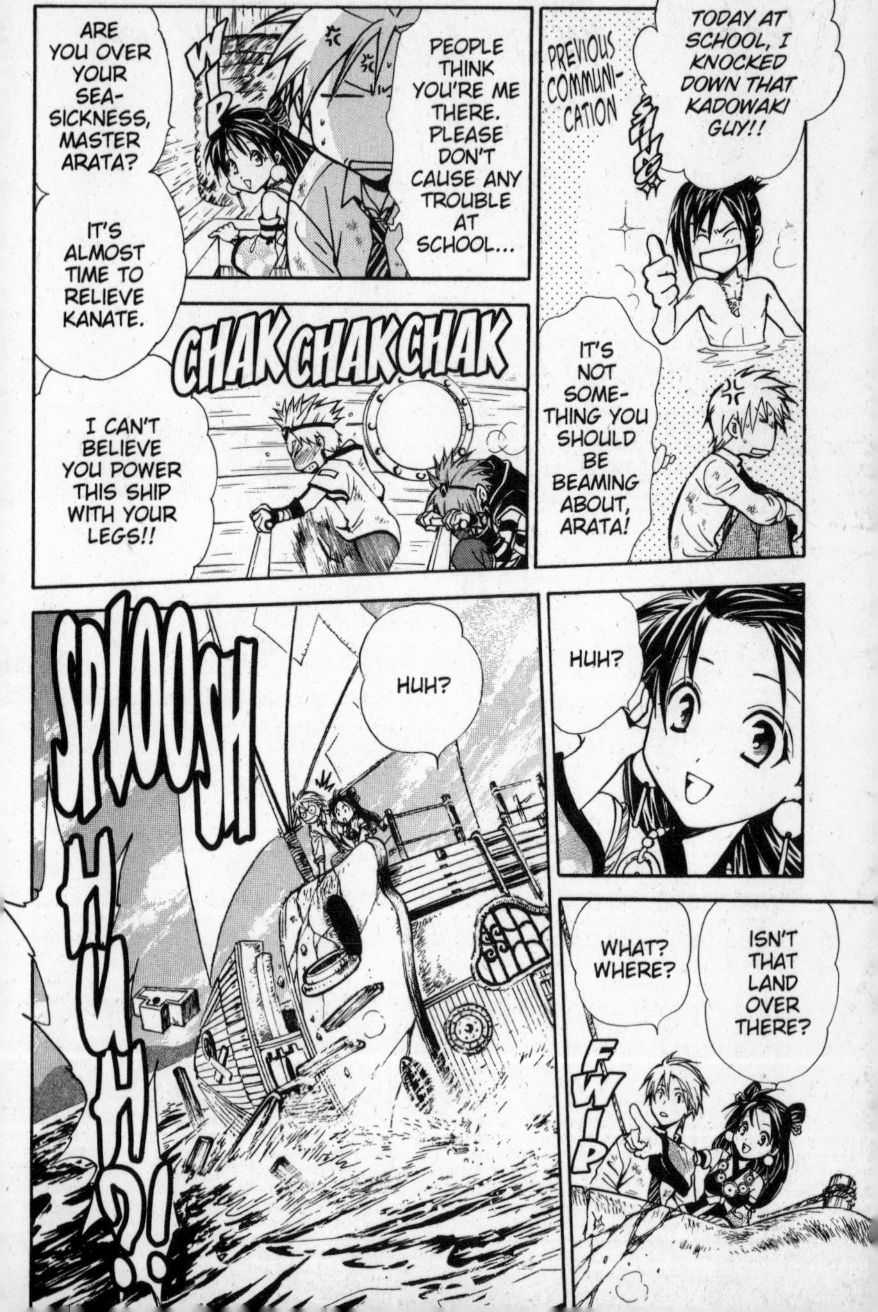
TODAY AT SCHOOL, I KNOCKED DOWN THAT KADOWAKI GUY!!
PREVIOUS COMMUNICATION
IT'S NOT SOMETHING YOU SHOULD BE BEAMING ABOUT, ARATA!
PEOPLE THINK YOU'RE ME THERE. PLEASE DON'T CAUSE ANY TROUBLE AT SCHOOL...
WIP
ARE YOU OVER YOUR SEA-SICKNESS, MASTER ARATA?
IT'S ALMOST TIME TO RELIEVE KANATE.
CHAK CHAK CHAK
I CAN'T BELIEVE YOU POWER THIS SHIP WITH YOUR LEGS!!
HUH?
ISN'T THAT LAND OVER THERE?
WHAT? WHERE?
FWIP
HUH?
SPLOOSH
HUUH?!

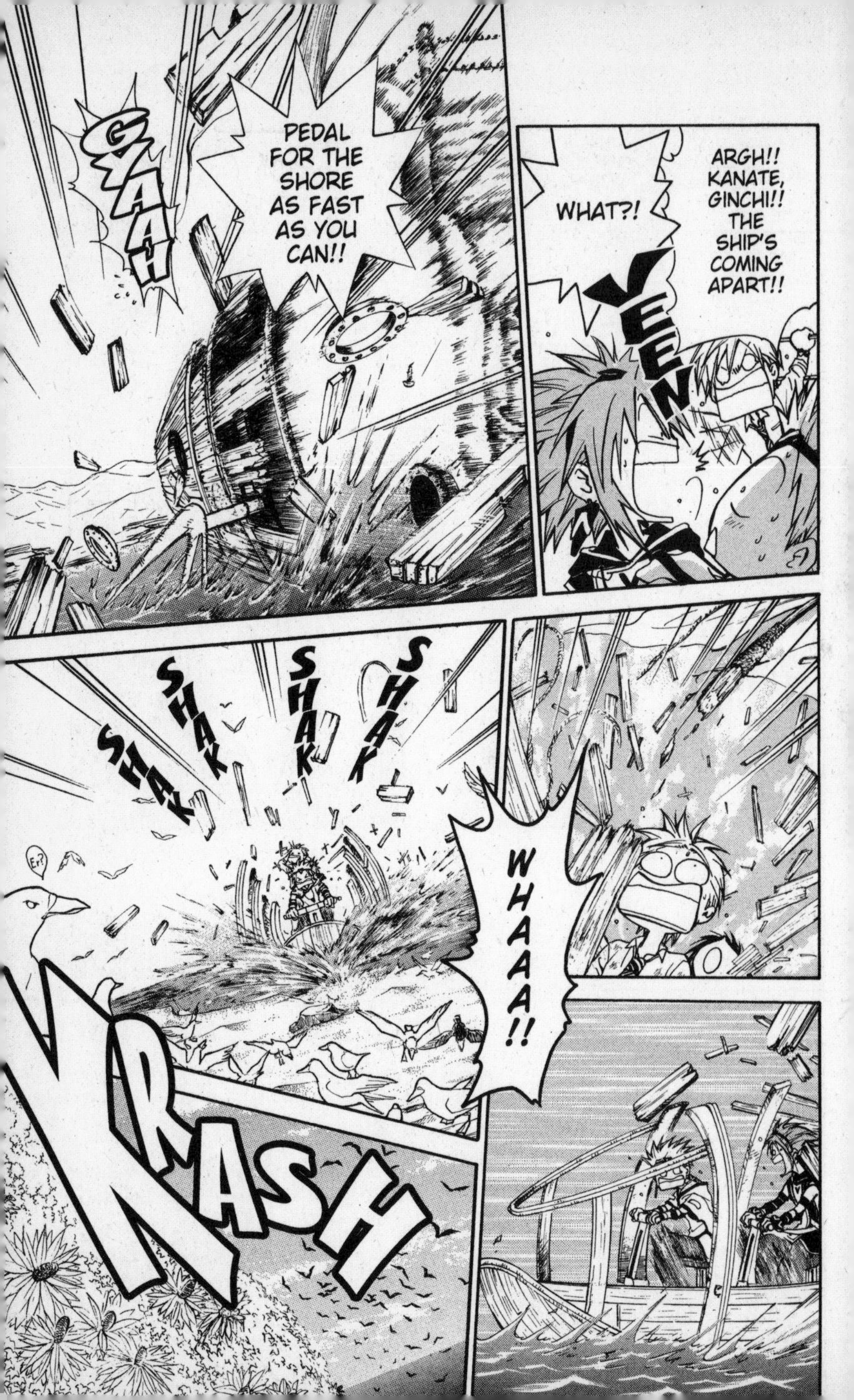
ARGH!! KANATE, GINCHI!! THE SHIP'S COMING APART!!
WHAT?!
YEEEN
PEDAL FOR THE SHORE AS FAST AS YOU CAN!!
GAAH
WHAAAA!!
SHAK
SHAK
SHAK
Er?
KRASH

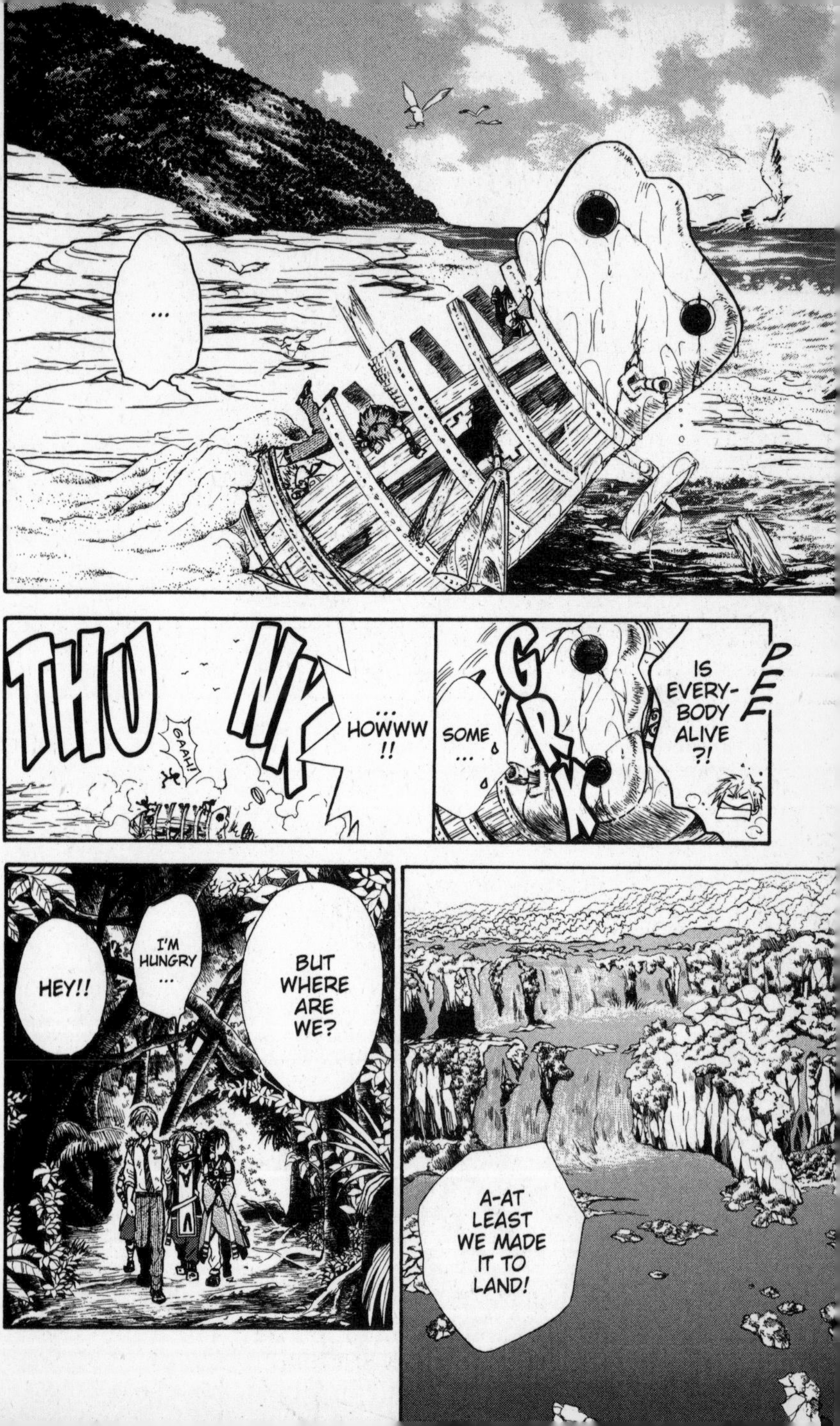
...
PEE
IS EVERY-BODY ALIVE?!
GRK
SOME...
...HOWWW!!
THUNK
GAAH!
A-AT LEAST WE MADE IT TO LAND!
BUT WHERE ARE WE?
I'M HUNGRY...
HEY!!

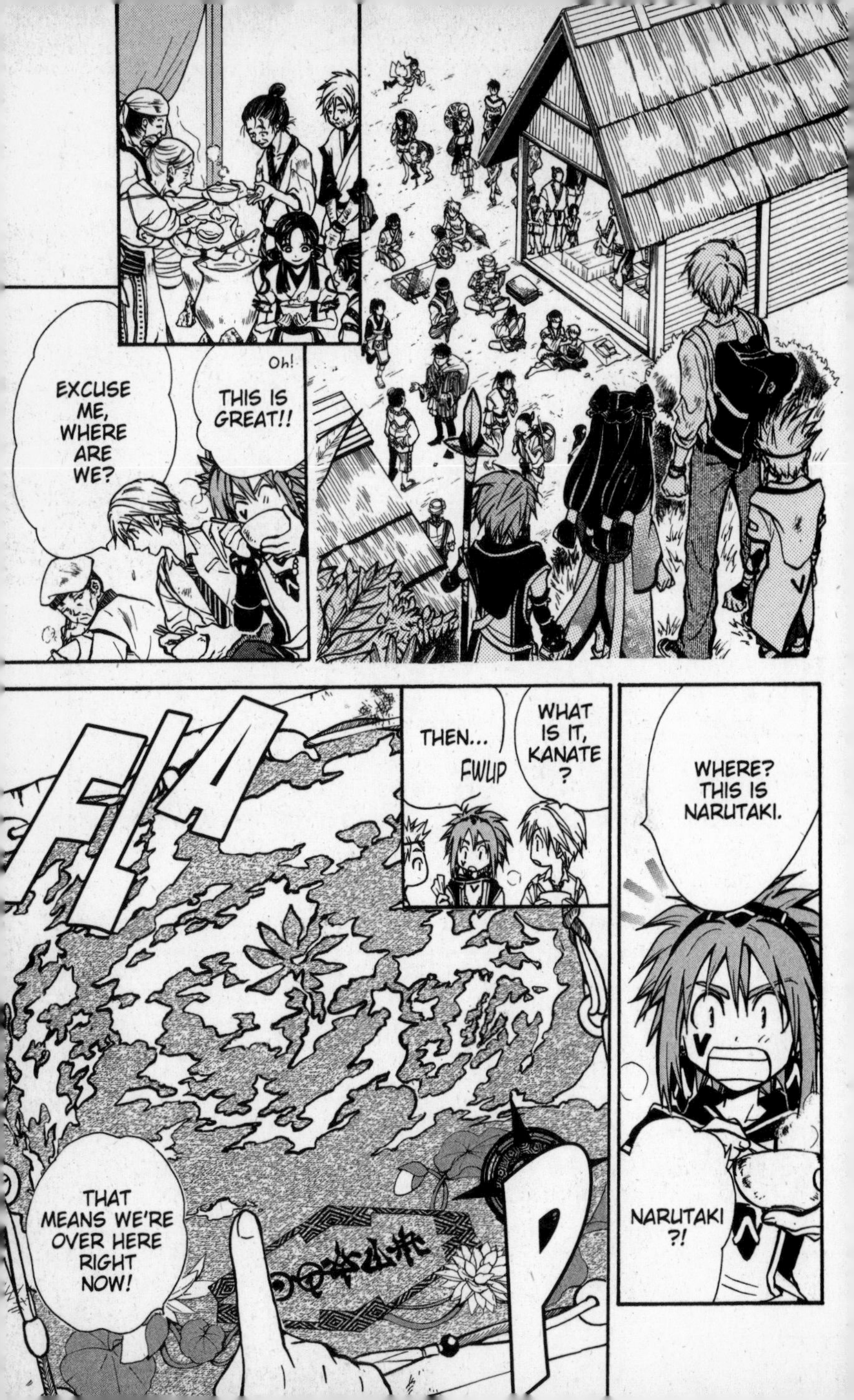
Oh!
THIS IS GREAT!!
EXCUSE ME, WHERE ARE WE?
WHERE? THIS IS NARUTAKI.
NARUTAKI ?!
WHAT IS IT, KANATE ?
FWUP
THEN...
THAT MEANS WE'RE OVER HERE RIGHT NOW!

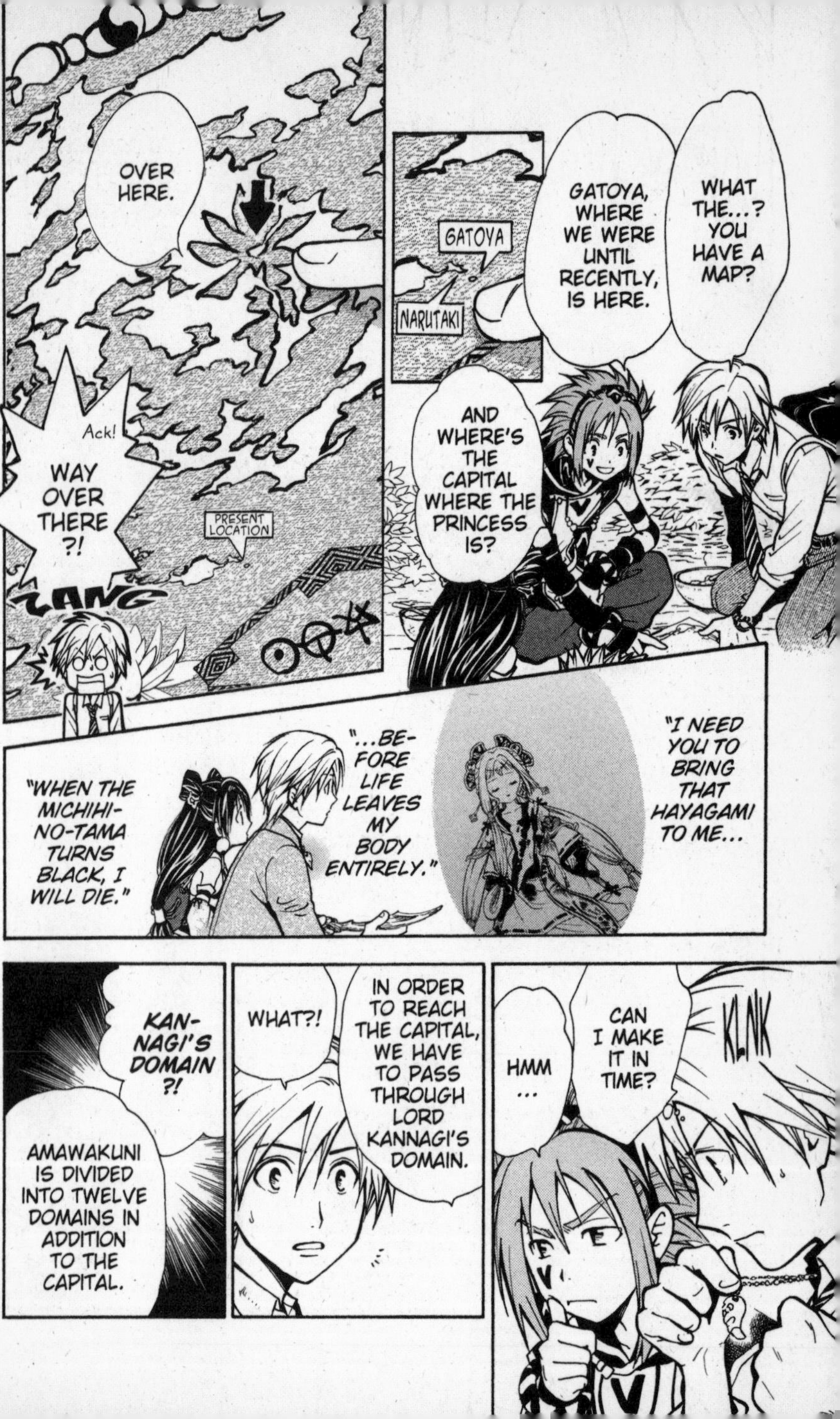
WHAT THE...? YOU HAVE A MAP?
GATOYA, WHERE WE WERE UNTIL RECENTLY, IS HERE.
GATOYA
NARUTAKI
AND WHERE'S THE CAPITAL WHERE THE PRINCESS IS?
OVER HERE.
PRESENT LOCATION
Ack!
WAY OVER THERE?!
ZANG
"I NEED YOU TO BRING THAT HAYAGAMI TO ME...
"...BEFORE LIFE LEAVES MY BODY ENTIRELY."
"WHEN THE MICHIHI-NO-TAMA TURNS BLACK, I WILL DIE."
KLNK
CAN I MAKE IT IN TIME?
HMM...
IN ORDER TO REACH THE CAPITAL, WE HAVE TO PASS THROUGH LORD KANNAGI'S DOMAIN.
WHAT?!
KANNAGI'S DOMAIN?!
AMAWAKUNI IS DIVIDED INTO TWELVE DOMAINS IN ADDITION TO THE CAPITAL.

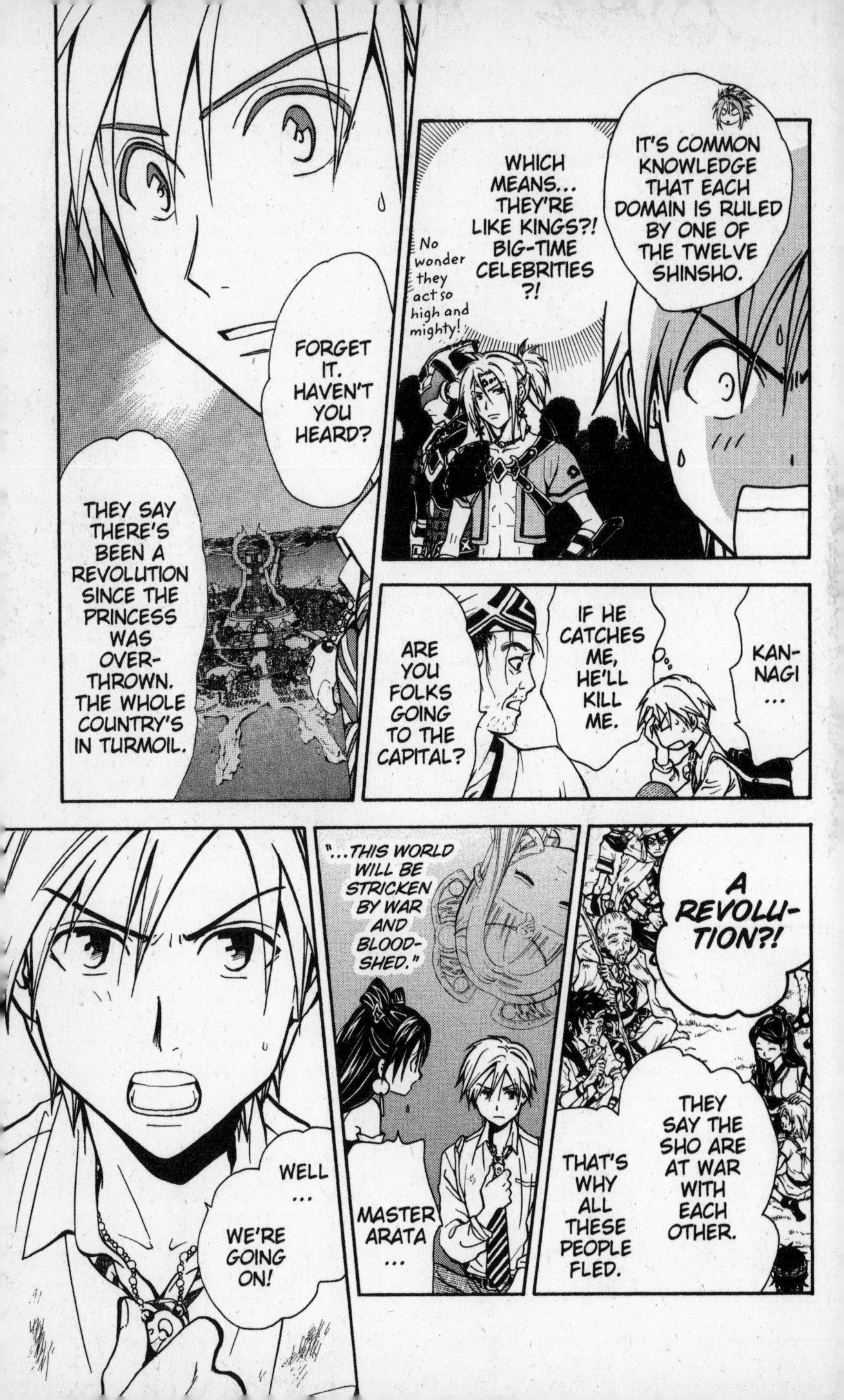
IT'S COMMON KNOWLEDGE THAT EACH DOMAIN IS RULED BY ONE OF THE TWELVE SHINSHO.
WHICH MEANS... THEY'RE LIKE KINGS?! BIG-TIME CELEBRITIES?!
No wonder they act so high and mighty!
KAN-NAGI...
IF HE CATCHES ME, HE'LL KILL ME.
ARE YOU FOLKS GOING TO THE CAPITAL?
FORGET IT. HAVEN'T YOU HEARD?
THEY SAY THERE'S BEEN A REVOLUTION SINCE THE PRINCESS WAS OVER-THROWN. THE WHOLE COUNTRY'S IN TURMOIL.
A REVOLU-TION?!
THEY SAY THE SHO ARE AT WAR WITH EACH OTHER.
THAT'S WHY ALL THESE PEOPLE FLED.
"...THIS WORLD WILL BE STRICKEN BY WAR AND BLOOD-SHED."
MASTER ARATA...
WELL...
WE'RE GOING ON!

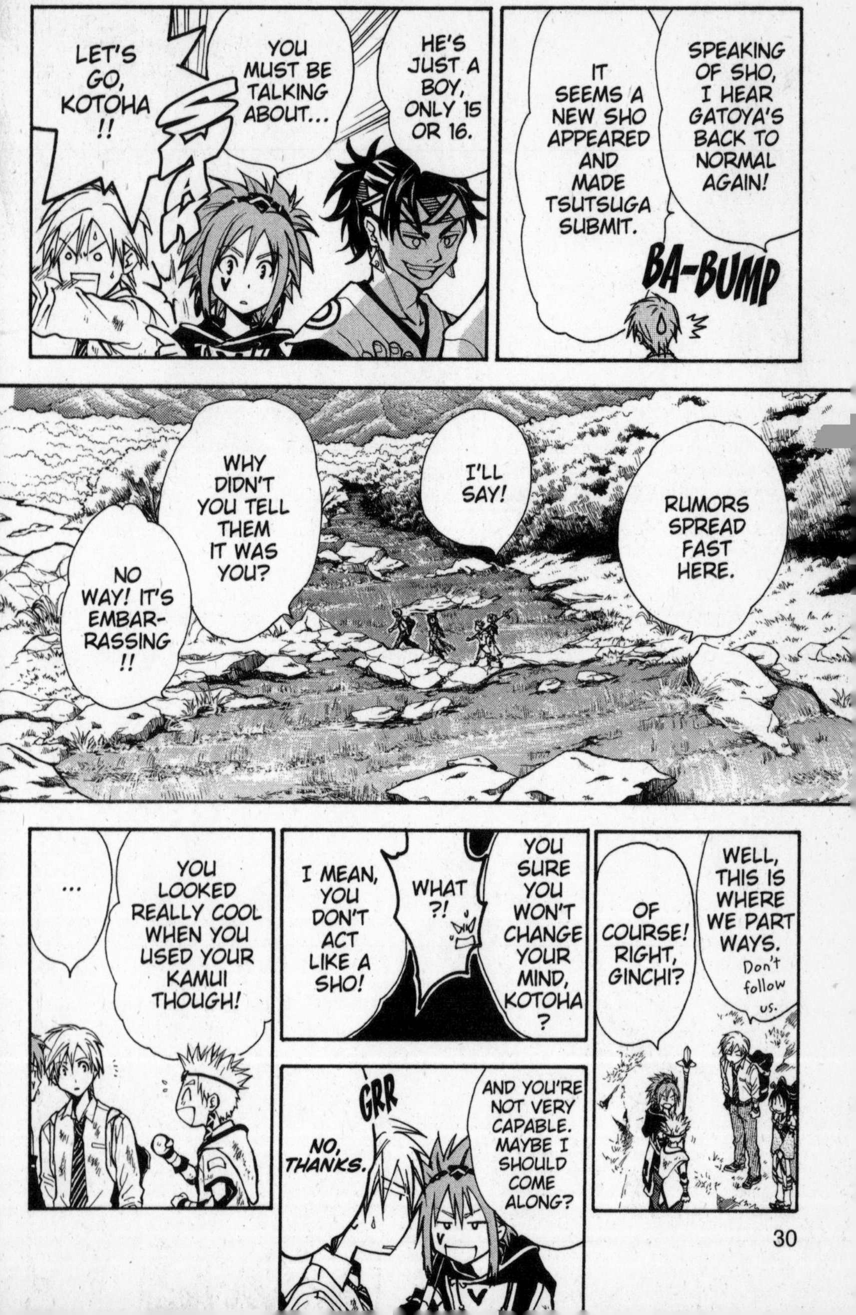
SPEAKING OF SHO, I HEAR GATOYA'S BACK TO NORMAL AGAIN!
IT SEEMS A NEW SHO APPEARED AND MADE TSUTSUGA SUBMIT.
BA-BUMP
HE'S JUST A BOY, ONLY 15 OR 16.
YOU MUST BE TALKING ABOUT...
LET'S GO, KOTOHA!!
RUMORS SPREAD FAST HERE.
I'LL SAY!
WHY DIDN'T YOU TELL THEM IT WAS YOU?
NO WAY! IT'S EMBARRASSING!!
WELL, THIS IS WHERE WE PART WAYS.
Don't follow us.
OF COURSE! RIGHT, GINCHI?
YOU SURE YOU WON'T CHANGE YOUR MIND, KOTOHA?
WHAT?!
I MEAN, YOU DON'T ACT LIKE A SHO!
AND YOU'RE NOT VERY CAPABLE. MAYBE I SHOULD COME ALONG?
GRR
NO, THANKS.
YOU LOOKED REALLY COOL WHEN YOU USED YOUR KAMUI THOUGH!
...

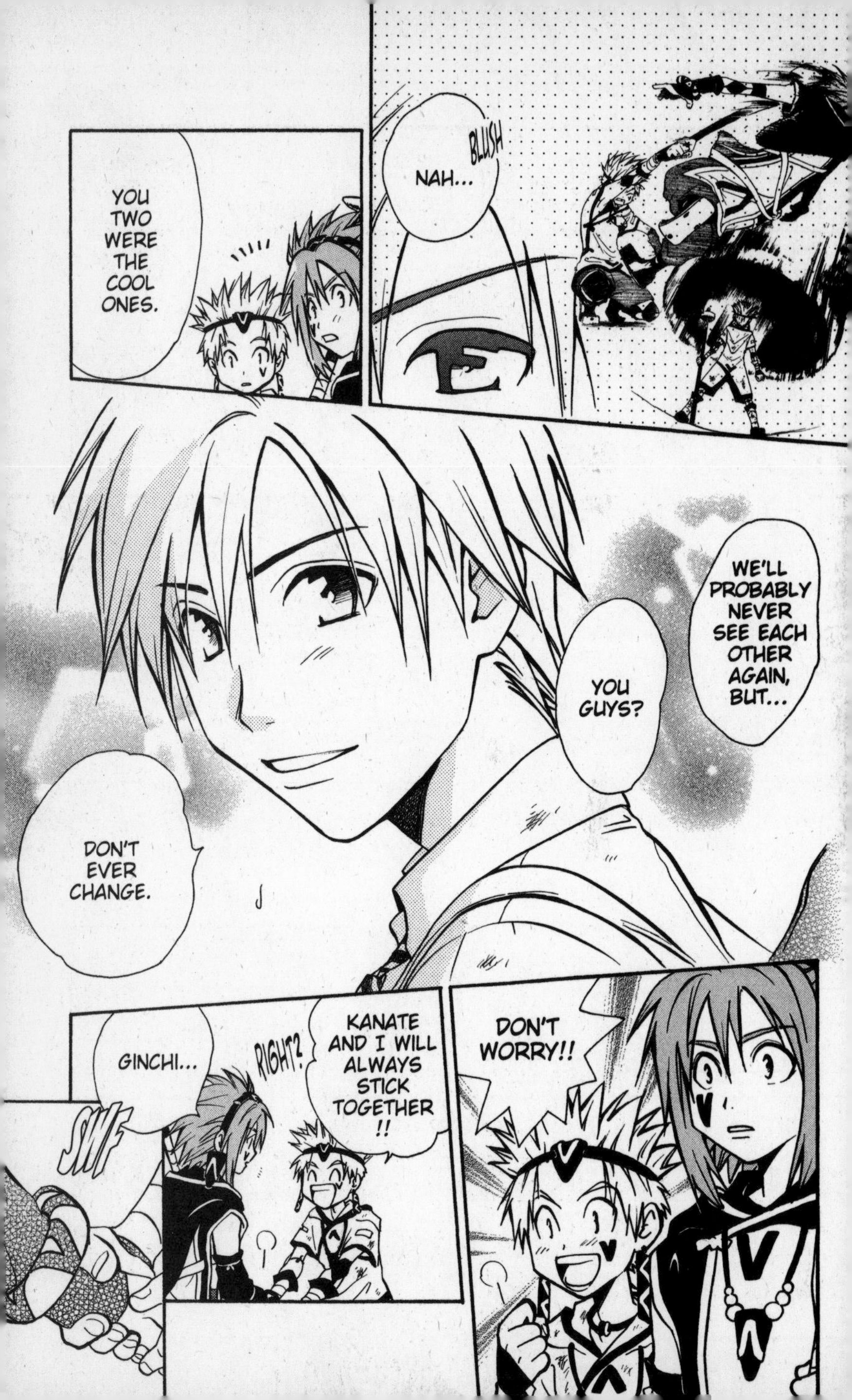
BLUSH
NAH...
YOU TWO WERE THE COOL ONES.
WE'LL PROBABLY NEVER SEE EACH OTHER AGAIN, BUT...
YOU GUYS?
DON'T EVER CHANGE.
DON'T WORRY!!
KANATE AND I WILL ALWAYS STICK TOGETHER!!
RIGHT?
GINCHI...

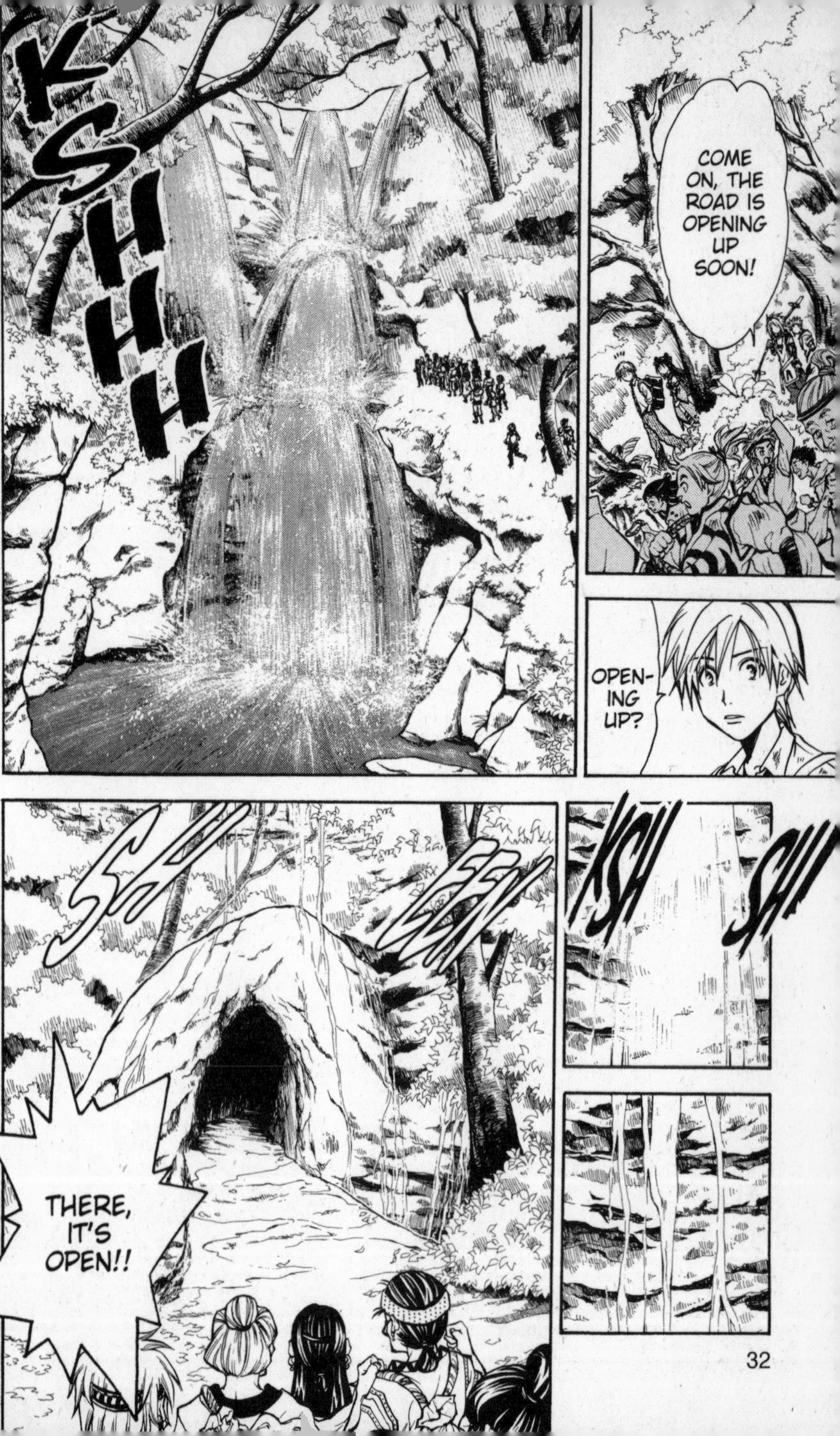
COME ON, THE ROAD IS OPENING UP SOON!
OPEN-ING UP?
KSHHHH
KSH
SH
THERE, IT'S OPEN!!

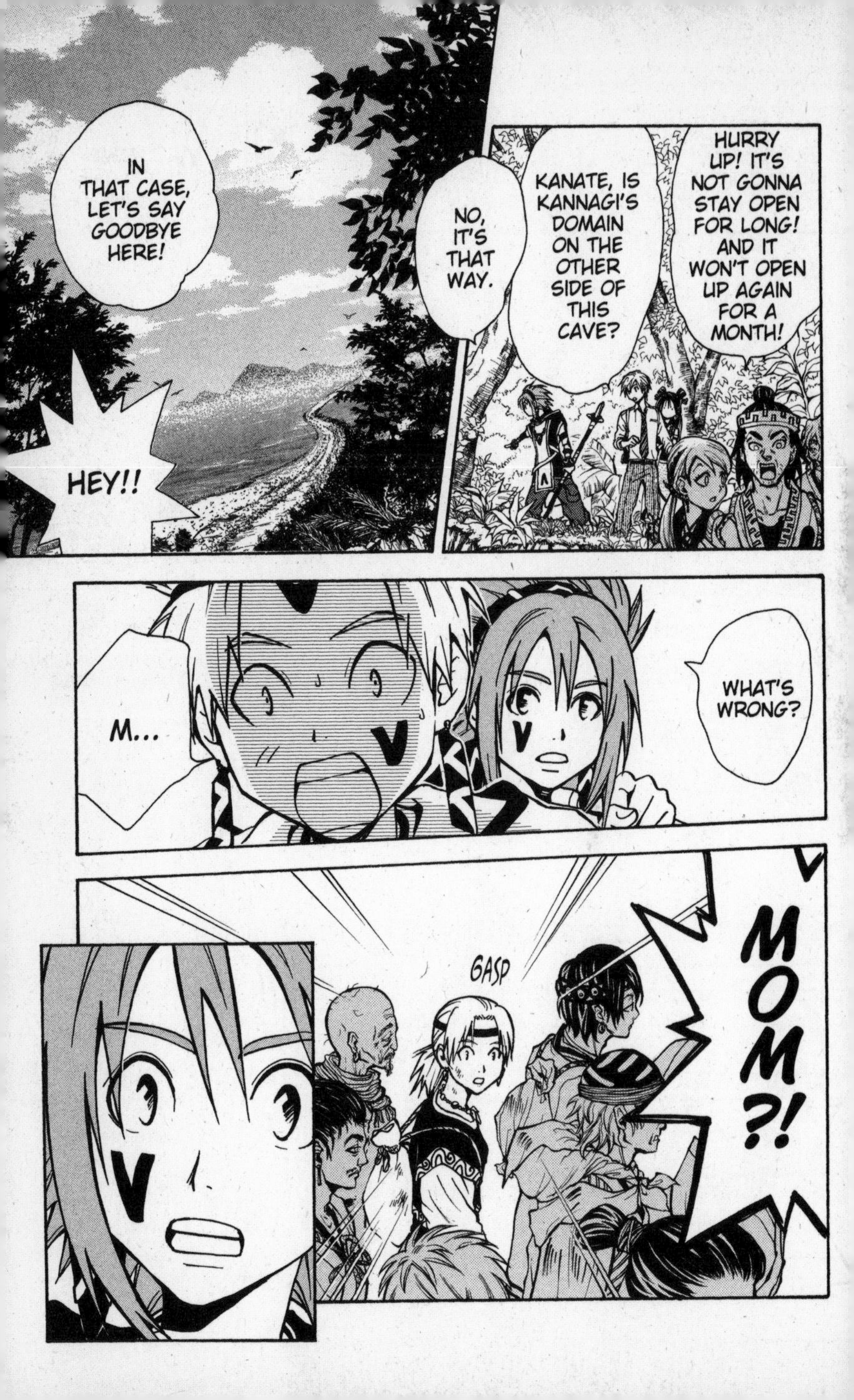
HURRY UP! IT'S NOT GONNA STAY OPEN FOR LONG! AND IT WON'T OPEN UP AGAIN FOR A MONTH!
KANATE, IS KANNAGI'S DOMAIN ON THE OTHER SIDE OF THIS CAVE?
NO, IT'S THAT WAY.
IN THAT CASE, LET'S SAY GOODBYE HERE!
HEY!!
WHAT'S WRONG?
M...
MOM?!
GASP

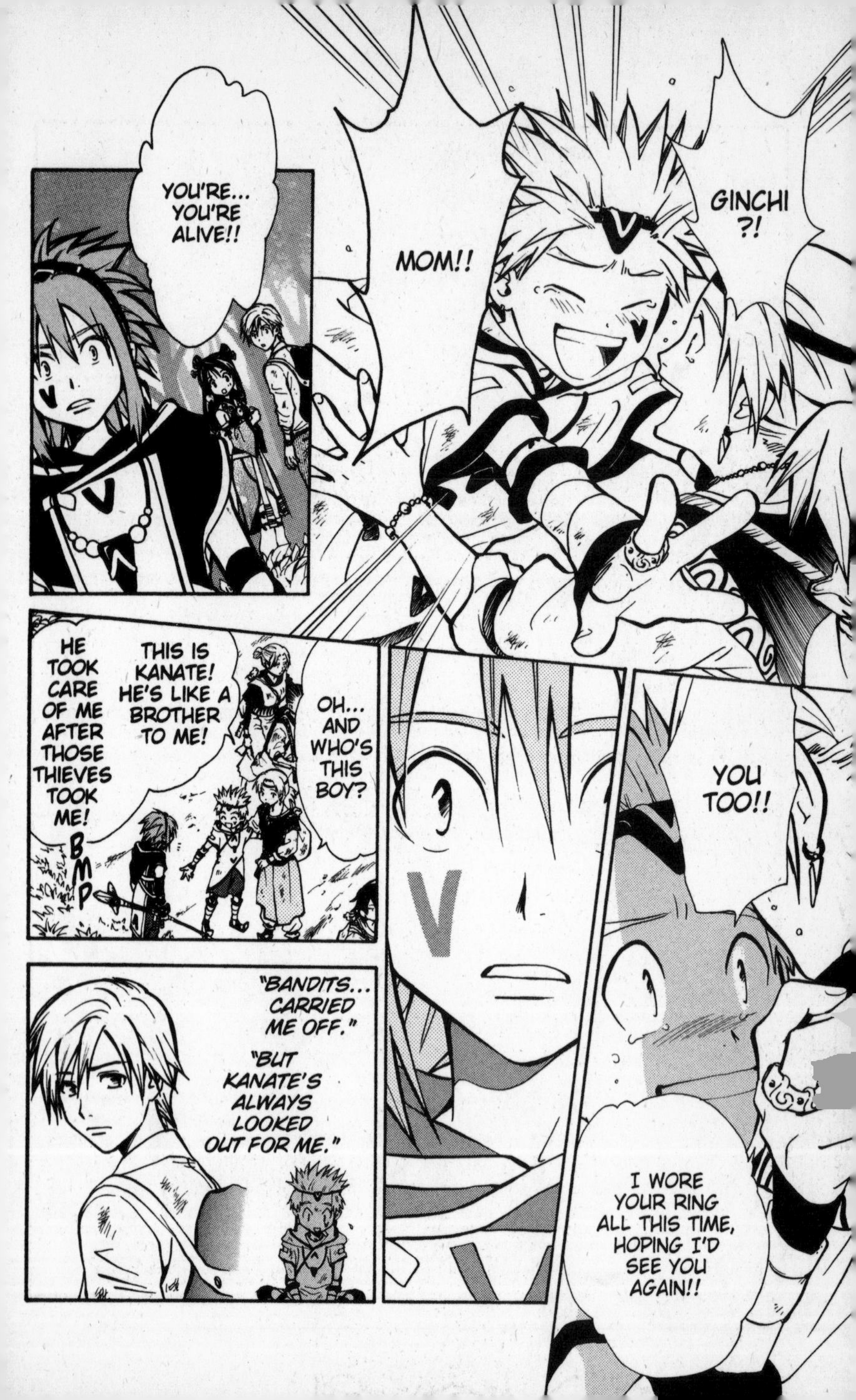
GINCHI ?!
MOM!!
YOU'RE... YOU'RE ALIVE!!
YOU TOO!!
I WORE YOUR RING ALL THIS TIME, HOPING I'D SEE YOU AGAIN!!
OH... AND WHO'S THIS BOY?
THIS IS KANATE! HE'S LIKE A BROTHER TO ME!
HE TOOK CARE OF ME AFTER THOSE THIEVES TOOK ME!
BMP
"BANDITS... CARRIED ME OFF."
"BUT KANATE'S ALWAYS LOOKED OUT FOR ME."

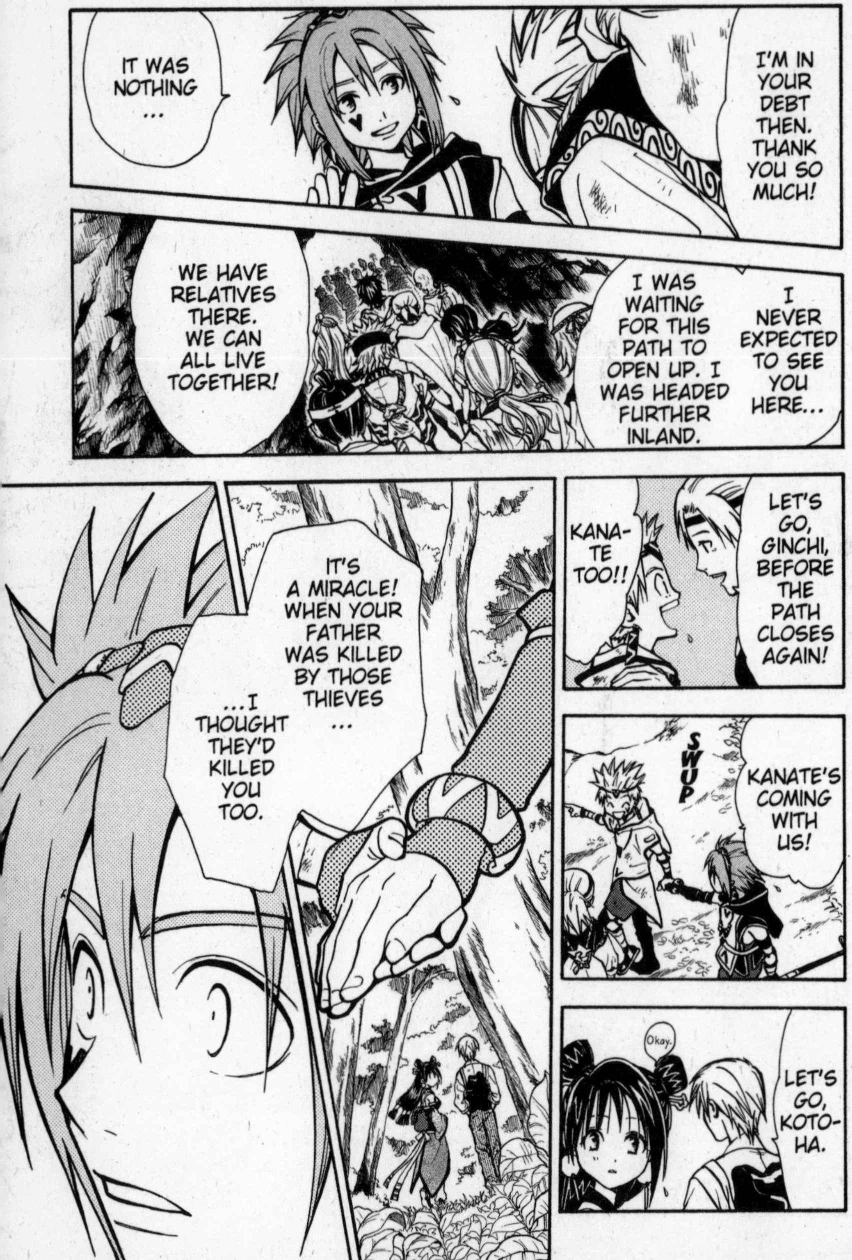
I'M IN YOUR DEBT THEN. THANK YOU SO MUCH!
IT WAS NOTHING ...
I NEVER EXPECTED TO SEE YOU HERE...
I WAS WAITING FOR THIS PATH TO OPEN UP. I WAS HEADED FURTHER INLAND.
WE HAVE RELATIVES THERE. WE CAN ALL LIVE TOGETHER!
LET'S GO, GINCHI, BEFORE THE PATH CLOSES AGAIN!
KANATE TOO!!
KANATE'S COMING WITH US!
SWUP
LET'S GO, KOTOHA.
Okay.
IT'S A MIRACLE! WHEN YOUR FATHER WAS KILLED BY THOSE THIEVES ...
...I THOUGHT THEY'D KILLED YOU TOO.

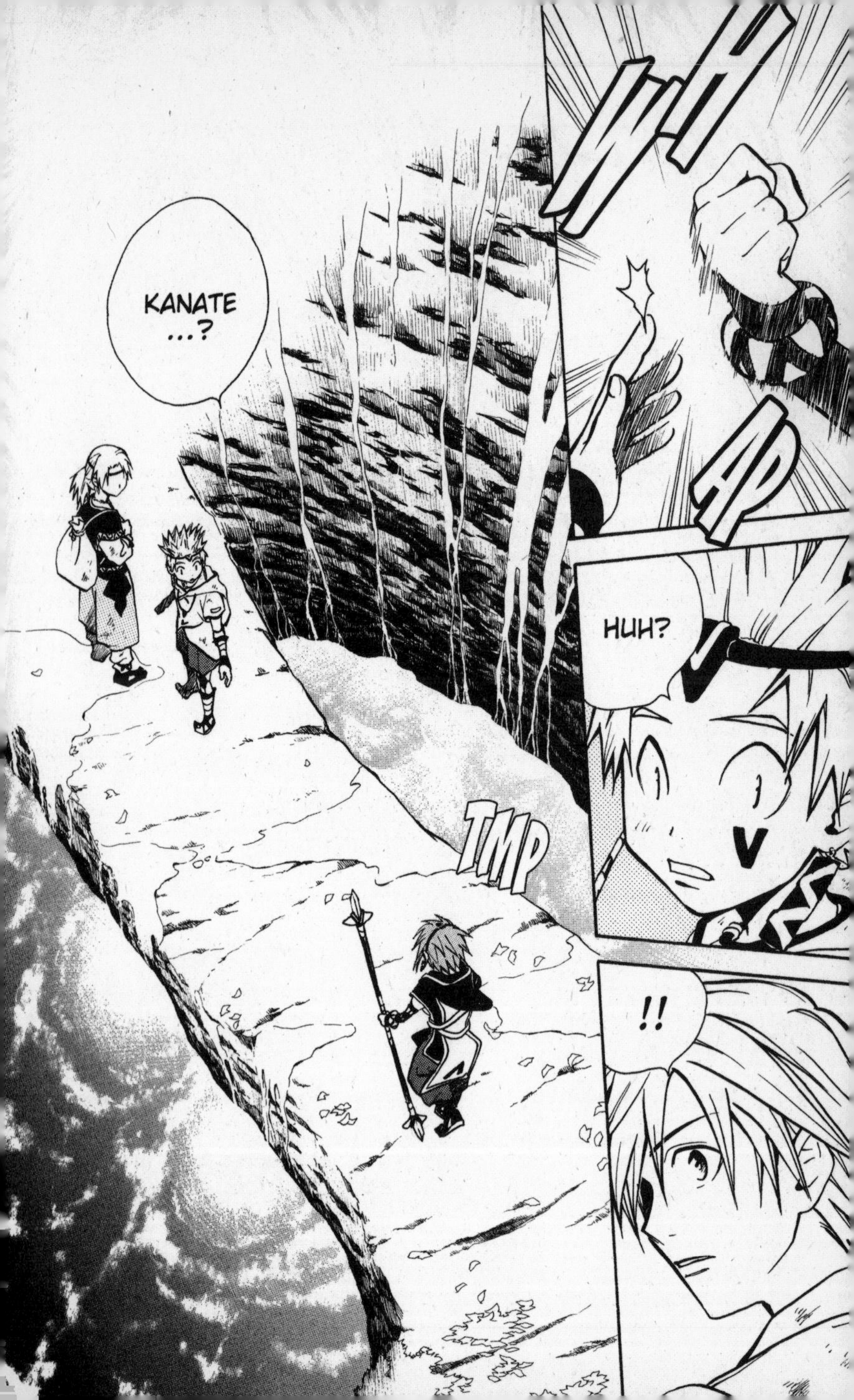
WHAP
HUH?
!!
KANATE ...?
TMP

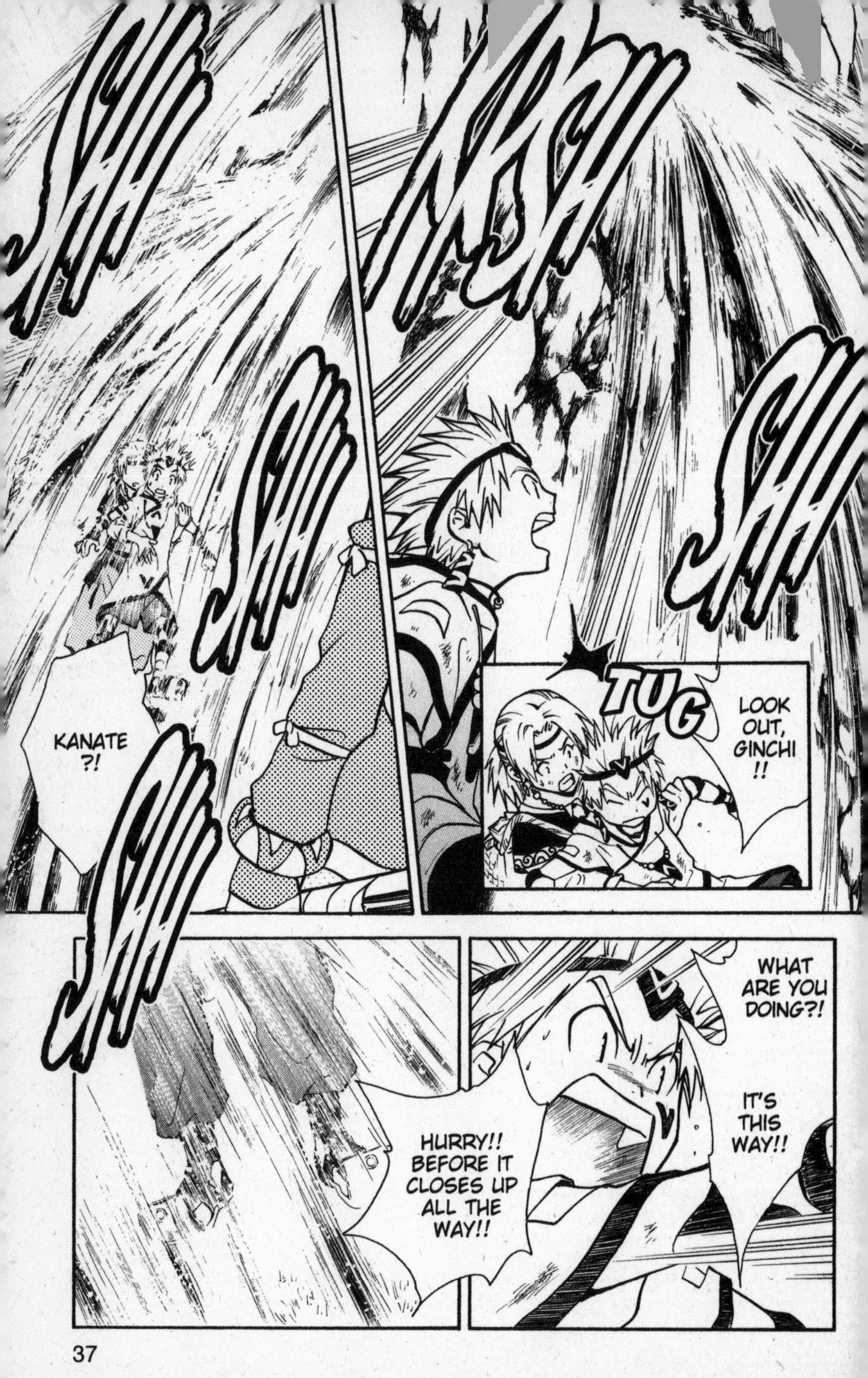
TUG
LOOK OUT, GINCHI!!
KANATE?!
WHAT ARE YOU DOING?!
IT'S THIS WAY!!
HURRY!! BEFORE IT CLOSES UP ALL THE WAY!!

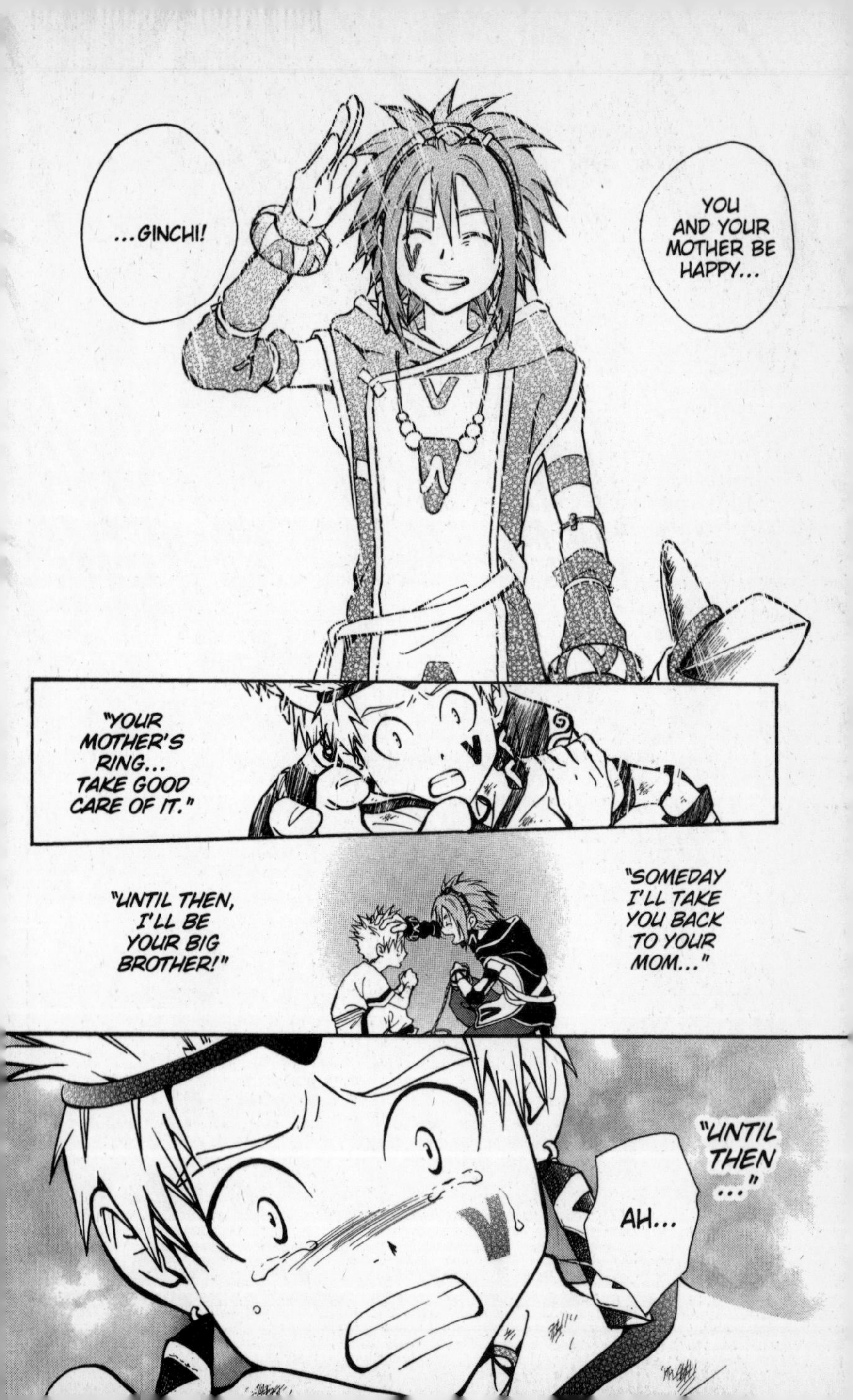
YOU AND YOUR MOTHER BE HAPPY...
...GINCHI!
"YOUR MOTHER'S RING... TAKE GOOD CARE OF IT."
"SOMEDAY I'LL TAKE YOU BACK TO YOUR MOM..."
"UNTIL THEN, I'LL BE YOUR BIG BROTHER!"
"UNTIL THEN ..."
AH...

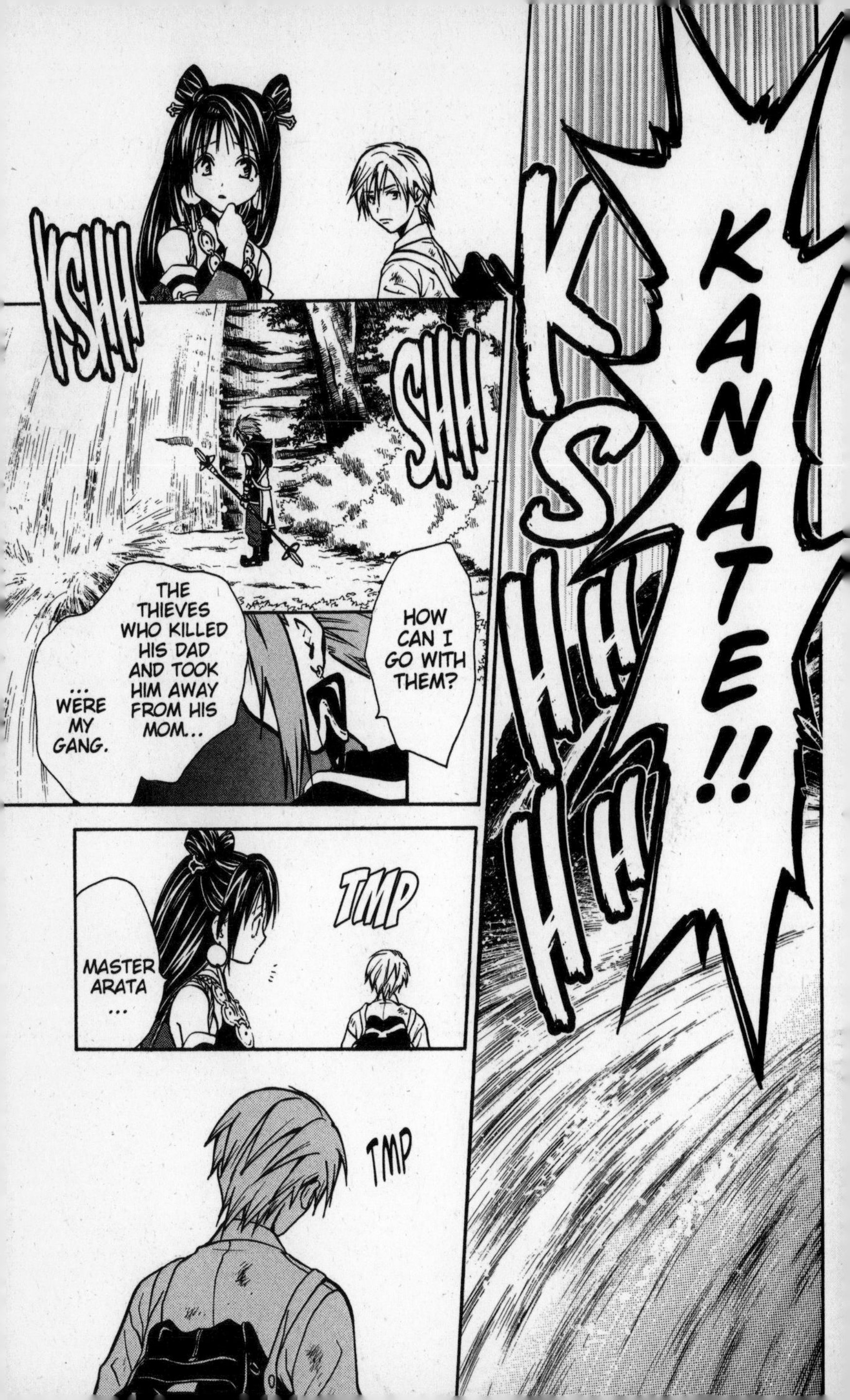
KANATE!!
KSHHH
KSHH
SHH
HOW CAN I GO WITH THEM?
THE THIEVES WHO KILLED HIS DAD AND TOOK HIM AWAY FROM HIS MOM...
...WERE MY GANG.
TMP
MASTER ARATA...
TMP

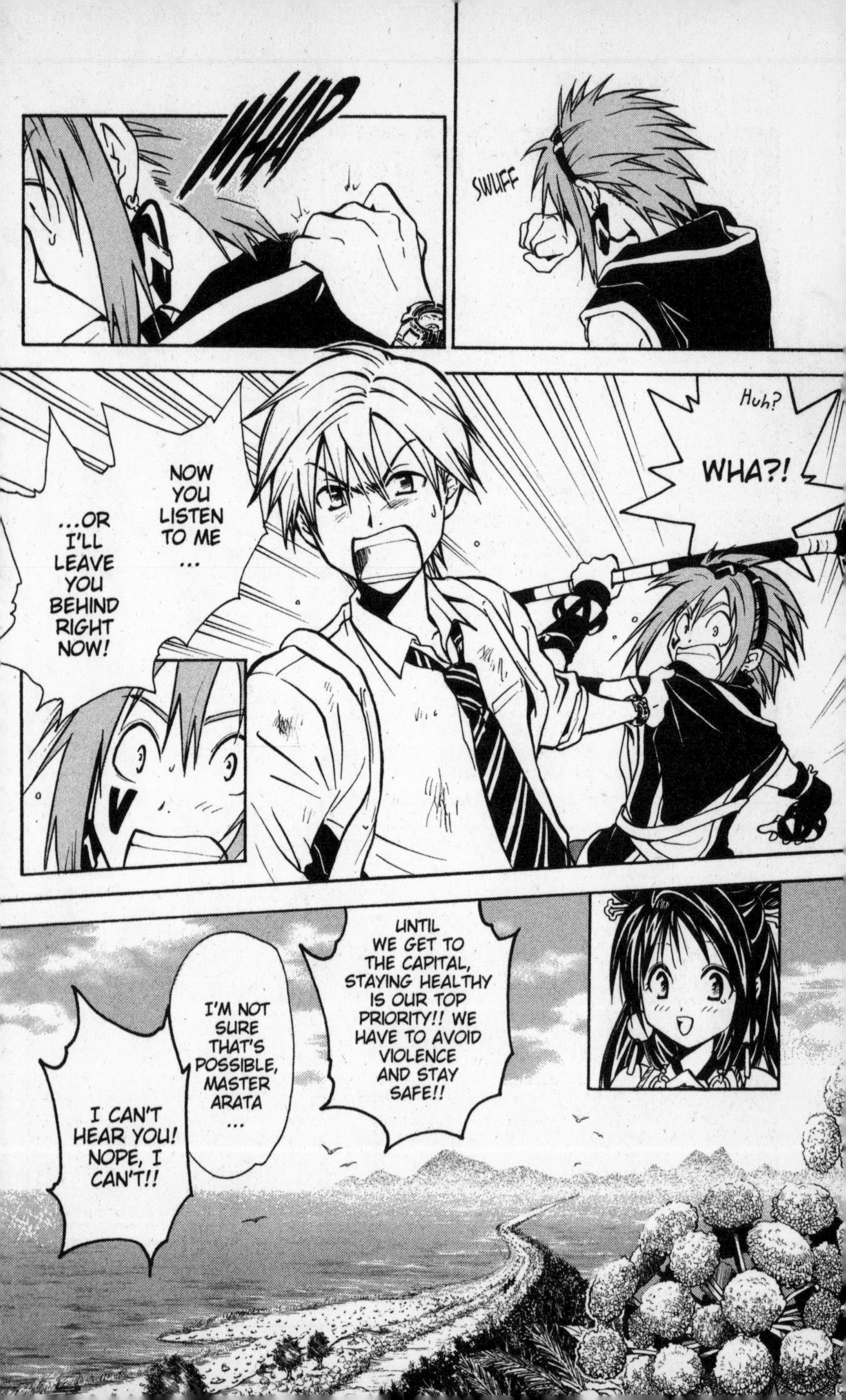
SWUFF
WHAP
Huh?
WHA?!
NOW YOU LISTEN TO ME ...
...OR I'LL LEAVE YOU BEHIND RIGHT NOW!
UNTIL WE GET TO THE CAPITAL, STAYING HEALTHY IS OUR TOP PRIORITY!! WE HAVE TO AVOID VIOLENCE AND STAY SAFE!!
I'M NOT SURE THAT'S POSSIBLE, MASTER ARATA ...
I CAN'T HEAR YOU! NOPE, I CAN'T!!

CHAPTER 20
KAGUTSUCHI

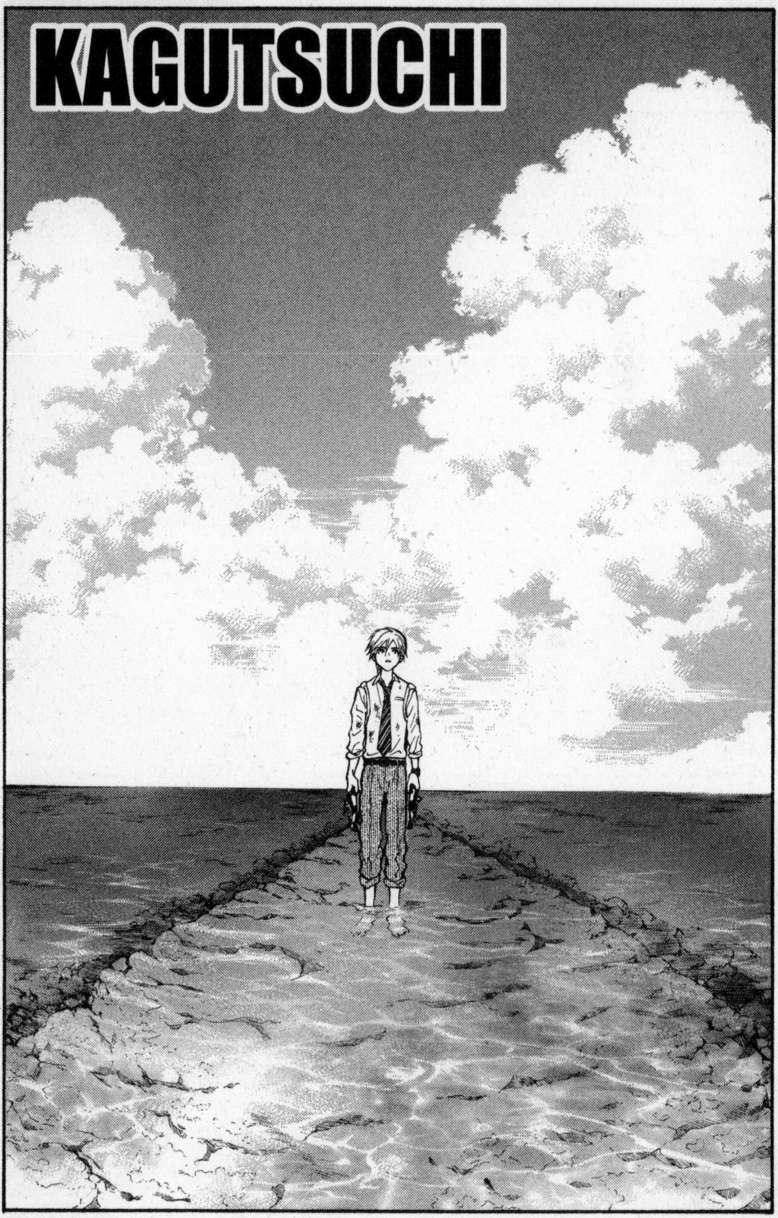

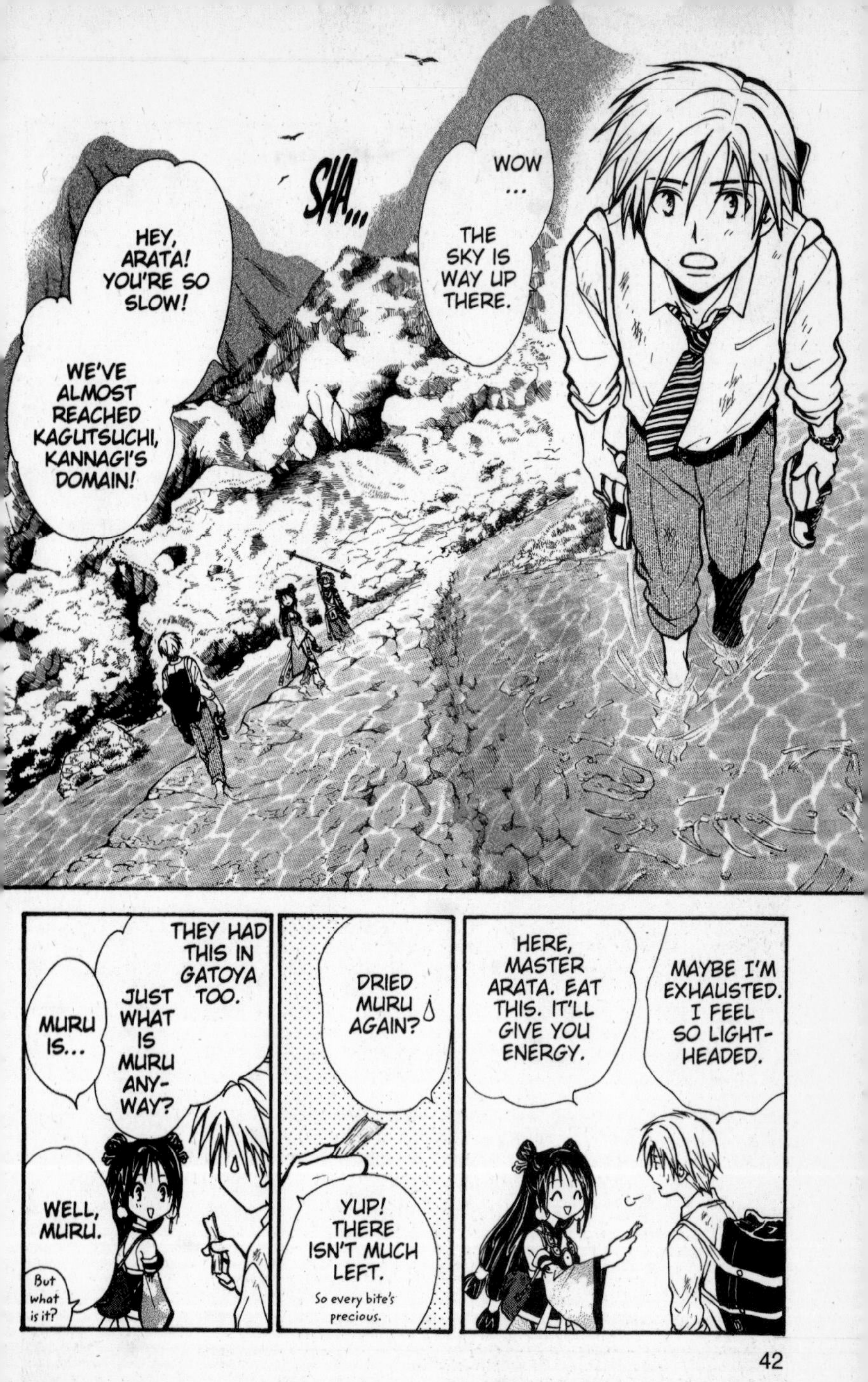
WOW ... THE SKY IS WAY UP THERE.
SHA...
HEY, ARATA! YOU'RE SO SLOW!
WE'VE ALMOST REACHED KAGUTSUCHI, KANNAGI'S DOMAIN!
MAYBE I'M EXHAUSTED. I FEEL SO LIGHT-HEADED.
HERE, MASTER ARATA. EAT THIS. IT'LL GIVE YOU ENERGY.
DRIED MURU AGAIN?
YUP! THERE ISN'T MUCH LEFT.
So every bite's precious.
THEY HAD THIS IN GATOYA TOO.
JUST WHAT IS MURU ANY-WAY?
MURU IS...
WELL, MURU.
But what is it?

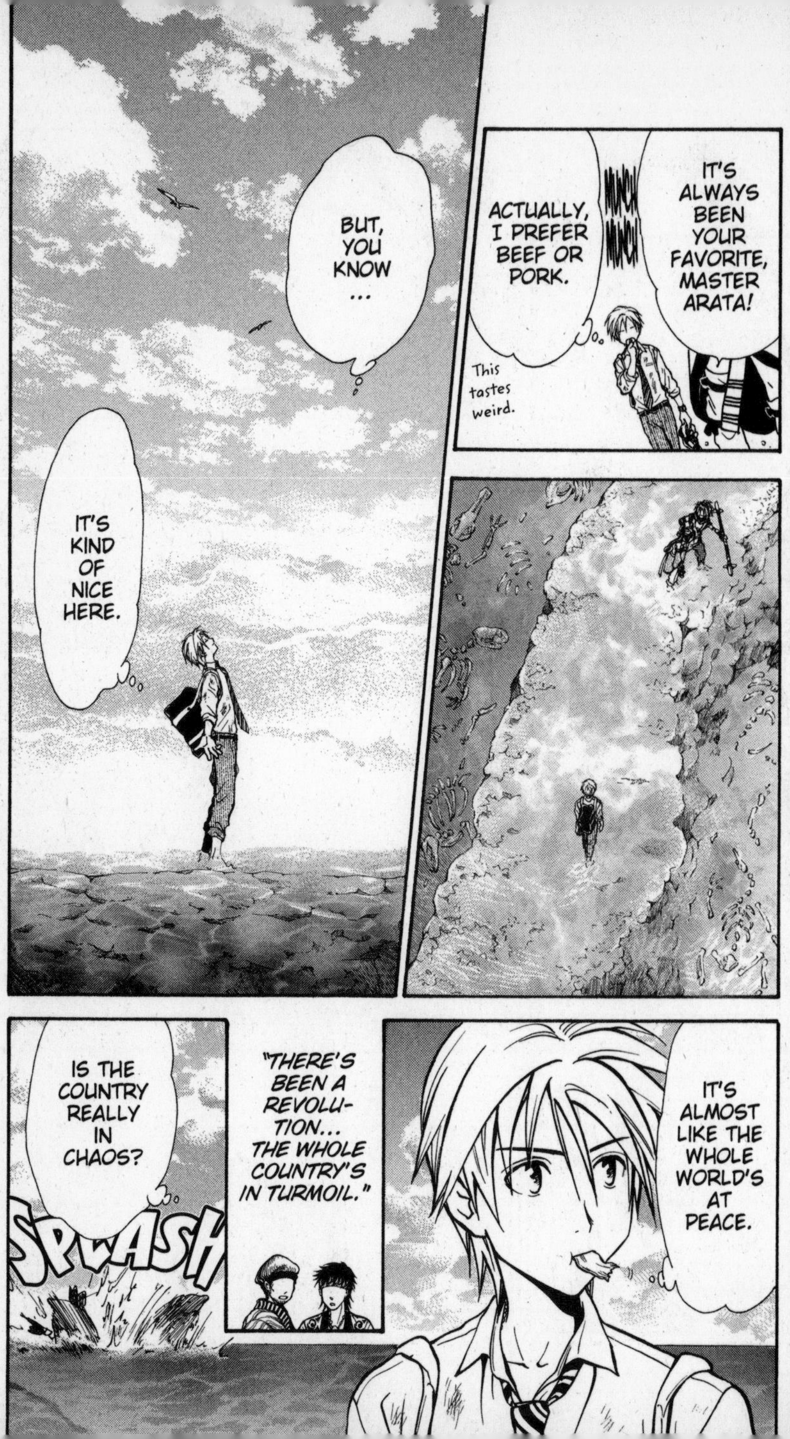
IT'S ALWAYS BEEN YOUR FAVORITE, MASTER ARATA!
MUNCH MUNCH
ACTUALLY, I PREFER BEEF OR PORK.
This tastes weird.
BUT, YOU KNOW ...
IT'S KIND OF NICE HERE.
IT'S ALMOST LIKE THE WHOLE WORLD'S AT PEACE.
"THERE'S BEEN A REVOLUTION... THE WHOLE COUNTRY'S IN TURMOIL."
IS THE COUNTRY REALLY IN CHAOS?
SPLASH

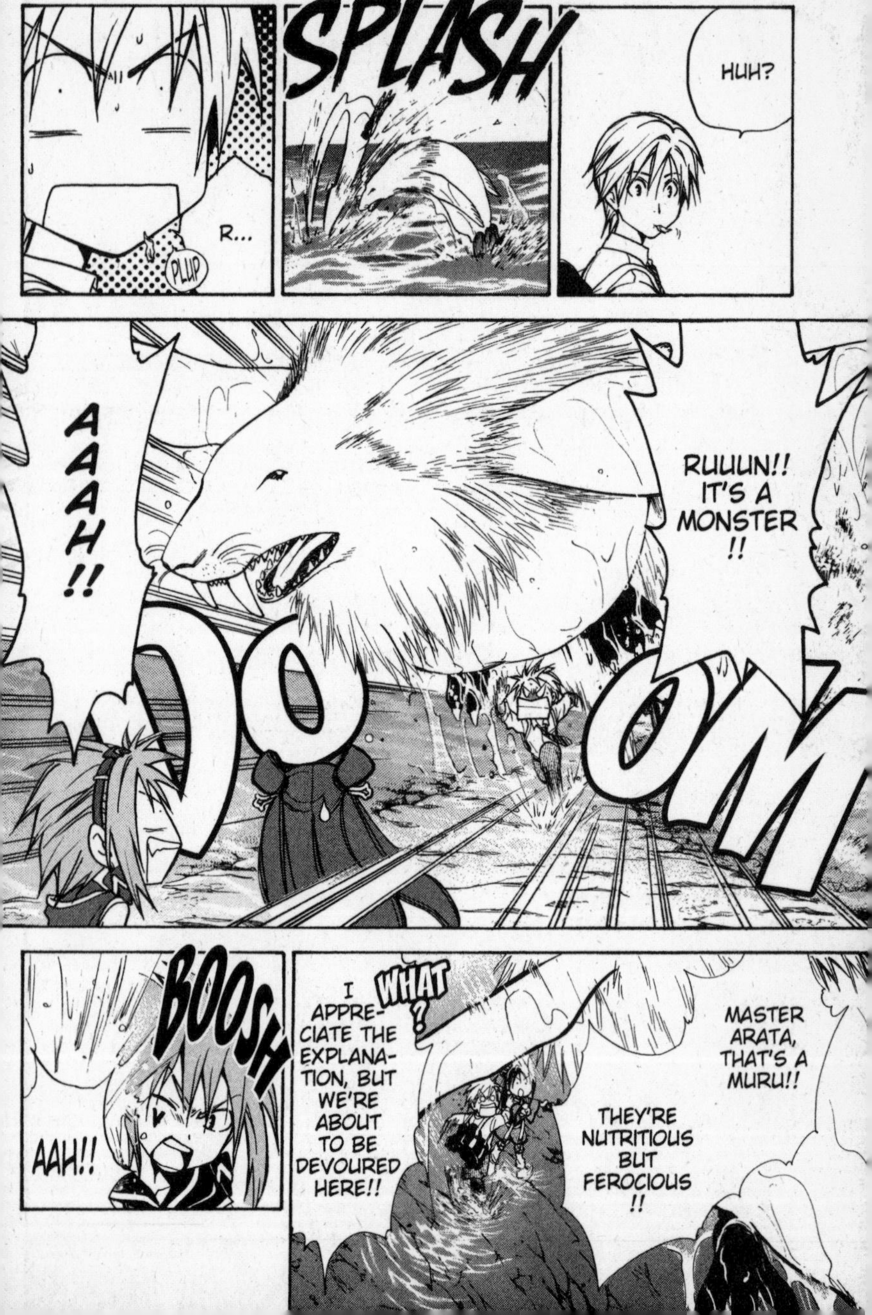
HUH?
SPLASH
R...
PLUP
RUUUN!! IT'S A MONSTER !!
DOOOM
AAAAH!!
MASTER ARATA, THAT'S A MURU!!
THEY'RE NUTRITIOUS BUT FEROCIOUS !!
WHAT ?
I APPRECIATE THE EXPLANATION, BUT WE'RE ABOUT TO BE DEVOURED HERE!!
BOOSH
AAH!!

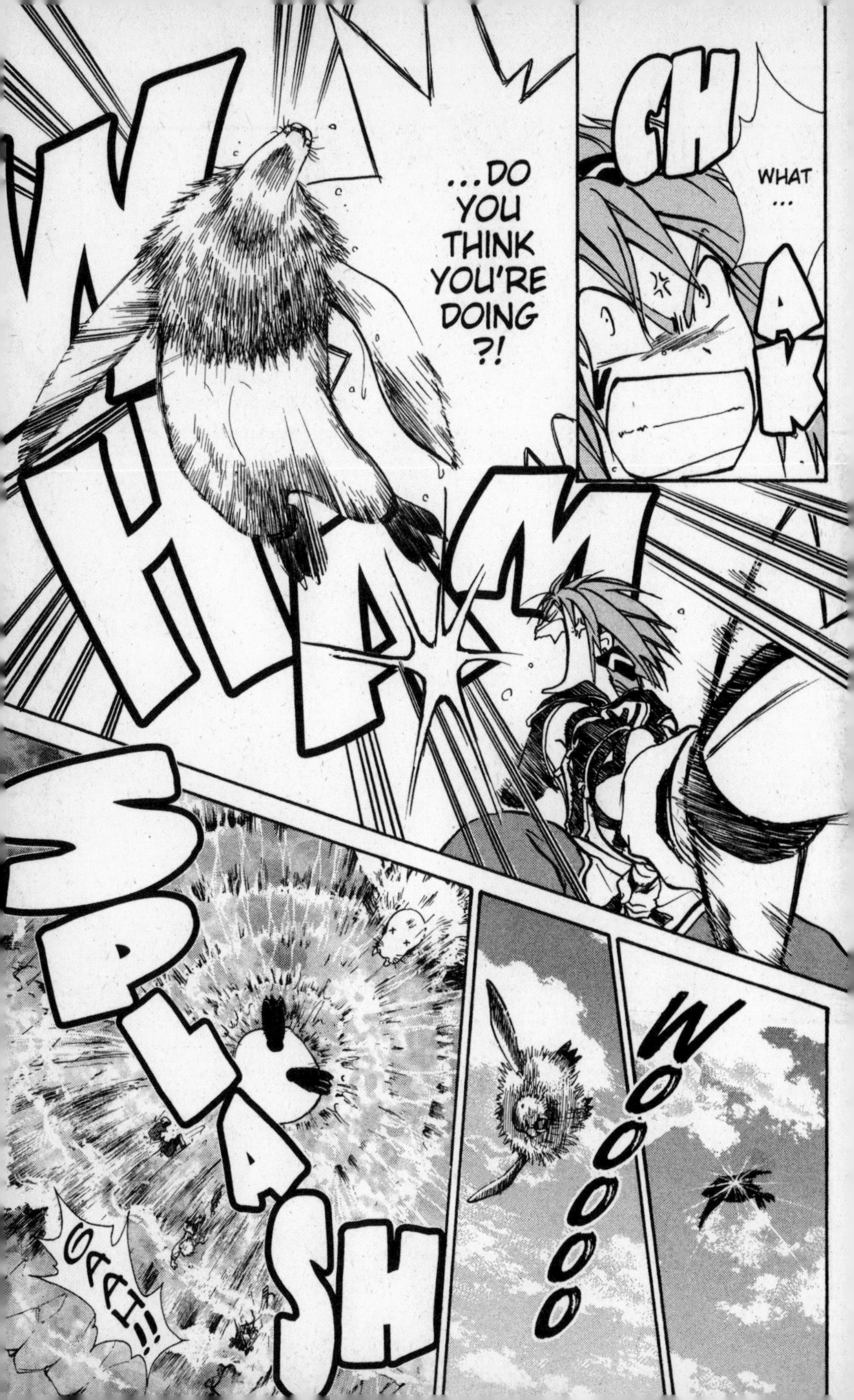
CHAK
WHAT...
WHAM
...DO YOU THINK YOU'RE DOING?!
WOOOOOOO
SPLASH
GAAH!!

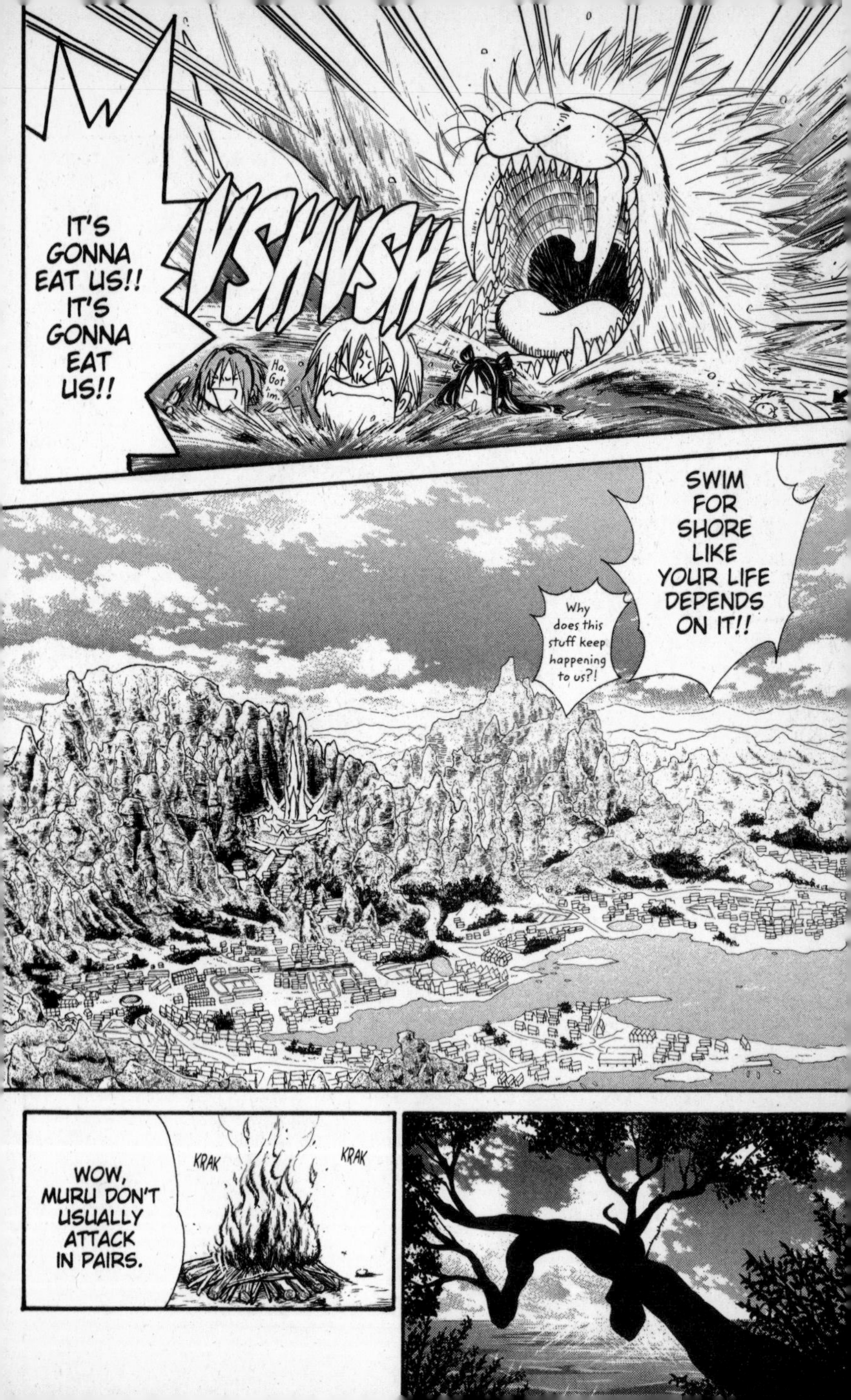
VSHVSH
IT'S GONNA EAT US!! IT'S GONNA EAT US!!
Ha. Got 'im.
SWIM FOR SHORE LIKE YOUR LIFE DEPENDS ON IT!!
Why does this stuff keep happening to us?!
KRAK
KRAK
WOW, MURU DON'T USUALLY ATTACK IN PAIRS.

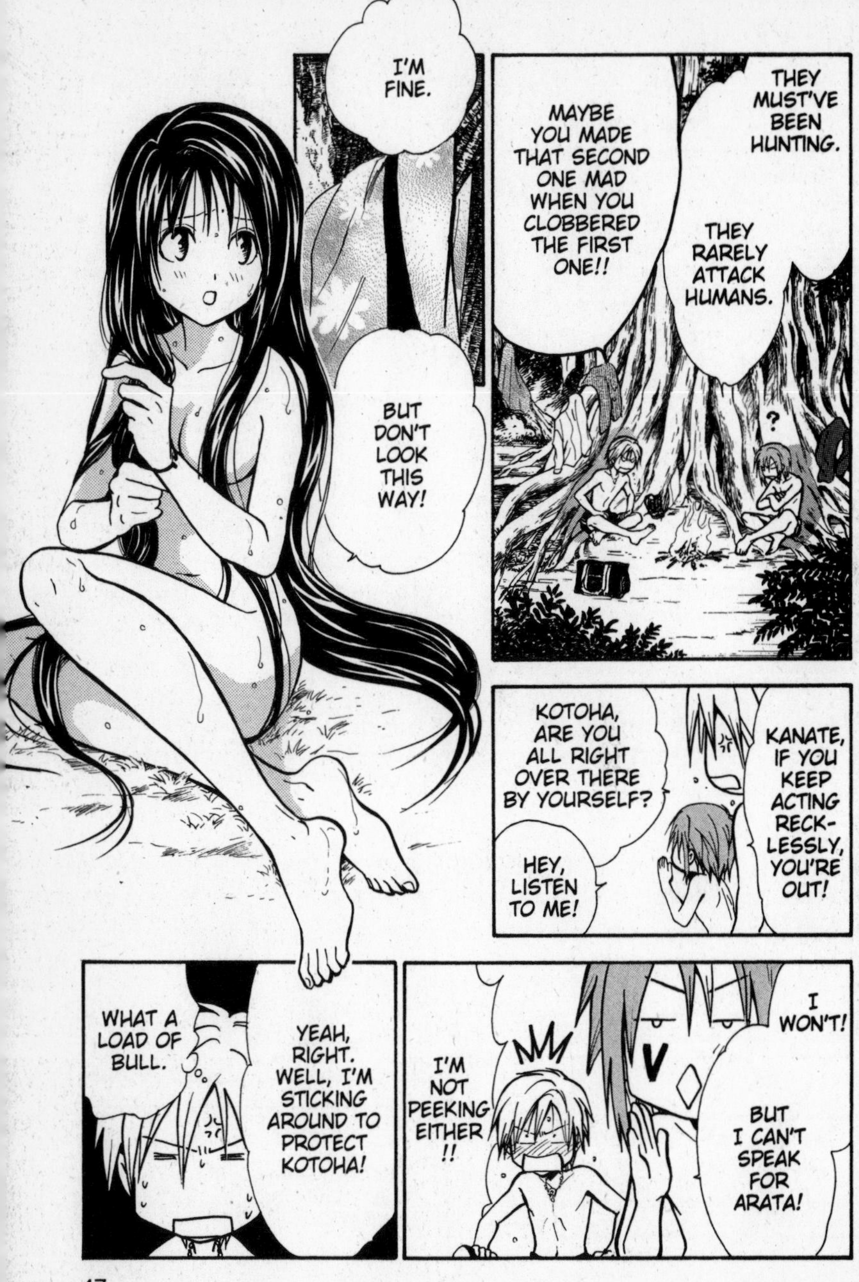
THEY MUST'VE BEEN HUNTING.
THEY RARELY ATTACK HUMANS.
MAYBE YOU MADE THAT SECOND ONE MAD WHEN YOU CLOBBERED THE FIRST ONE!!
KANATE, IF YOU KEEP ACTING RECK-LESSLY, YOU'RE OUT!
KOTOHA, ARE YOU ALL RIGHT OVER THERE BY YOURSELF?
HEY, LISTEN TO ME!
I'M FINE.
BUT DON'T LOOK THIS WAY!
I WON'T!
BUT I CAN'T SPEAK FOR ARATA!
I'M NOT PEEKING EITHER!!
YEAH, RIGHT. WELL, I'M STICKING AROUND TO PROTECT KOTOHA!
WHAT A LOAD OF BULL.

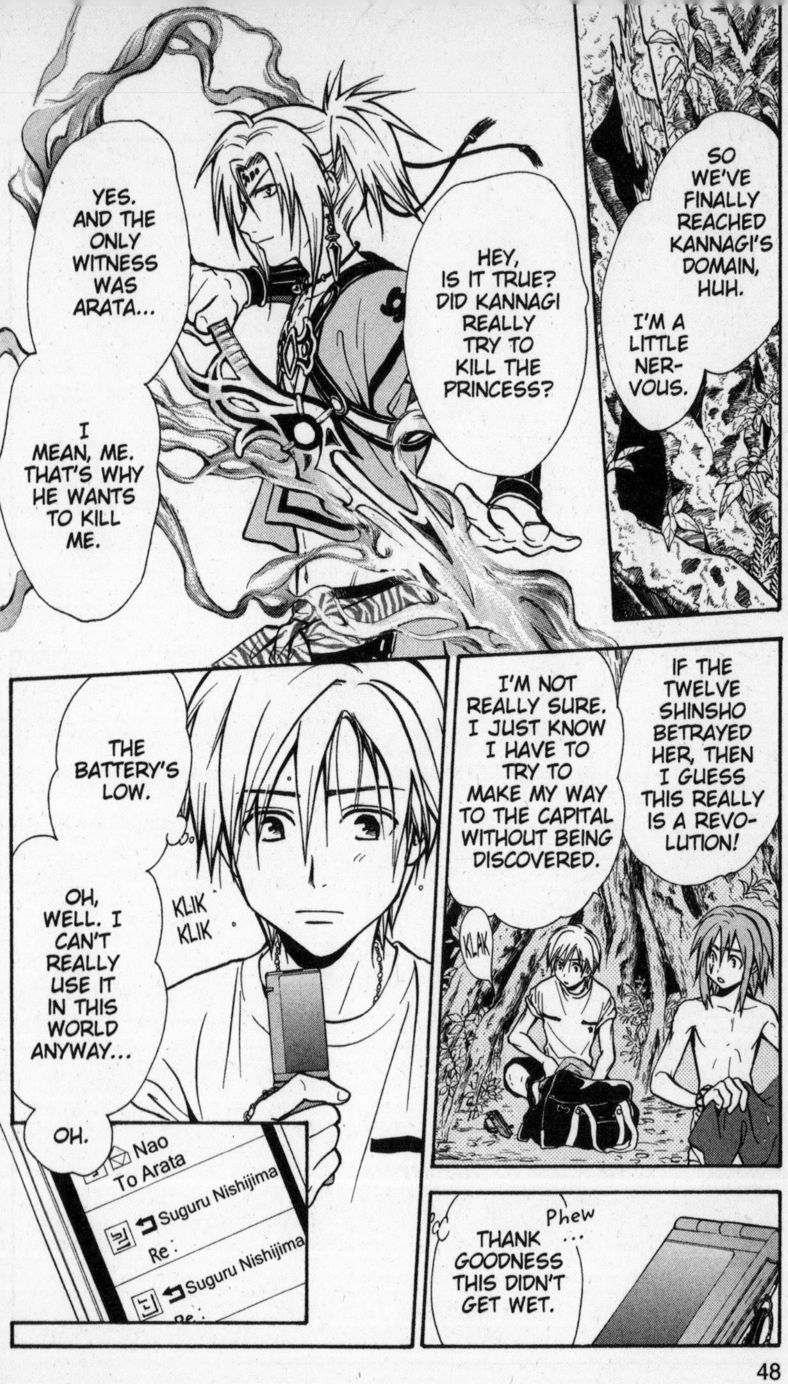
SO WE'VE FINALLY REACHED KANNAGI'S DOMAIN, HUH.
I'M A LITTLE NER-VOUS.
HEY, IS IT TRUE? DID KANNAGI REALLY TRY TO KILL THE PRINCESS?
YES. AND THE ONLY WITNESS WAS ARATA...
I MEAN, ME. THAT'S WHY HE WANTS TO KILL ME.
IF THE TWELVE SHINSHO BETRAYED HER, THEN I GUESS THIS REALLY IS A REVO-LUTION!
I'M NOT REALLY SURE. I JUST KNOW I HAVE TO TRY TO MAKE MY WAY TO THE CAPITAL WITHOUT BEING DISCOVERED.
KLAK
THANK GOODNESS THIS DIDN'T GET WET.
Phew ...
THE BATTERY'S LOW.
KLIK KLIK
OH, WELL. I CAN'T REALLY USE IT IN THIS WORLD ANYWAY...
OH.
Nao
To Arata
Suguru Nishijima
Re:
Suguru Nishijima

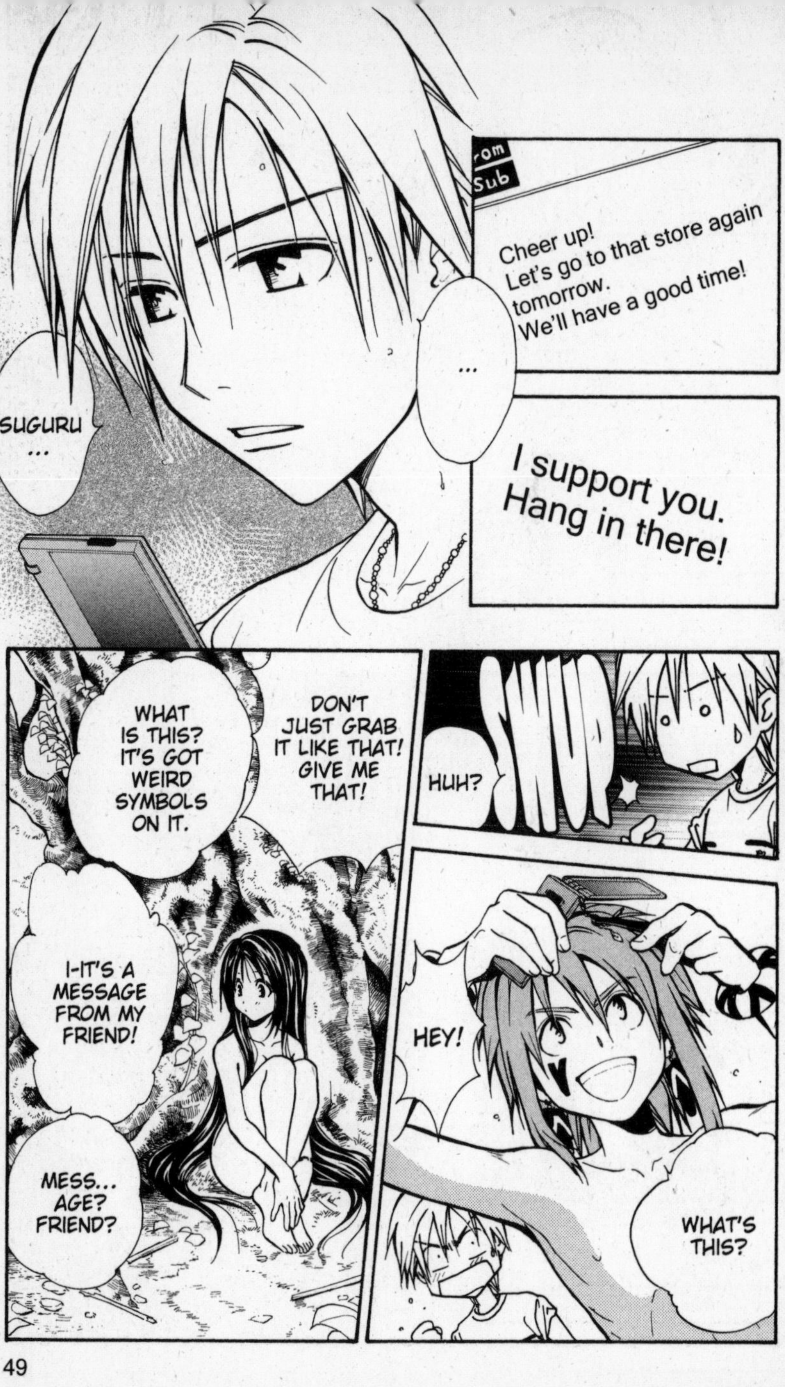
rom
Sub
Cheer up! Let's go to that store again tomorrow. We'll have a good time!
...
I support you. Hang in there!
SUGURU ...
HUH?
HEY!
WHAT'S THIS?
DON'T JUST GRAB IT LIKE THAT! GIVE ME THAT!
WHAT IS THIS? IT'S GOT WEIRD SYMBOLS ON IT.
I-IT'S A MESSAGE FROM MY FRIEND!
MESS... AGE? FRIEND?

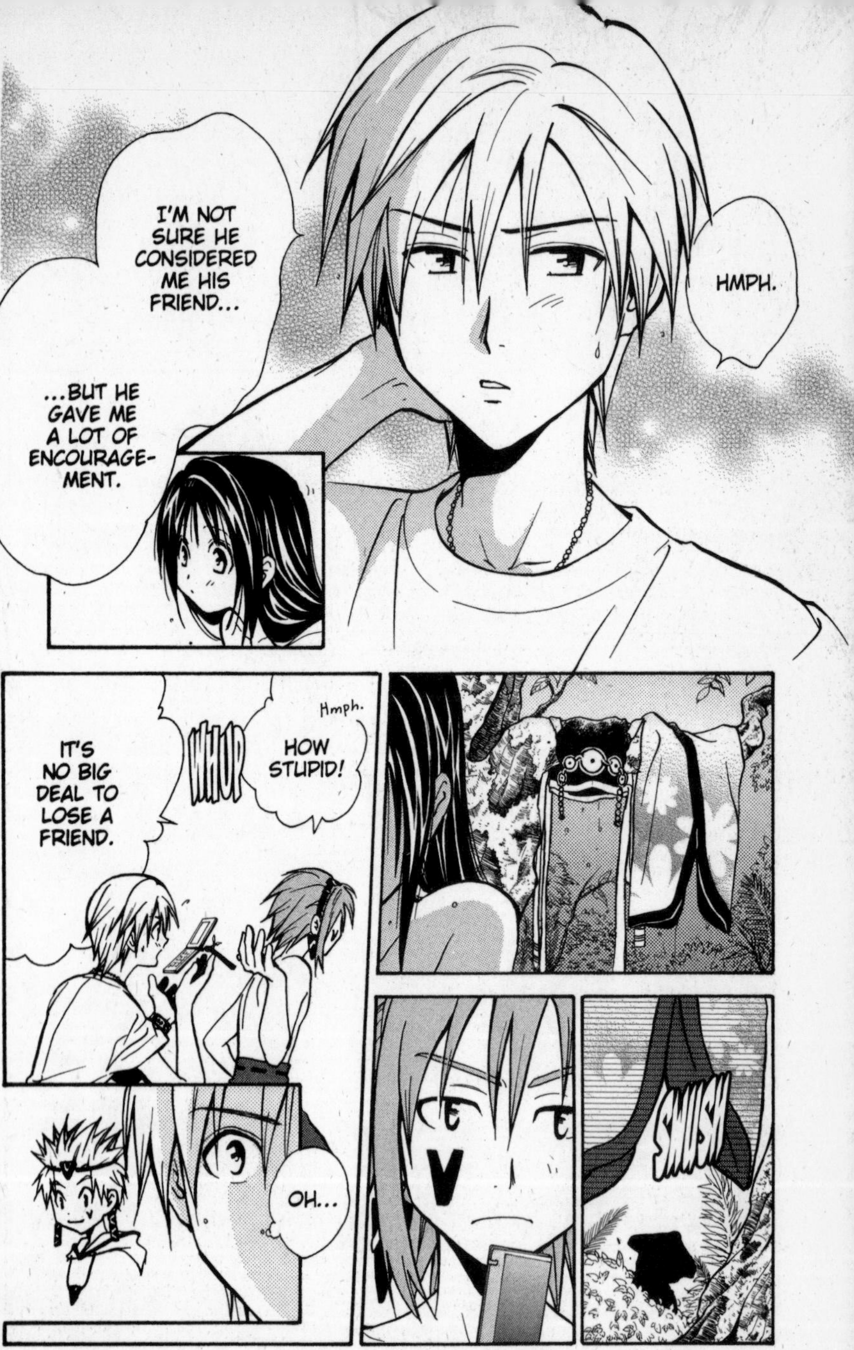
HMPH.
I'M NOT SURE HE CONSIDERED ME HIS FRIEND...
...BUT HE GAVE ME A LOT OF ENCOURAGE-MENT.
Hmph.
HOW STUPID!
WHOP
IT'S NO BIG DEAL TO LOSE A FRIEND.
SWISH
OH...

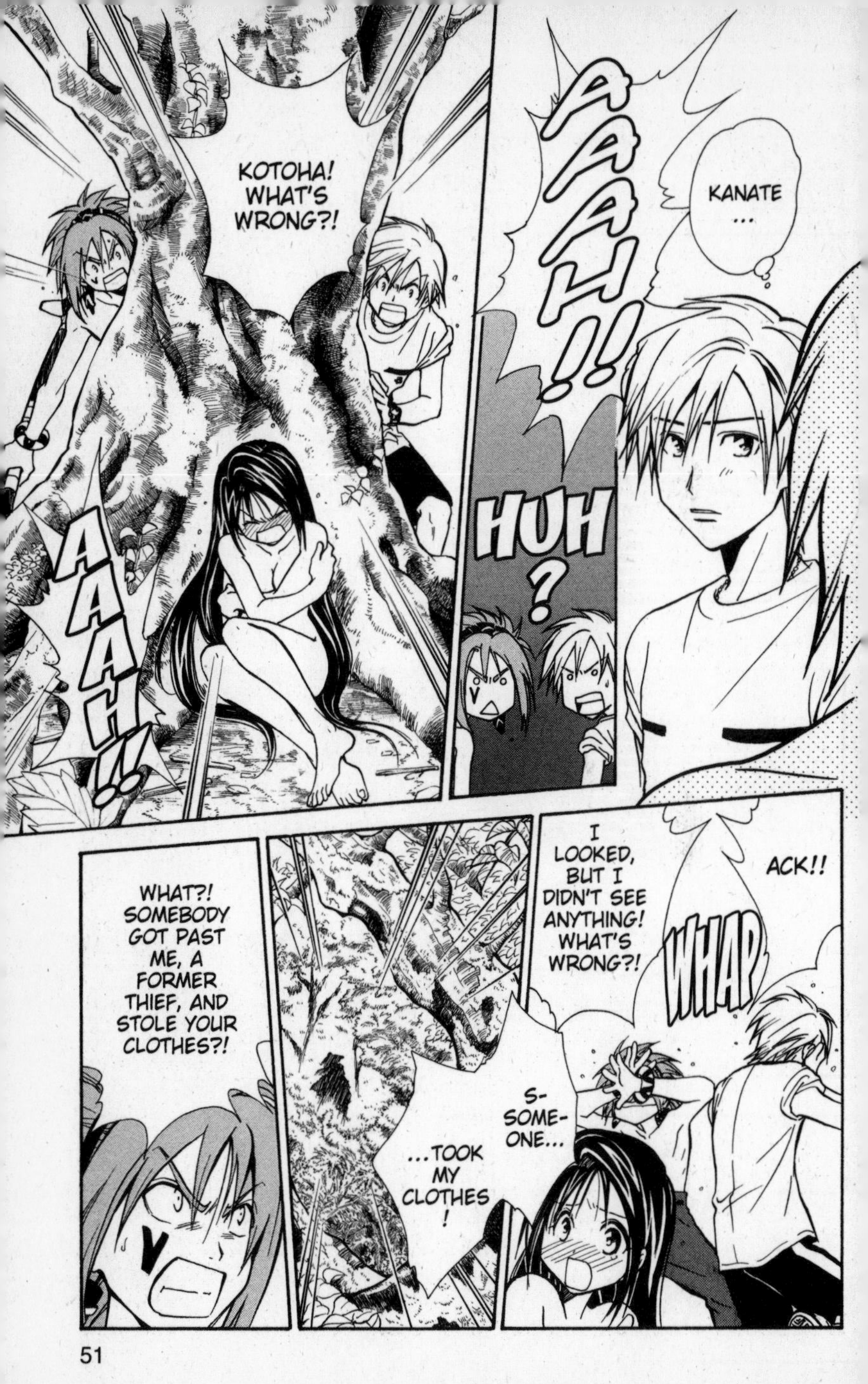
KANATE ...
AAAAH!!
HUH ?
KOTOHA! WHAT'S WRONG?!
AAAAH!!
I LOOKED, BUT I DIDN'T SEE ANYTHING! WHAT'S WRONG?!
ACK!!
WHAP
S-SOME-ONE...
...TOOK MY CLOTHES !
WHAT?! SOMEBODY GOT PAST ME, A FORMER THIEF, AND STOLE YOUR CLOTHES?!

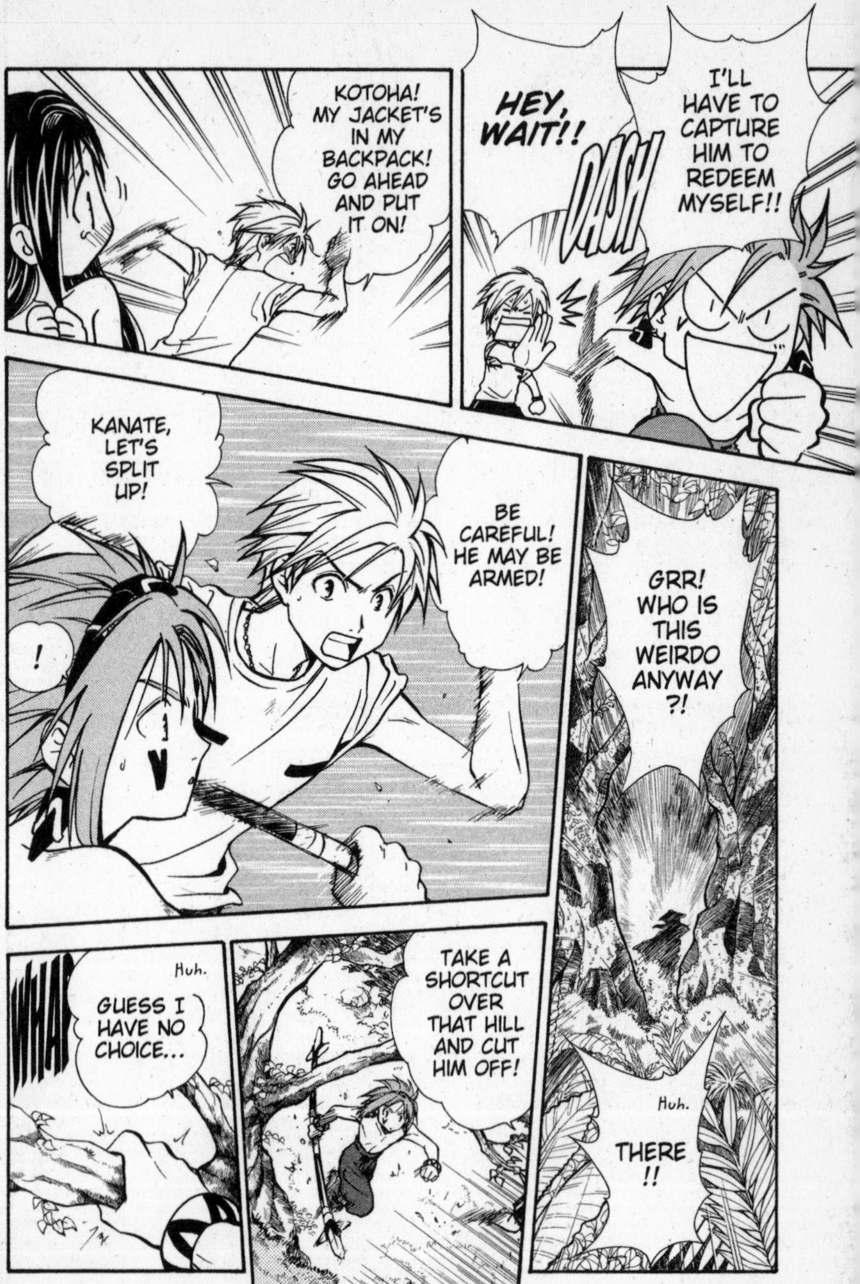
I'LL HAVE TO CAPTURE HIM TO REDEEM MYSELF!!
HEY, WAIT!!
DASH
KOTOHA! MY JACKET'S IN MY BACKPACK! GO AHEAD AND PUT IT ON!
GRR! WHO IS THIS WEIRDO ANYWAY ?!
Huh.
THERE !!
KANATE, LET'S SPLIT UP!
BE CAREFUL! HE MAY BE ARMED!
!
TAKE A SHORTCUT OVER THAT HILL AND CUT HIM OFF!
Huh.
GUESS I HAVE NO CHOICE...
WHAP

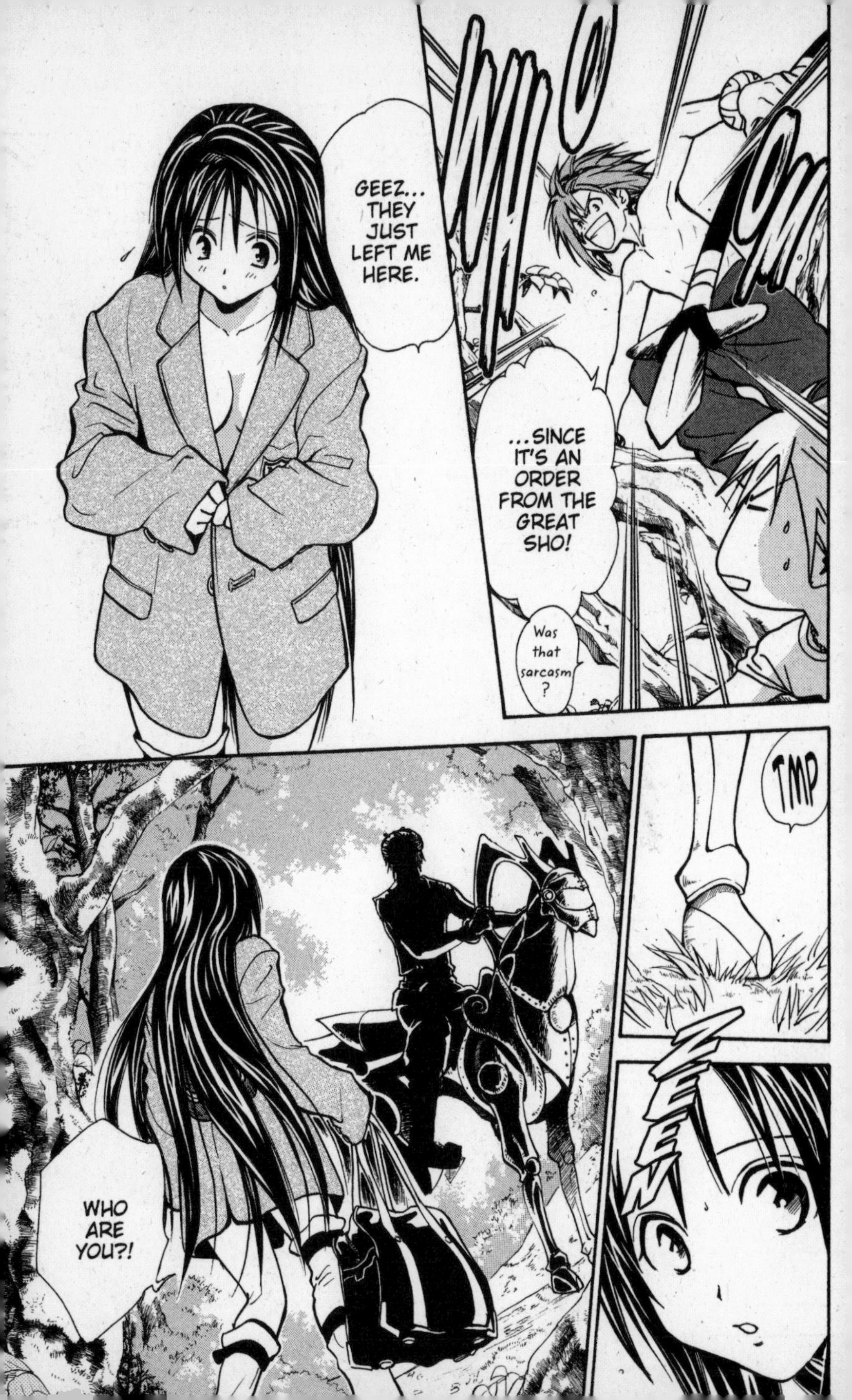
...SINCE IT'S AN ORDER FROM THE GREAT SHO!
Was that sarcasm?
GEEZ... THEY JUST LEFT ME HERE.
TMP
WHO ARE YOU?!

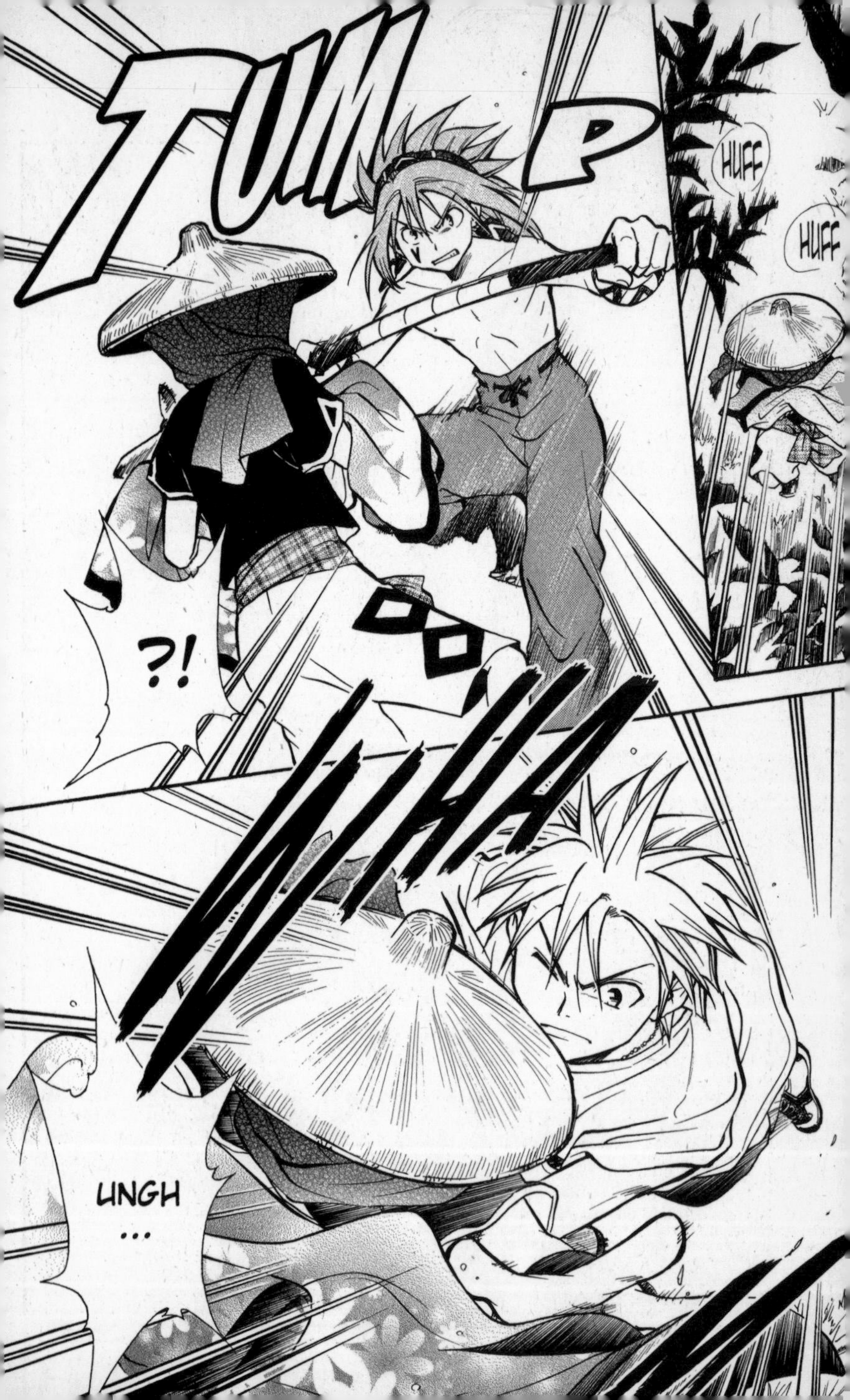
HUFF
HUFF
TUMP
?!
WHA
UNGH
...

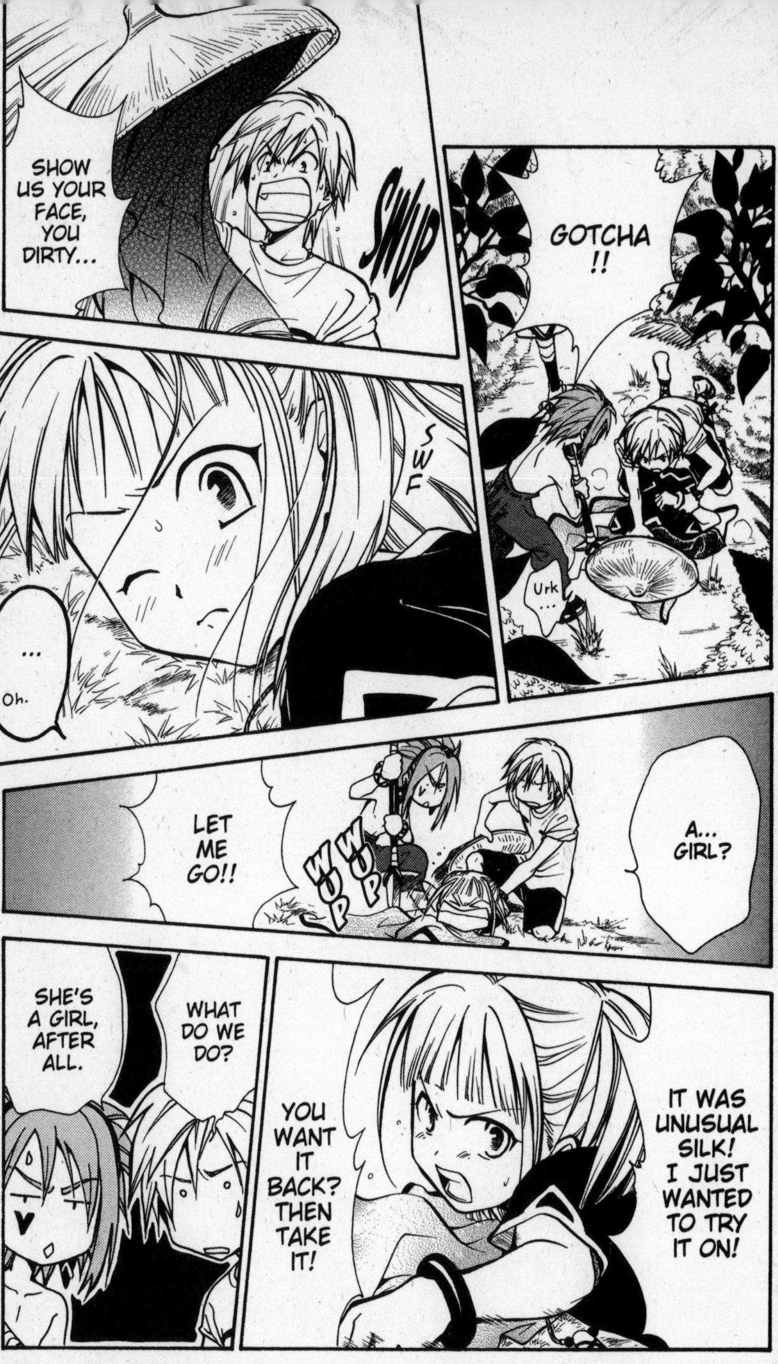
GOTCHA !!
Urk...
SHOW US YOUR FACE, YOU DIRTY...
SHIP
SWF
... Oh.
A... GIRL?
LET ME GO!!
WUP WUP
IT WAS UNUSUAL SILK! I JUST WANTED TO TRY IT ON!
YOU WANT IT BACK? THEN TAKE IT!
WHAT DO WE DO?
SHE'S A GIRL, AFTER ALL.

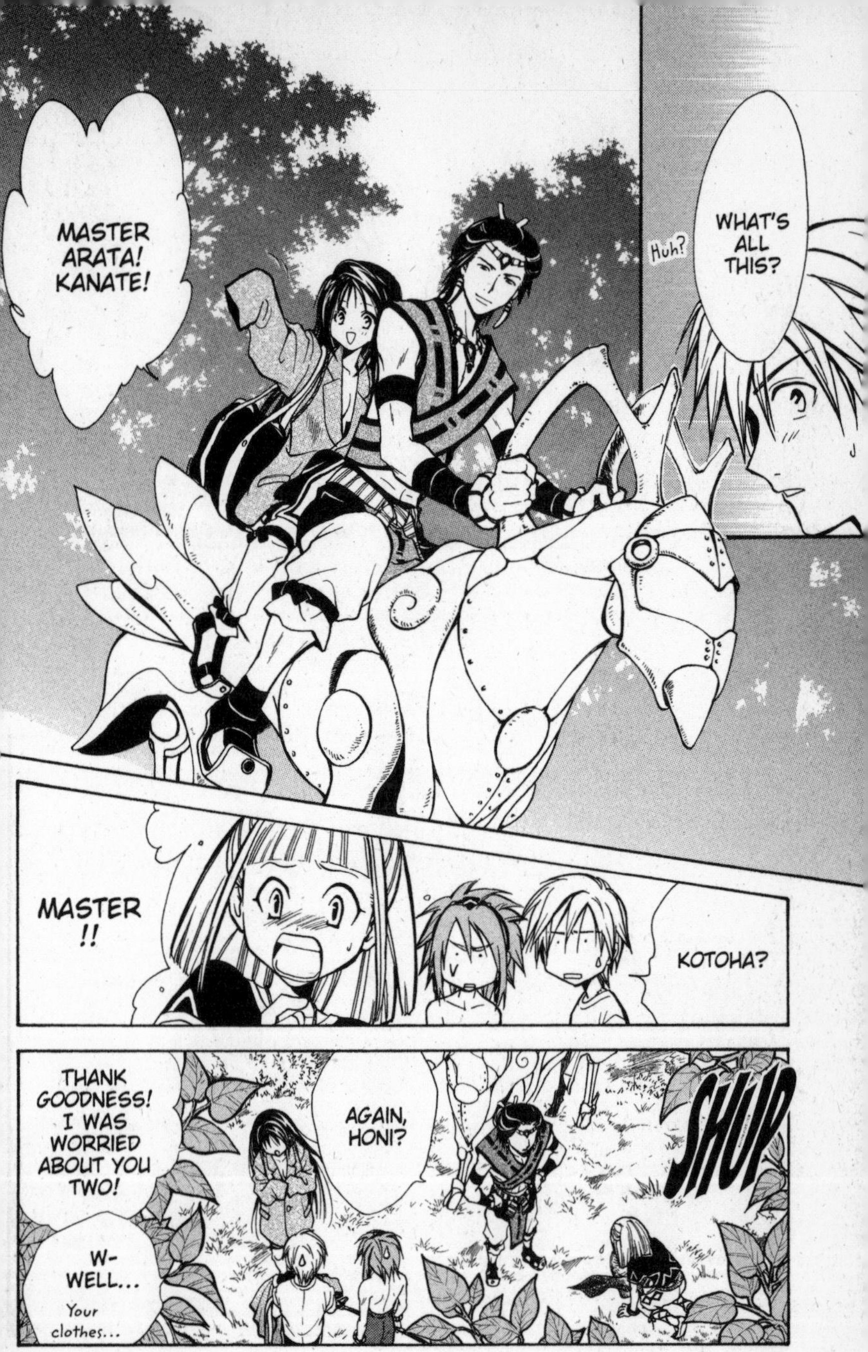
WHAT'S ALL THIS?
Huh?
MASTER ARATA! KANATE!
KOTOHA?
MASTER !!
SHUP
AGAIN, HONI?
THANK GOODNESS! I WAS WORRIED ABOUT YOU TWO!
W-WELL...
Your clothes...

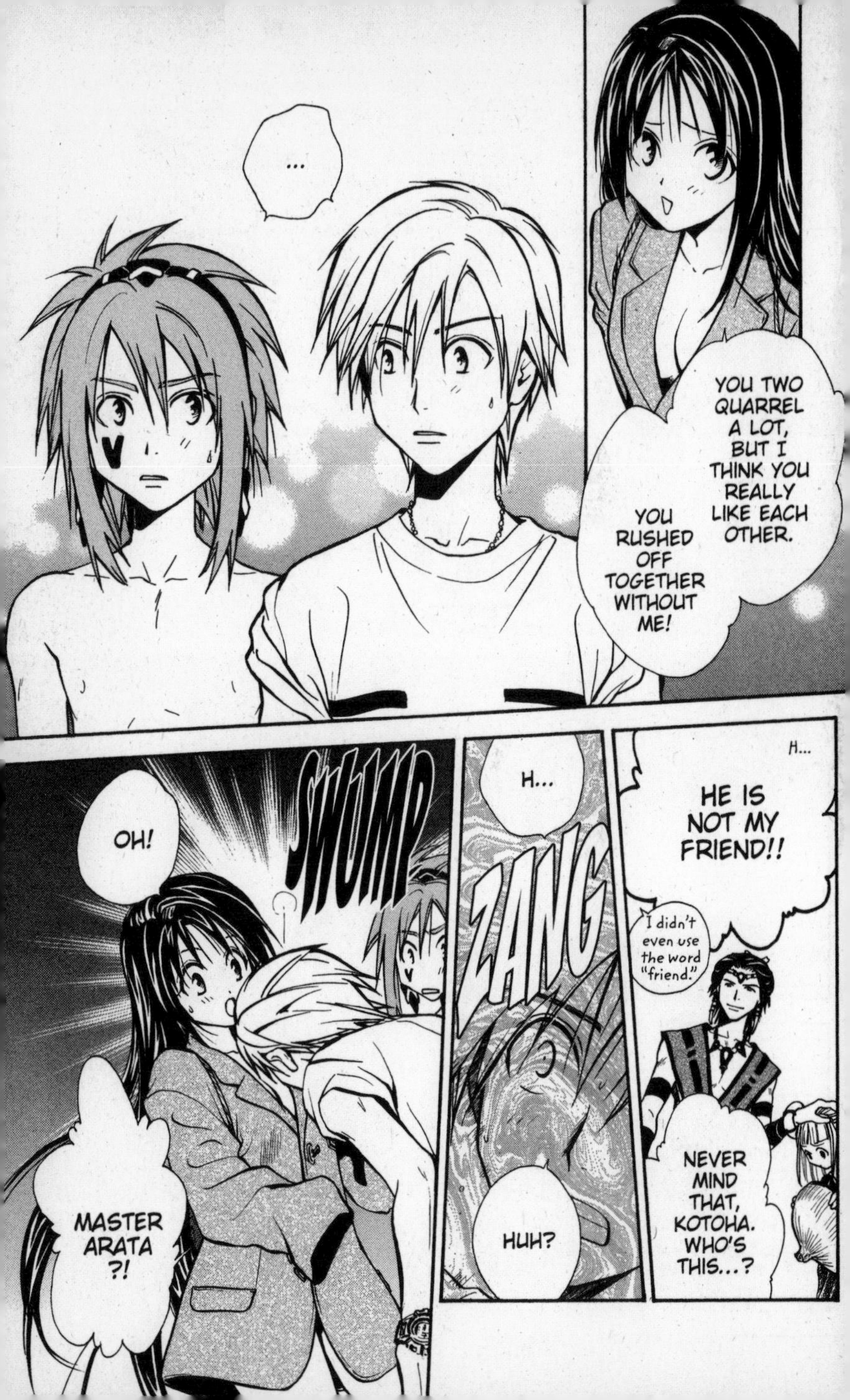
YOU TWO QUARREL A LOT, BUT I THINK YOU REALLY LIKE EACH OTHER.
YOU RUSHED OFF TOGETHER WITHOUT ME!
...
H...
HE IS NOT MY FRIEND!!
I didn't even use the word "friend."
NEVER MIND THAT, KOTOHA. WHO'S THIS...?
H...
ZANG
HUH?
SWUMP
OH!
MASTER ARATA?!

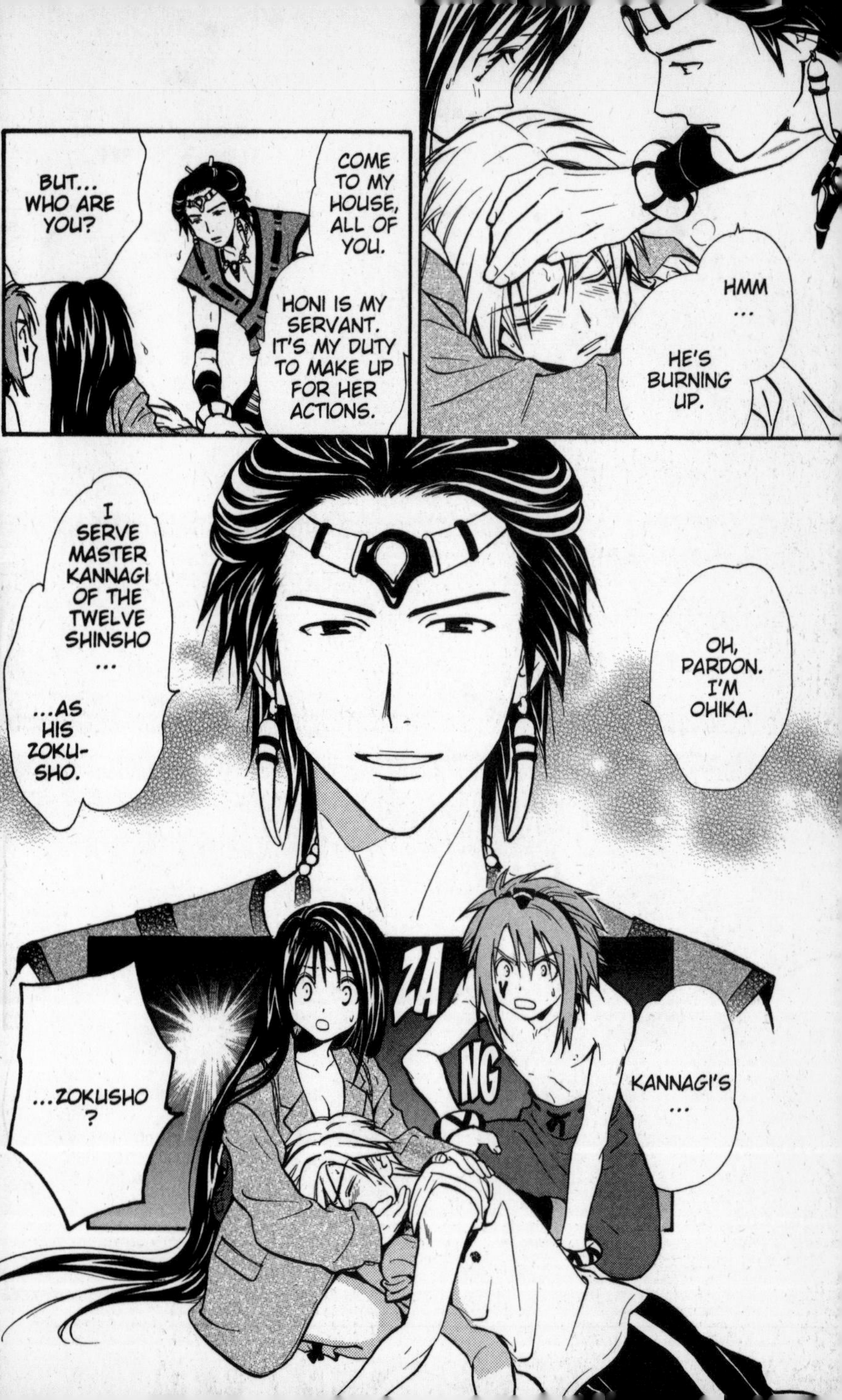
HMM ...
HE'S BURNING UP.
COME TO MY HOUSE, ALL OF YOU.
HONI IS MY SERVANT. IT'S MY DUTY TO MAKE UP FOR HER ACTIONS.
BUT... WHO ARE YOU?
OH, PARDON. I'M OHIKA.
I SERVE MASTER KANNAGI OF THE TWELVE SHINSHO ...
...AS HIS ZOKU-SHO.
KANNAGI'S ...
ZANG
...ZOKUSHO ?

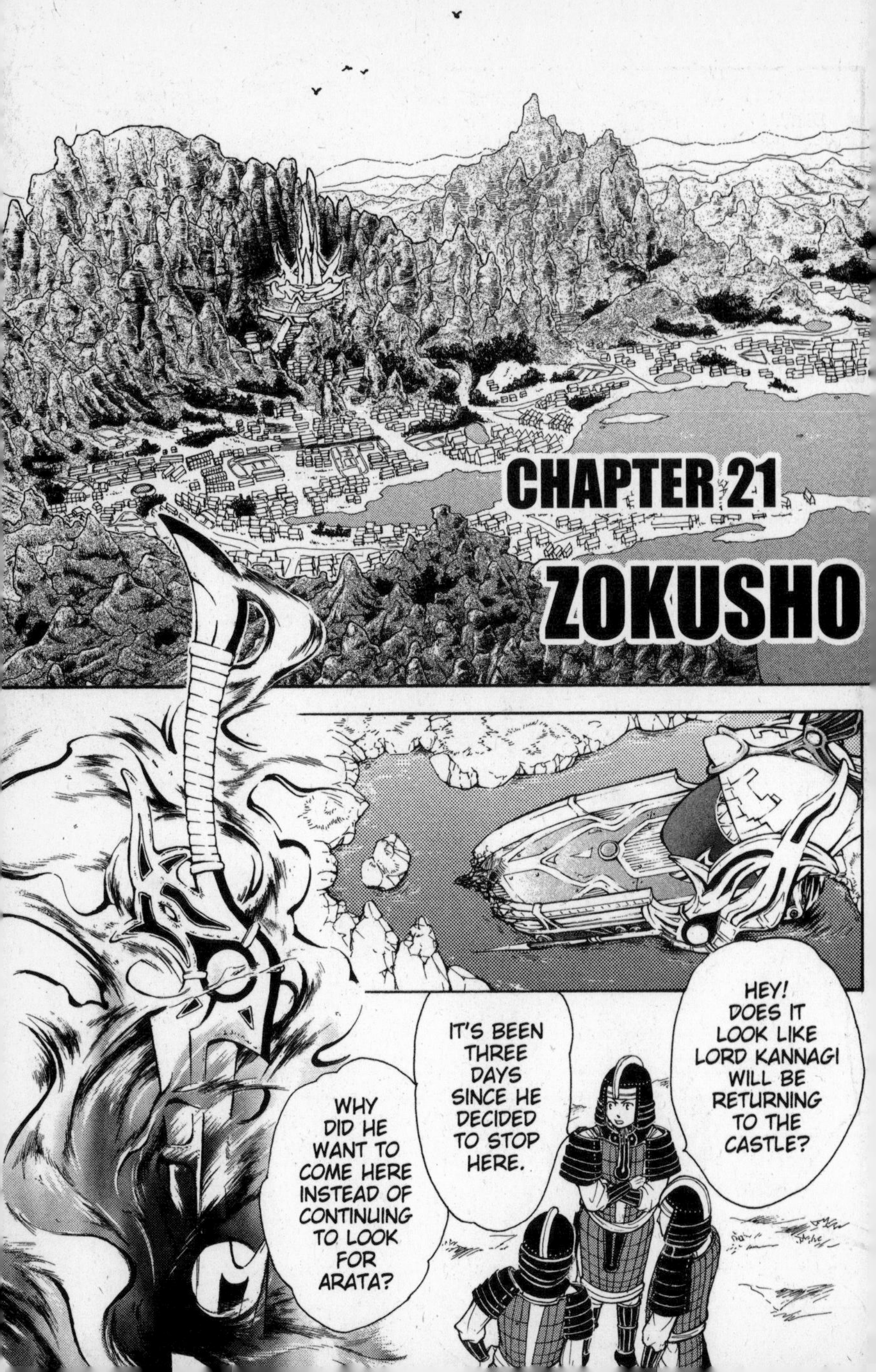
CHAPTER 21
ZOKUSHO
HEY! DOES IT LOOK LIKE LORD KANNAGI WILL BE RETURNING TO THE CASTLE?
IT'S BEEN THREE DAYS SINCE HE DECIDED TO STOP HERE.
WHY DID HE WANT TO COME HERE INSTEAD OF CONTINUING TO LOOK FOR ARATA?

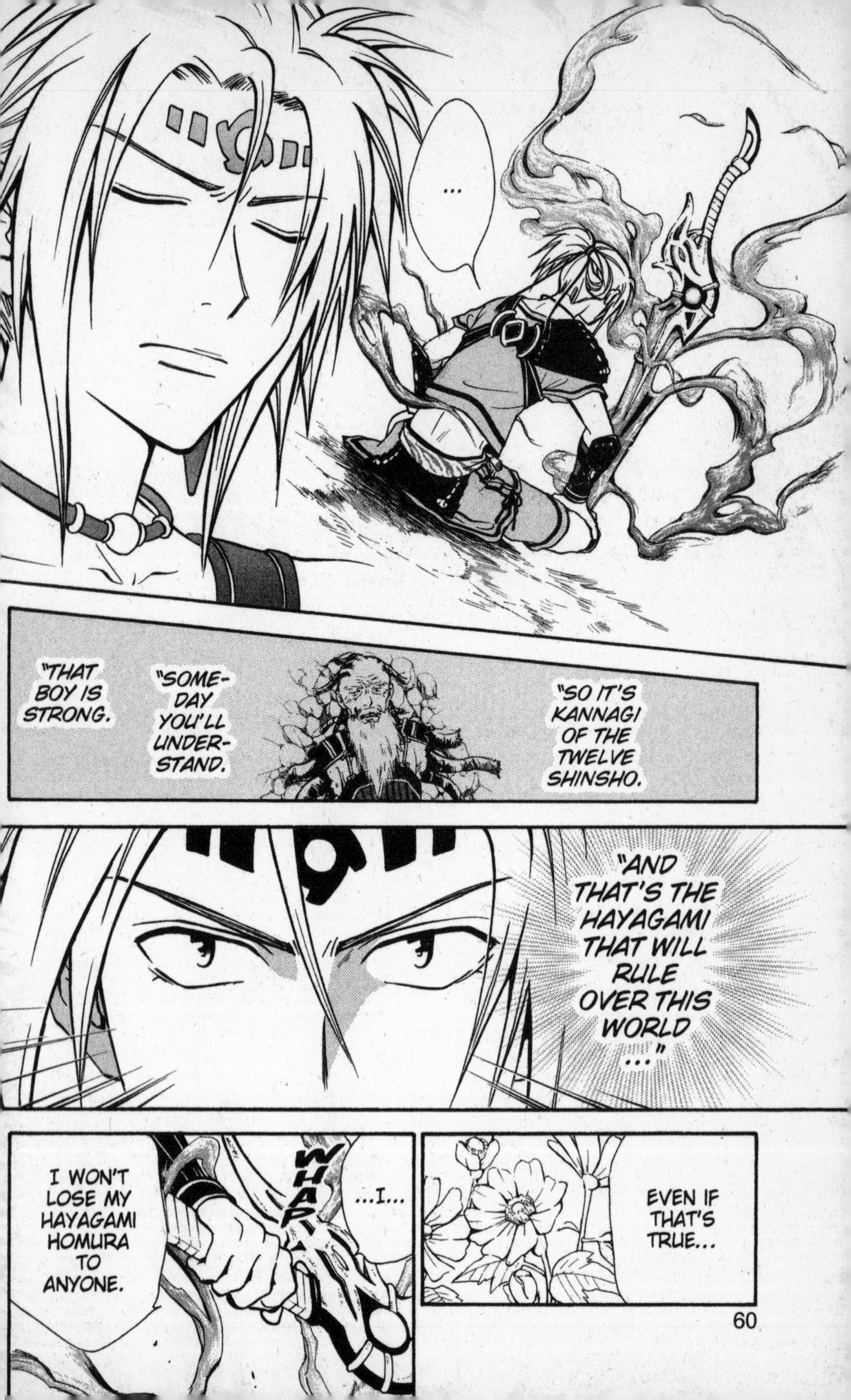
...
"SO IT'S KANNAGI OF THE TWELVE SHINSHO.
"SOME-DAY YOU'LL UNDER-STAND.
"THAT BOY IS STRONG.
"AND THAT'S THE HAYAGAMI THAT WILL RULE OVER THIS WORLD ..."
EVEN IF THAT'S TRUE...
...I...
WHAP
I WON'T LOSE MY HAYAGAMI HOMURA TO ANYONE.

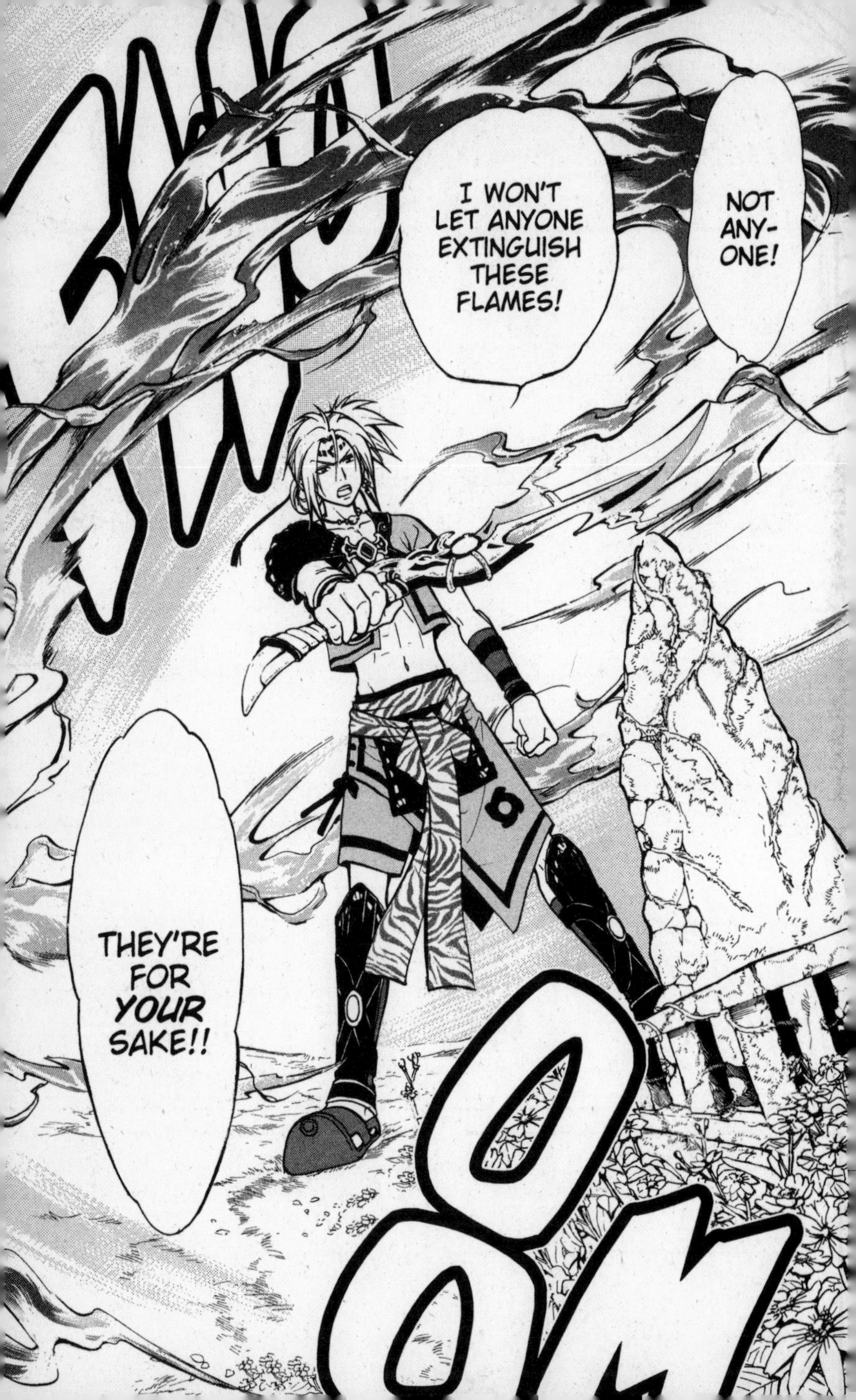
NOT ANY- ONE!
I WON'T LET ANYONE EXTINGUISH THESE FLAMES!
THEY'RE FOR *YOUR* SAKE!!

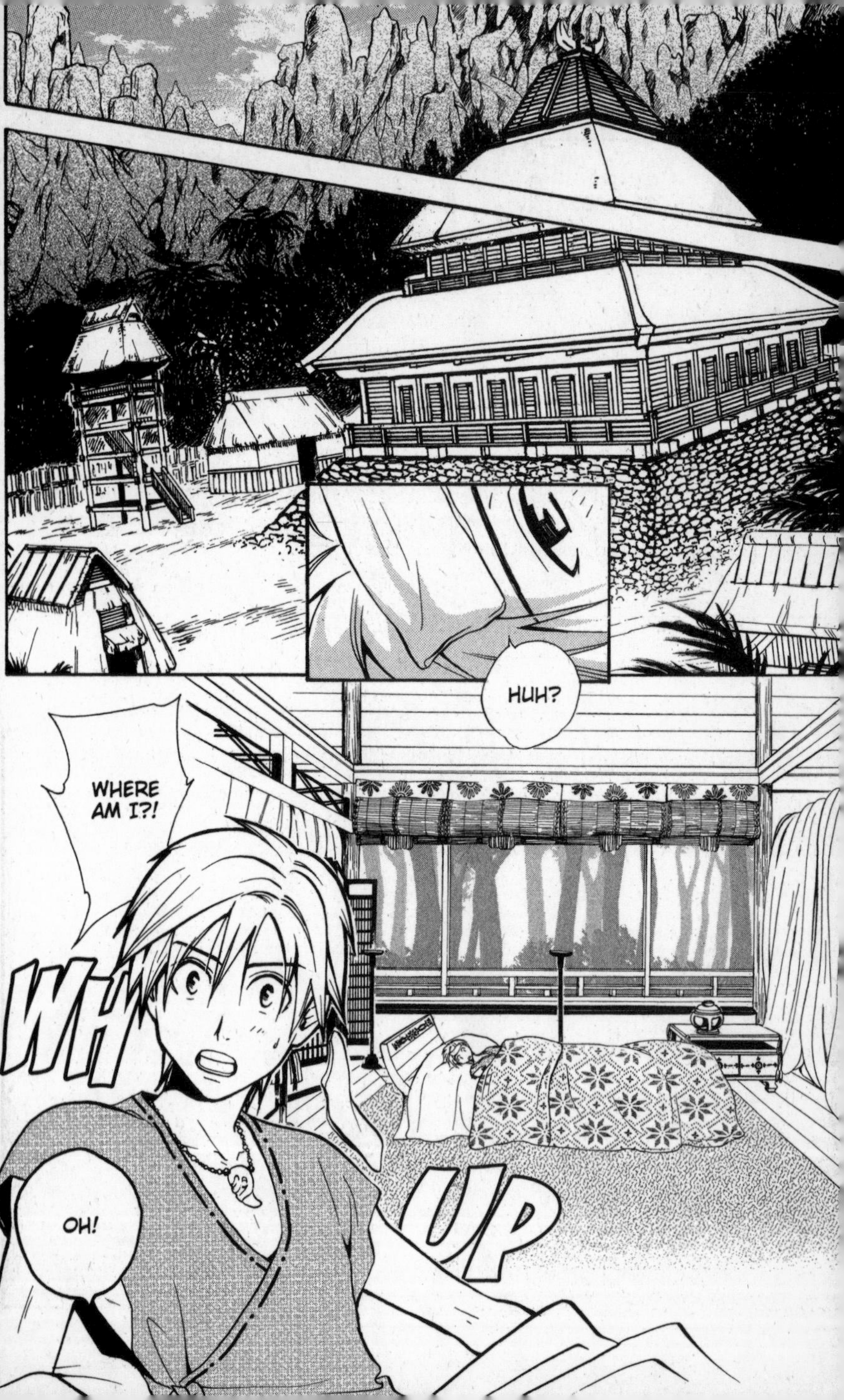
HUH?
WHERE AM I?!
WH UP
OH!

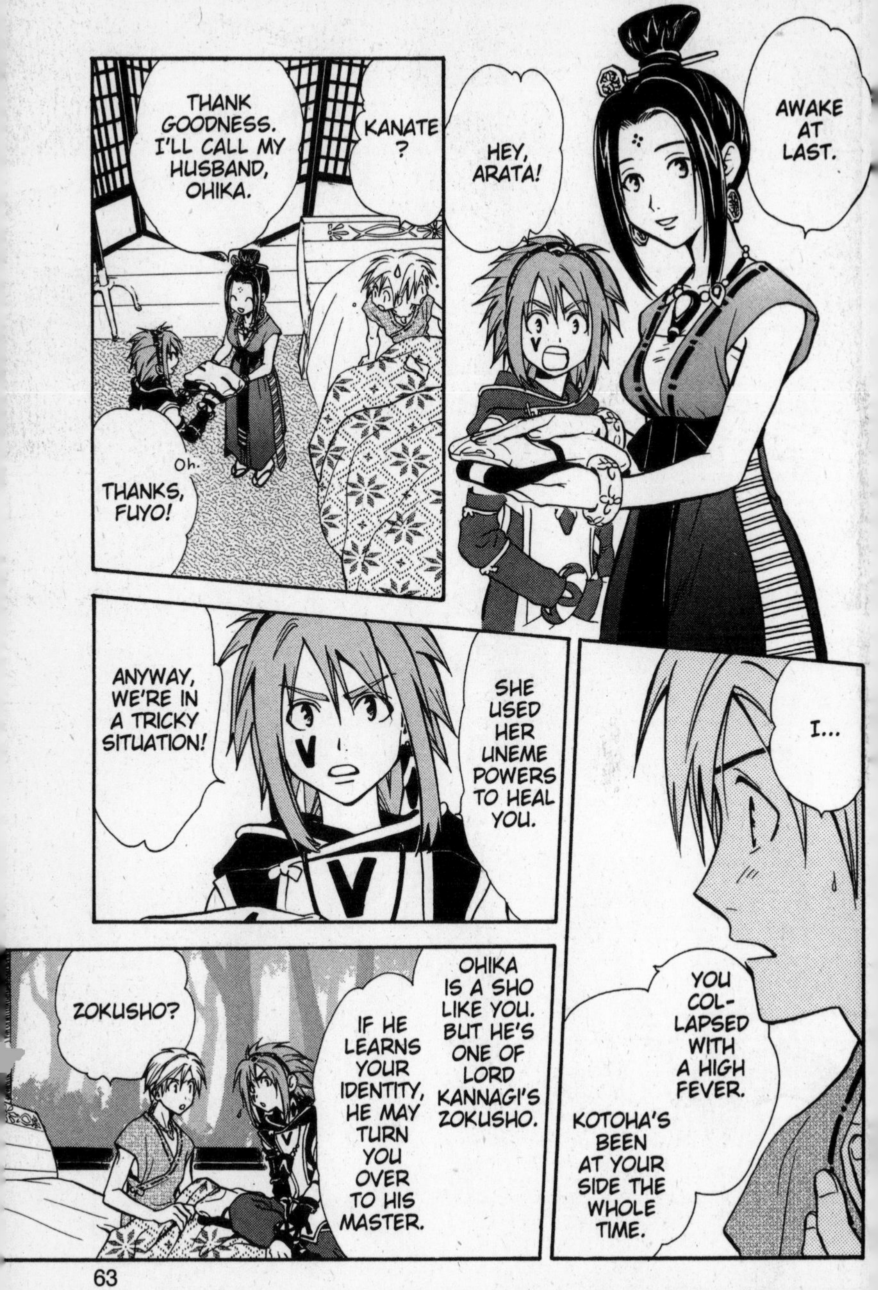
AWAKE AT LAST.
HEY, ARATA!
KANATE?
THANK GOODNESS. I'LL CALL MY HUSBAND, OHIKA.
Oh.
THANKS, FUYO!
I...
YOU COL-LAPSED WITH A HIGH FEVER.
KOTOHA'S BEEN AT YOUR SIDE THE WHOLE TIME.
SHE USED HER UNEME POWERS TO HEAL YOU.
ANYWAY, WE'RE IN A TRICKY SITUATION!
OHIKA IS A SHO LIKE YOU. BUT HE'S ONE OF LORD KANNAGI'S ZOKUSHO.
IF HE LEARNS YOUR IDENTITY, HE MAY TURN YOU OVER TO HIS MASTER.
ZOKUSHO?

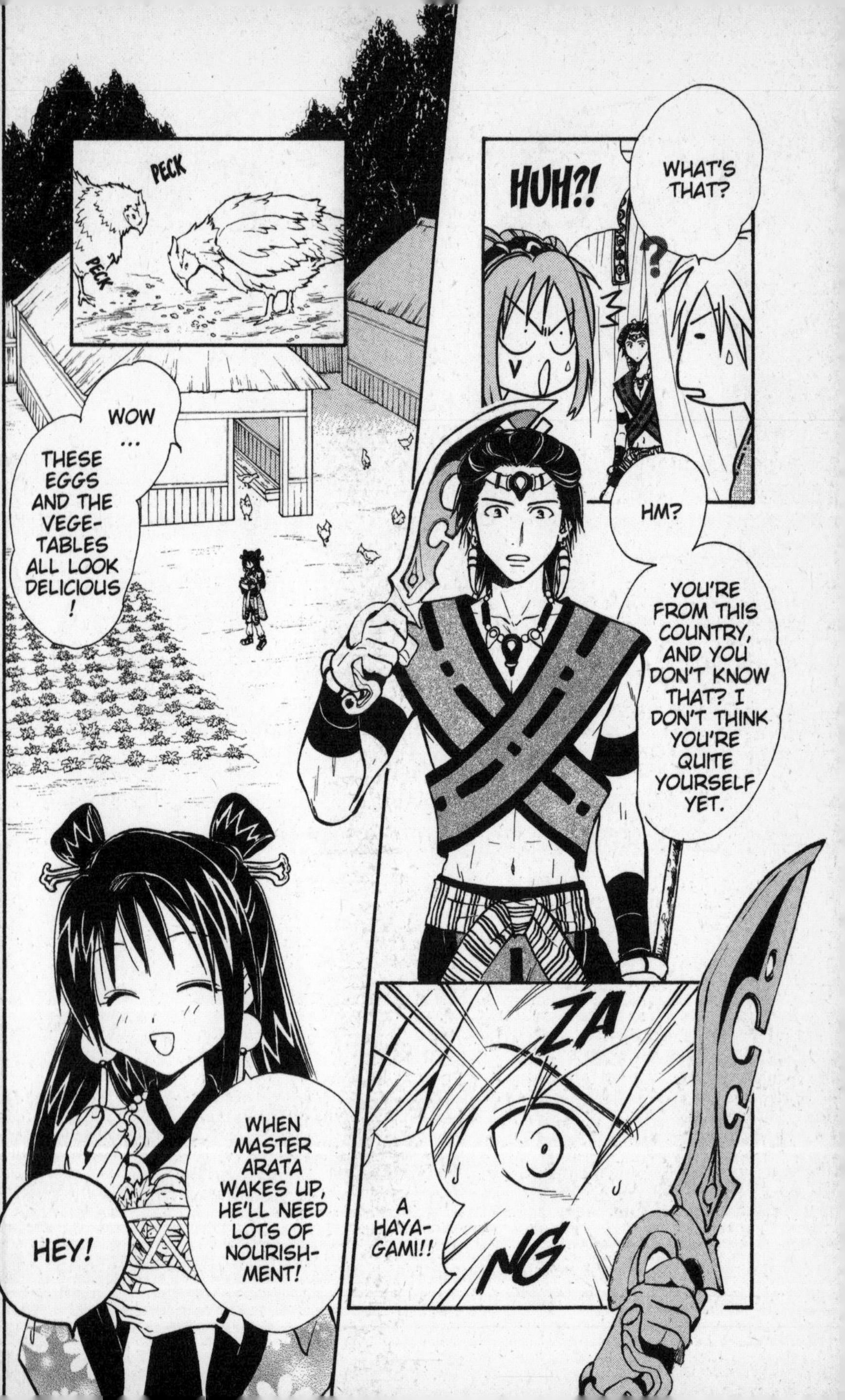

WHAT'S THAT?
HUH?!
PECK
PECK
WOW ...
THESE EGGS AND THE VEGE-TABLES ALL LOOK DELICIOUS!
WHEN MASTER ARATA WAKES UP, HE'LL NEED LOTS OF NOURISH-MENT!
HEY!
HM?
YOU'RE FROM THIS COUNTRY, AND YOU DON'T KNOW THAT? I DON'T THINK YOU'RE QUITE YOURSELF YET.
ZA
NG
A HAYA-GAMI!!

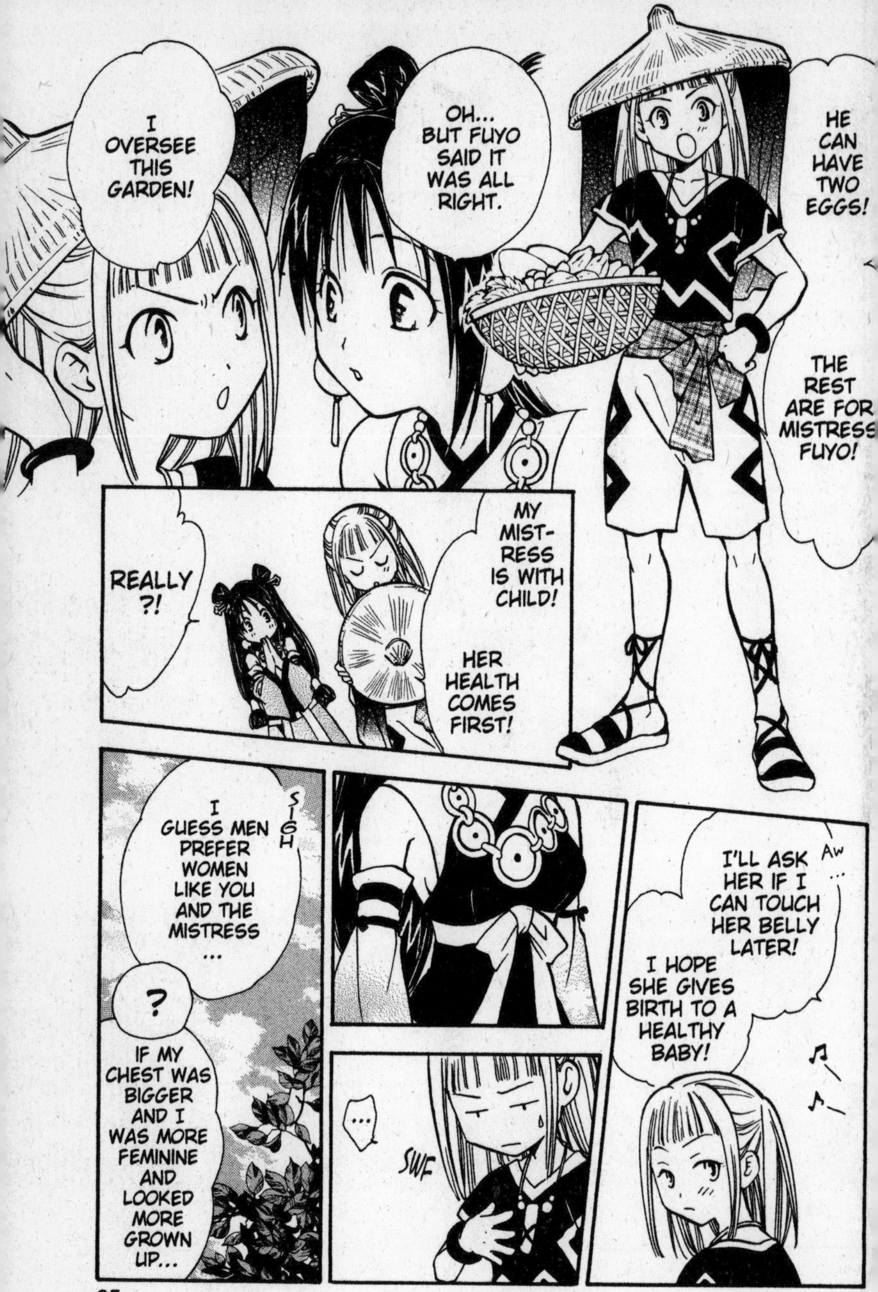
HE CAN HAVE TWO EGGS!
THE REST ARE FOR MISTRESS FUYO!
OH... BUT FUYO SAID IT WAS ALL RIGHT.
I OVERSEE THIS GARDEN!
MY MISTRESS IS WITH CHILD!
HER HEALTH COMES FIRST!
REALLY ?!
I'LL ASK HER IF I CAN TOUCH HER BELLY LATER!
AW...
I HOPE SHE GIVES BIRTH TO A HEALTHY BABY!
♪
...
SWF
SIGH
I GUESS MEN PREFER WOMEN LIKE YOU AND THE MISTRESS...
?
IF MY CHEST WAS BIGGER AND I WAS MORE FEMININE AND LOOKED MORE GROWN UP...

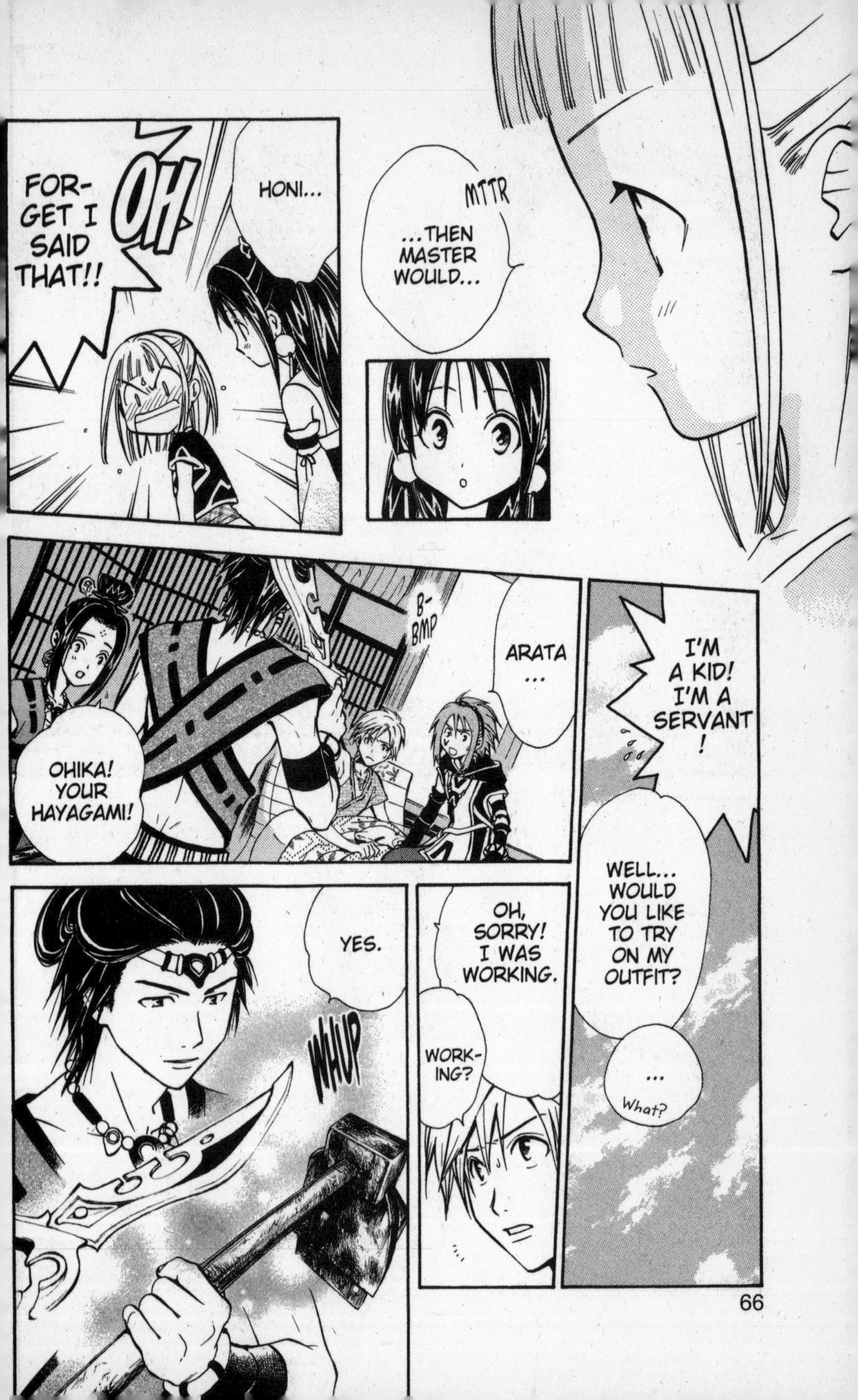
MTTR
...THEN MASTER WOULD...
HONI...
OH
FOR-GET I SAID THAT!!
I'M A KID! I'M A SERVANT!
WELL... WOULD YOU LIKE TO TRY ON MY OUTFIT?
...
What?
B-BMP
ARATA...
OHIKA! YOUR HAYAGAMI!
OH, SORRY! I WAS WORKING.
WORK-ING?
YES.
WHUP

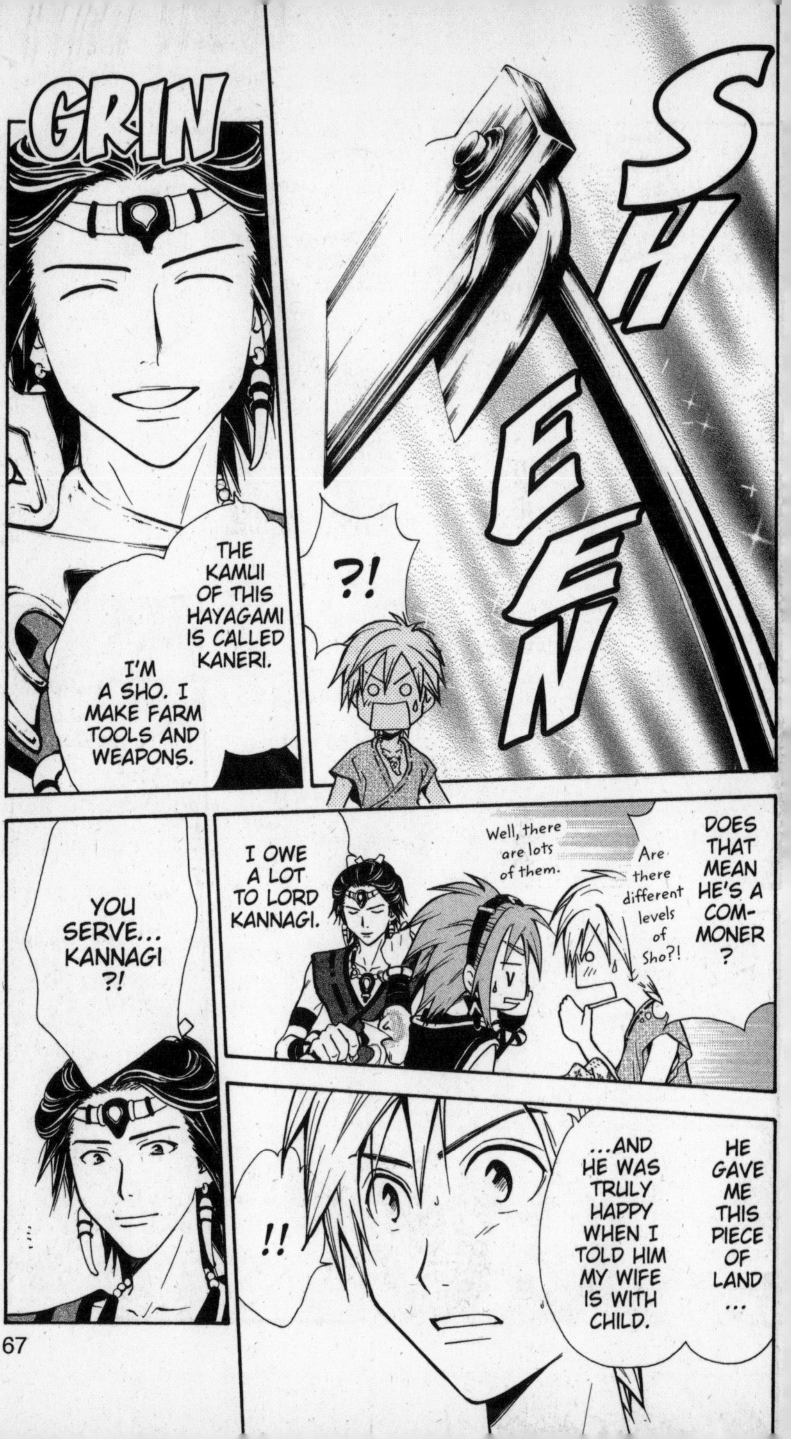
SHEEN
?!
GRIN
THE KAMUI OF THIS HAYAGAMI IS CALLED KANERI.
I'M A SHO. I MAKE FARM TOOLS AND WEAPONS.
DOES THAT MEAN HE'S A COMMONER?
Are there different levels of Sho?!
Well, there are lots of them.
I OWE A LOT TO LORD KANNAGI.
HE GAVE ME THIS PIECE OF LAND...
...AND HE WAS TRULY HAPPY WHEN I TOLD HIM MY WIFE IS WITH CHILD.
!!
YOU SERVE... KANNAGI?!

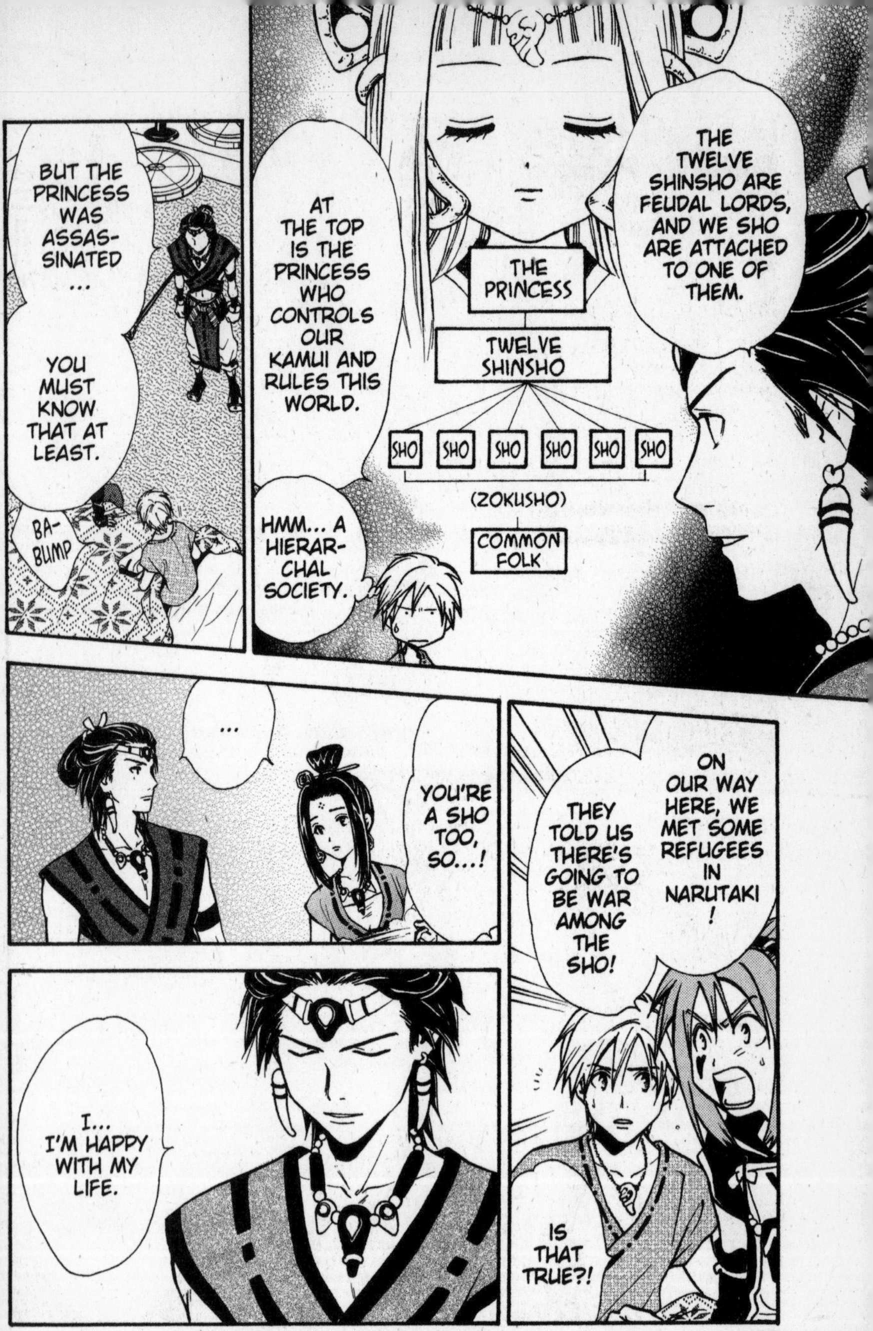
THE TWELVE SHINSHO ARE FEUDAL LORDS, AND WE SHO ARE ATTACHED TO ONE OF THEM.
AT THE TOP IS THE PRINCESS WHO CONTROLS OUR KAMUI AND RULES THIS WORLD.
THE PRINCESS
TWELVE SHINSHO
SHO
SHO
SHO
SHO
SHO
SHO
(ZOKUSHO)
COMMON FOLK
HMM... A HIERARCHAL SOCIETY.
BUT THE PRINCESS WAS ASSASSINATED...
YOU MUST KNOW THAT AT LEAST.
BA-BUMP
ON OUR WAY HERE, WE MET SOME REFUGEES IN NARUTAKI!
THEY TOLD US THERE'S GOING TO BE WAR AMONG THE SHO!
IS THAT TRUE?!
YOU'RE A SHO TOO, SO...!
...
I... I'M HAPPY WITH MY LIFE.

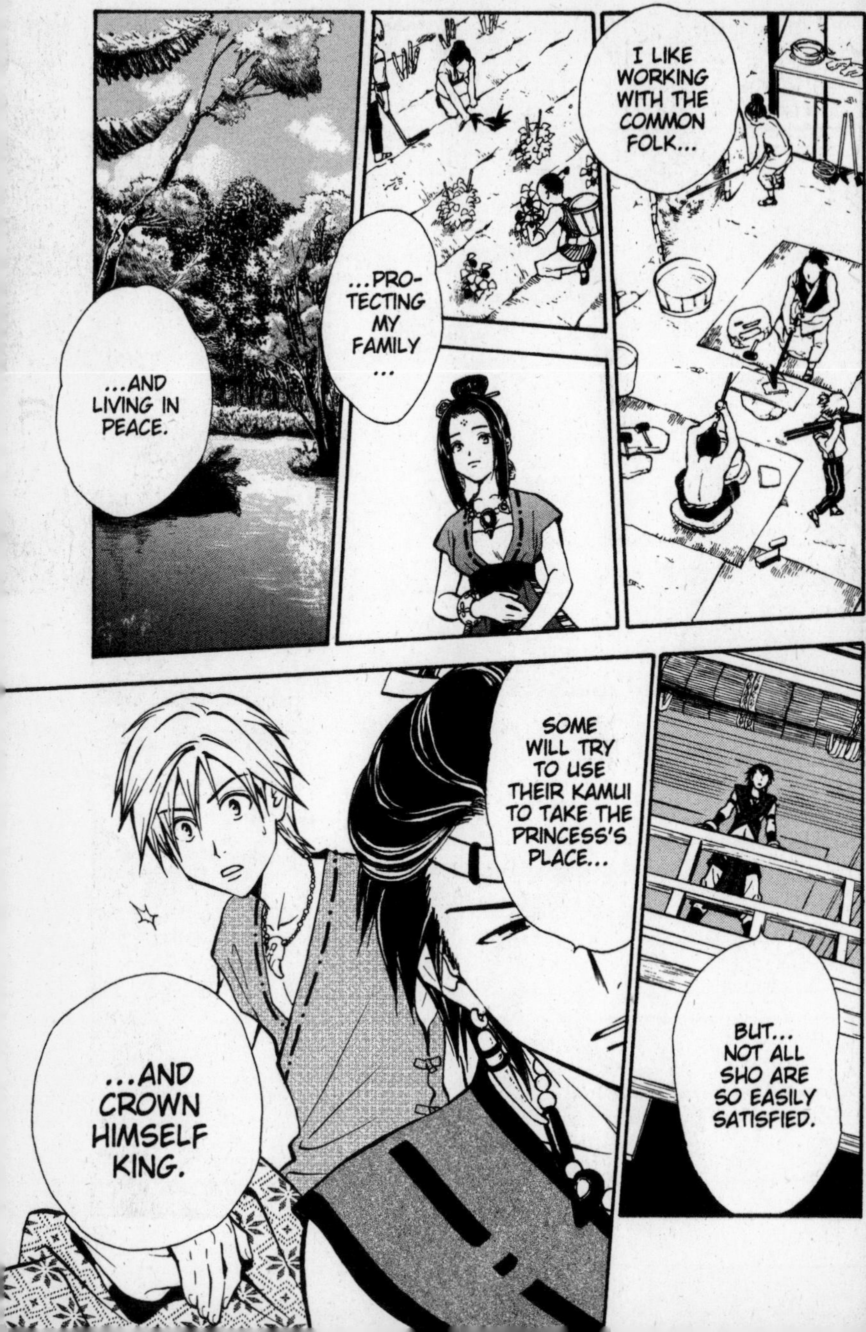
I LIKE WORKING WITH THE COMMON FOLK...
...PRO-TECTING MY FAMILY...
...AND LIVING IN PEACE.
BUT... NOT ALL SHO ARE SO EASILY SATISFIED.
SOME WILL TRY TO USE THEIR KAMUI TO TAKE THE PRINCESS'S PLACE...
...AND CROWN HIMSELF KING.

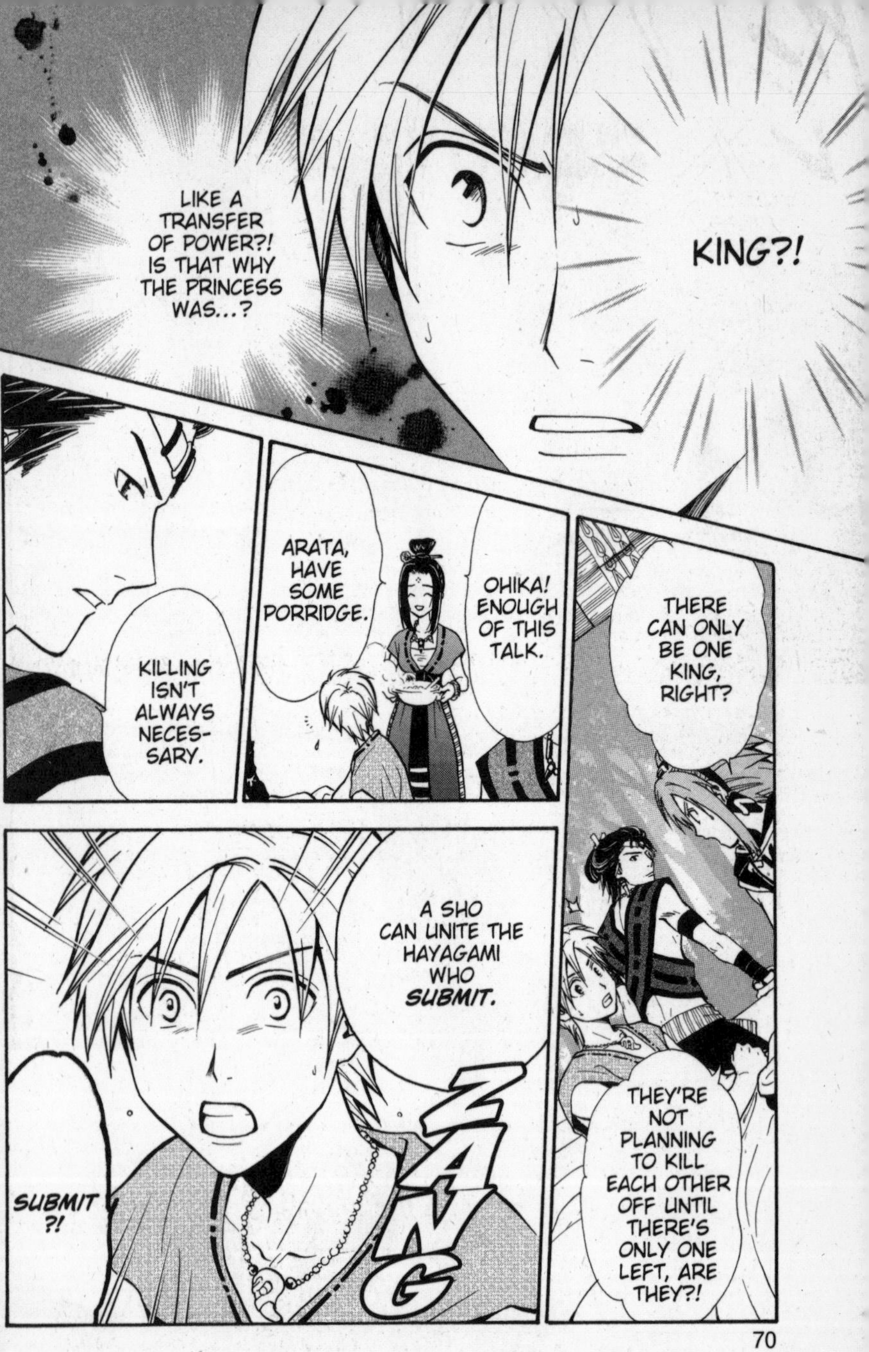
KING?!
LIKE A TRANSFER OF POWER?! IS THAT WHY THE PRINCESS WAS...?
THERE CAN ONLY BE ONE KING, RIGHT?
THEY'RE NOT PLANNING TO KILL EACH OTHER OFF UNTIL THERE'S ONLY ONE LEFT, ARE THEY?!
OHIKA! ENOUGH OF THIS TALK.
ARATA, HAVE SOME PORRIDGE.
KILLING ISN'T ALWAYS NECES-SARY.
A SHO CAN UNITE THE HAYAGAMI WHO SUBMIT.
ZANG
SUBMIT ?!

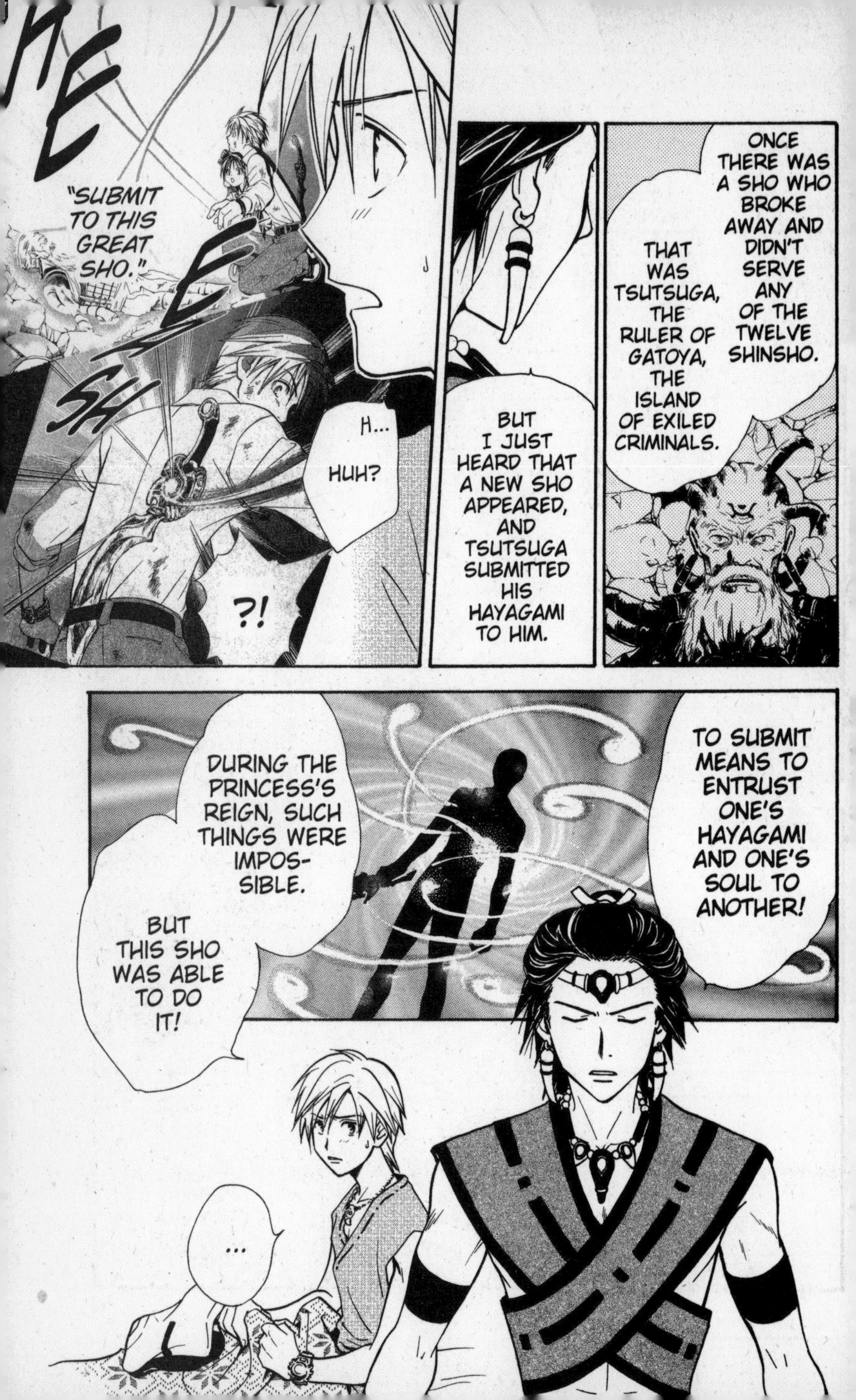
ONCE THERE WAS A SHO WHO BROKE AWAY AND DIDN'T SERVE ANY OF THE TWELVE SHINSHO.
THAT WAS TSUTSUGA, THE RULER OF GATOYA, THE ISLAND OF EXILED CRIMINALS.
BUT I JUST HEARD THAT A NEW SHO APPEARED, AND TSUTSUGA SUBMITTED HIS HAYAGAMI TO HIM.
H...
HUH?
"SUBMIT TO THIS GREAT SHO."
?!
TO SUBMIT MEANS TO ENTRUST ONE'S HAYAGAMI AND ONE'S SOUL TO ANOTHER!
DURING THE PRINCESS'S REIGN, SUCH THINGS WERE IMPOS-SIBLE.
BUT THIS SHO WAS ABLE TO DO IT!
...

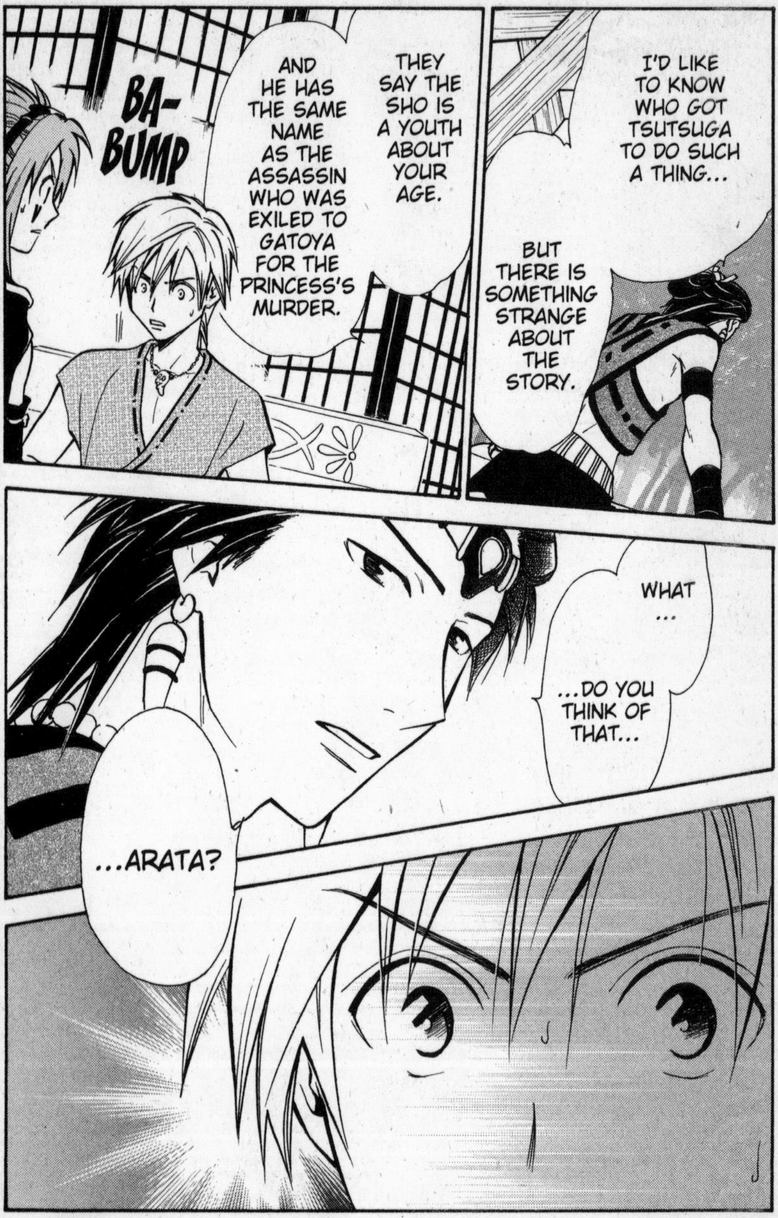
I'D LIKE TO KNOW WHO GOT TSUTSUGA TO DO SUCH A THING...
BUT THERE IS SOMETHING STRANGE ABOUT THE STORY.
THEY SAY THE SHO IS A YOUTH ABOUT YOUR AGE.
AND HE HAS THE SAME NAME AS THE ASSASSIN WHO WAS EXILED TO GATOYA FOR THE PRINCESS'S MURDER.
BA-BUMP
WHAT...
...DO YOU THINK OF THAT...
...ARATA?

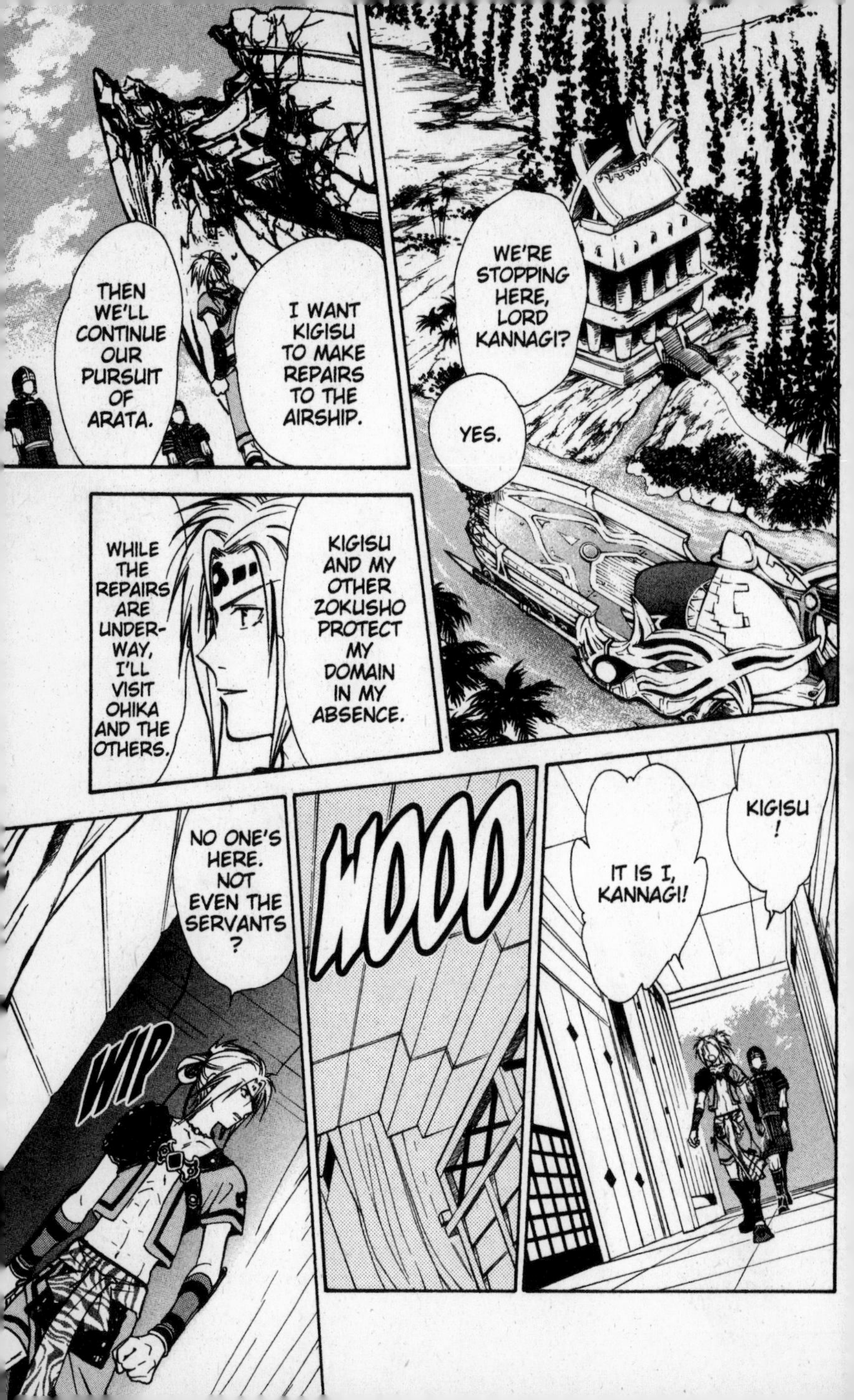
WE'RE STOPPING HERE, LORD KANNAGI?
YES.
I WANT KIGISU TO MAKE REPAIRS TO THE AIRSHIP.
THEN WE'LL CONTINUE OUR PURSUIT OF ARATA.
KIGISU AND MY OTHER ZOKUSHO PROTECT MY DOMAIN IN MY ABSENCE.
WHILE THE REPAIRS ARE UNDER-WAY, I'LL VISIT OHIKA AND THE OTHERS.
KIGISU!
IT IS I, KANNAGI!
WOOO
NO ONE'S HERE. NOT EVEN THE SERVANTS?
WHIP

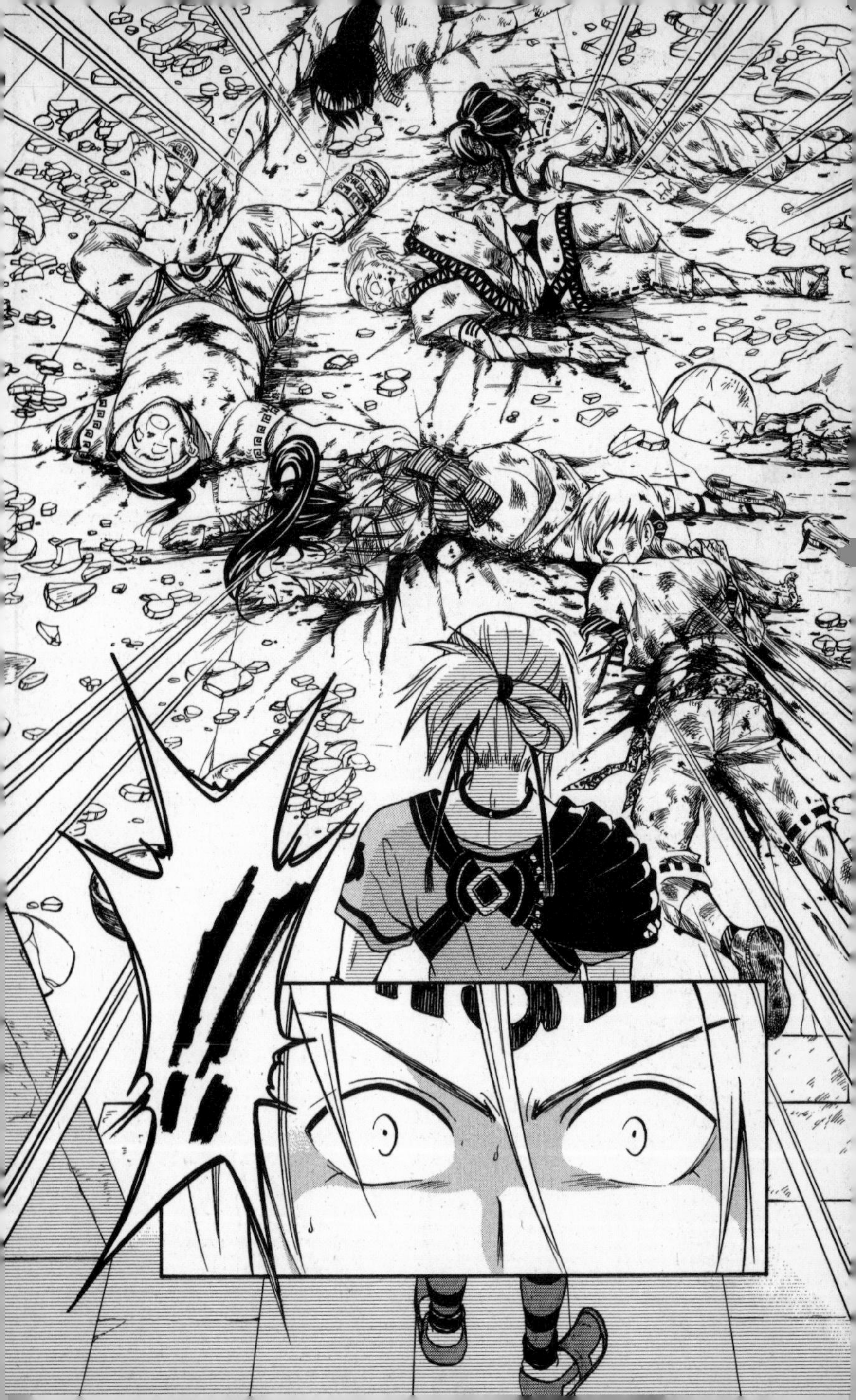
!!

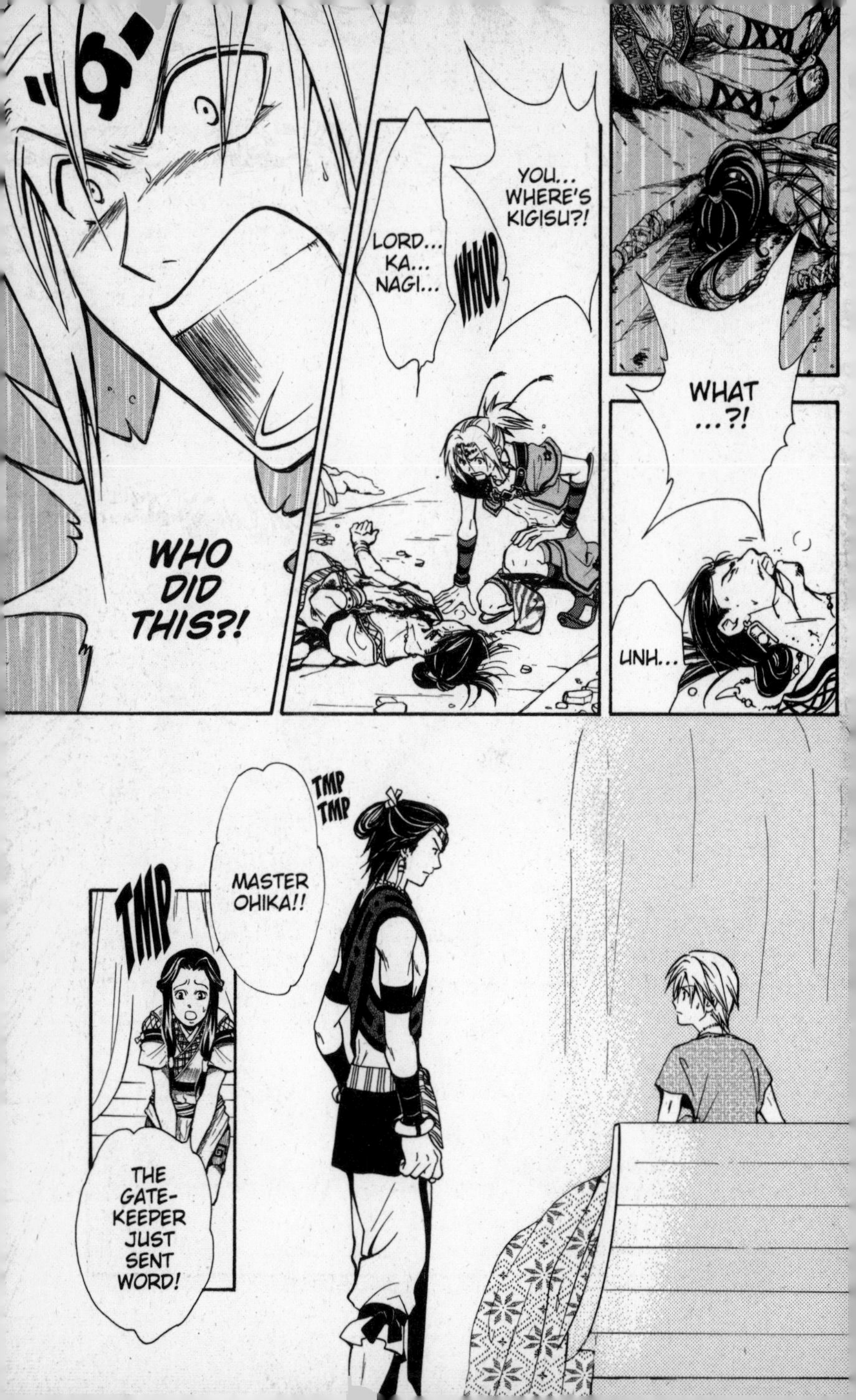
WHAT...?!
UNH...
YOU... WHERE'S KIGISU?!
LORD... KA... NAGI...
WHUP
WHO DID THIS?!
TMP TMP
MASTER OHIKA!!
TMP
THE GATE-KEEPER JUST SENT WORD!

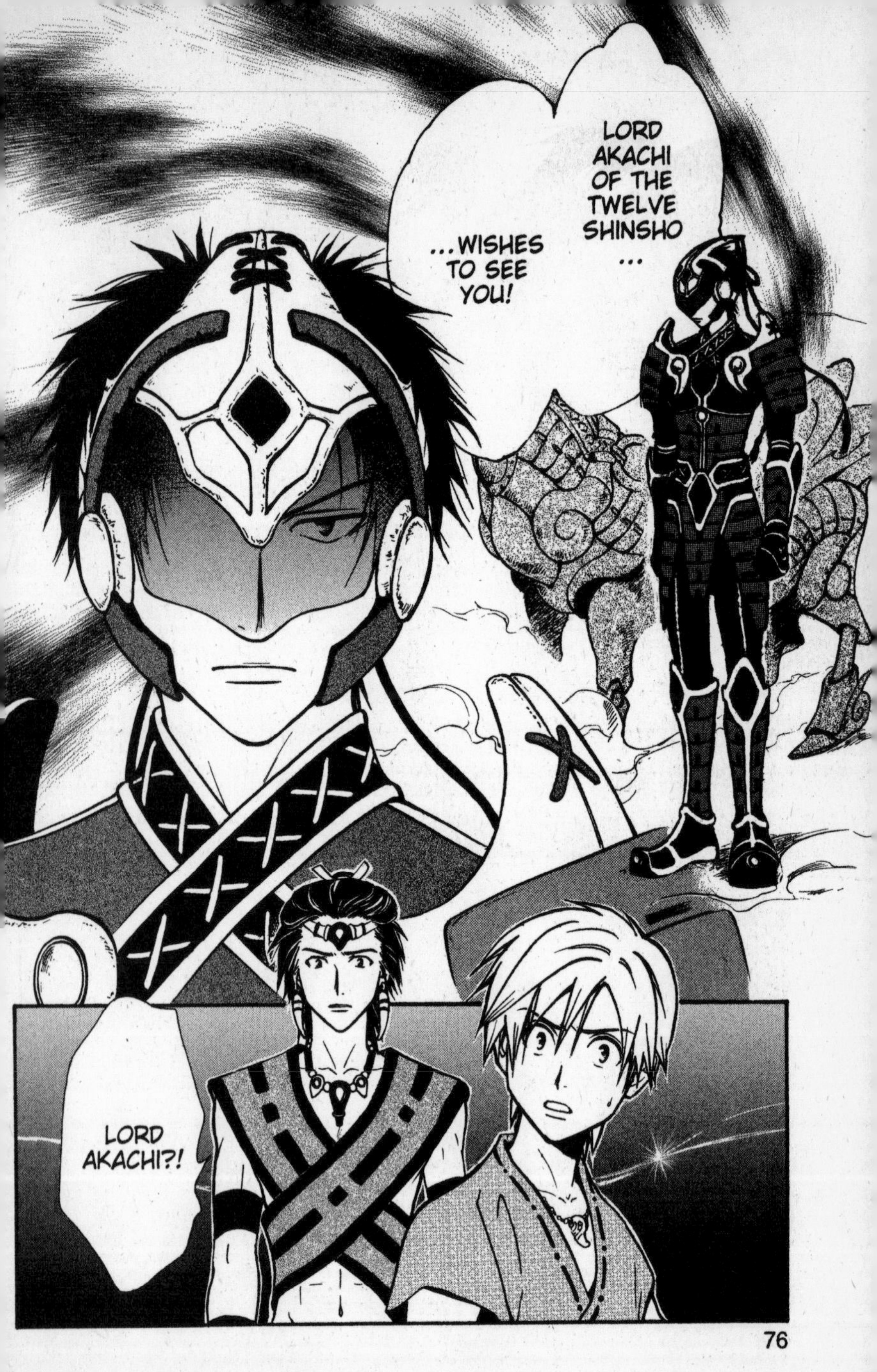
LORD AKACHI OF THE TWELVE SHINSHO ...
...WISHES TO SEE YOU!
LORD AKACHI?!

CHAPTER 22
AKACHI

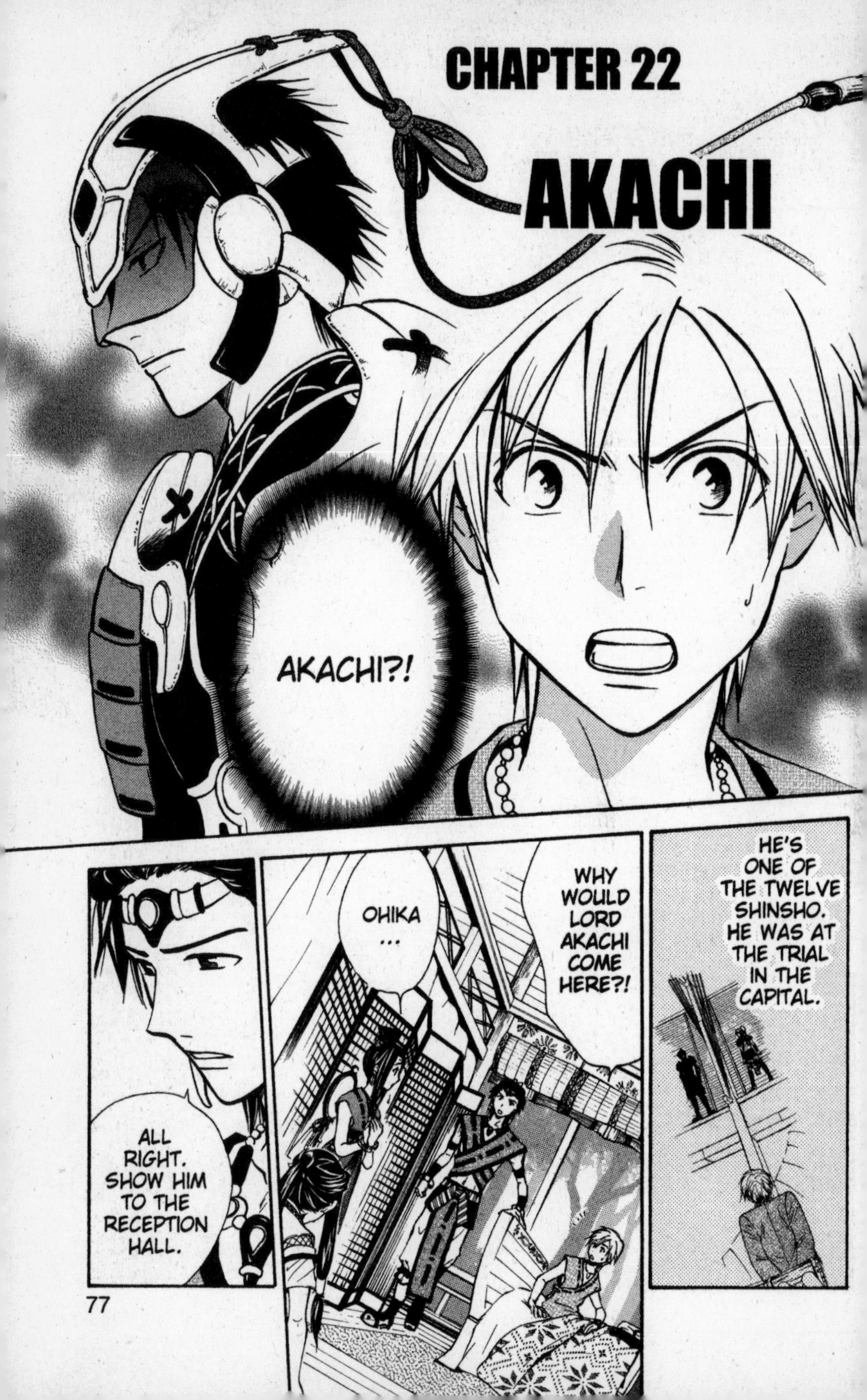
AKACHI?!
HE'S ONE OF THE TWELVE SHINSHO. HE WAS AT THE TRIAL IN THE CAPITAL.
WHY WOULD LORD AKACHI COME HERE?!
OHIKA ...
ALL RIGHT. SHOW HIM TO THE RECEPTION HALL.

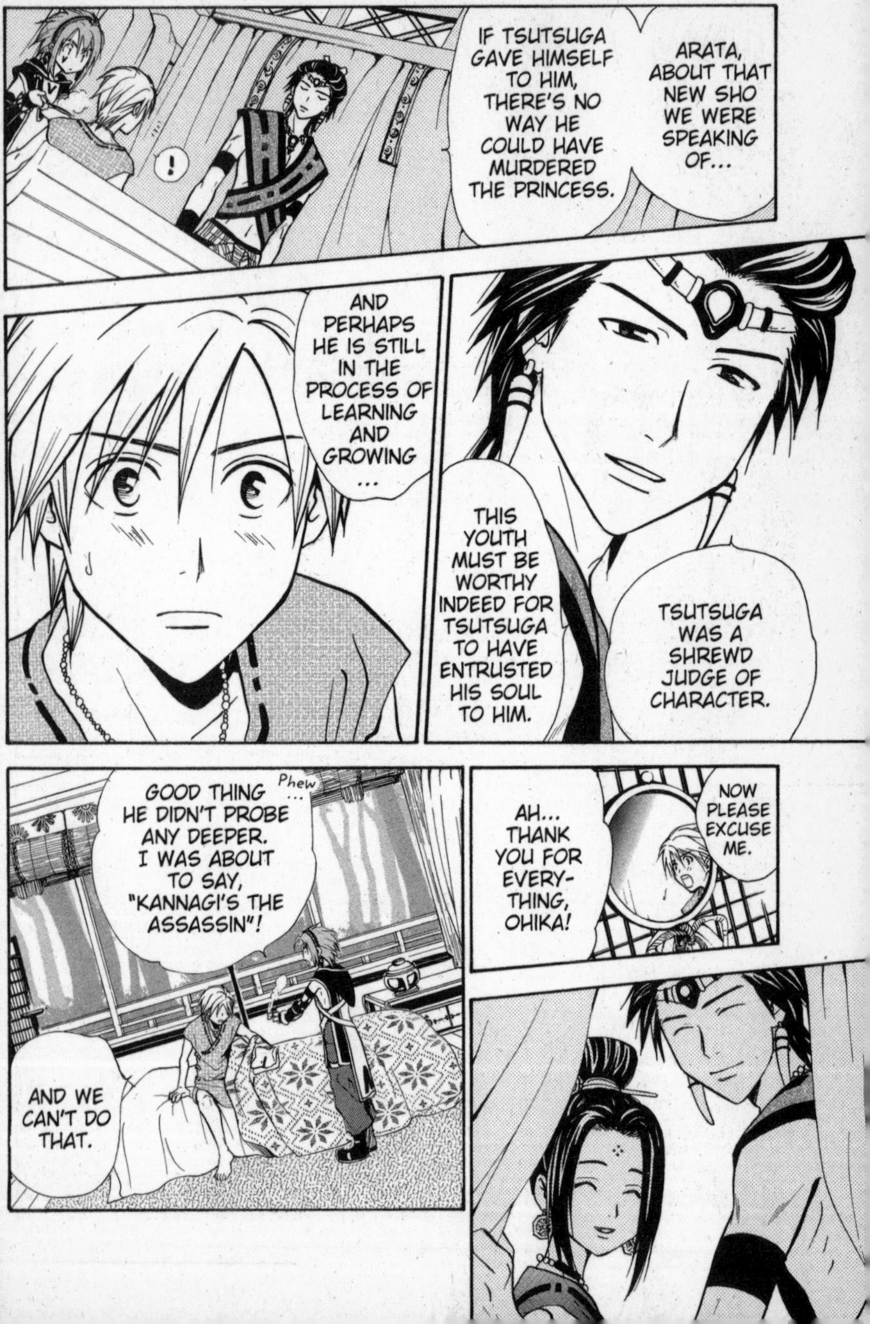
ARATA, ABOUT THAT NEW SHO WE WERE SPEAKING OF...
IF TSUTSUGA GAVE HIMSELF TO HIM, THERE'S NO WAY HE COULD HAVE MURDERED THE PRINCESS.
!
TSUTSUGA WAS A SHREWD JUDGE OF CHARACTER.
THIS YOUTH MUST BE WORTHY INDEED FOR TSUTSUGA TO HAVE ENTRUSTED HIS SOUL TO HIM.
AND PERHAPS HE IS STILL IN THE PROCESS OF LEARNING AND GROWING...
NOW PLEASE EXCUSE ME.
AH... THANK YOU FOR EVERYTHING, OHIKA!
Phew...
GOOD THING HE DIDN'T PROBE ANY DEEPER. I WAS ABOUT TO SAY, "KANNAGI'S THE ASSASSIN"!
AND WE CAN'T DO THAT.

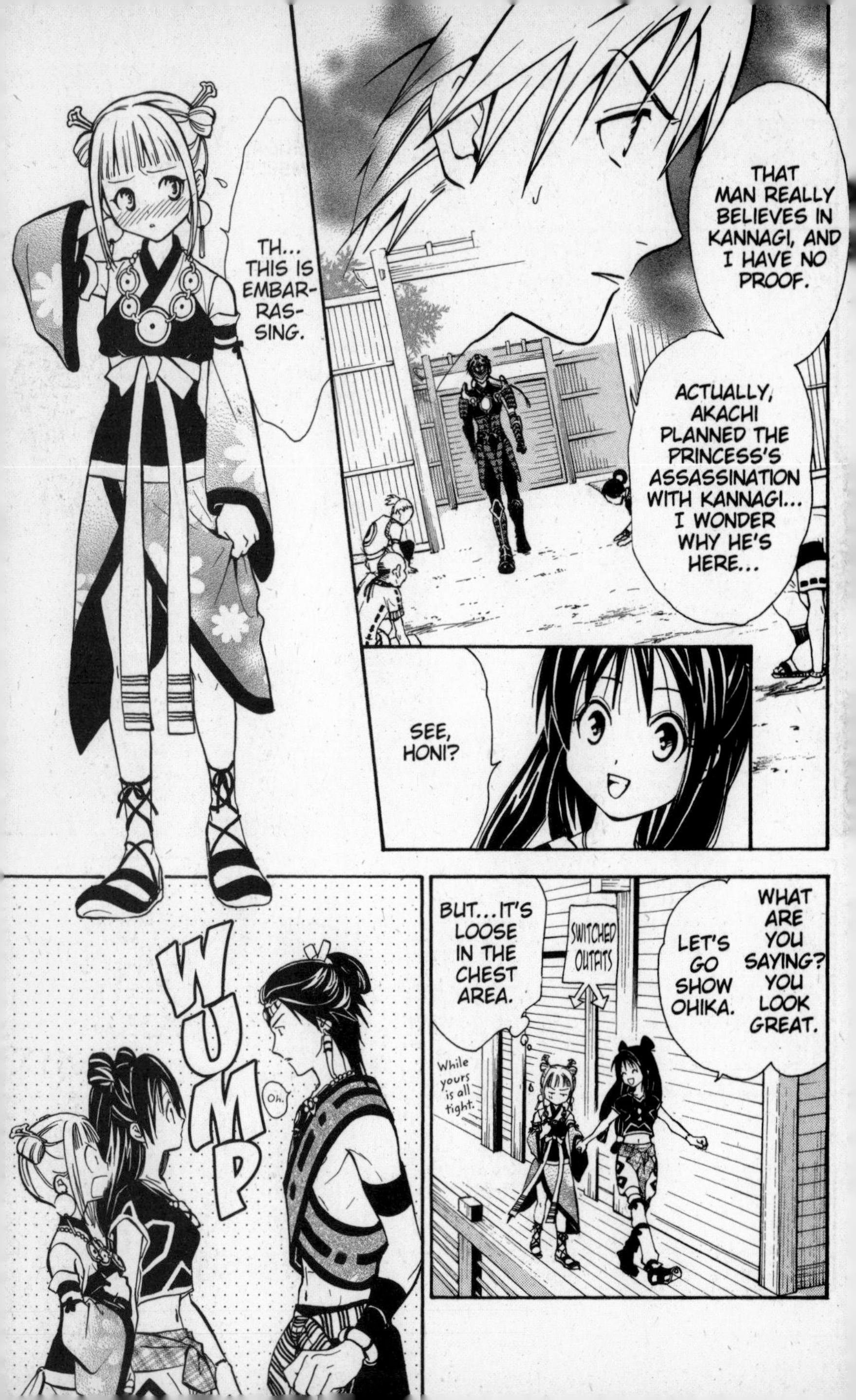
THAT MAN REALLY BELIEVES IN KANNAGI, AND I HAVE NO PROOF.
ACTUALLY, AKACHI PLANNED THE PRINCESS'S ASSASSINATION WITH KANNAGI... I WONDER WHY HE'S HERE...
SEE, HONI?
TH... THIS IS EMBARRASSING.
WHAT ARE YOU SAYING? YOU LOOK GREAT.
LET'S GO SHOW OHIKA.
SWITCHED OUTFITS
BUT...IT'S LOOSE IN THE CHEST AREA.
While yours is all tight.
WUMP
Oh.

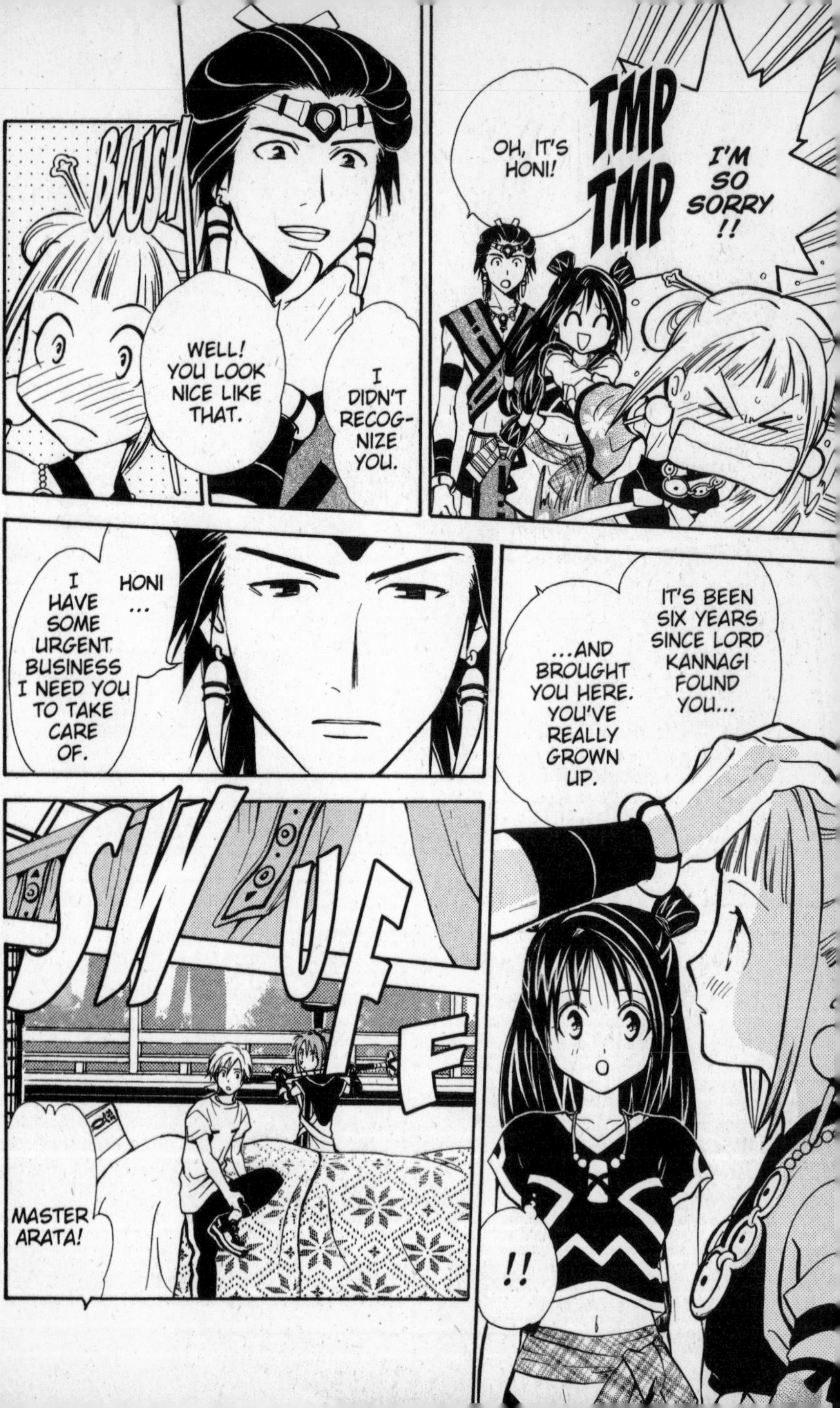
I'M SO SORRY!!
TMP TMP
OH, IT'S HONI!
I DIDN'T RECOGNIZE YOU.
WELL! YOU LOOK NICE LIKE THAT.
BLUSH
IT'S BEEN SIX YEARS SINCE LORD KANNAGI FOUND YOU...
...AND BROUGHT YOU HERE. YOU'VE REALLY GROWN UP.
!!
HONI...
I HAVE SOME URGENT BUSINESS I NEED YOU TO TAKE CARE OF.
SWOOF
MASTER ARATA!

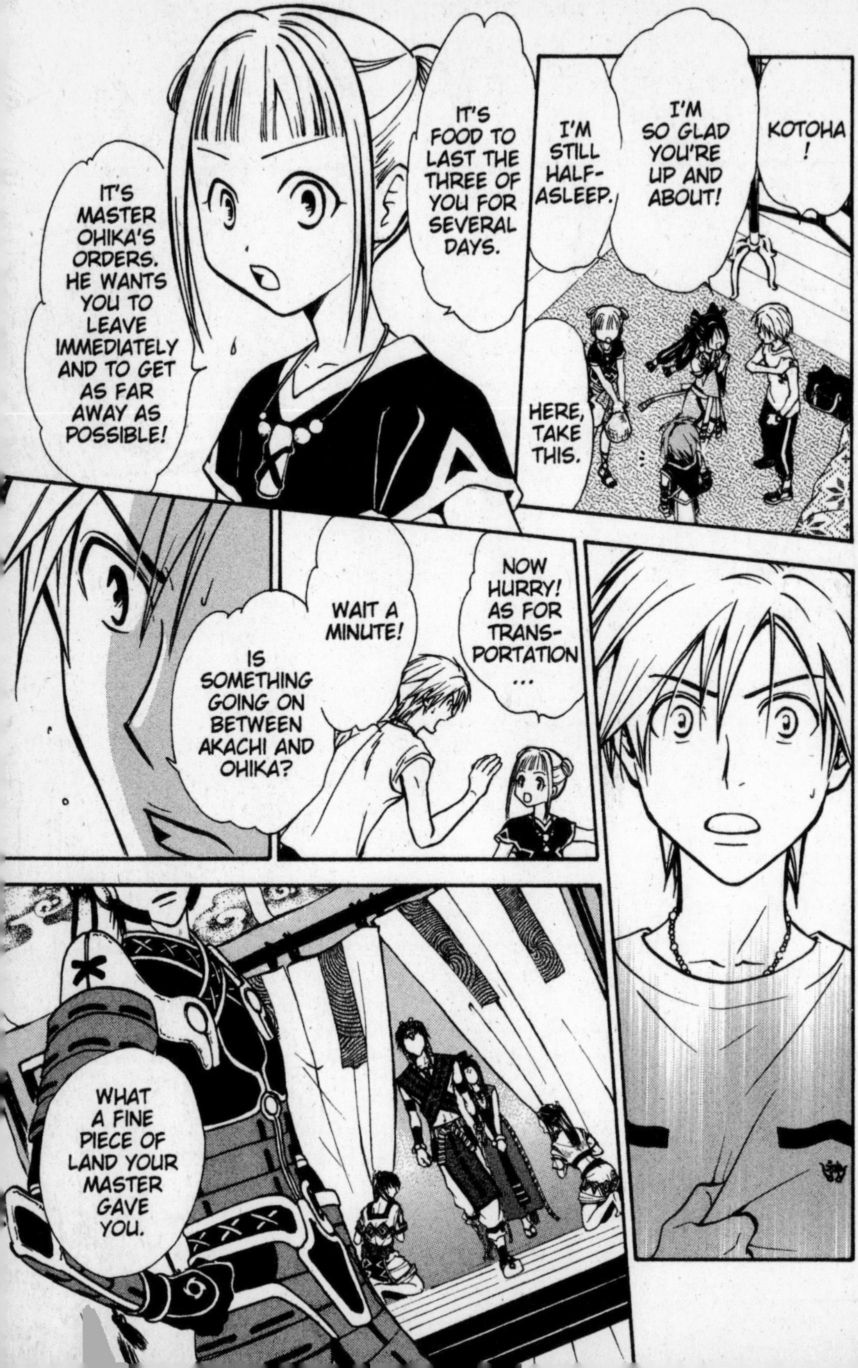
KOTOHA!
I'M SO GLAD YOU'RE UP AND ABOUT!
I'M STILL HALF-ASLEEP.
HERE, TAKE THIS.
...
IT'S FOOD TO LAST THE THREE OF YOU FOR SEVERAL DAYS.
IT'S MASTER OHIKA'S ORDERS. HE WANTS YOU TO LEAVE IMMEDIATELY AND TO GET AS FAR AWAY AS POSSIBLE!
NOW HURRY! AS FOR TRANSPORTATION ...
WAIT A MINUTE!
IS SOMETHING GOING ON BETWEEN AKACHI AND OHIKA?
WHAT A FINE PIECE OF LAND YOUR MASTER GAVE YOU.

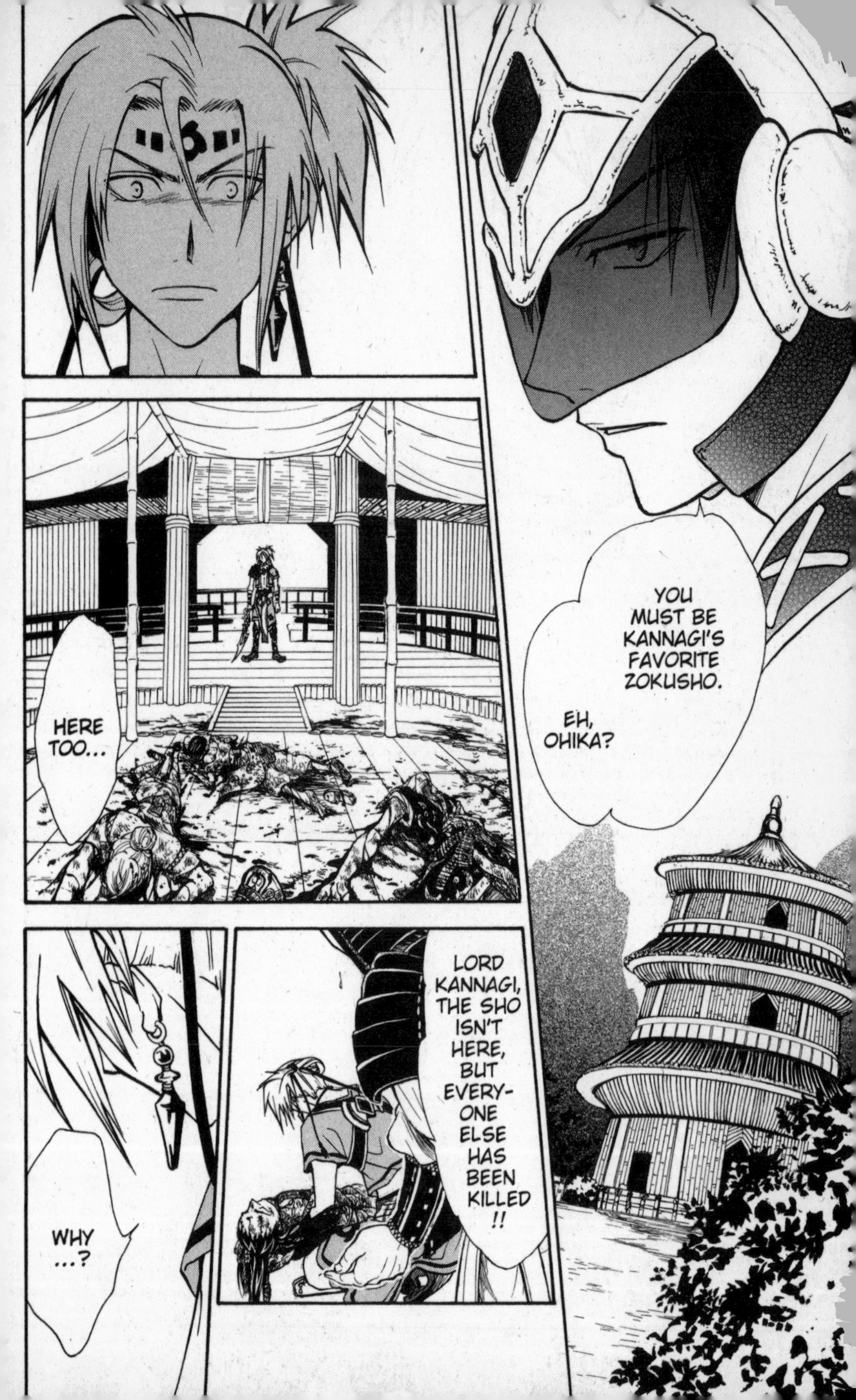
YOU MUST BE KANNAGI'S FAVORITE ZOKUSHO.
EH, OHIKA?
HERE TOO...
LORD KANNAGI, THE SHO ISN'T HERE, BUT EVERY-ONE ELSE HAS BEEN KILLED!!
WHY ...?

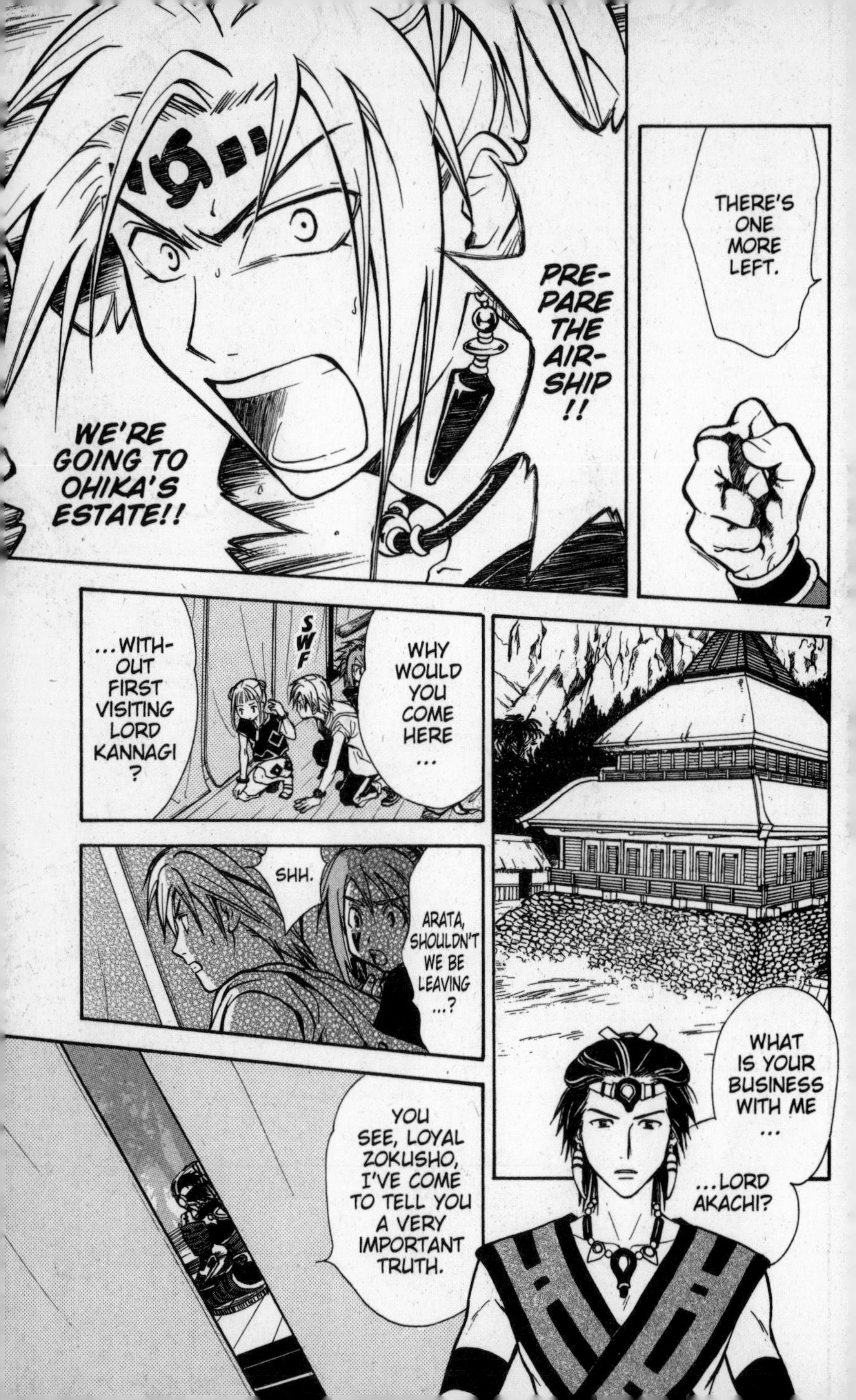
THERE'S ONE MORE LEFT.
PRE-PARE THE AIR-SHIP!!
WE'RE GOING TO OHIKA'S ESTATE!!
7
WHAT IS YOUR BUSINESS WITH ME ...
...LORD AKACHI?
SWF
WHY WOULD YOU COME HERE ...
...WITH-OUT FIRST VISITING LORD KANNAGI?
ARATA, SHOULDN'T WE BE LEAVING ...?
SHH.
YOU SEE, LOYAL ZOKUSHO, I'VE COME TO TELL YOU A VERY IMPORTANT TRUTH.

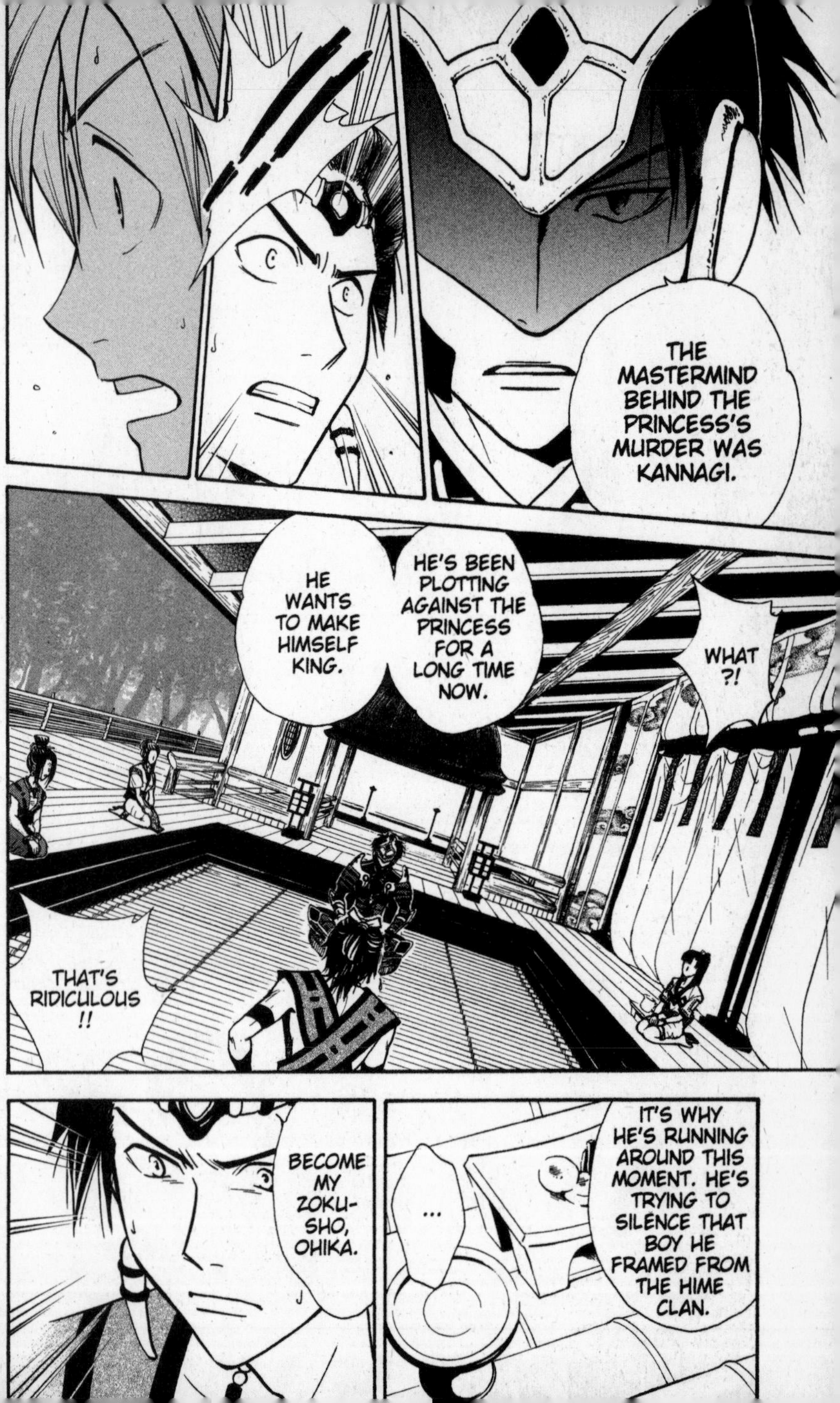
THE MASTERMIND BEHIND THE PRINCESS'S MURDER WAS KANNAGI.
HE'S BEEN PLOTTING AGAINST THE PRINCESS FOR A LONG TIME NOW.
HE WANTS TO MAKE HIMSELF KING.
WHAT?!
THAT'S RIDICULOUS!!
IT'S WHY HE'S RUNNING AROUND THIS MOMENT. HE'S TRYING TO SILENCE THAT BOY HE FRAMED FROM THE HIME CLAN.
...
BECOME MY ZOKU-SHO, OHIKA.

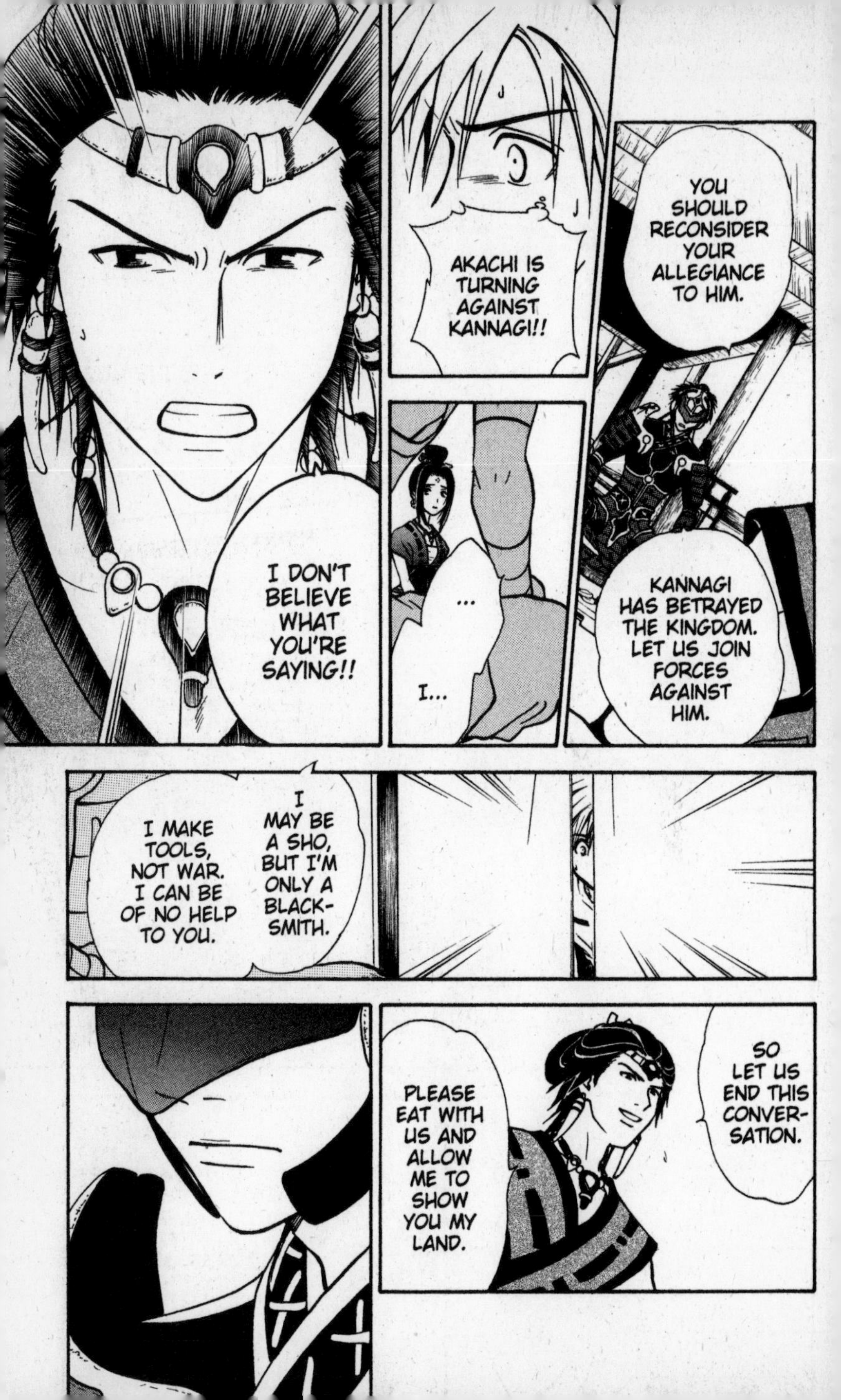
YOU SHOULD RECONSIDER YOUR ALLEGIANCE TO HIM.
KANNAGI HAS BETRAYED THE KINGDOM. LET US JOIN FORCES AGAINST HIM.
AKACHI IS TURNING AGAINST KANNAGI!!
...
I...
I DON'T BELIEVE WHAT YOU'RE SAYING!!
I MAY BE A SHO, BUT I'M ONLY A BLACK-SMITH.
I MAKE TOOLS, NOT WAR. I CAN BE OF NO HELP TO YOU.
SO LET US END THIS CONVER-SATION.
PLEASE EAT WITH US AND ALLOW ME TO SHOW YOU MY LAND.

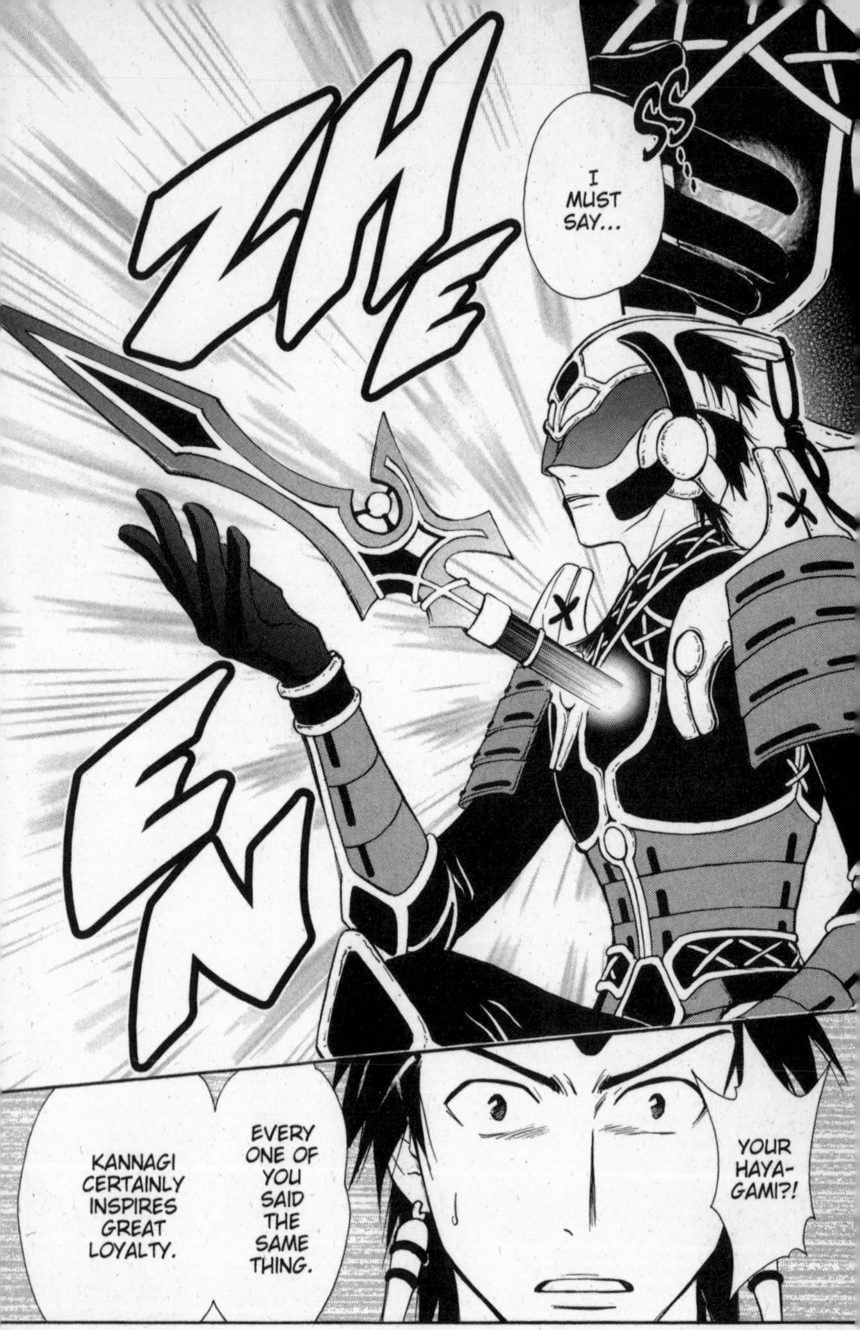
I MUST SAY...
YOUR HAYA-GAMI?!
EVERY ONE OF YOU SAID THE SAME THING.
KANNAGI CERTAINLY INSPIRES GREAT LOYALTY.

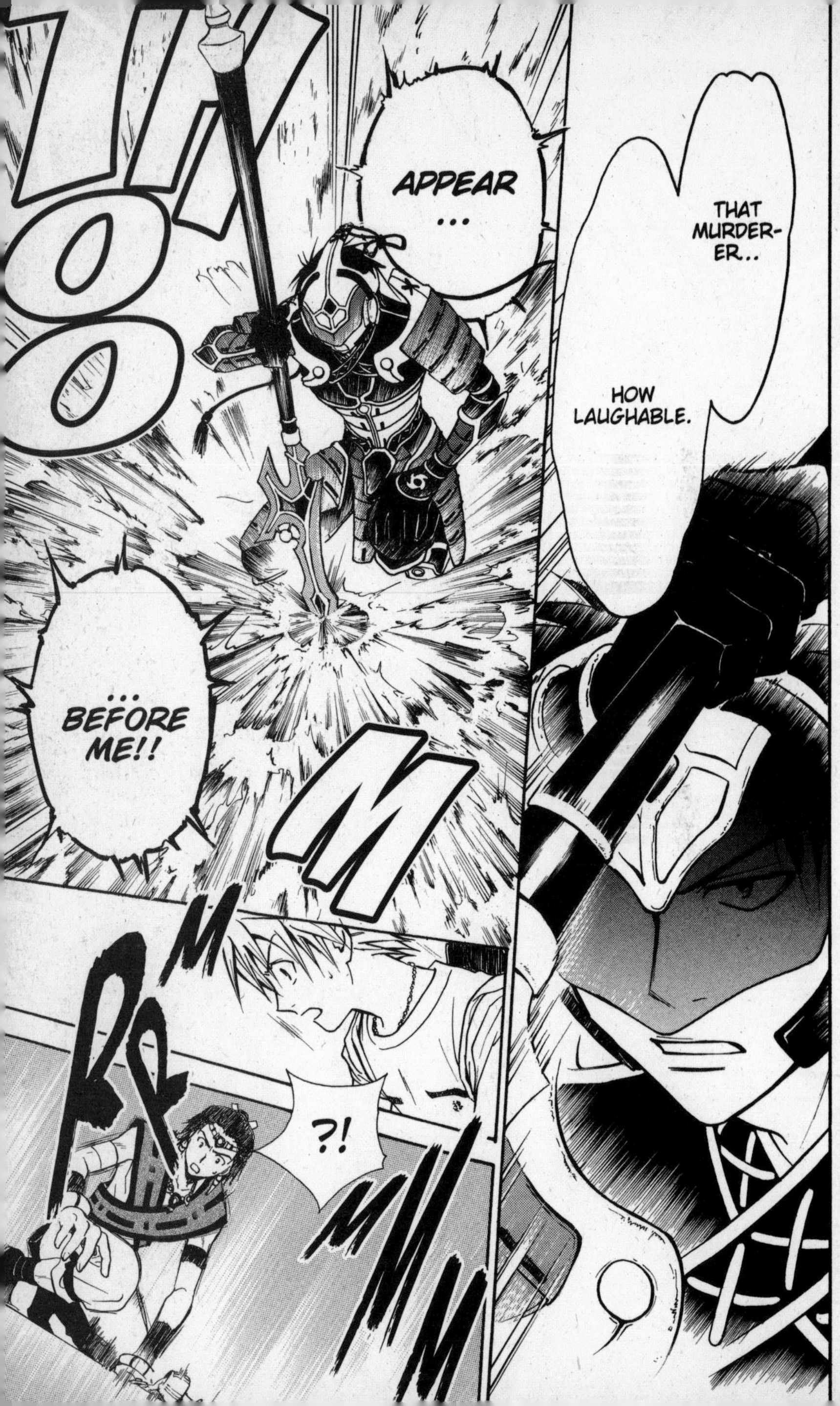
THAT MURDER-ER...
HOW LAUGHABLE.
APPEAR ...
... BEFORE ME!!
?!

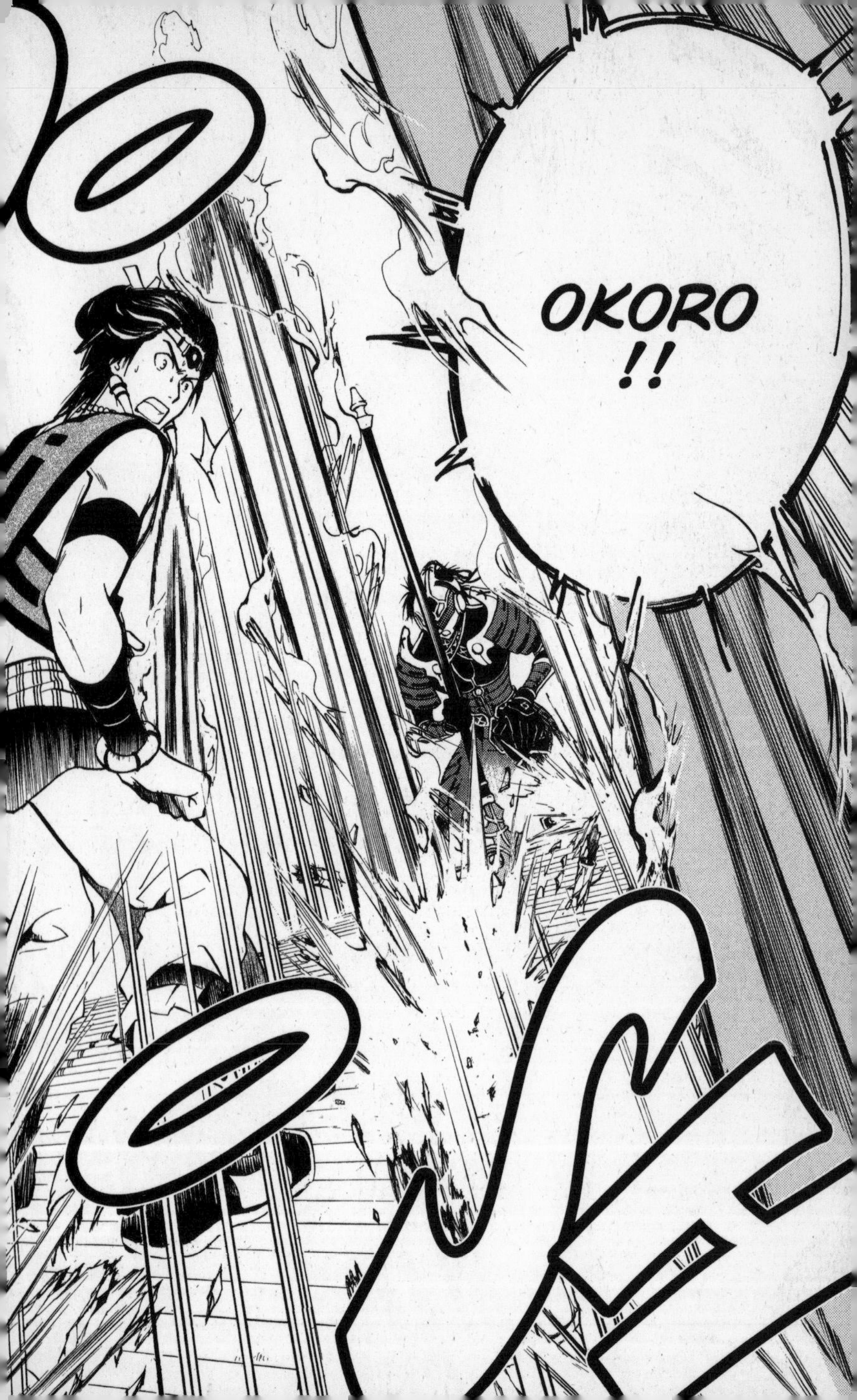
OKORO !!

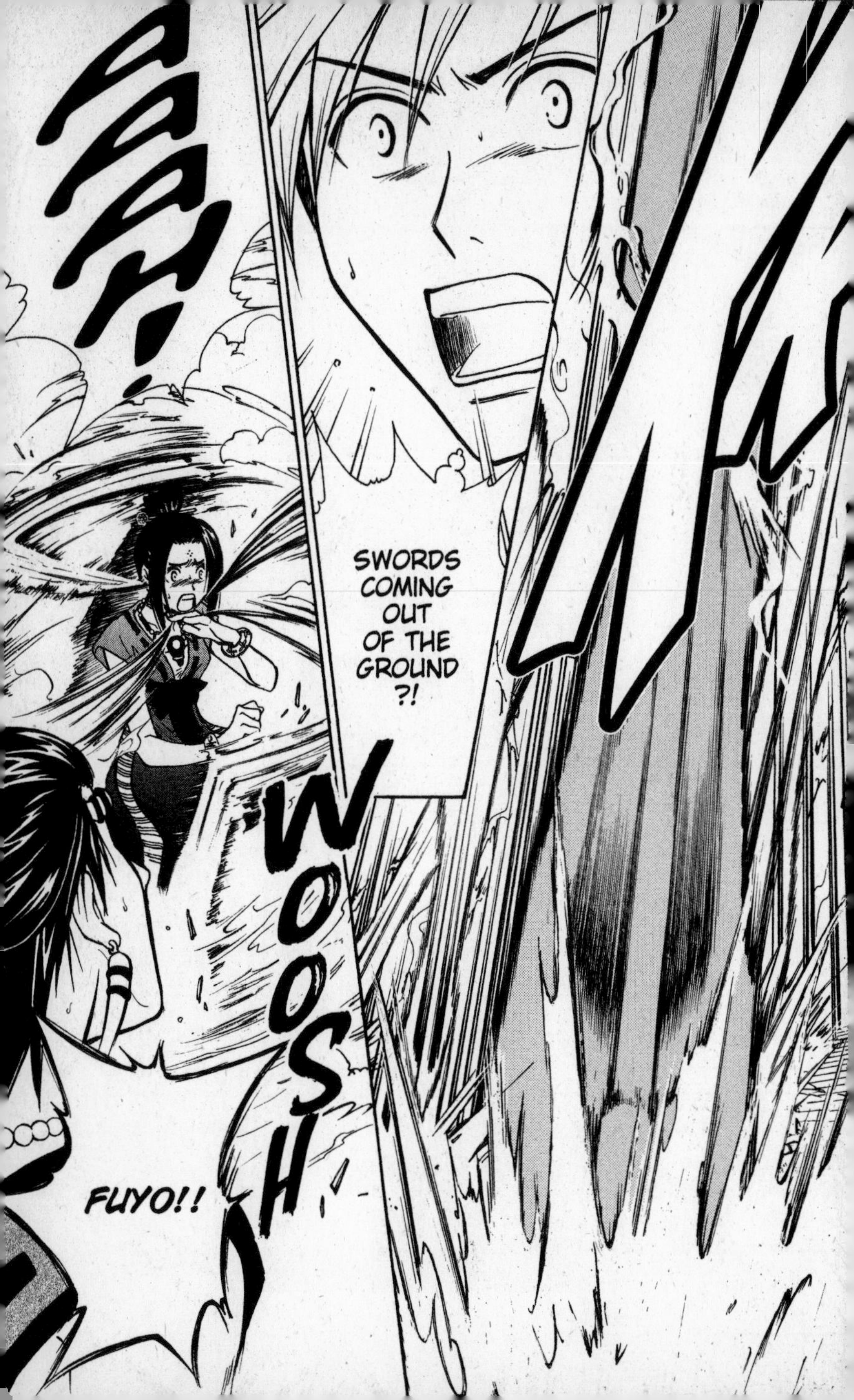
SWORDS COMING OUT OF THE GROUND ?!
WOOSH
FUYO!!

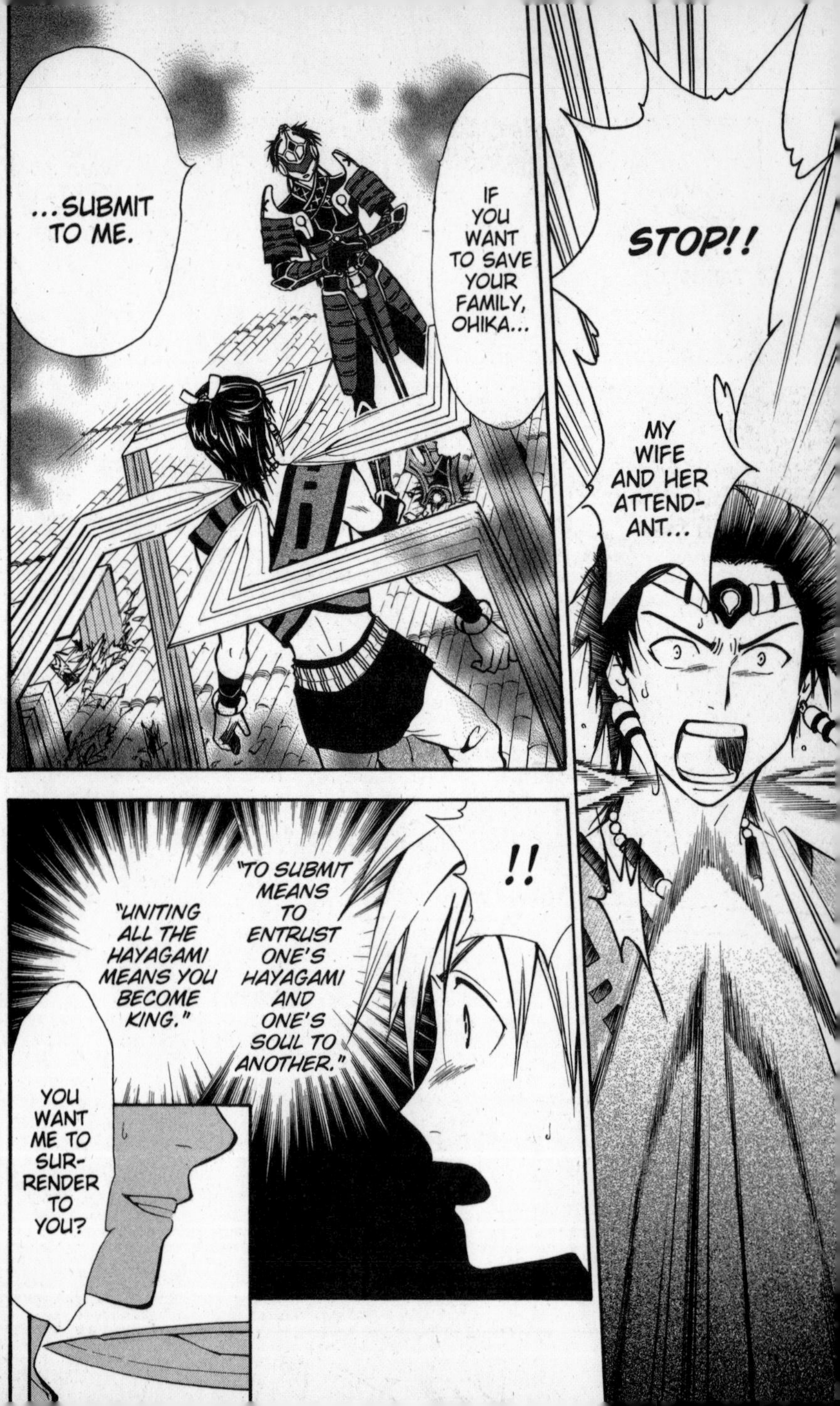
STOP!!
MY WIFE AND HER ATTENDANT...
IF YOU WANT TO SAVE YOUR FAMILY, OHIKA...
...SUBMIT TO ME.
!!
"TO SUBMIT MEANS TO ENTRUST ONE'S HAYAGAMI AND ONE'S SOUL TO ANOTHER."
"UNITING ALL THE HAYAGAMI MEANS YOU BECOME KING."
YOU WANT ME TO SURRENDER TO YOU?

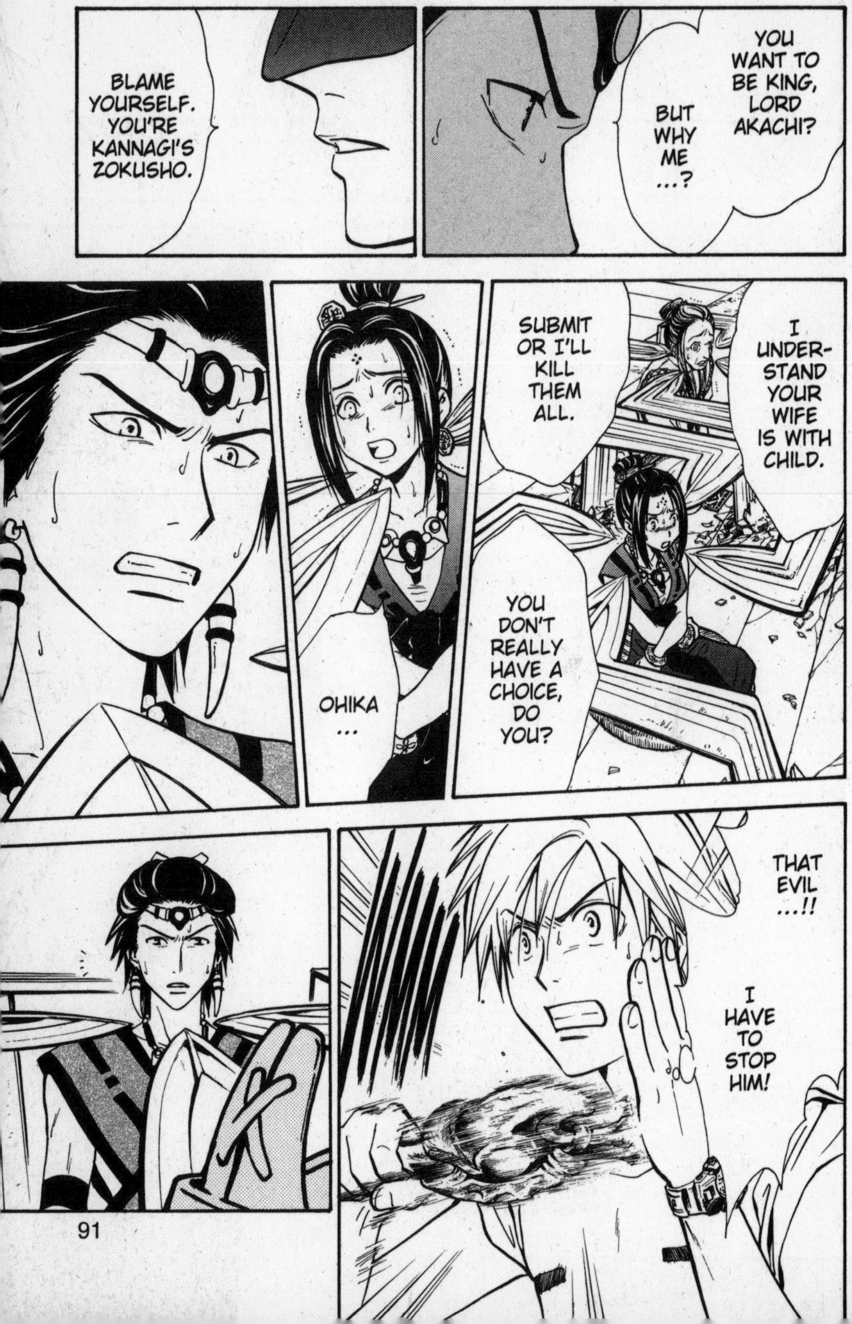
YOU WANT TO BE KING, LORD AKACHI?
BUT WHY ME ...?
BLAME YOURSELF. YOU'RE KANNAGI'S ZOKUSHO.
I UNDERSTAND YOUR WIFE IS WITH CHILD.
SUBMIT OR I'LL KILL THEM ALL.
YOU DON'T REALLY HAVE A CHOICE, DO YOU?
OHIKA ...
THAT EVIL ...!!
I HAVE TO STOP HIM!

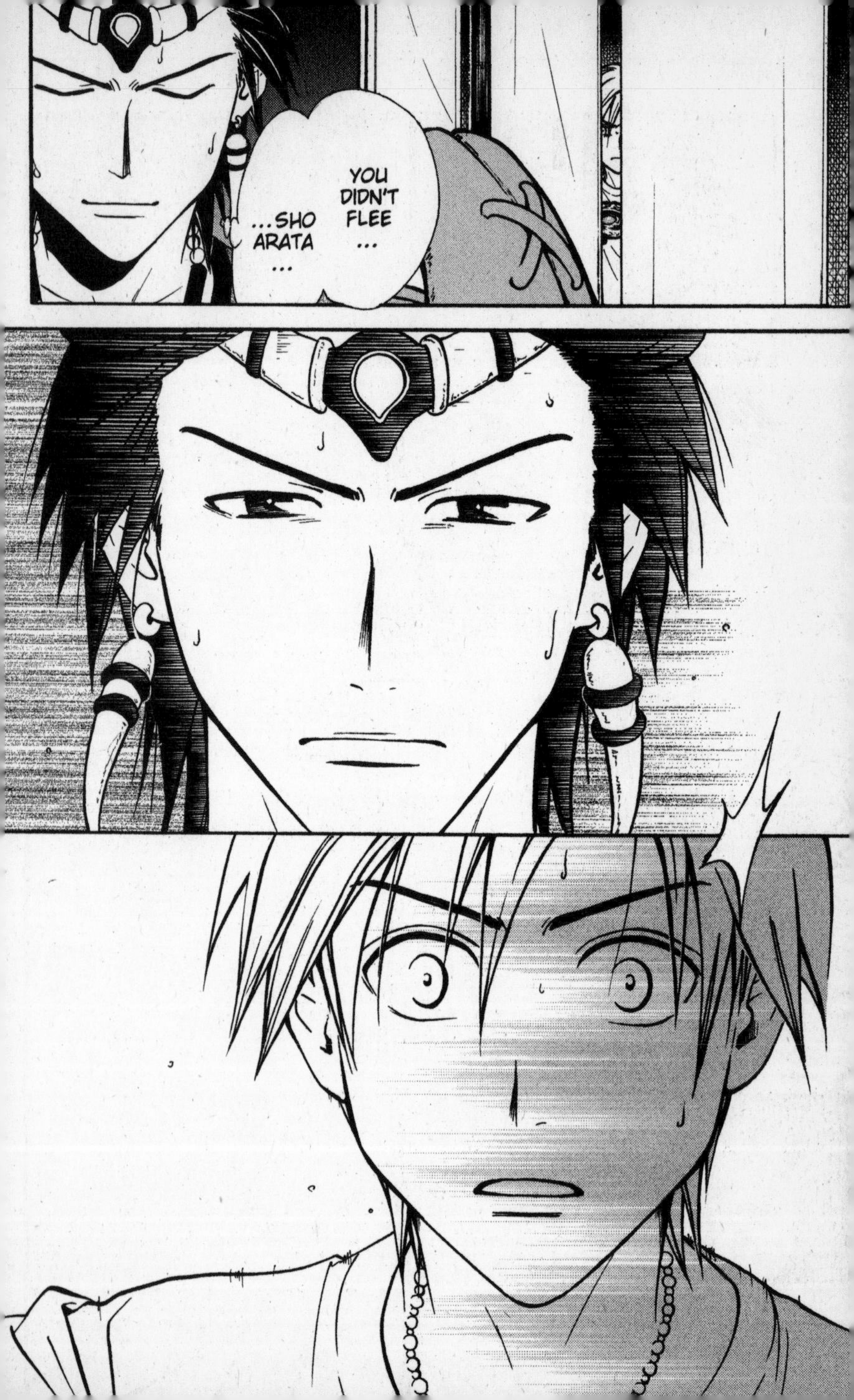
YOU DIDN'T FLEE ... ...SHO ARATA ...

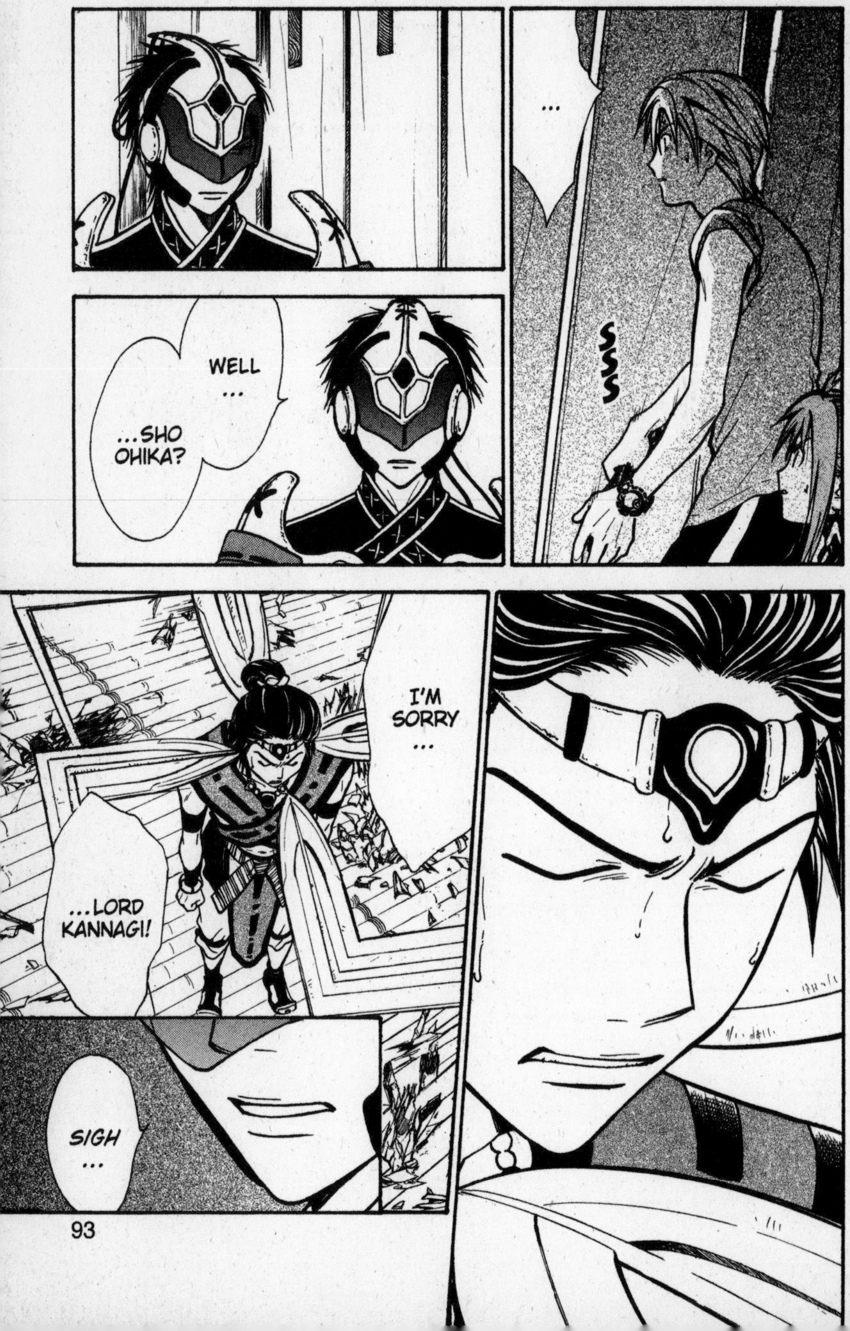
...
SSS
WELL ...
...SHO OHIKA?
I'M SORRY ...
...LORD KANNAGI!
SIGH ...

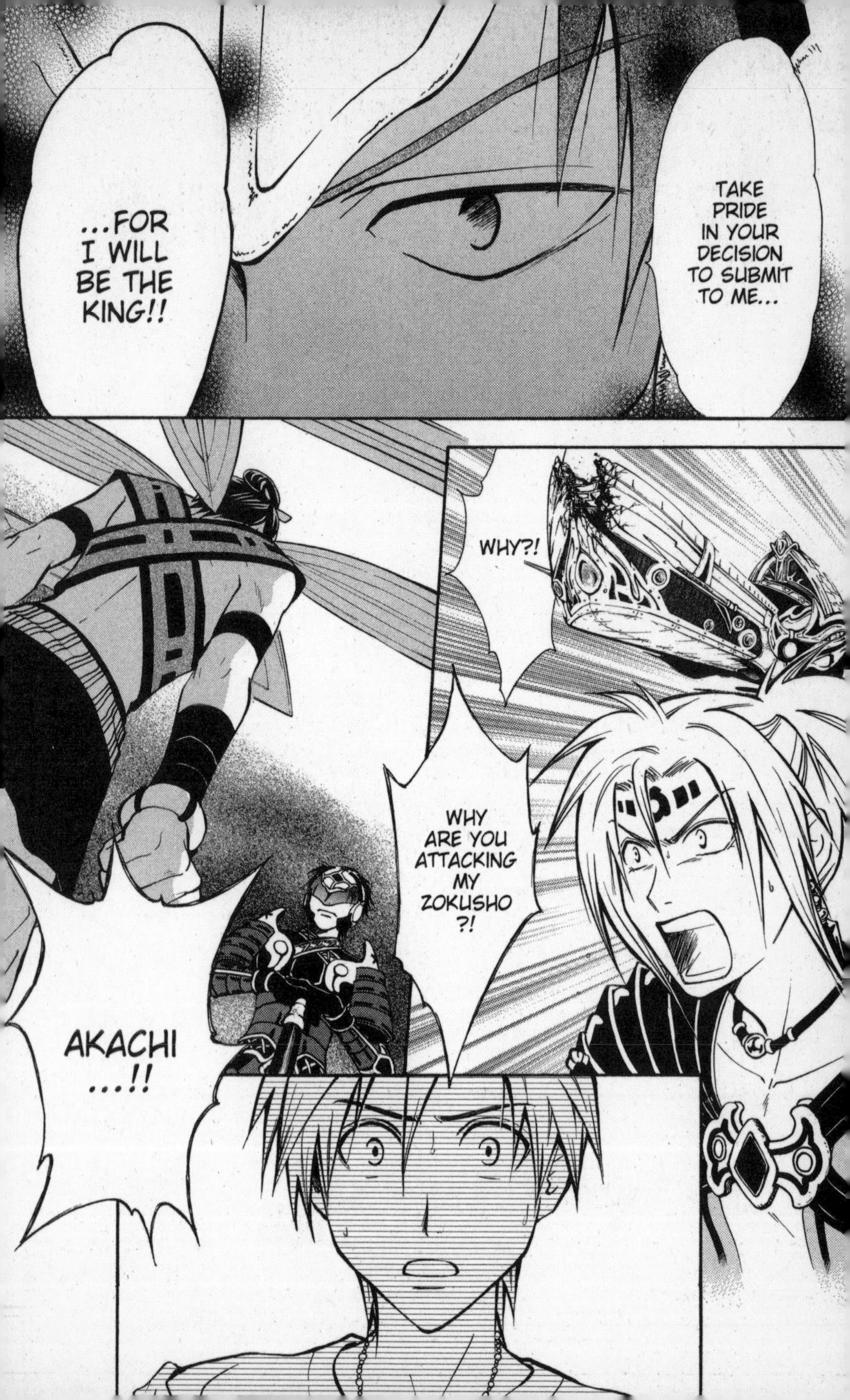
TAKE PRIDE IN YOUR DECISION TO SUBMIT TO ME...
...FOR I WILL BE THE KING!!
WHY?!
WHY ARE YOU ATTACKING MY ZOKUSHO ?!
AKACHI ...!!

CHAPTER 23
BEHIND THE CURTAIN

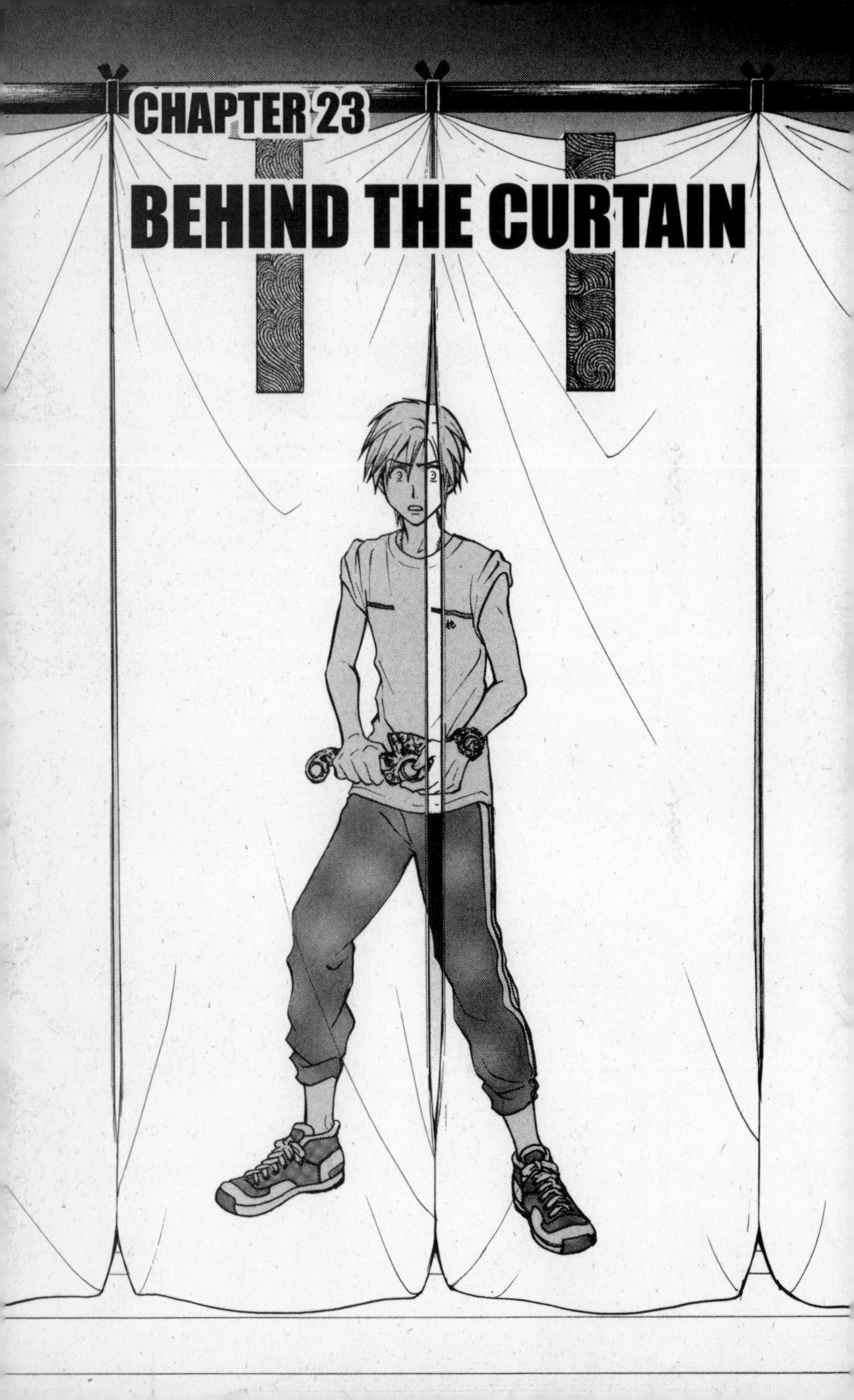

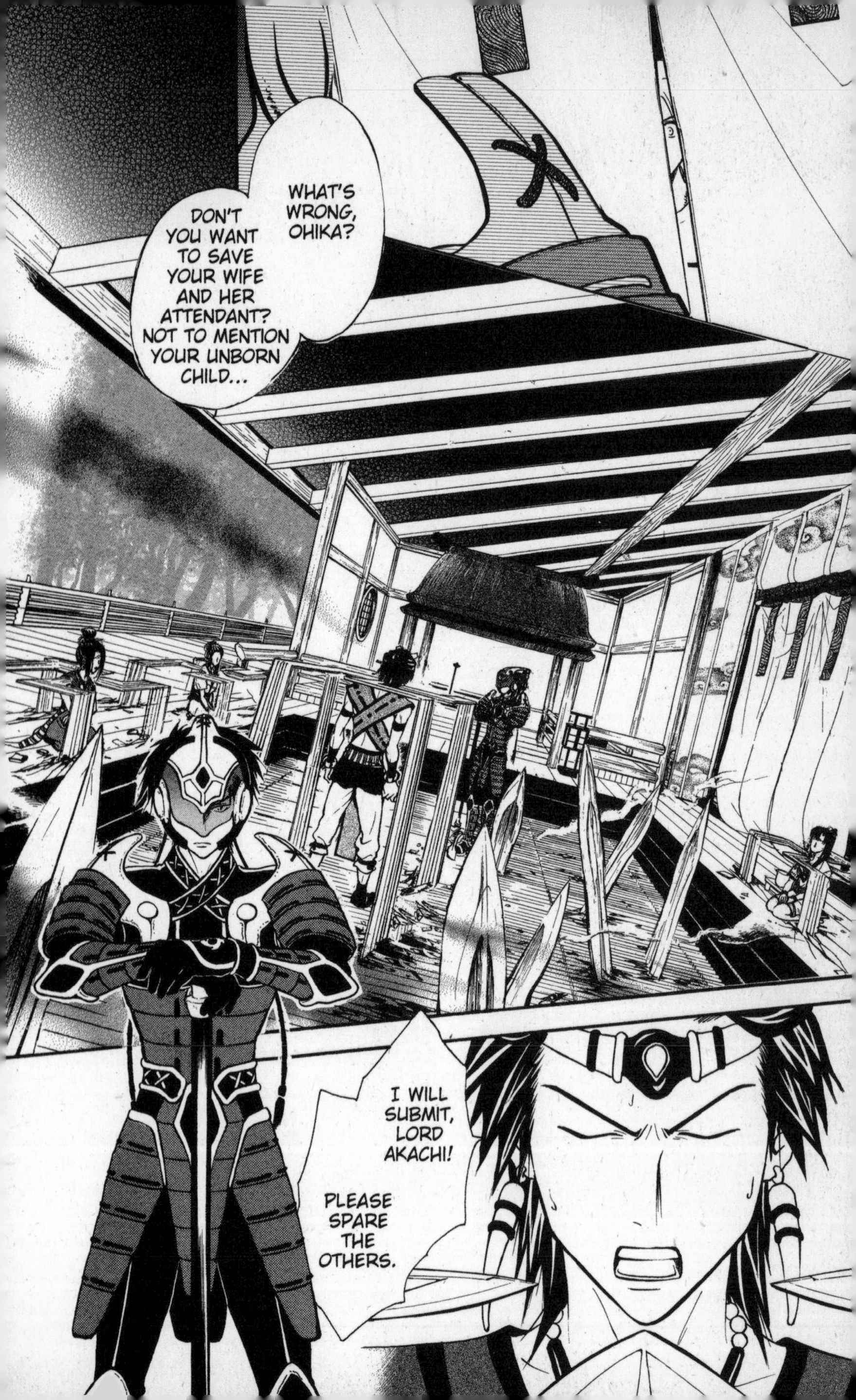
WHAT'S WRONG, OHIKA?
DON'T YOU WANT TO SAVE YOUR WIFE AND HER ATTENDANT? NOT TO MENTION YOUR UNBORN CHILD...
I WILL SUBMIT, LORD AKACHI!
PLEASE SPARE THE OTHERS.

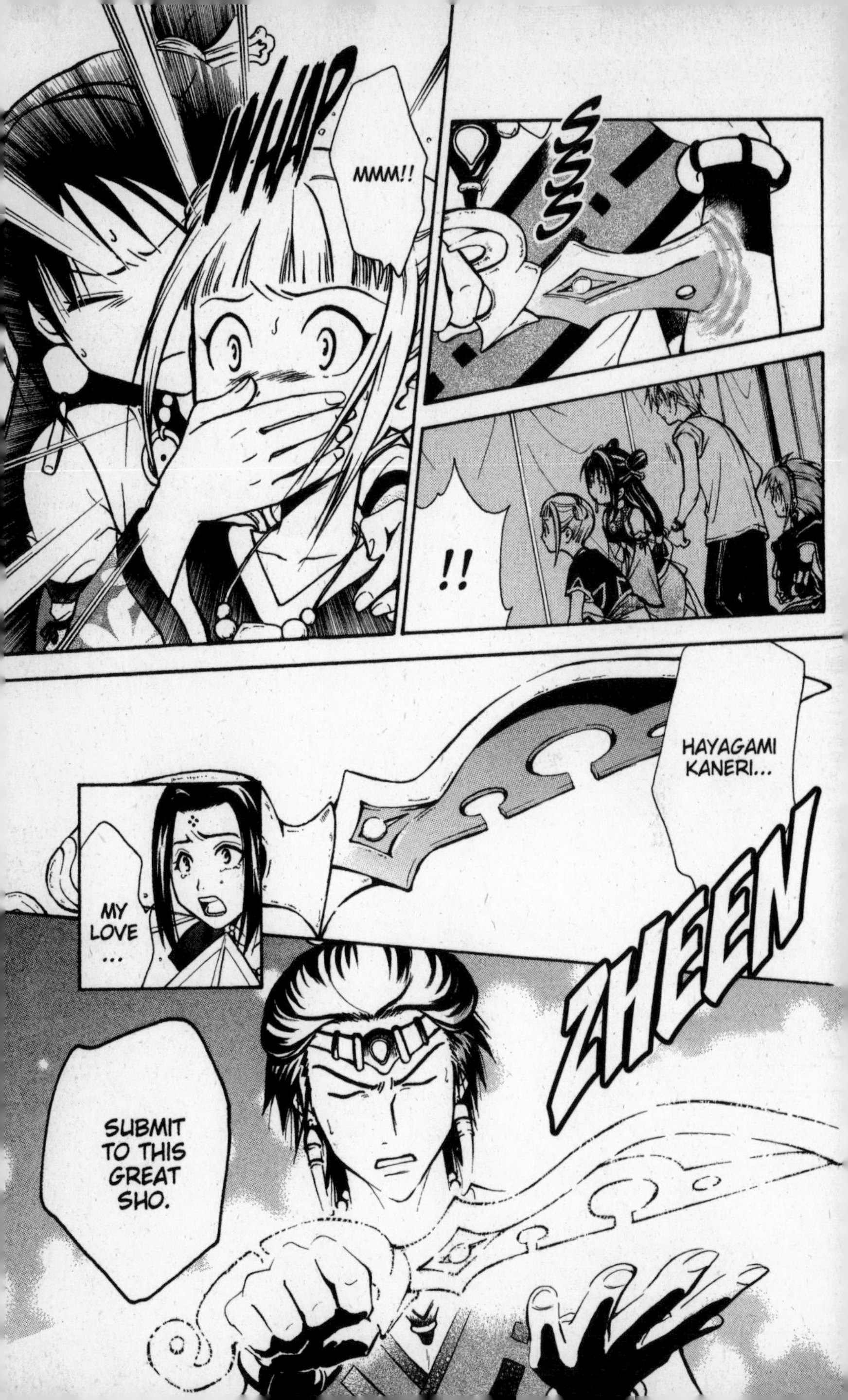
SSSS
!!
WHAP
MMMM!!
HAYAGAMI KANERI...
ZHEEN
MY LOVE...
SUBMIT TO THIS GREAT SHO.

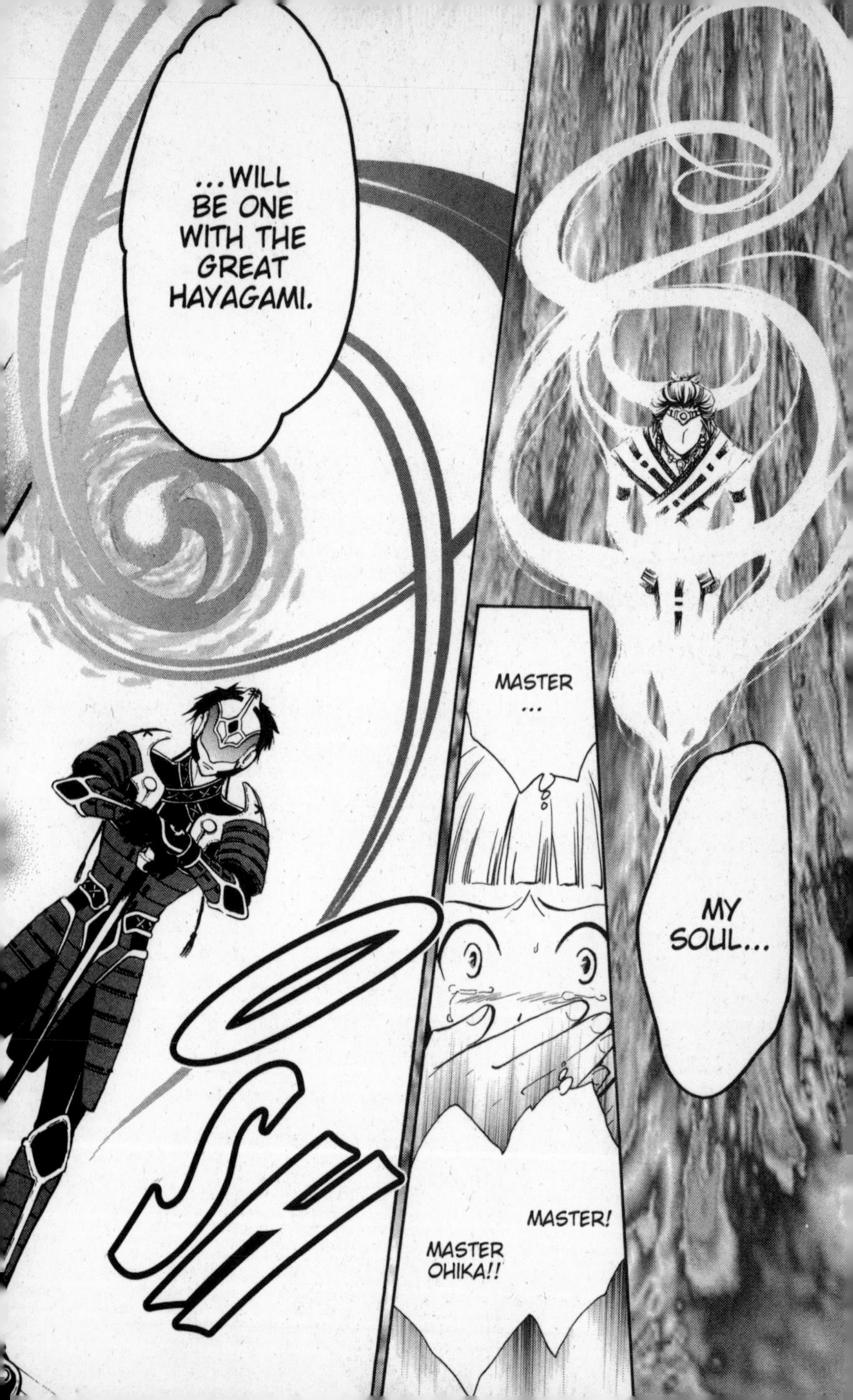
MY SOUL...
...WILL BE ONE WITH THE GREAT HAYAGAMI.
MASTER ...
MASTER!
MASTER OHIKA!!

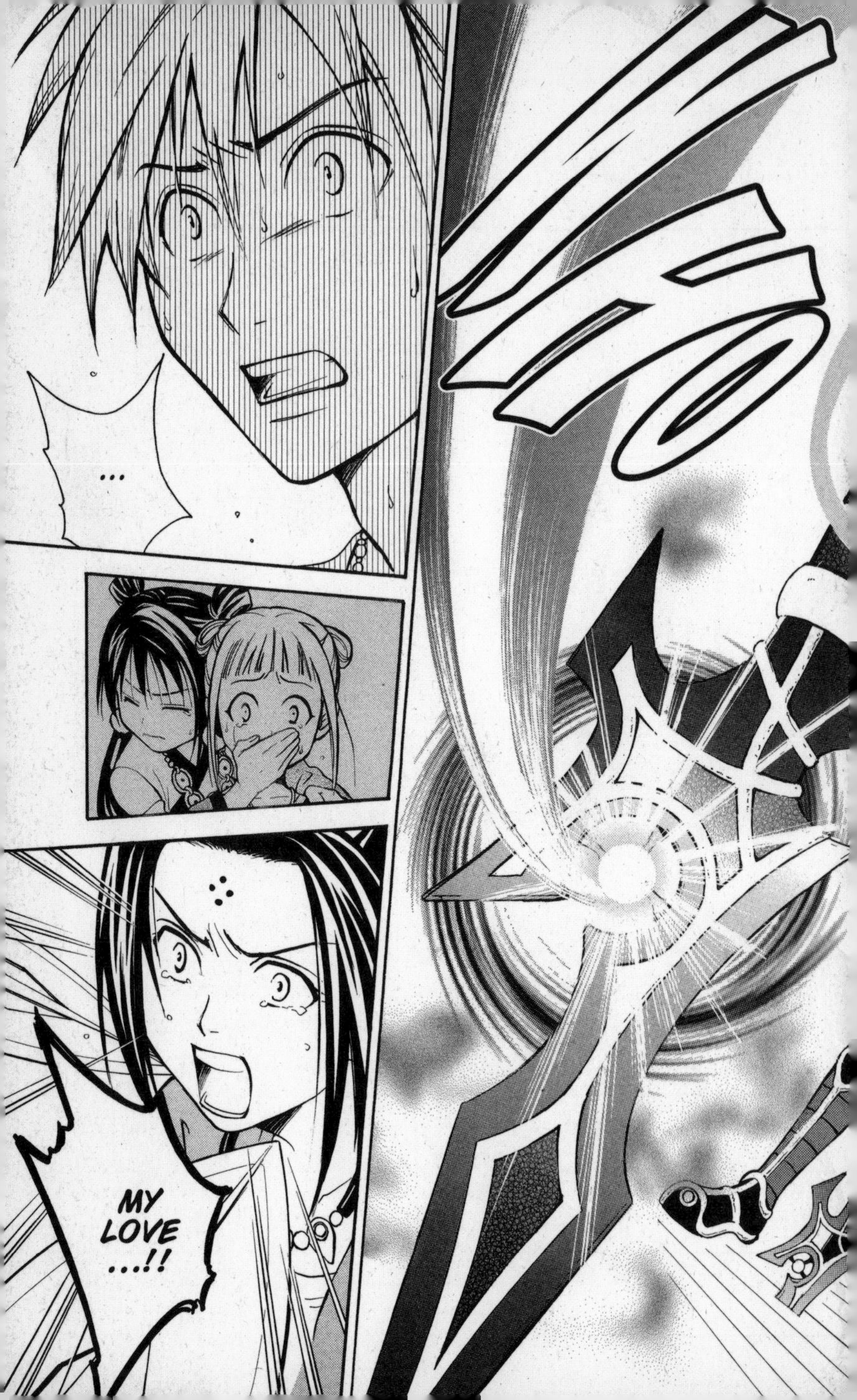
...
MY LOVE ...!!

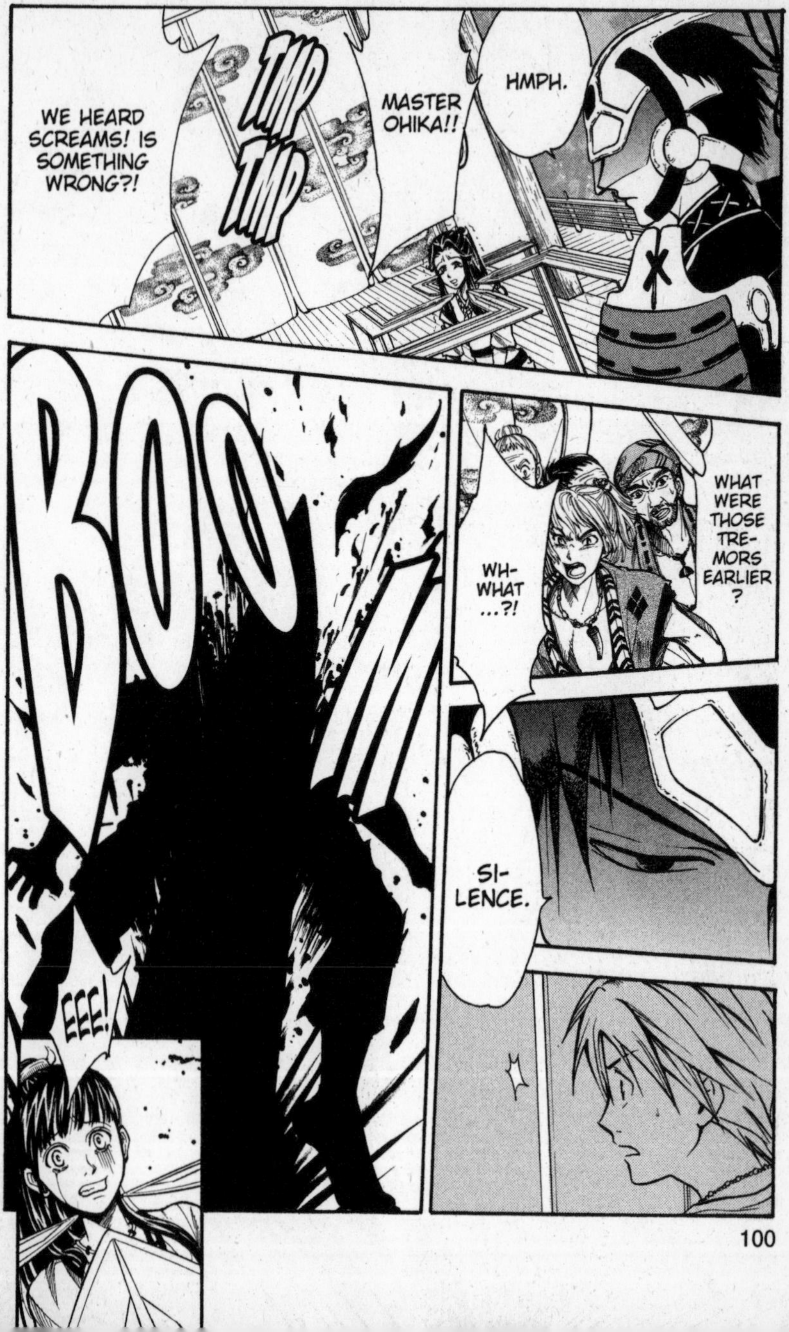
HMPH.
MASTER OHIKA!!
TMP TMP
WE HEARD SCREAMS! IS SOMETHING WRONG?!
WHAT WERE THOSE TRE-MORS EARLIER?
WH- WHAT ...?!
SI- LENCE.
BOOOM
EEE!

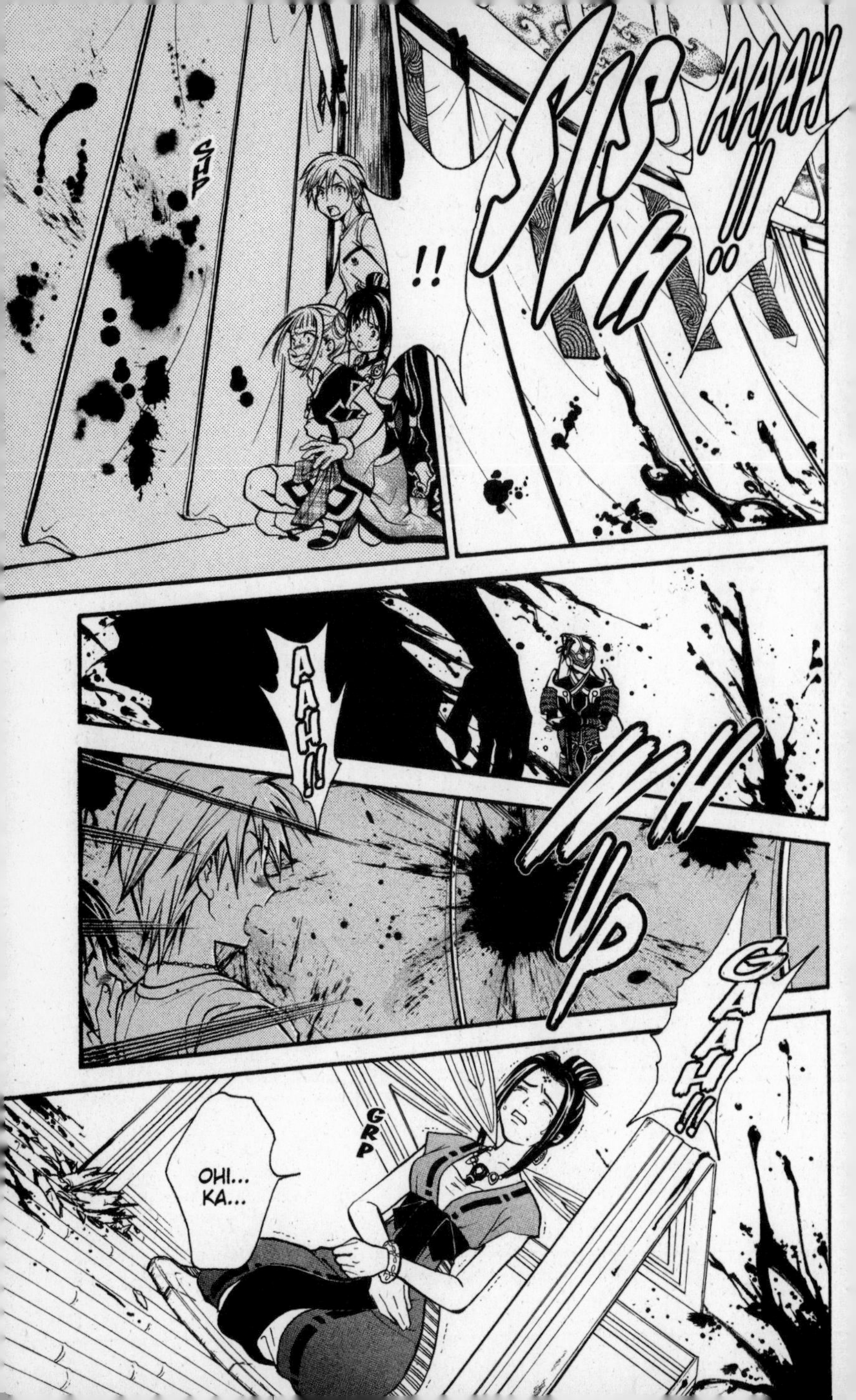
AAAAH!!
!!
SHP
AAAH!!
GAAAH!!
GRP
OHI... KA...

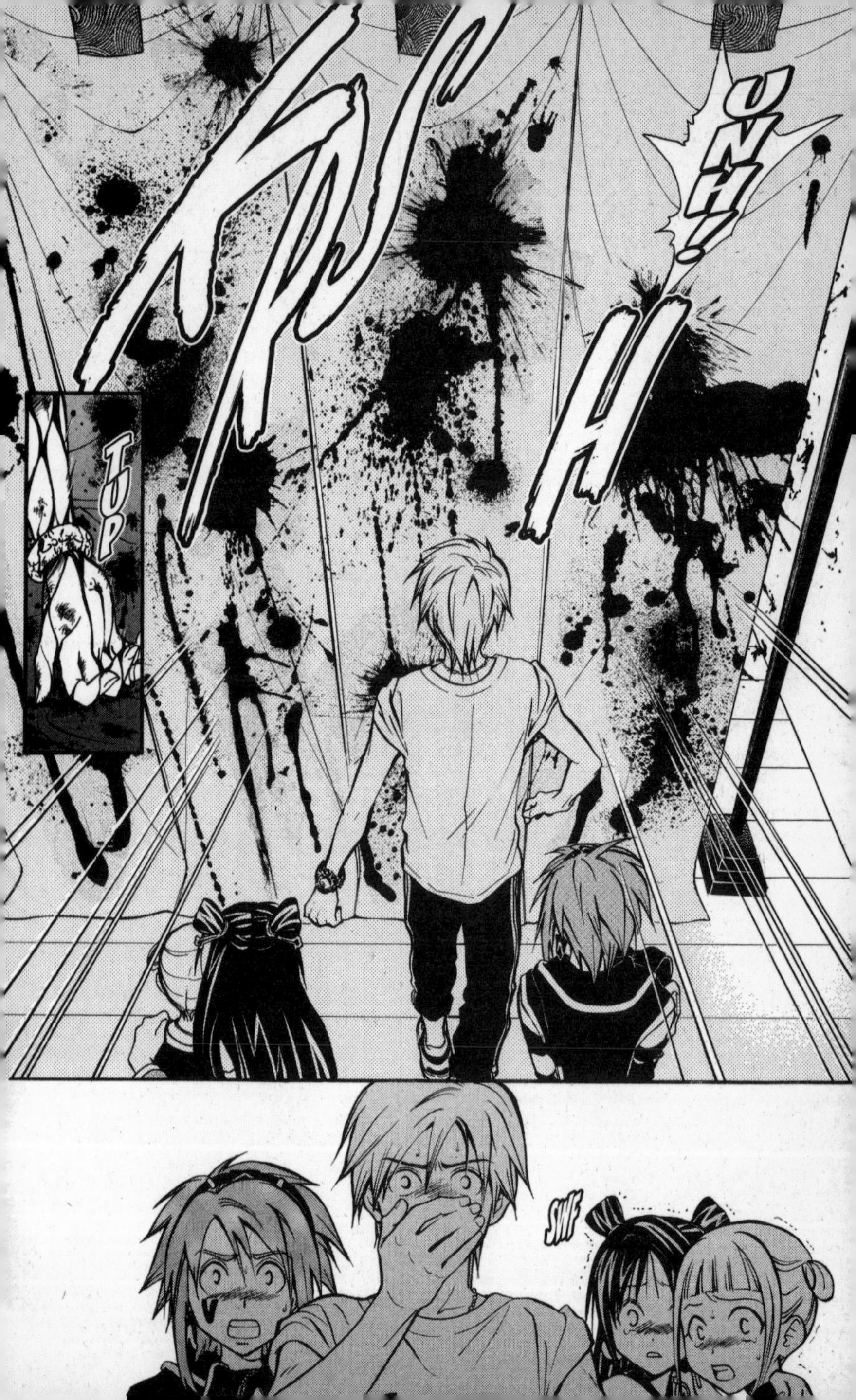
UNH!
TUP
SWF

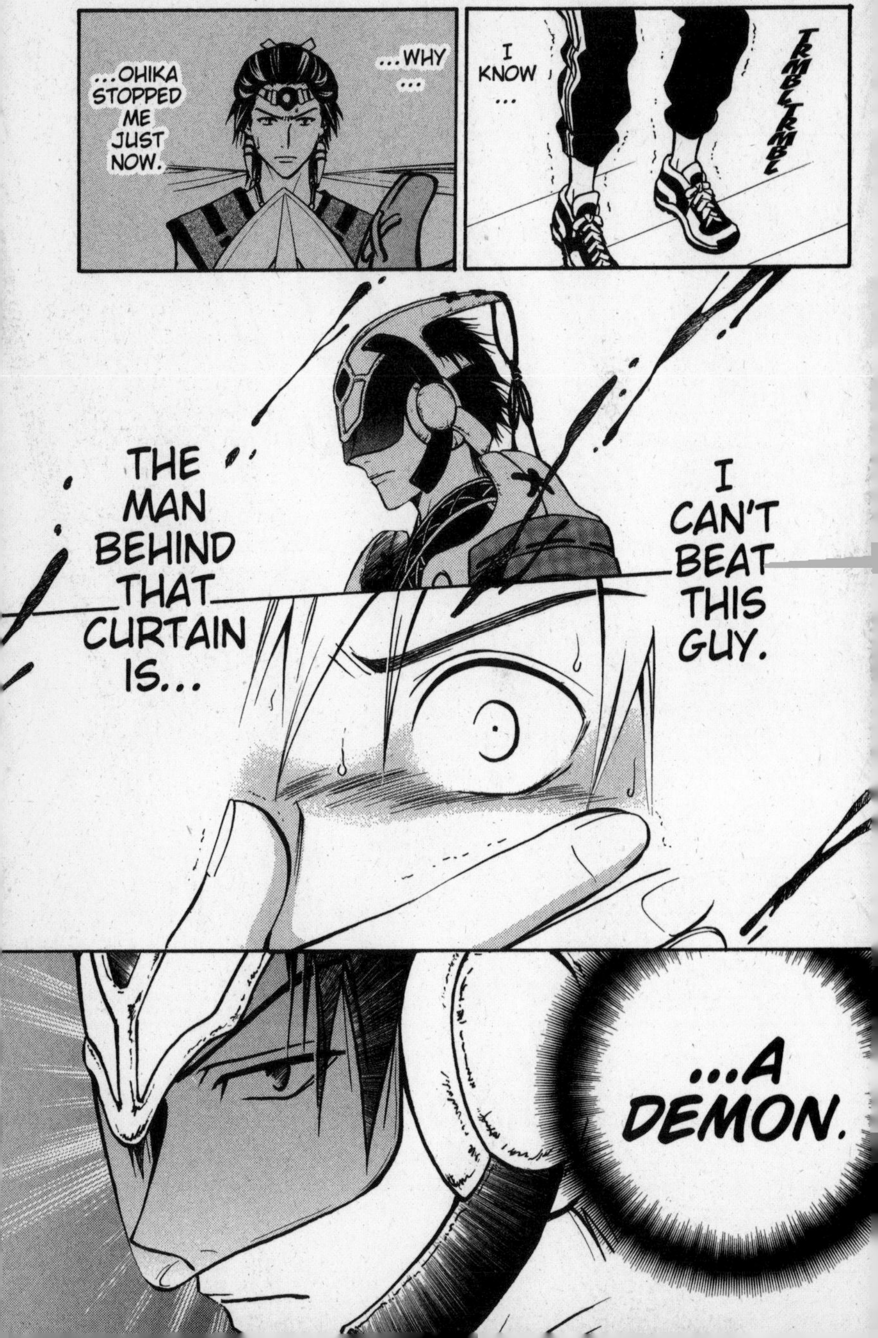
I KNOW ...
TREMBL TREMBL
...WHY ...
...OHIKA STOPPED ME JUST NOW.
I CAN'T BEAT THIS GUY.
THE MAN BEHIND THAT CURTAIN IS...
...A DEMON.

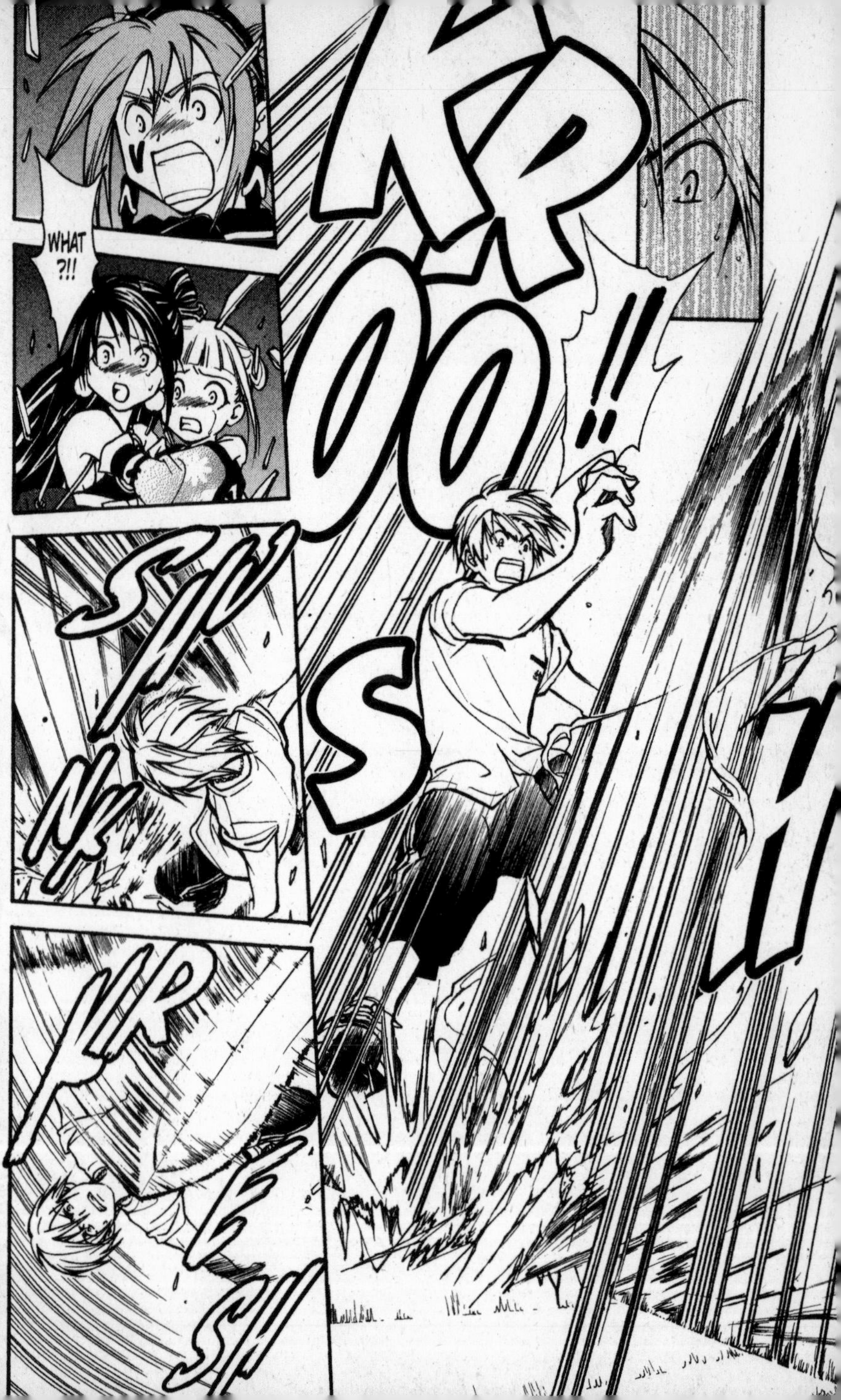
KROO!!
WHAT ?!!

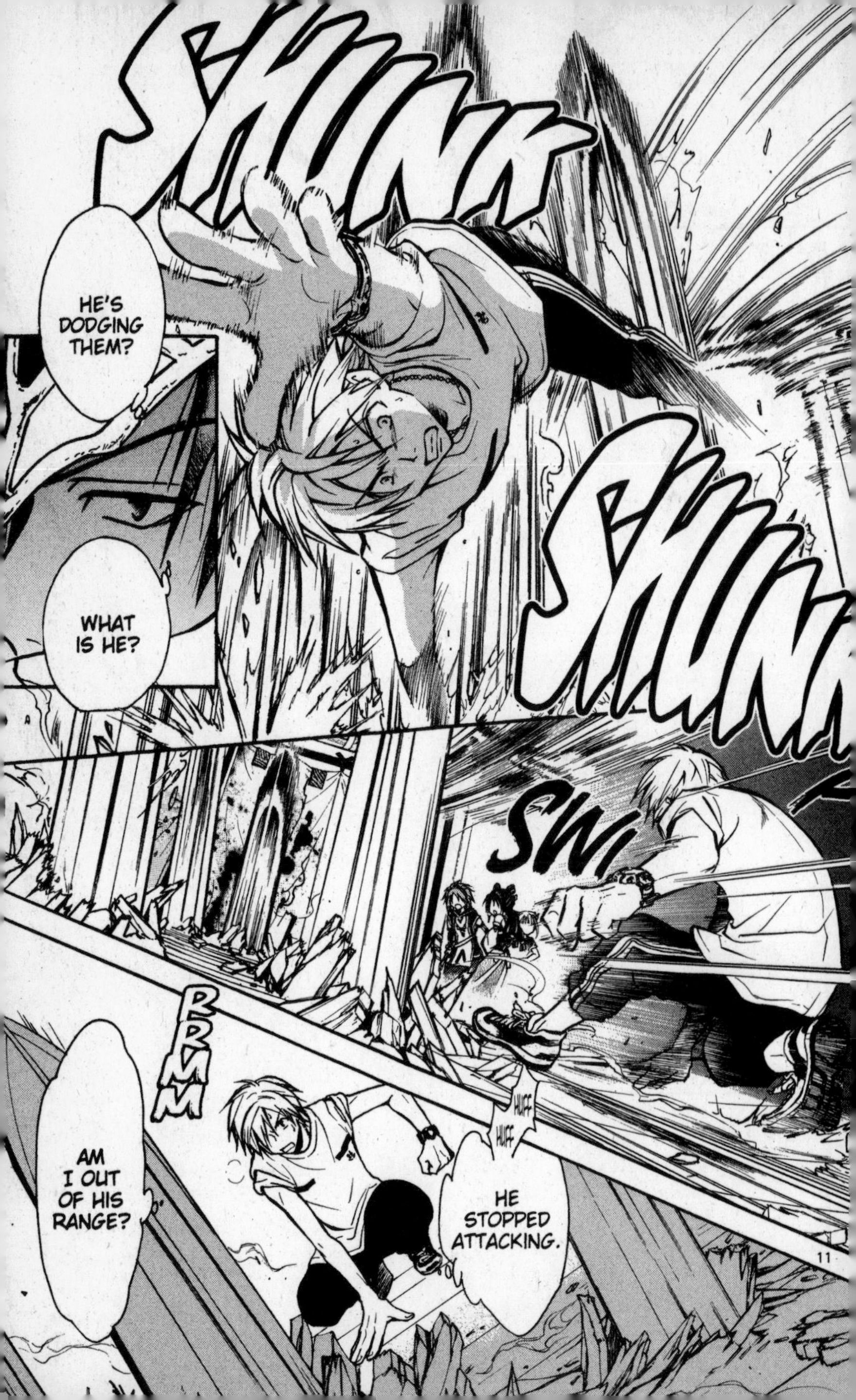
SHUNK
SHUN
HE'S DODGING THEM?
WHAT IS HE?
SWI
HUFF
HUFF
HE STOPPED ATTACKING.
RRUMM
AM I OUT OF HIS RANGE?

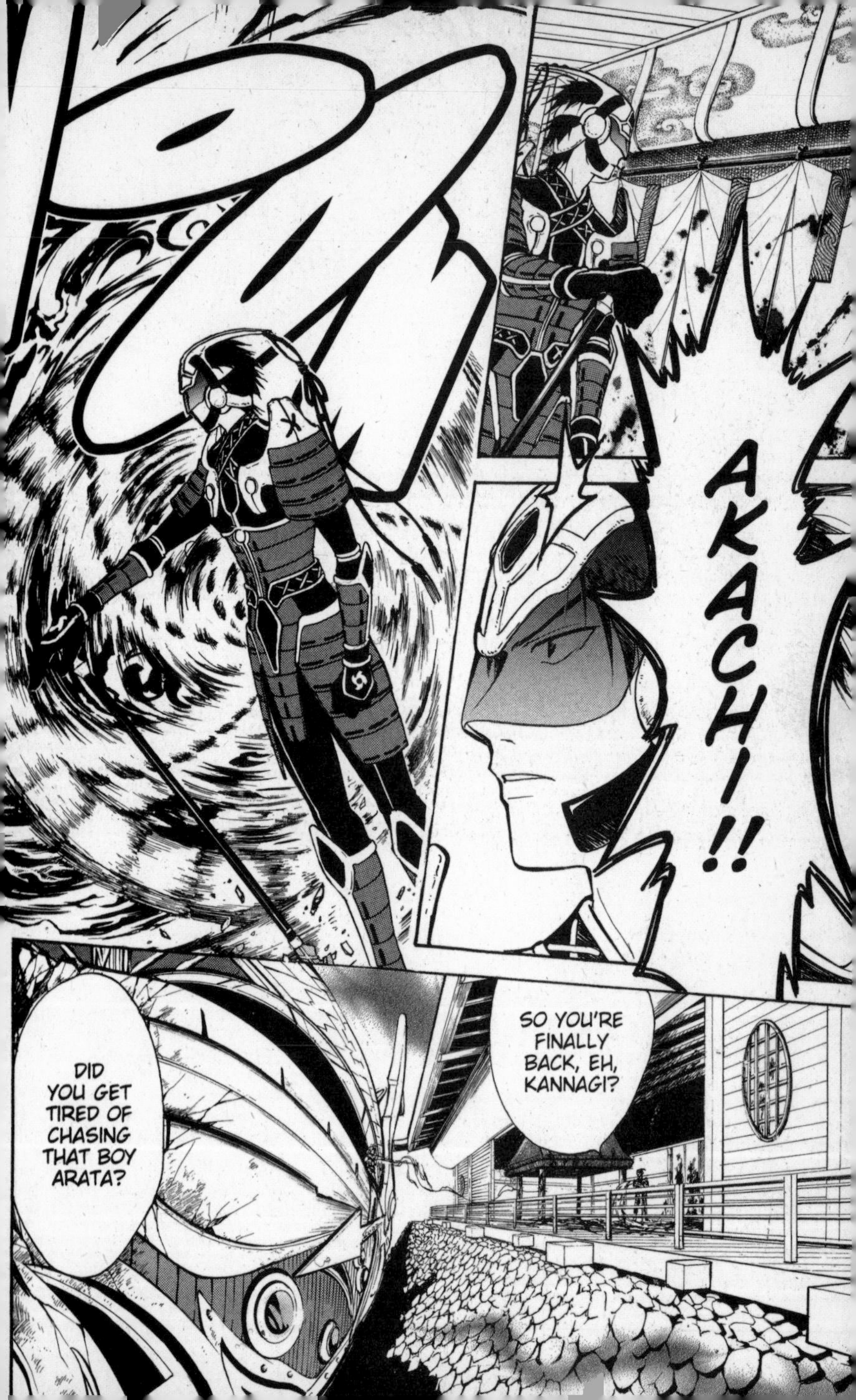
AKACHI!!
SO YOU'RE FINALLY BACK, EH, KANNAGI?
DID YOU GET TIRED OF CHASING THAT BOY ARATA?

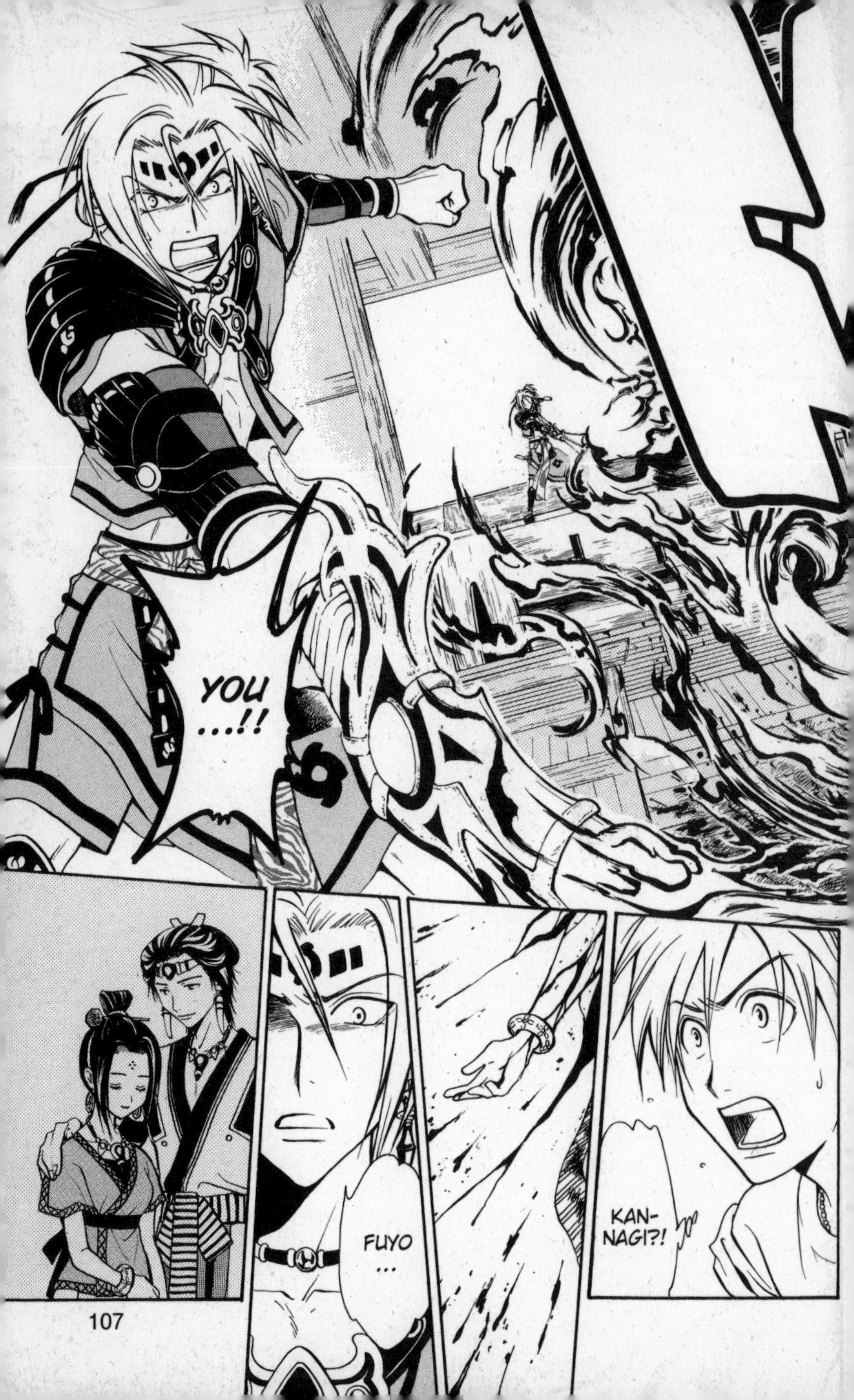
YOU ...!!
KAN-NAGI?!
FUYO ...

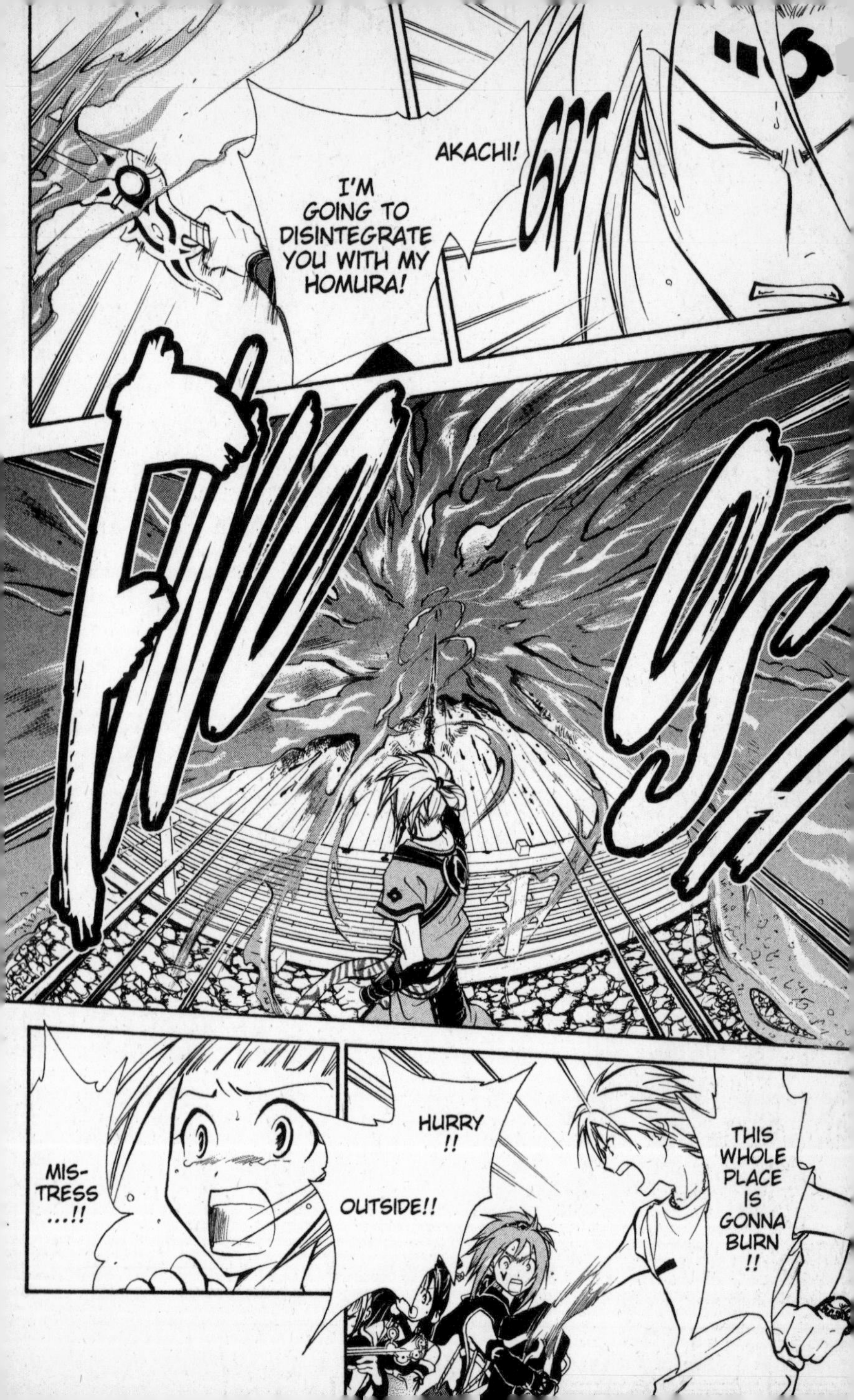
GPT
AKACHI!
I'M GOING TO DISINTEGRATE YOU WITH MY HOMURA!
THIS WHOLE PLACE IS GONNA BURN!!
HURRY!!
OUTSIDE!!
MIS-TRESS ...!!

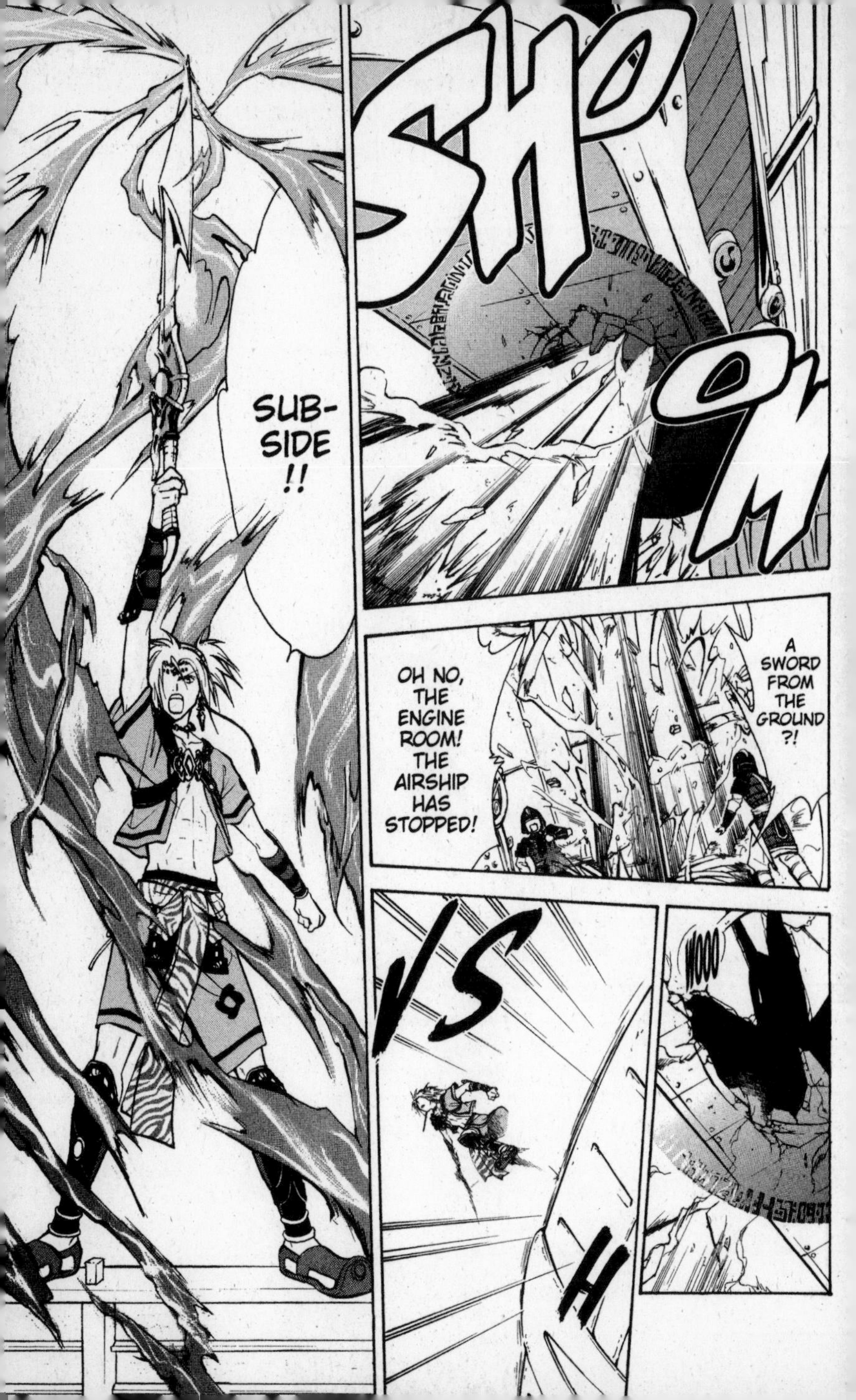
SHOOM
A SWORD FROM THE GROUND?!
OH NO, THE ENGINE ROOM! THE AIRSHIP HAS STOPPED!
WOOO
VS
H
SUB-SIDE!!

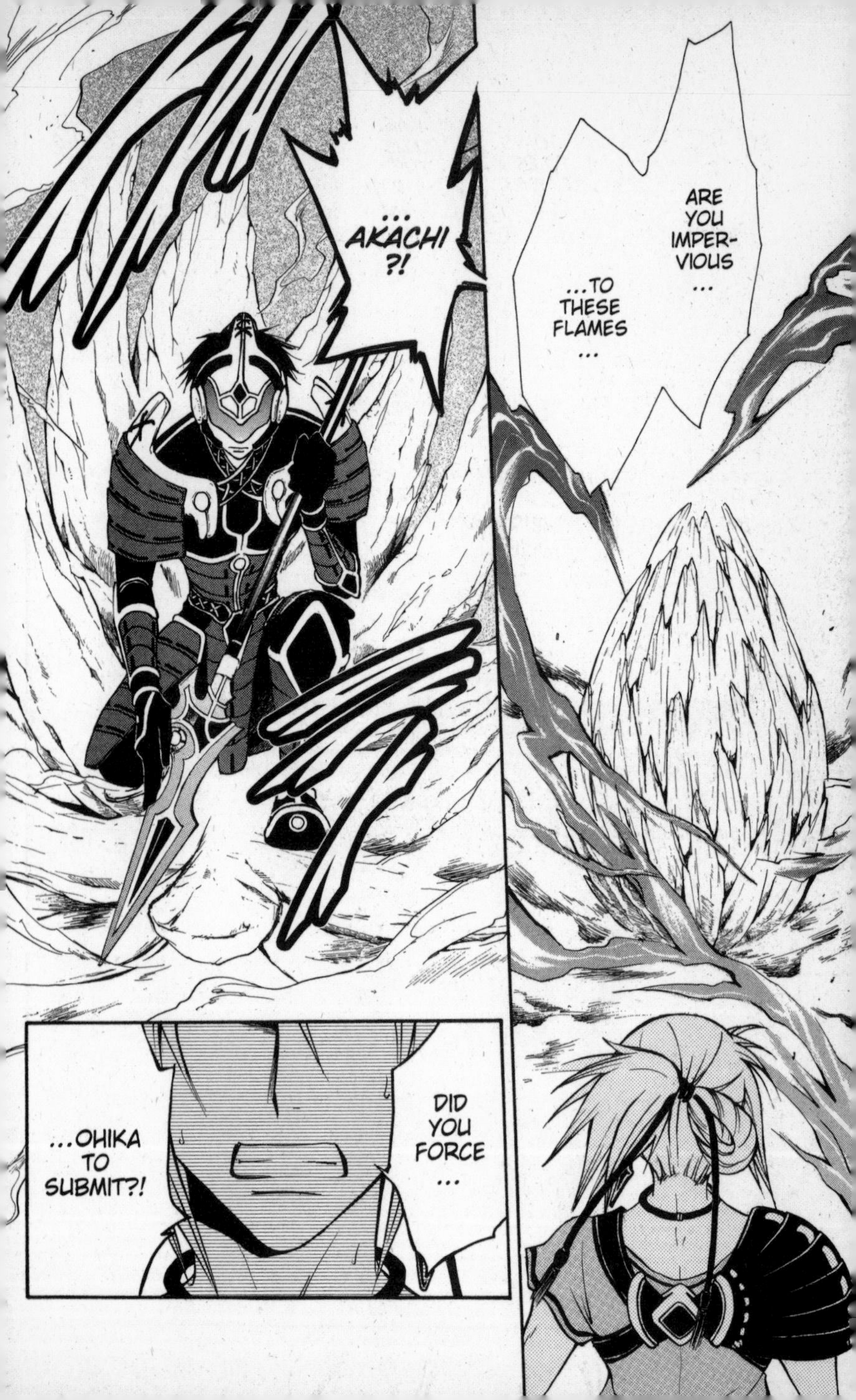
ARE YOU IMPERVIOUS...
...TO THESE FLAMES...
...AKACHI?!
DID YOU FORCE...
...OHIKA TO SUBMIT?!

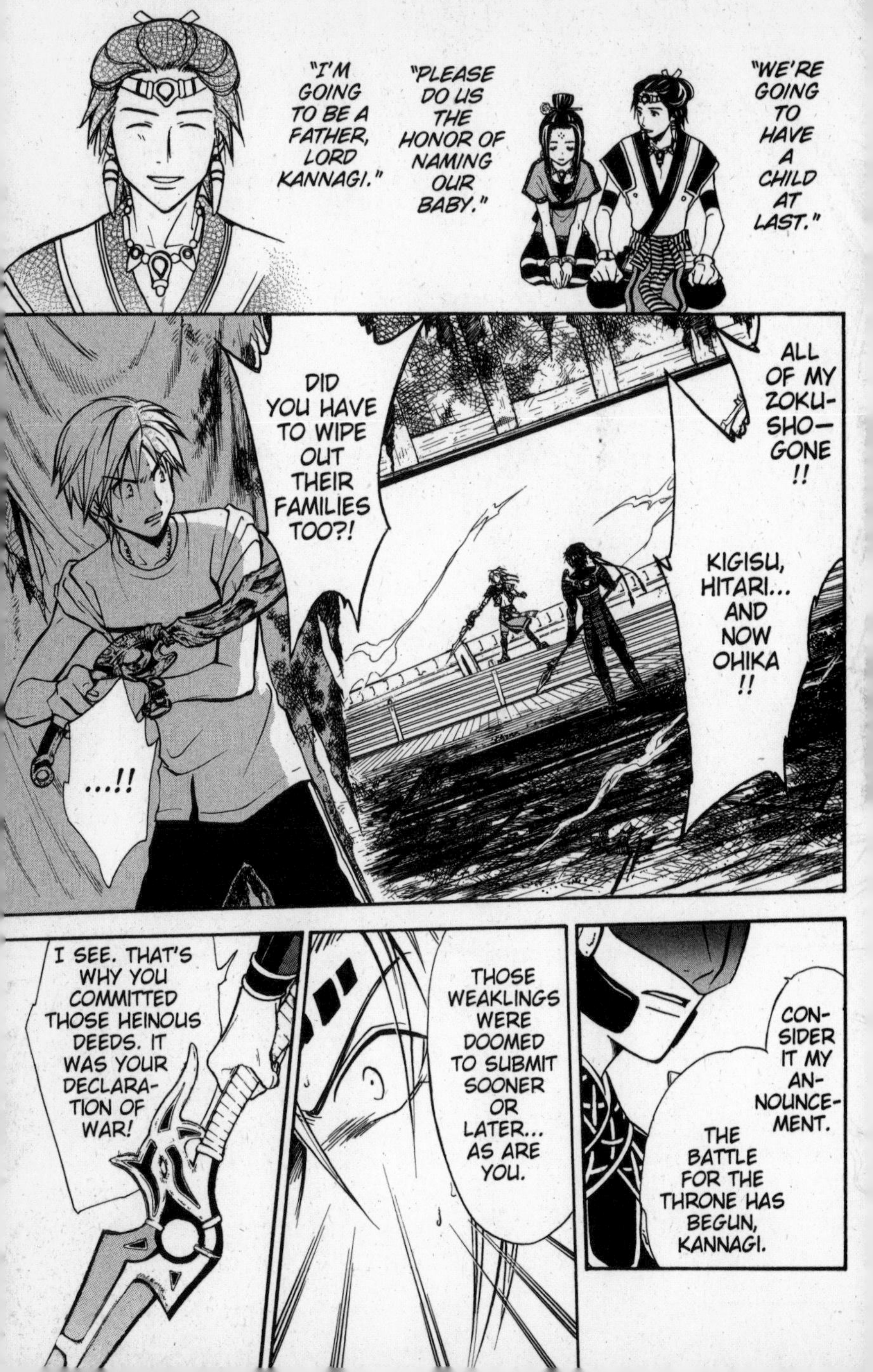
"WE'RE GOING TO HAVE A CHILD AT LAST."
"PLEASE DO US THE HONOR OF NAMING OUR BABY."
"I'M GOING TO BE A FATHER, LORD KANNAGI."
ALL OF MY ZOKU-SHO—GONE!!
KIGISU, HITARI... AND NOW OHIKA!!
DID YOU HAVE TO WIPE OUT THEIR FAMILIES TOO?!
...!!
CONSIDER IT MY ANNOUNCEMENT.
THE BATTLE FOR THE THRONE HAS BEGUN, KANNAGI.
THOSE WEAKLINGS WERE DOOMED TO SUBMIT SOONER OR LATER... AS ARE YOU.
I SEE. THAT'S WHY YOU COMMITTED THOSE HEINOUS DEEDS. IT WAS YOUR DECLARATION OF WAR!

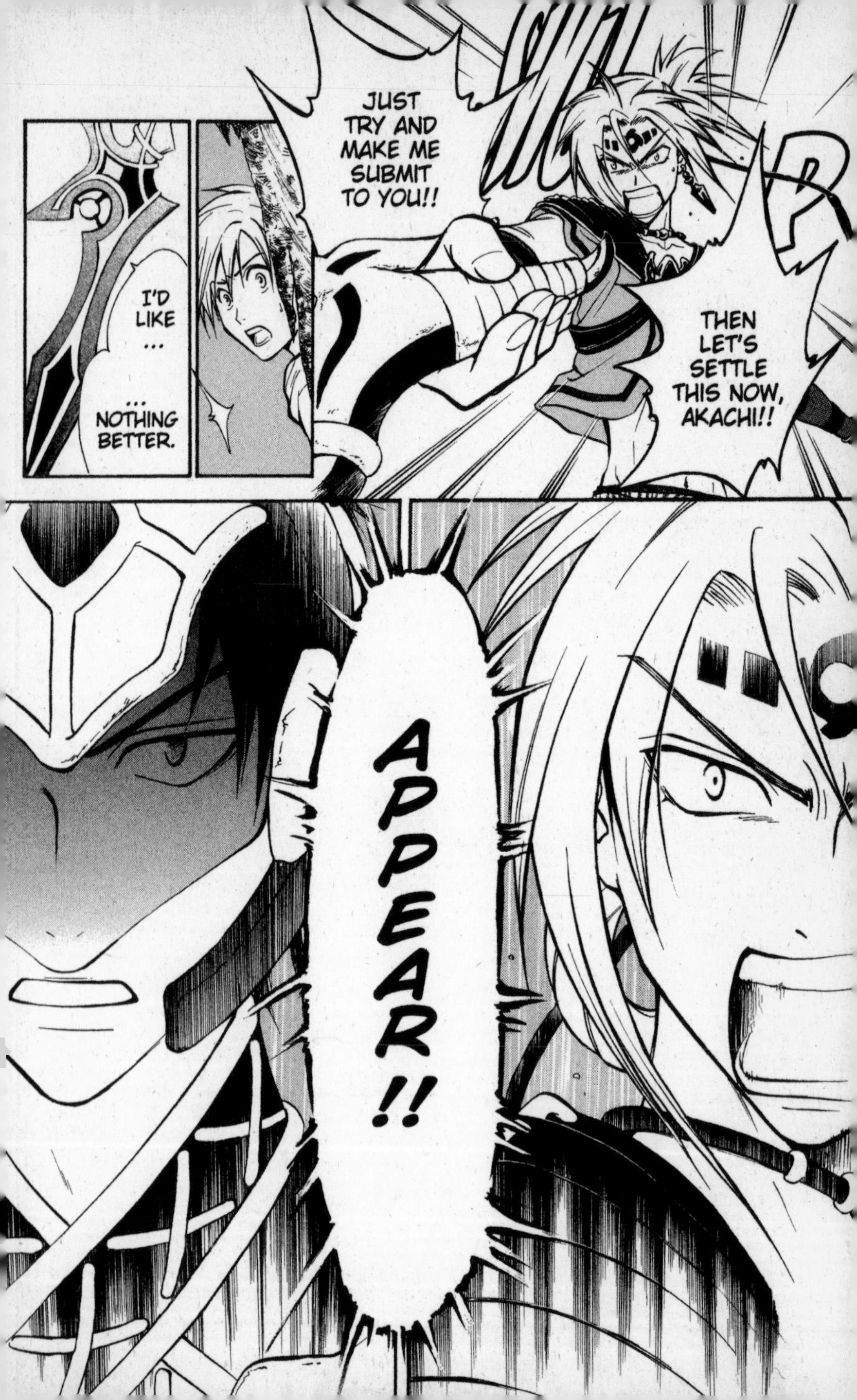
THEN LET'S SETTLE THIS NOW, AKACHI!!
JUST TRY AND MAKE ME SUBMIT TO YOU!!
I'D LIKE ...
... NOTHING BETTER.
APPEAR!!

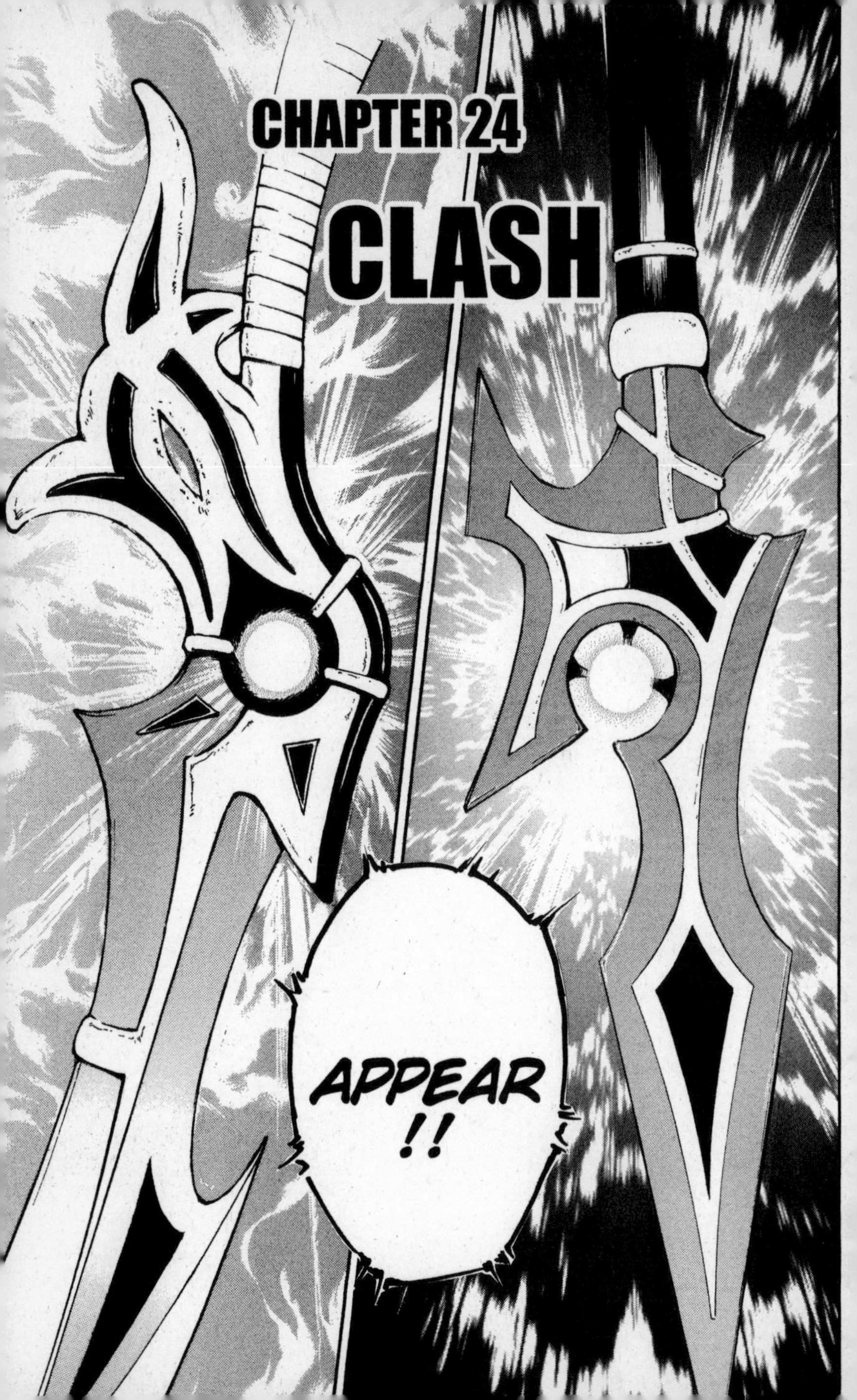
CHAPTER 24
CLASH
APPEAR !!

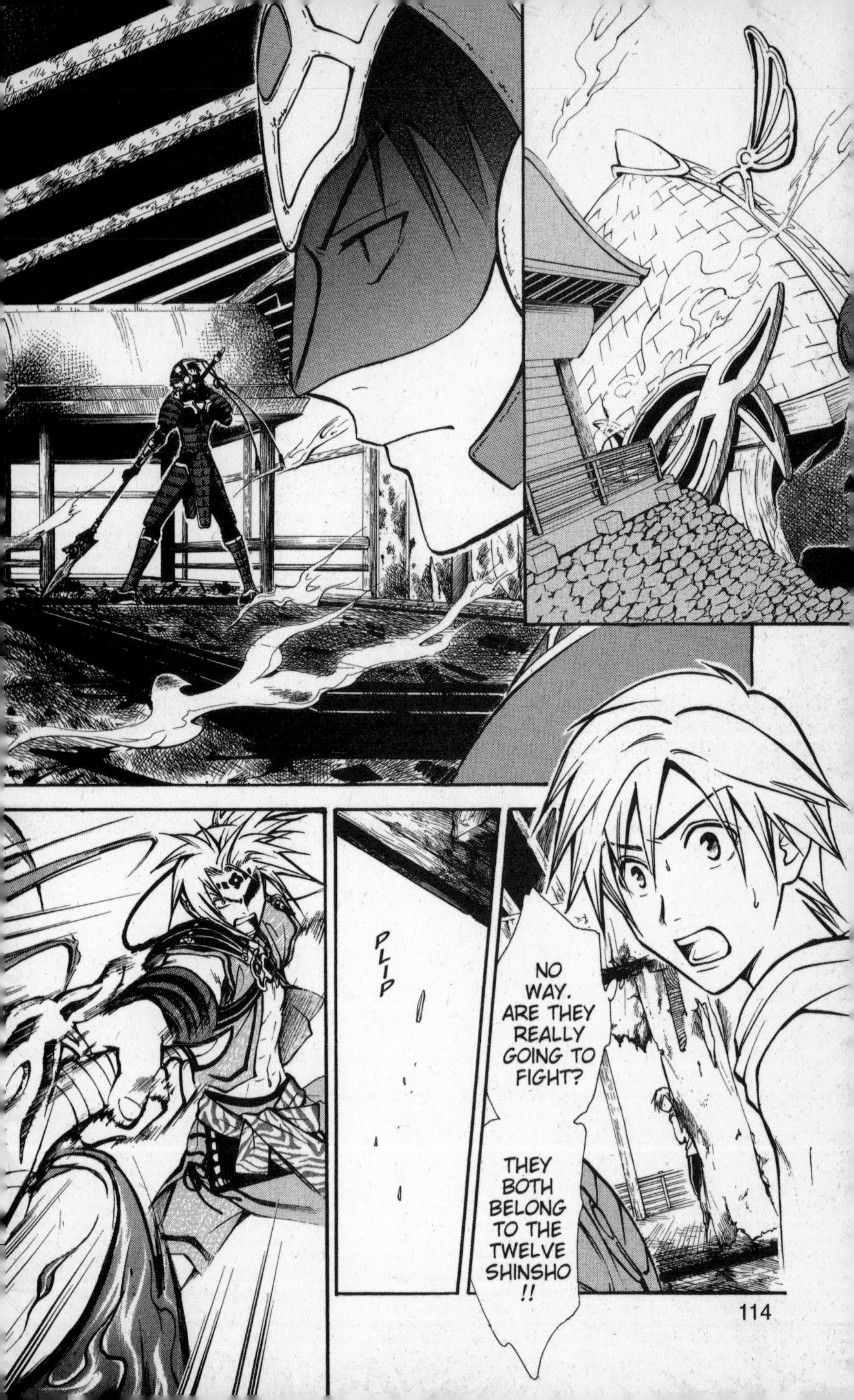
NO WAY. ARE THEY REALLY GOING TO FIGHT?
THEY BOTH BELONG TO THE TWELVE SHINSHO!!
PLIP

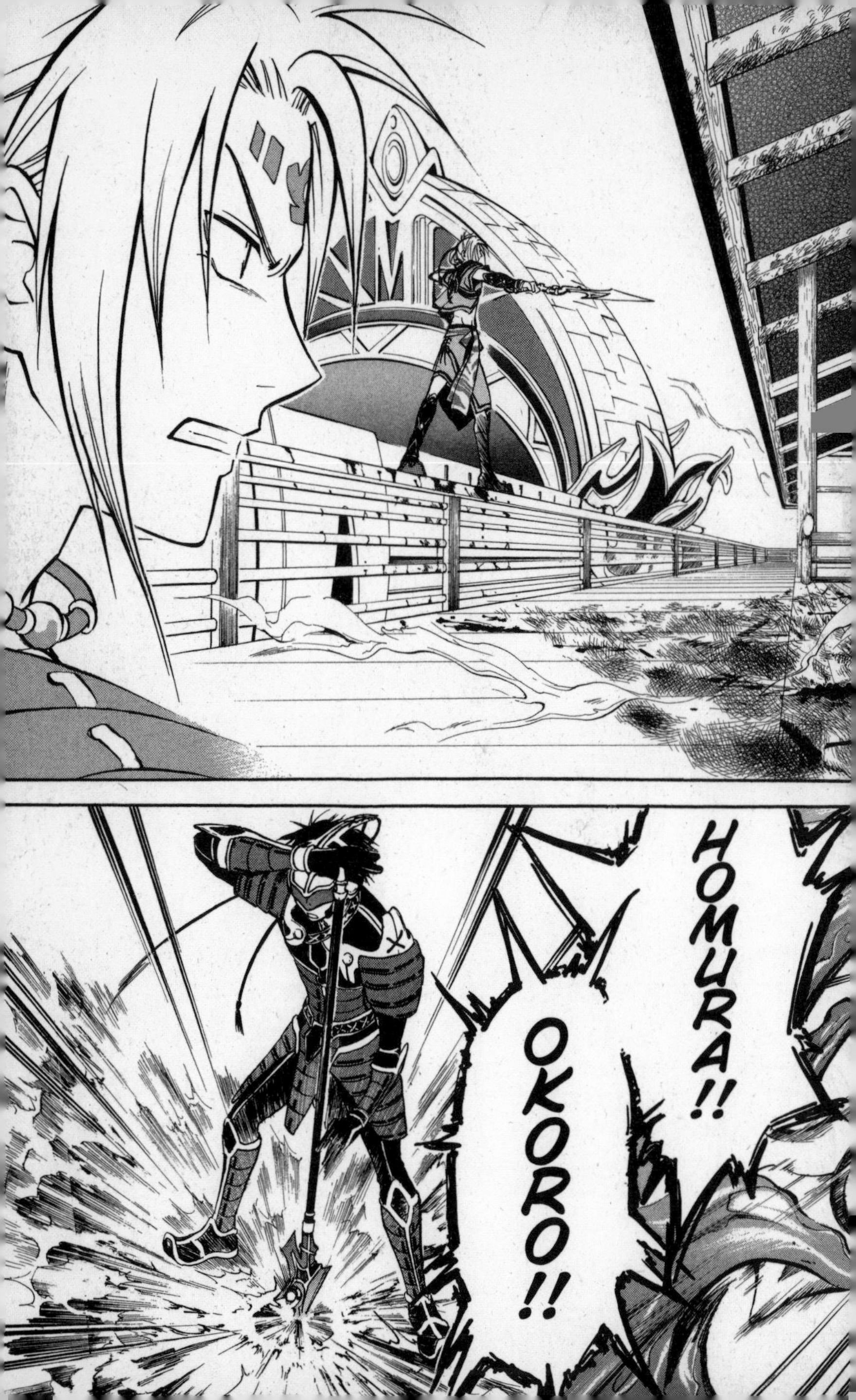
HOMURA!!
OKORO!!

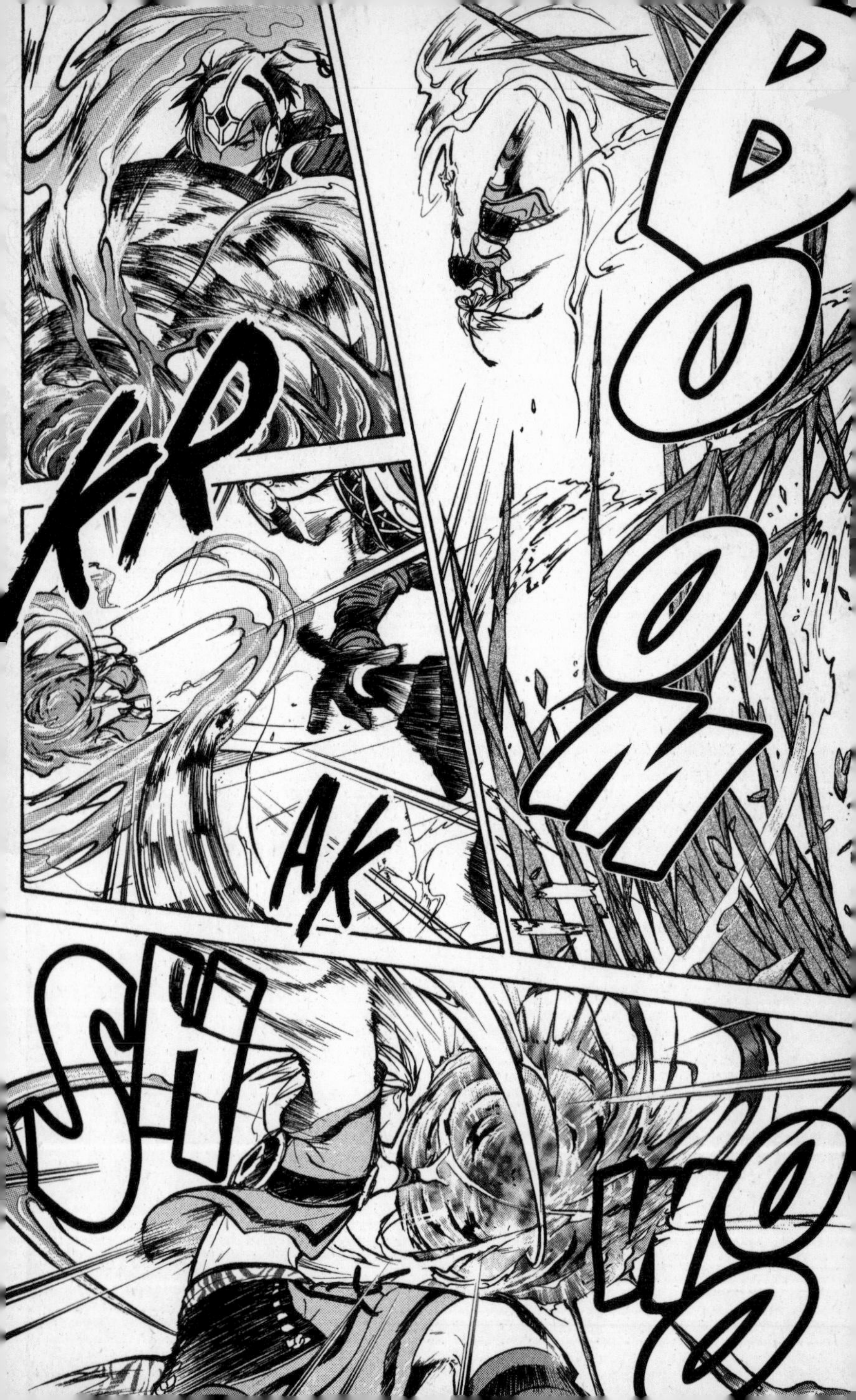
DOOM
KRAK

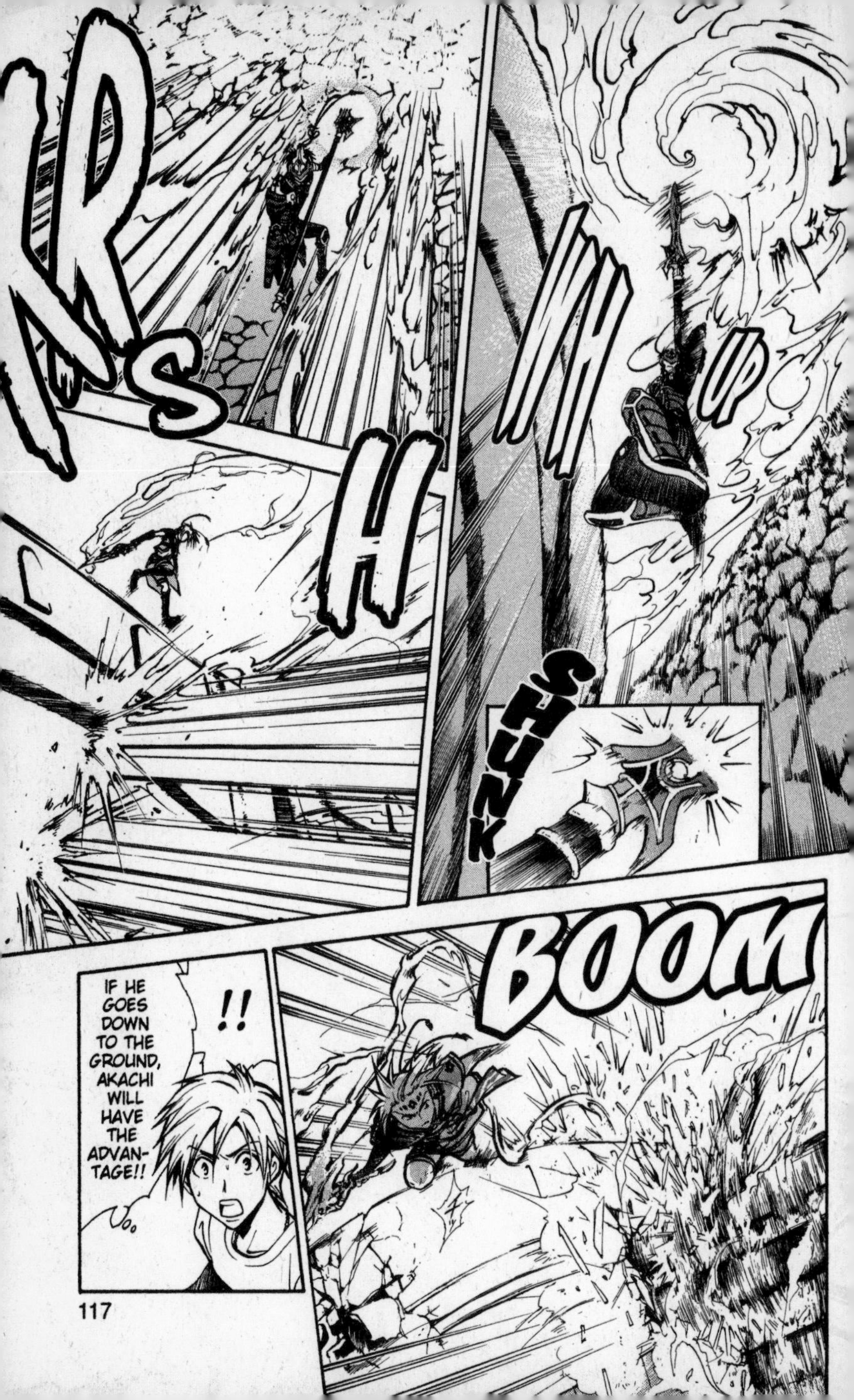
WHUP
SHUNK
BOOM
!!
IF HE GOES DOWN TO THE GROUND, AKACHI WILL HAVE THE ADVANTAGE!!

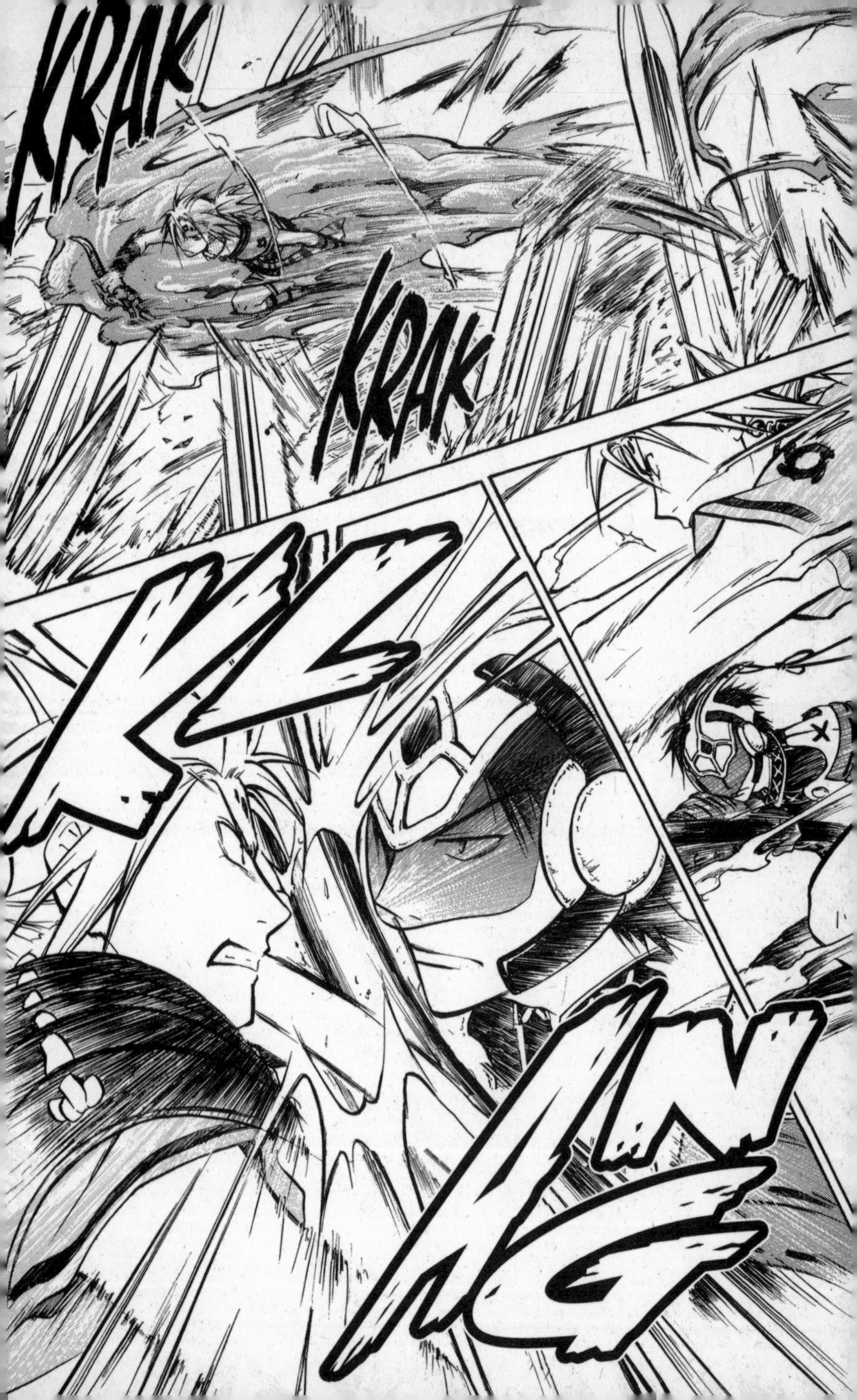
KRAK
KRAK
KLANG

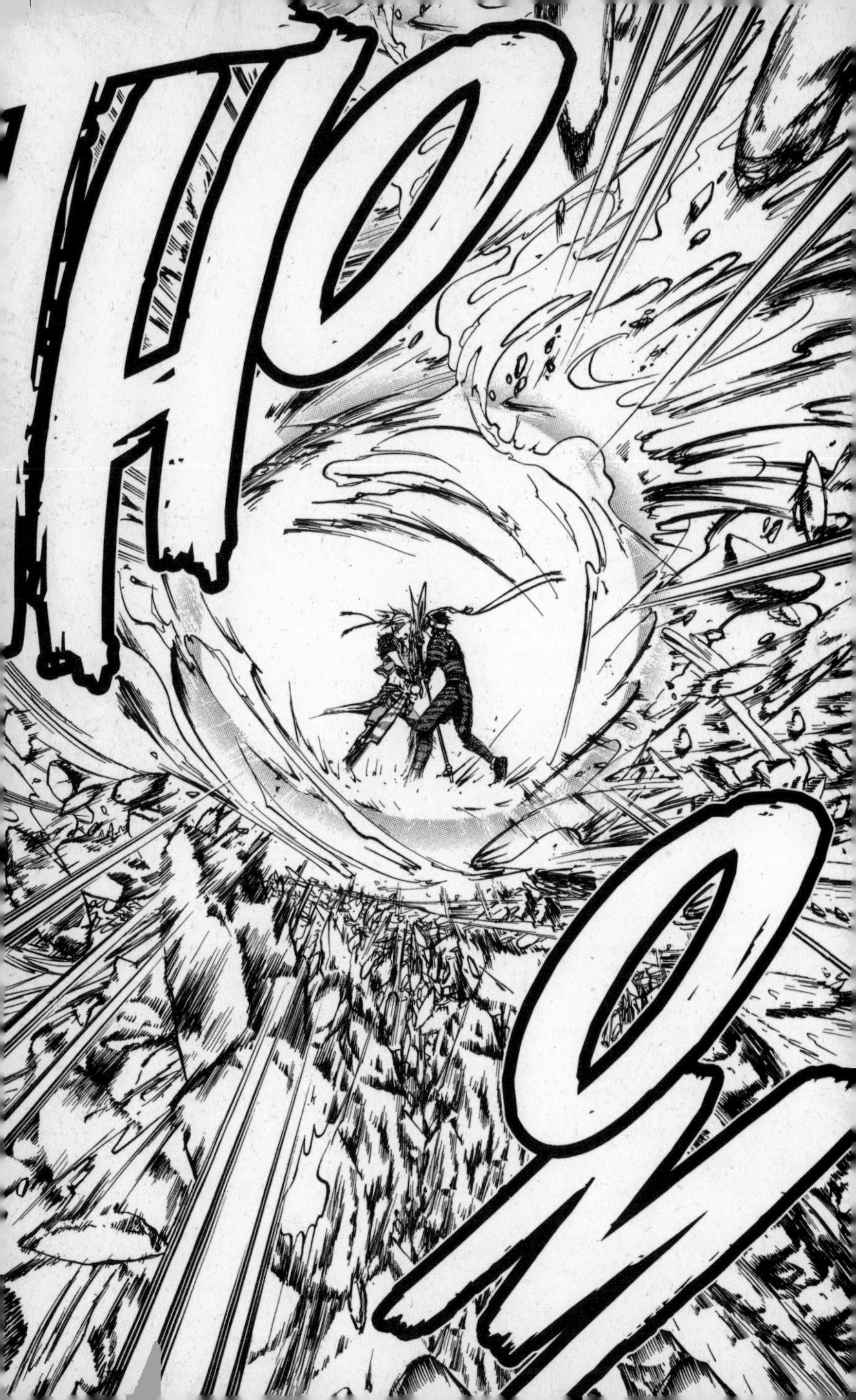

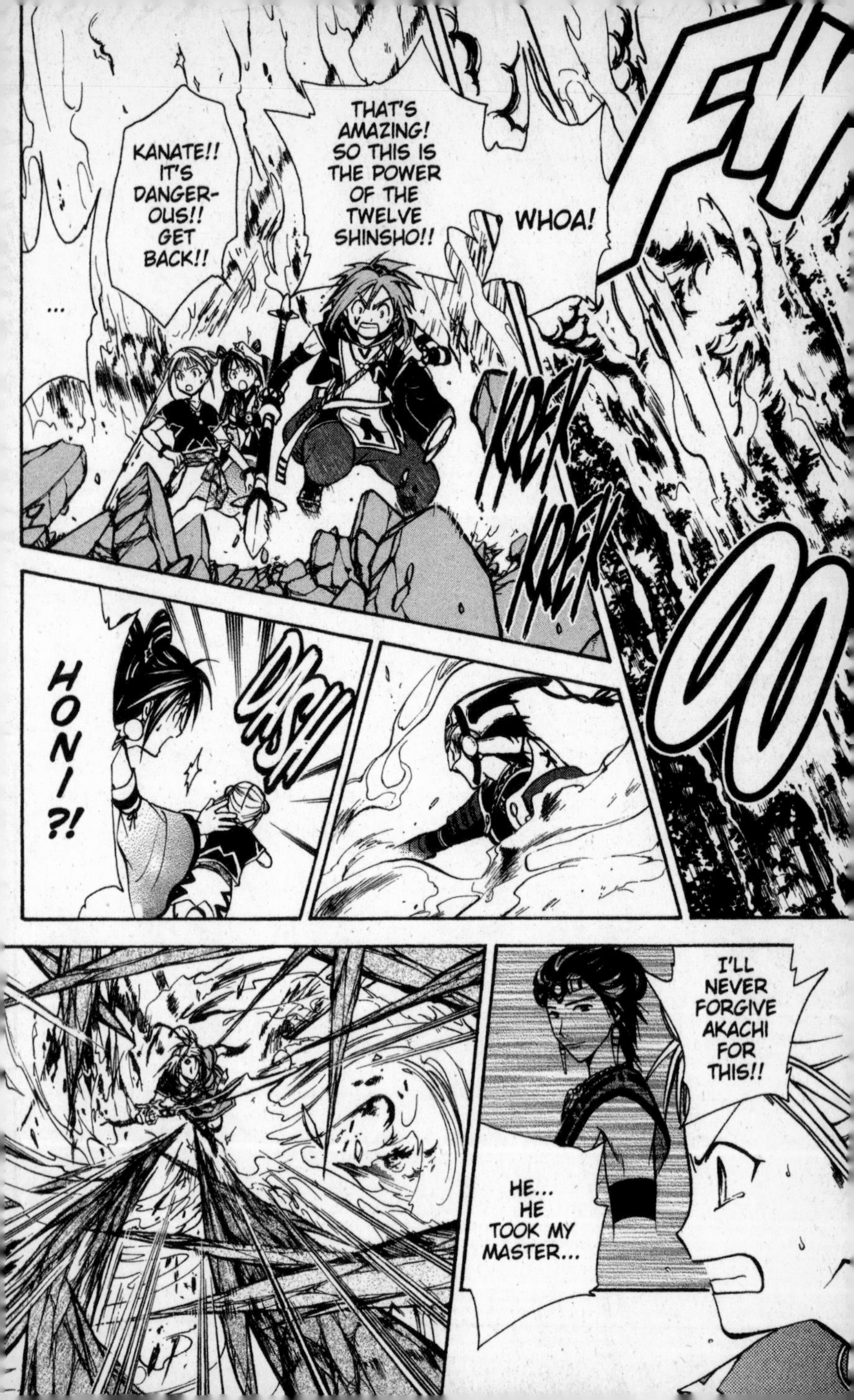
FWOO
WHOA!
THAT'S AMAZING! SO THIS IS THE POWER OF THE TWELVE SHINSHO!!
KANATE!! IT'S DANGER-OUS!! GET BACK!!
...
KREK KREK
DASH!
HONI?!
I'LL NEVER FORGIVE AKACHI FOR THIS!!
HE... HE TOOK MY MASTER...

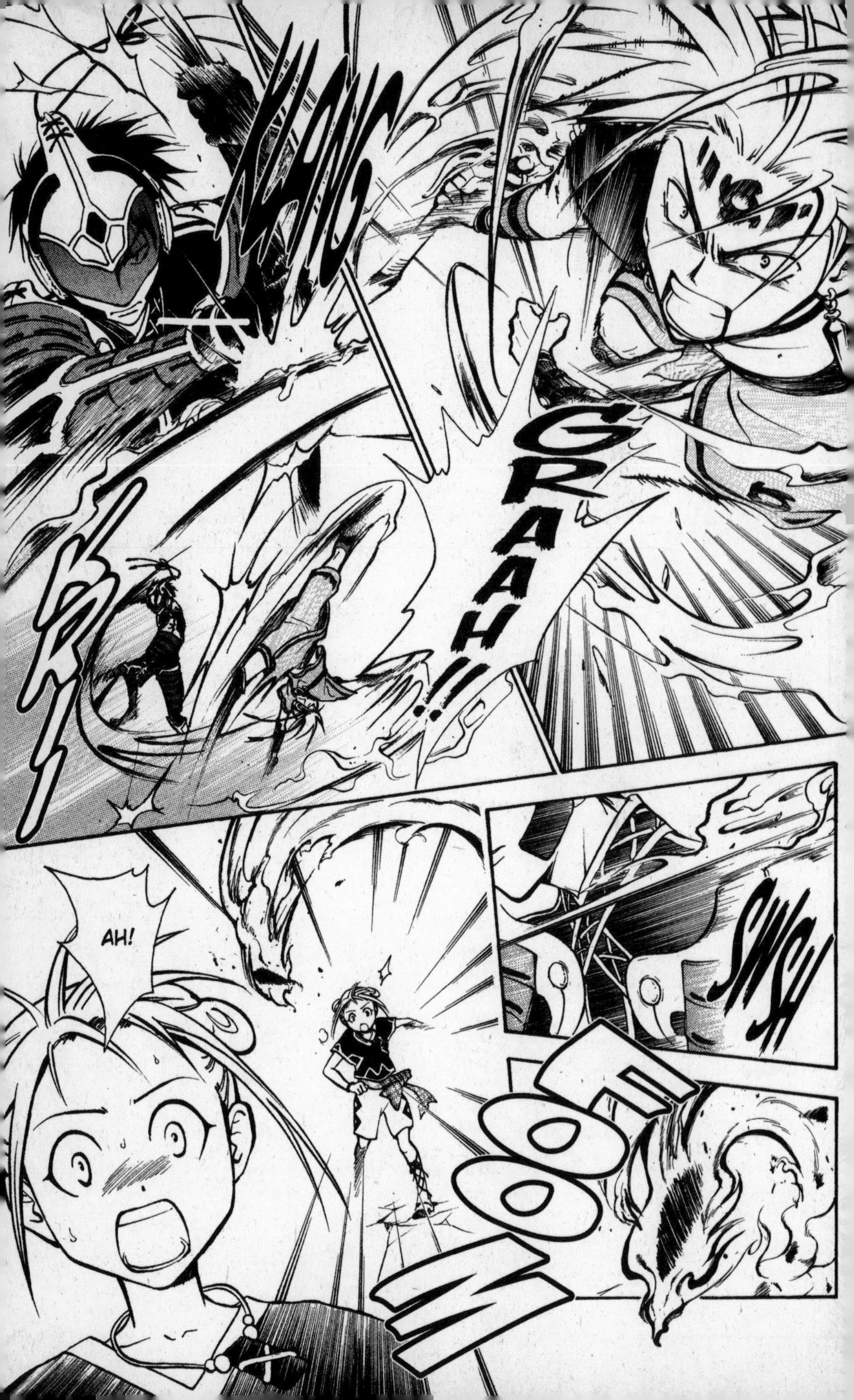
GRAAH!!
SWISH
FOOOM
AH!

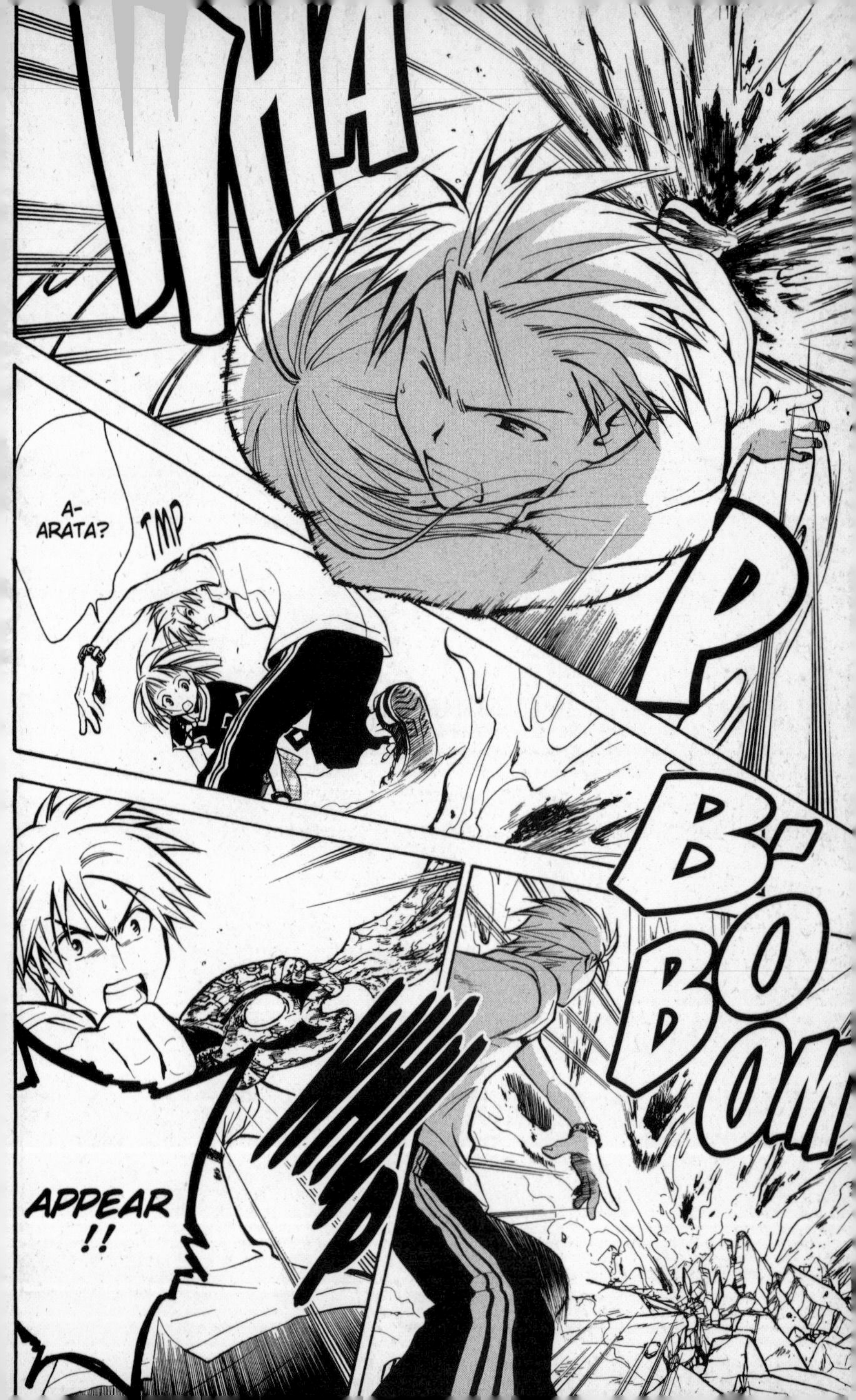
WHA
A-
ARATA?
TMP
P
APPEAR
!!

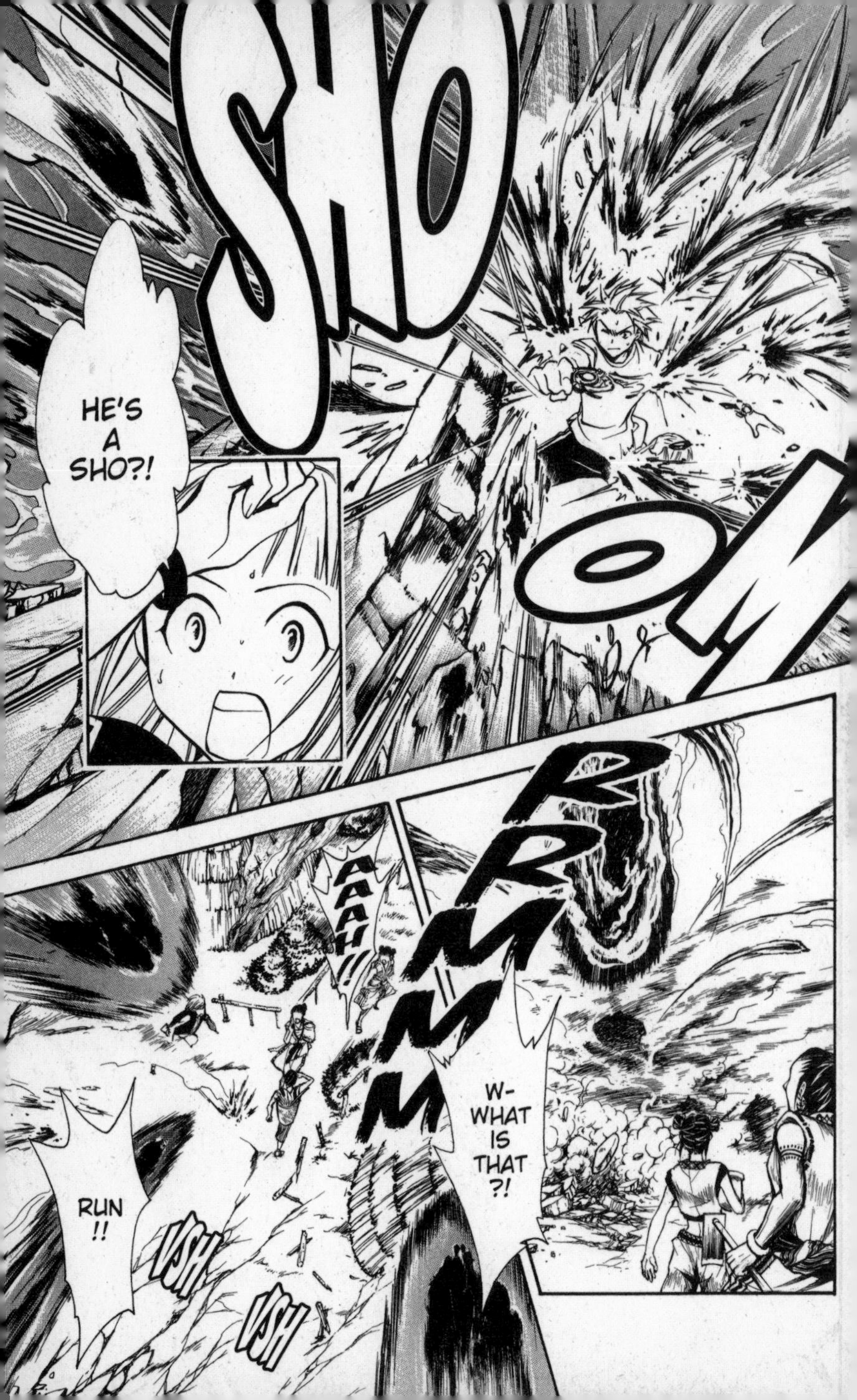
SHO
OM
HE'S A SHO?!
W-WHAT IS THAT?!
RRMMM
AAAH!!
RUN!!
VSH
VSH

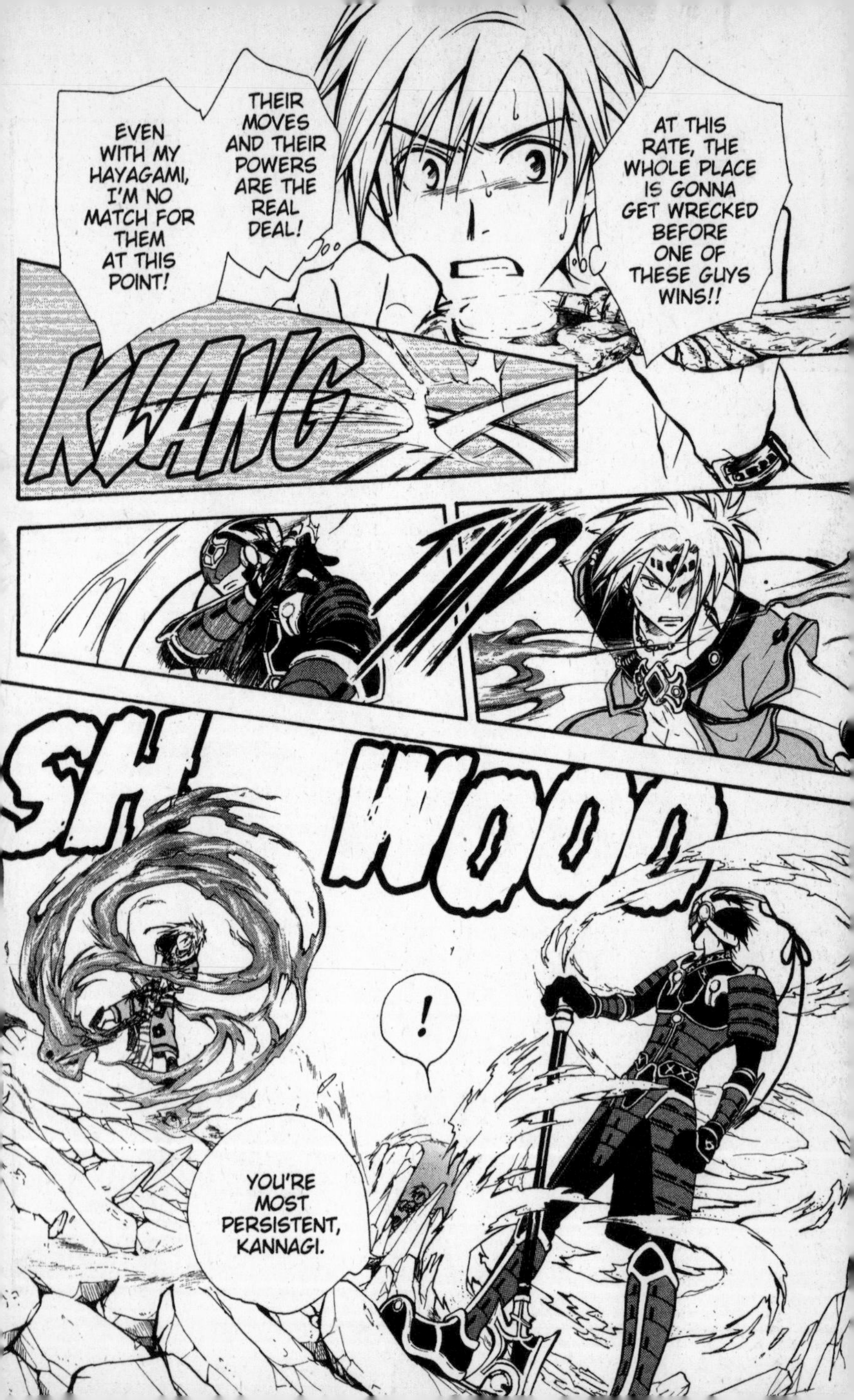
AT THIS RATE, THE WHOLE PLACE IS GONNA GET WRECKED BEFORE ONE OF THESE GUYS WINS!!
THEIR MOVES AND THEIR POWERS ARE THE REAL DEAL!
EVEN WITH MY HAYAGAMI, I'M NO MATCH FOR THEM AT THIS POINT!
KLANG
SHWOOO
!
YOU'RE MOST PERSISTENT, KANNAGI.

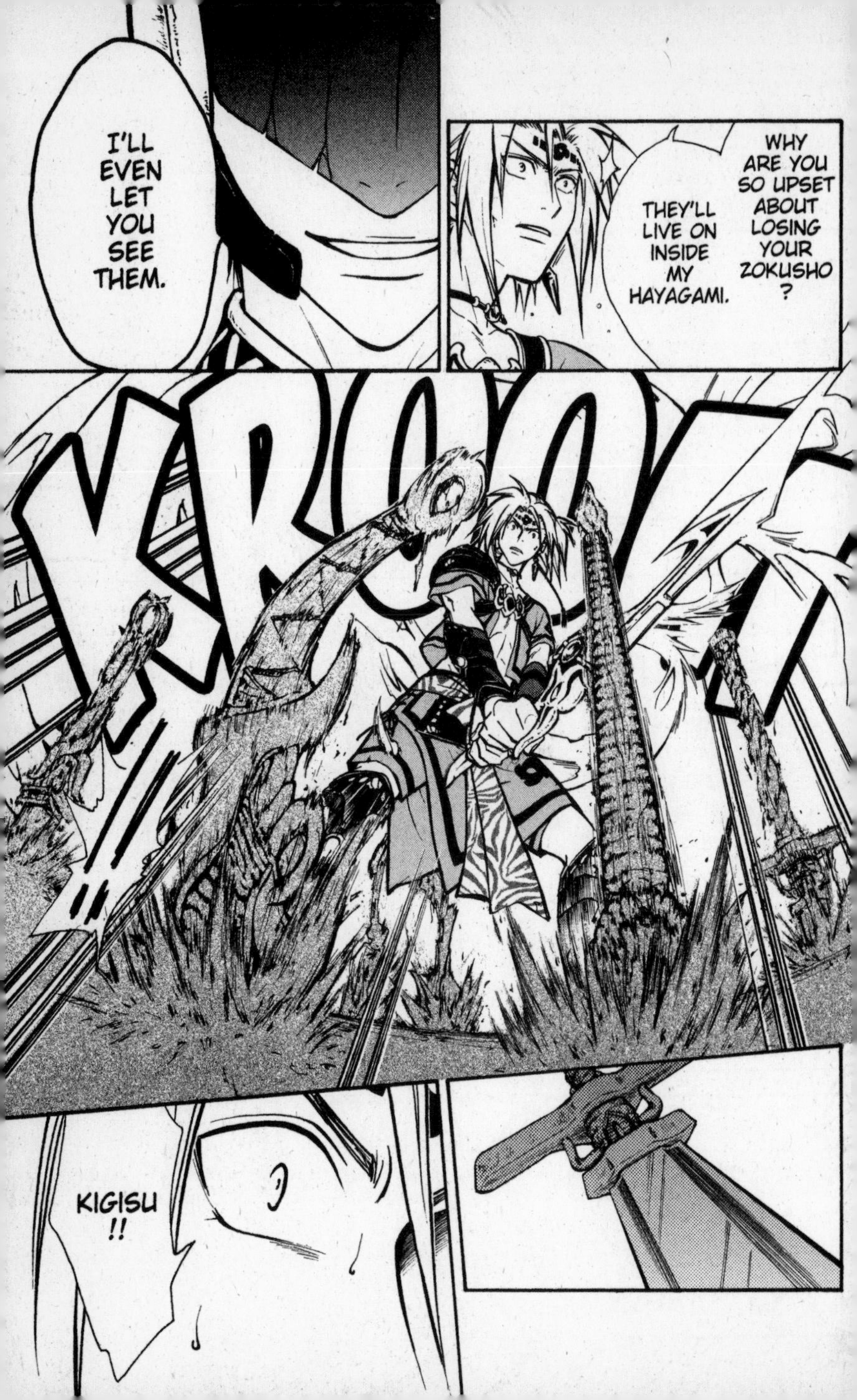
WHY ARE YOU SO UPSET ABOUT LOSING YOUR ZOKUSHO?
THEY'LL LIVE ON INSIDE MY HAYAGAMI.
I'LL EVEN LET YOU SEE THEM.
KIGISU!!

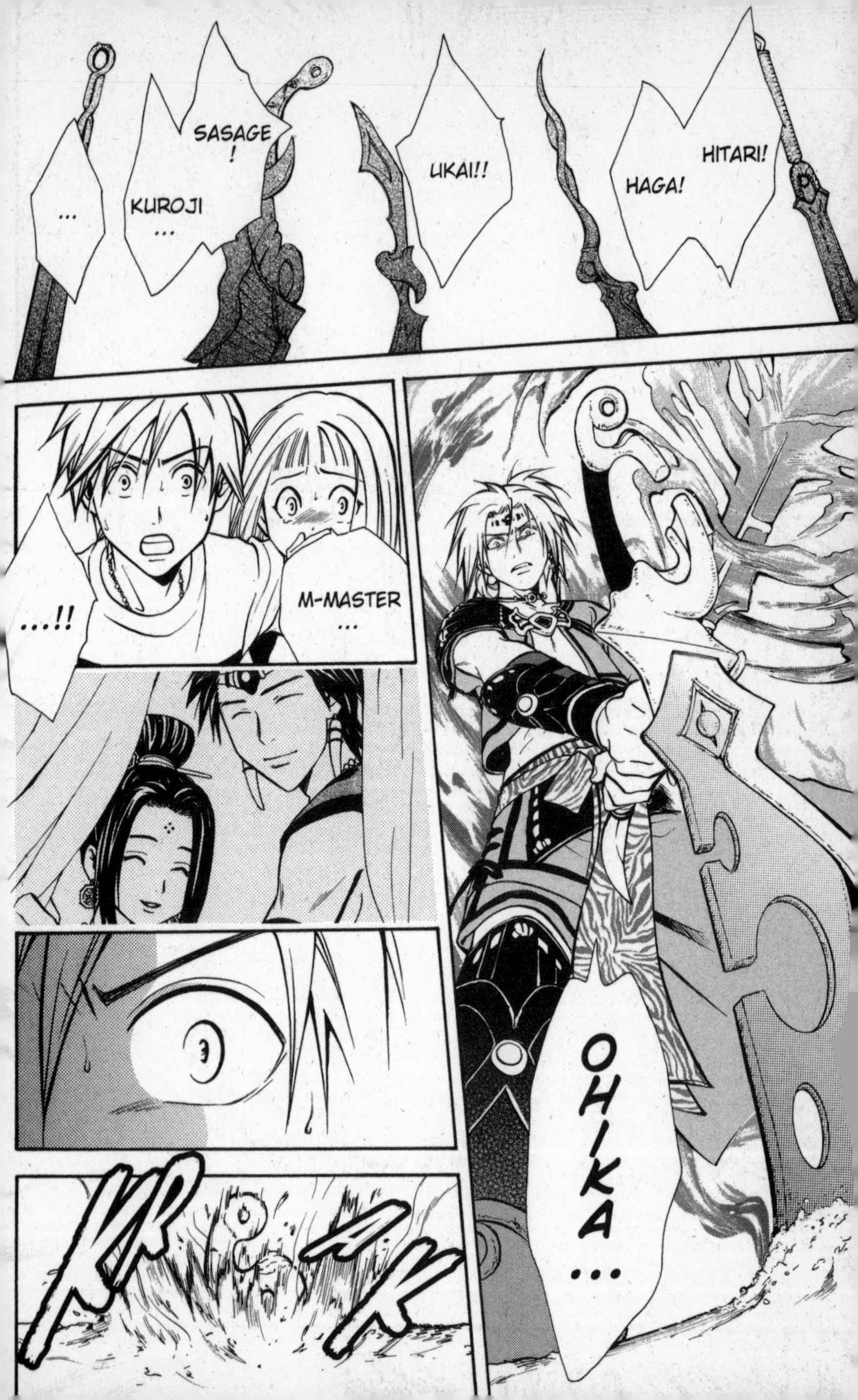
HITARI!
HAGA!
UKAI!!
SASAGE!
KUROJI...
...
OHIKA...
M-MASTER...
...!!
KRAK

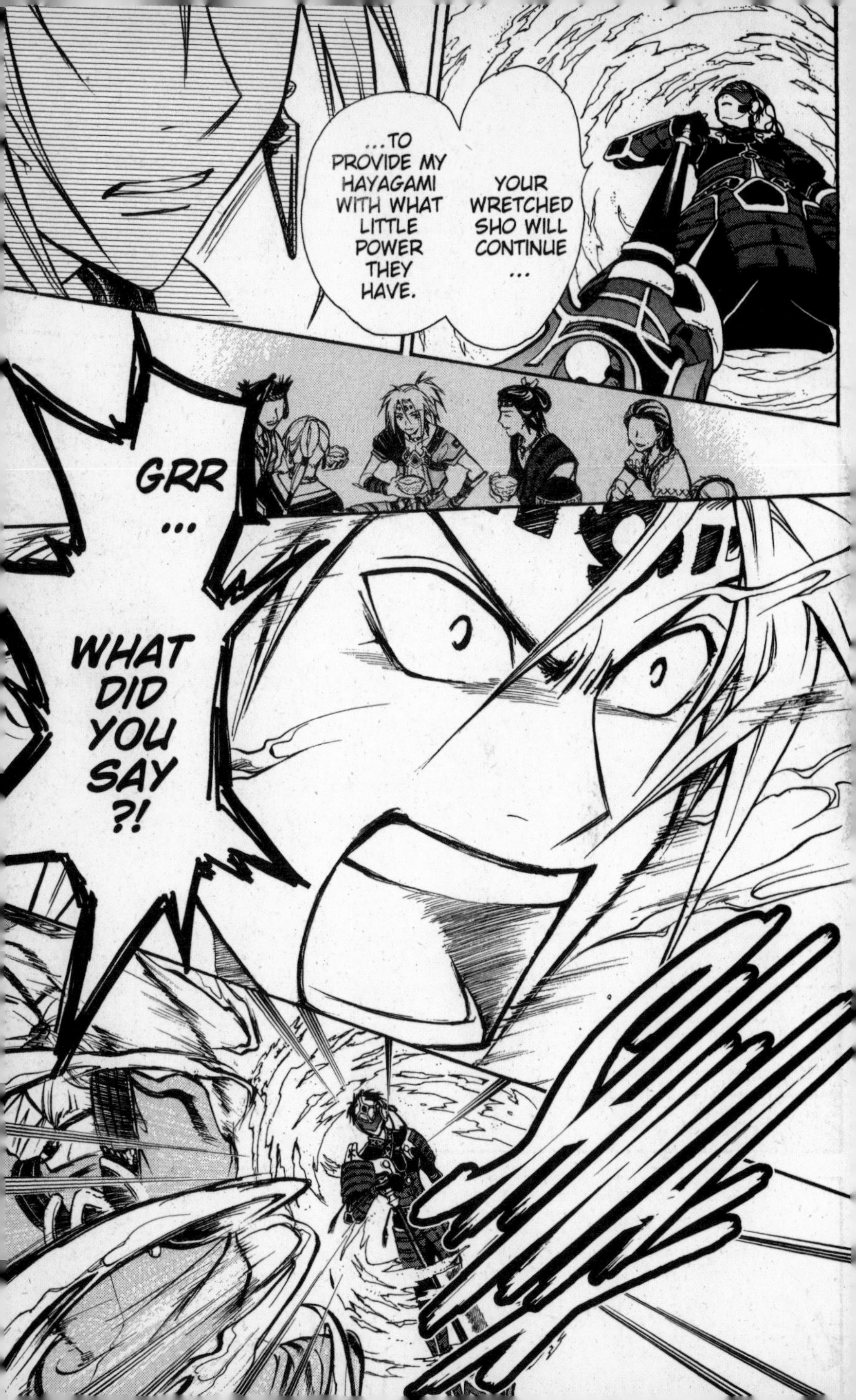
YOUR WRETCHED SHO WILL CONTINUE...
...TO PROVIDE MY HAYAGAMI WITH WHAT LITTLE POWER THEY HAVE.
GRR...
WHAT DID YOU SAY?!

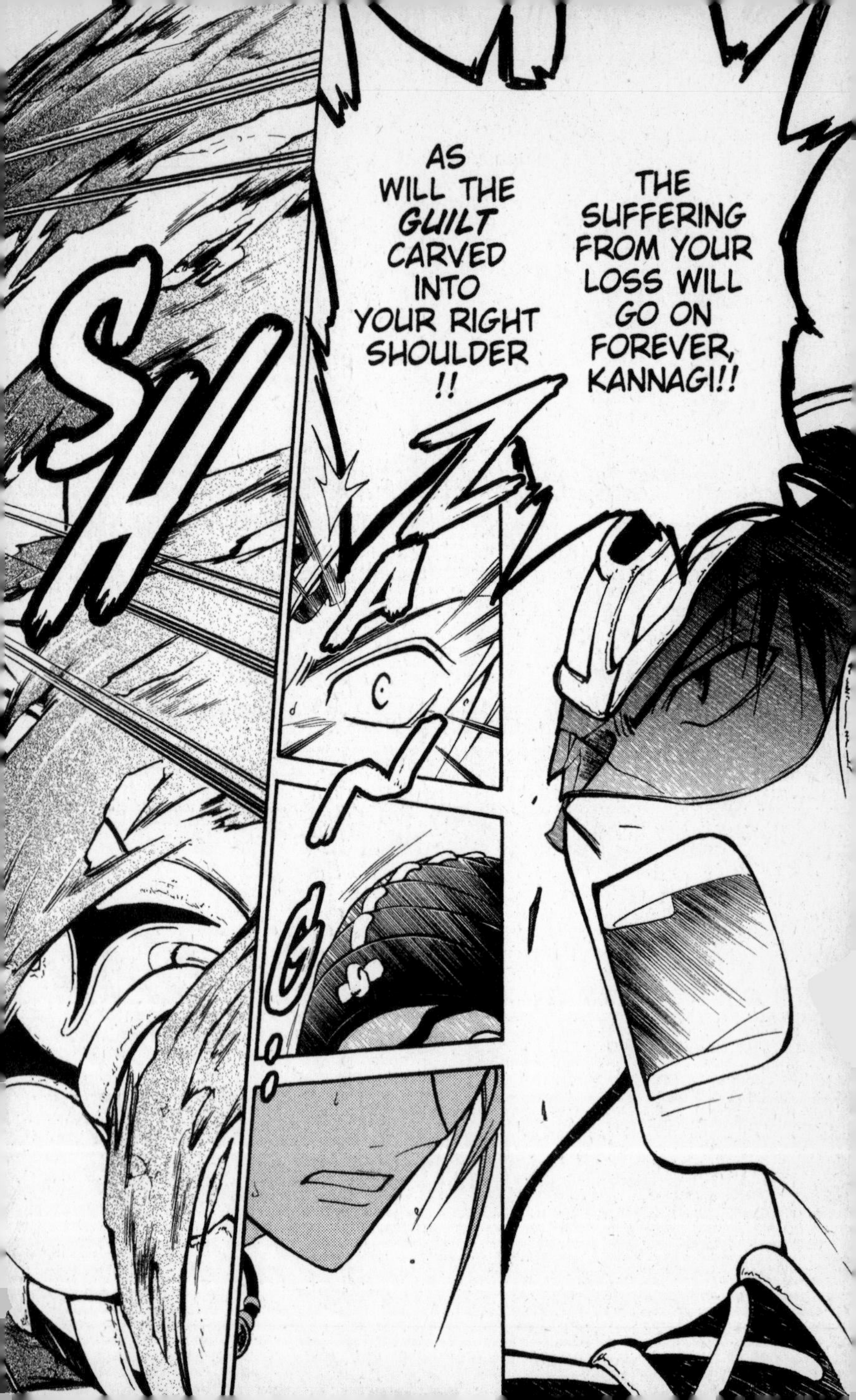
THE SUFFERING FROM YOUR LOSS WILL GO ON FOREVER, KANNAGI!!
AS WILL THE GUILT CARVED INTO YOUR RIGHT SHOULDER !!

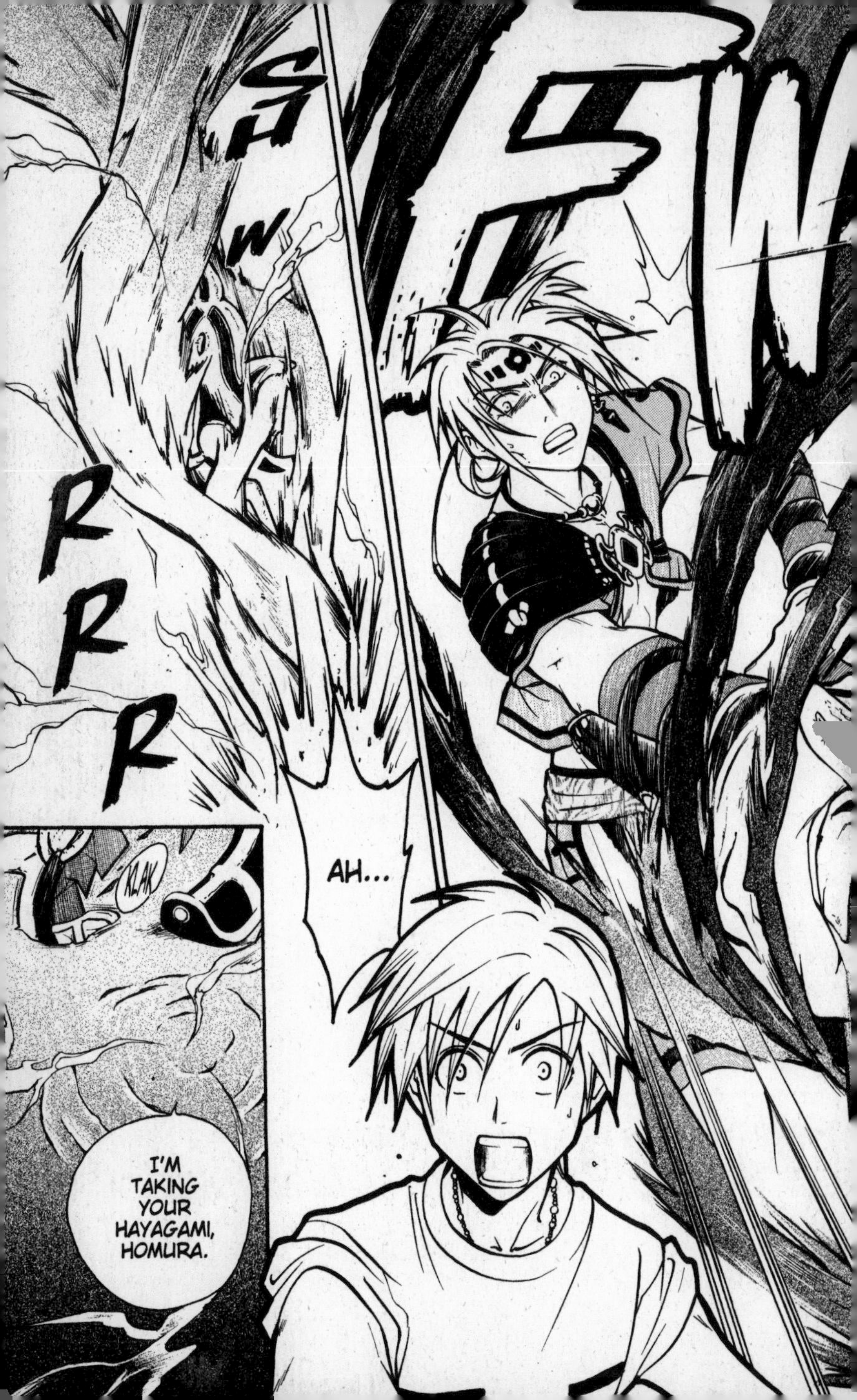
SHAW
RRR
AH...
KLAK
I'M TAKING YOUR HAYAGAMI, HOMURA.

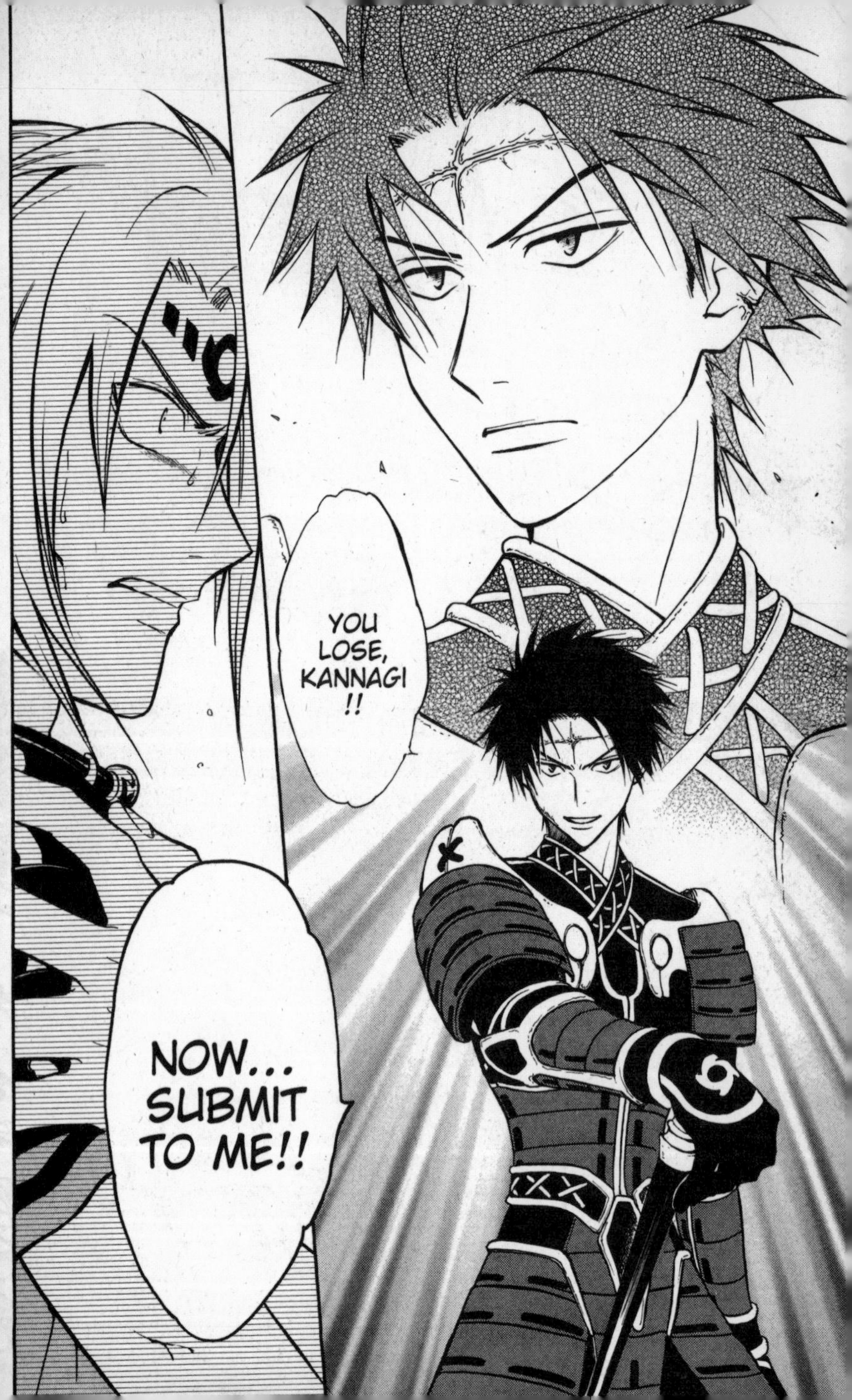
YOU LOSE, KANNAGI!!
NOW... SUBMIT TO ME!!

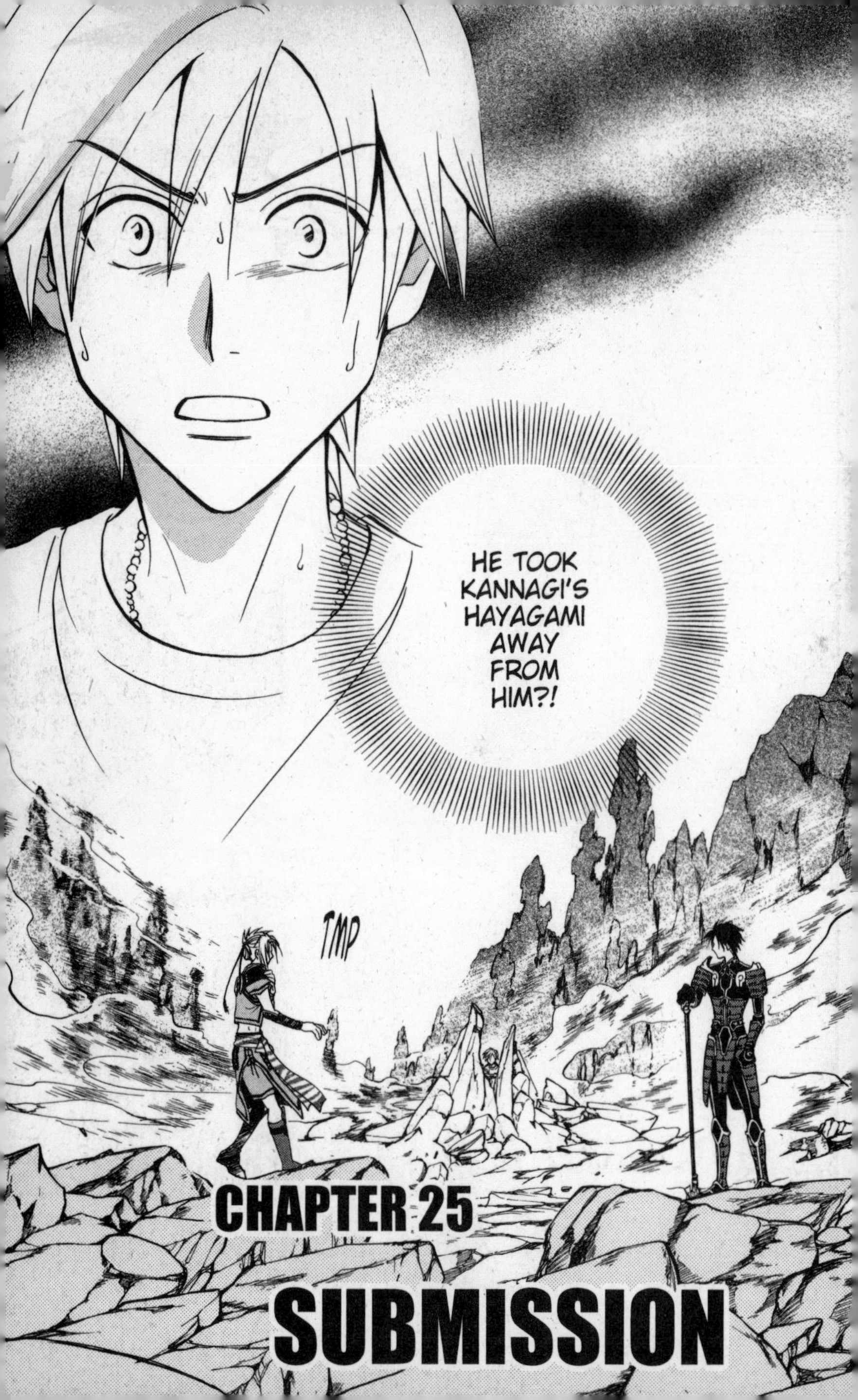
HE TOOK KANNAGI'S HAYAGAMI AWAY FROM HIM?!
TMP
CHAPTER 25
SUBMISSION

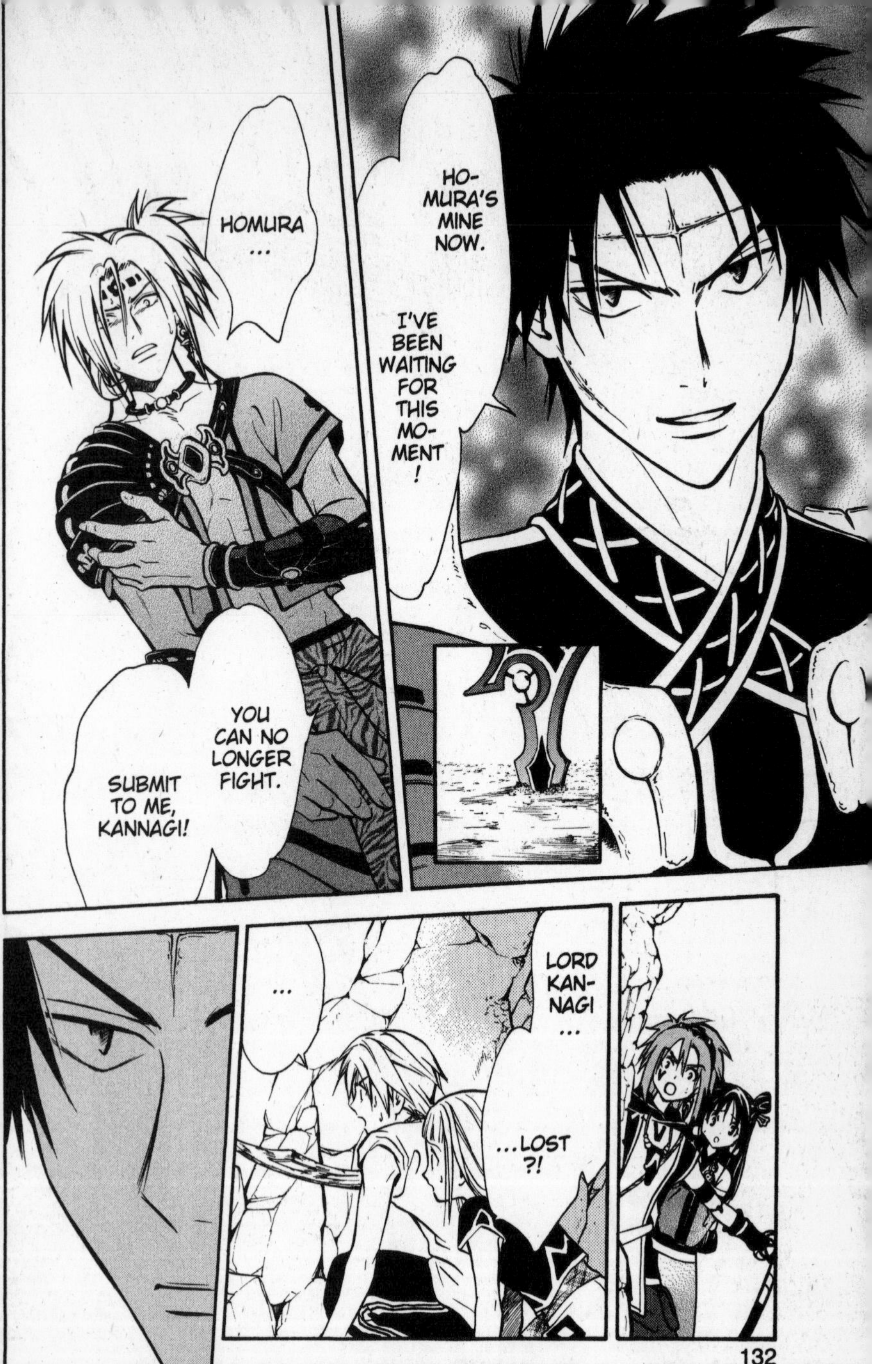
HO-MURA'S MINE NOW.
I'VE BEEN WAITING FOR THIS MO-MENT!
HOMURA ...
YOU CAN NO LONGER FIGHT.
SUBMIT TO ME, KANNAGI!
LORD KAN-NAGI ...
...LOST ?!
...

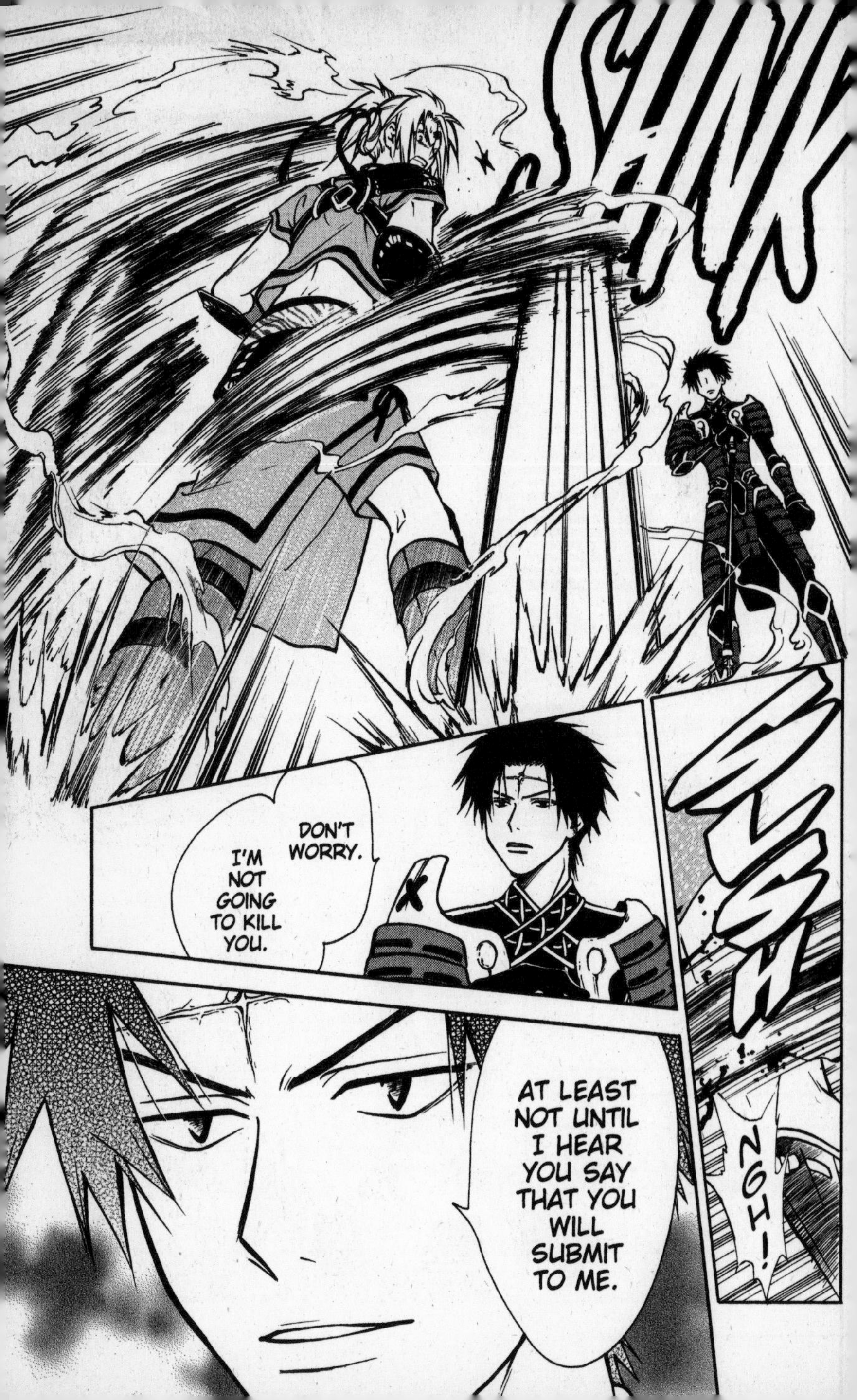
SHINK
WHOOSH
DON'T WORRY.
I'M NOT GOING TO KILL YOU.
NGH!
AT LEAST NOT UNTIL I HEAR YOU SAY THAT YOU WILL SUBMIT TO ME.

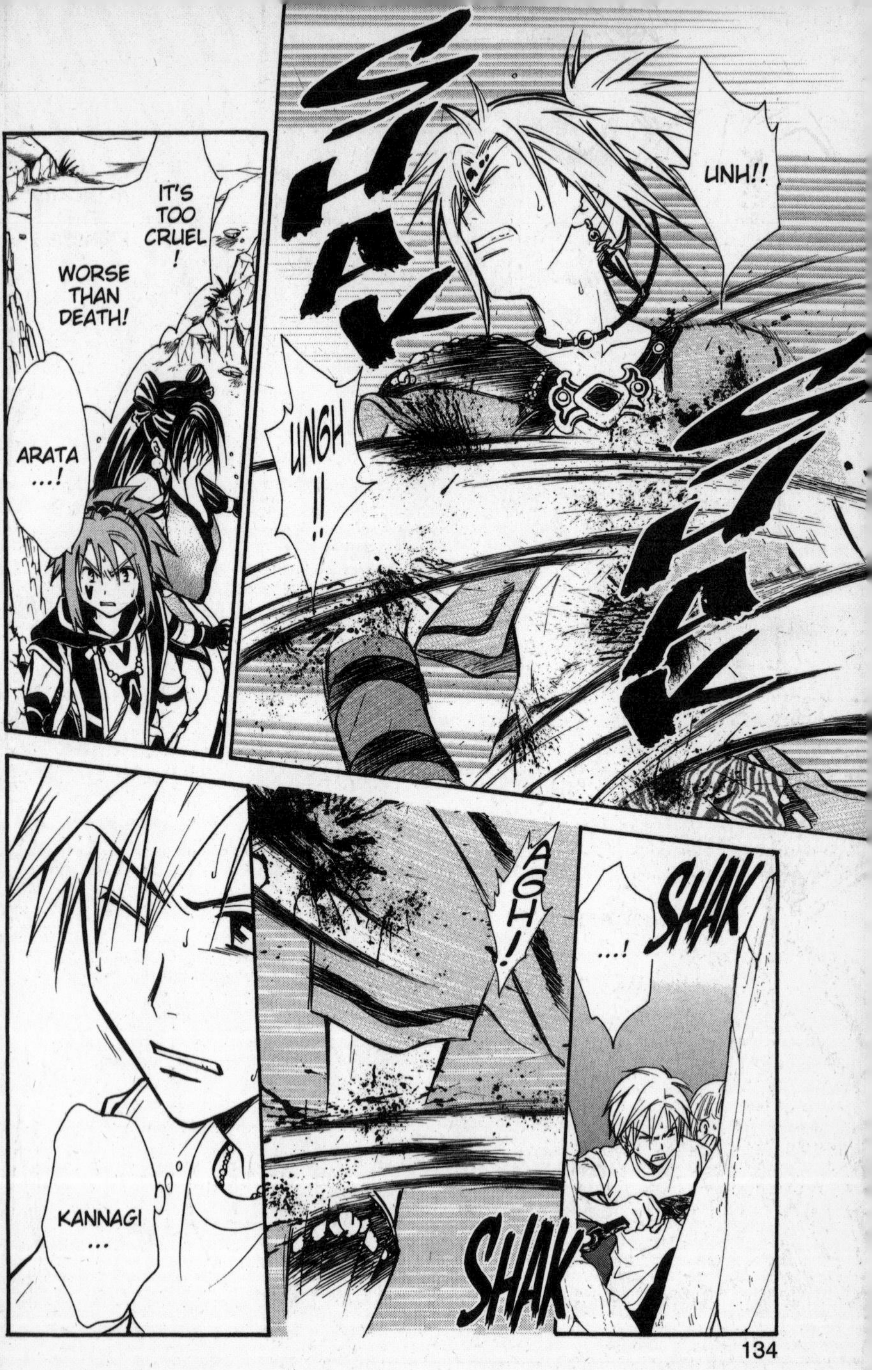
SHAK
UNH!!
UNGH!!
SHAK
IT'S TOO CRUEL!
WORSE THAN DEATH!
ARATA...!
SHAK
...!
SHAK
AGH!
KANNAGI...

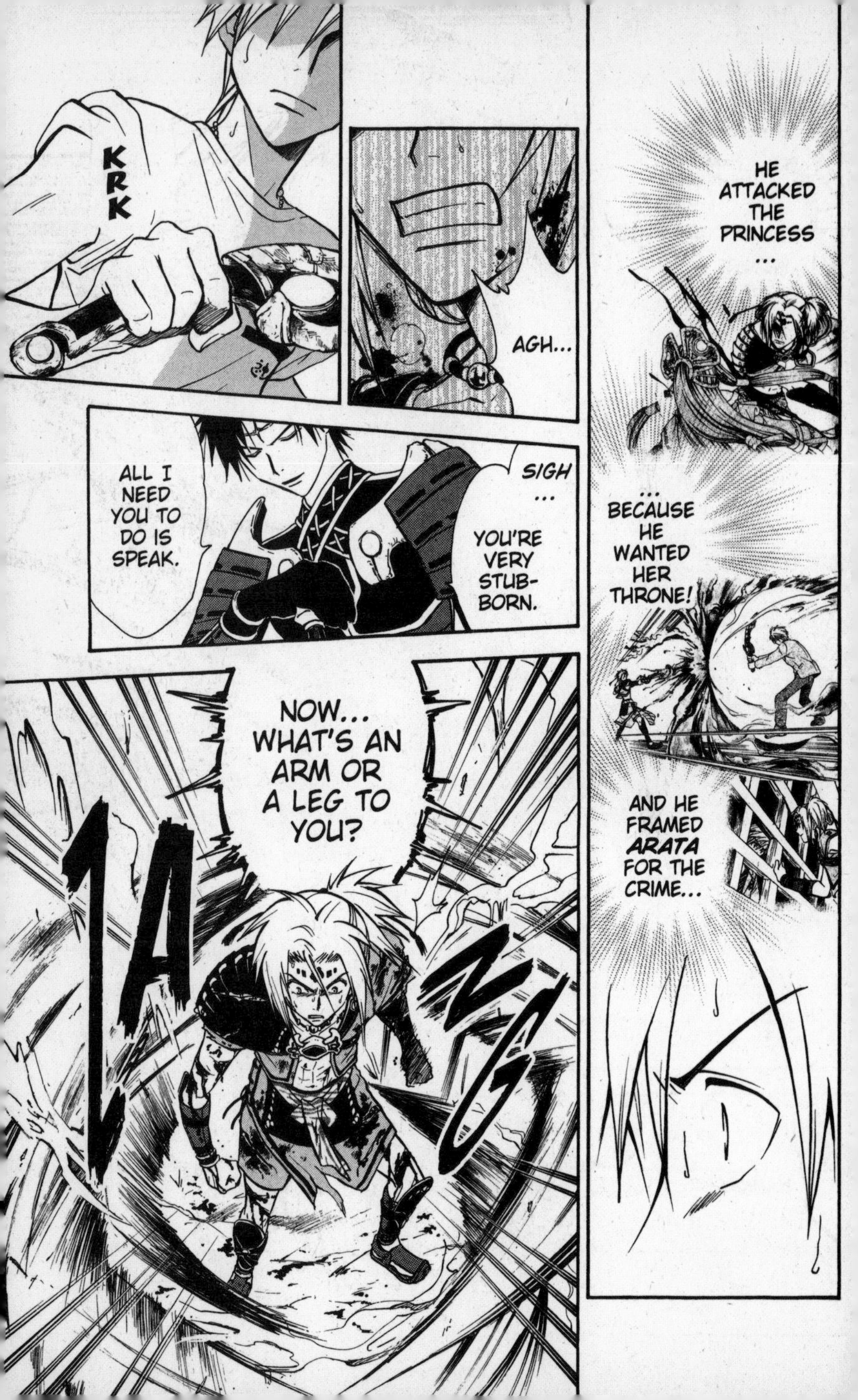
HE ATTACKED THE PRINCESS...
...BECAUSE HE WANTED HER THRONE!
AND HE FRAMED ARATA FOR THE CRIME...
AGH...
KRK
SIGH...
YOU'RE VERY STUB-BORN.
ALL I NEED YOU TO DO IS SPEAK.
NOW... WHAT'S AN ARM OR A LEG TO YOU?

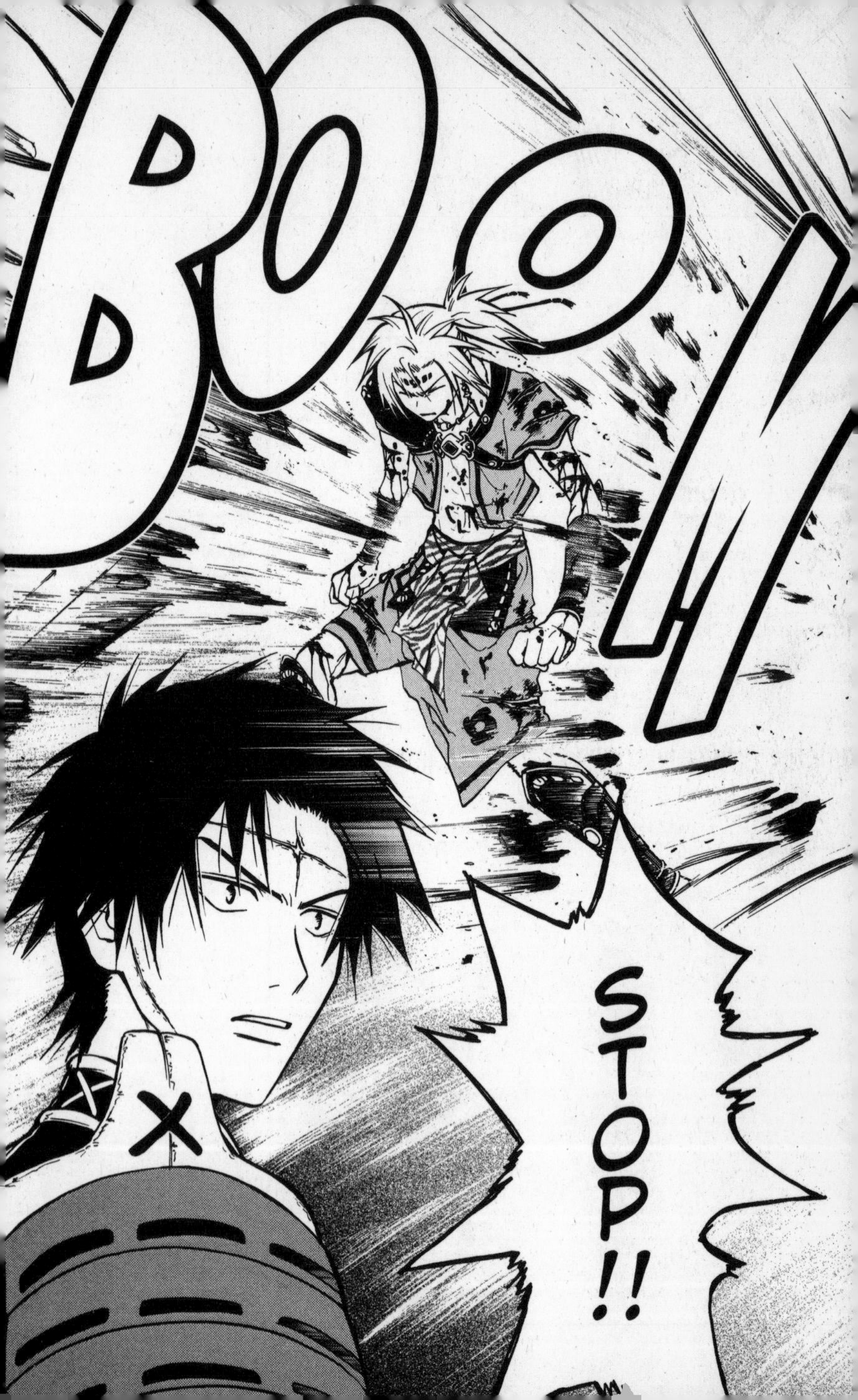
BOOM
STOP!!

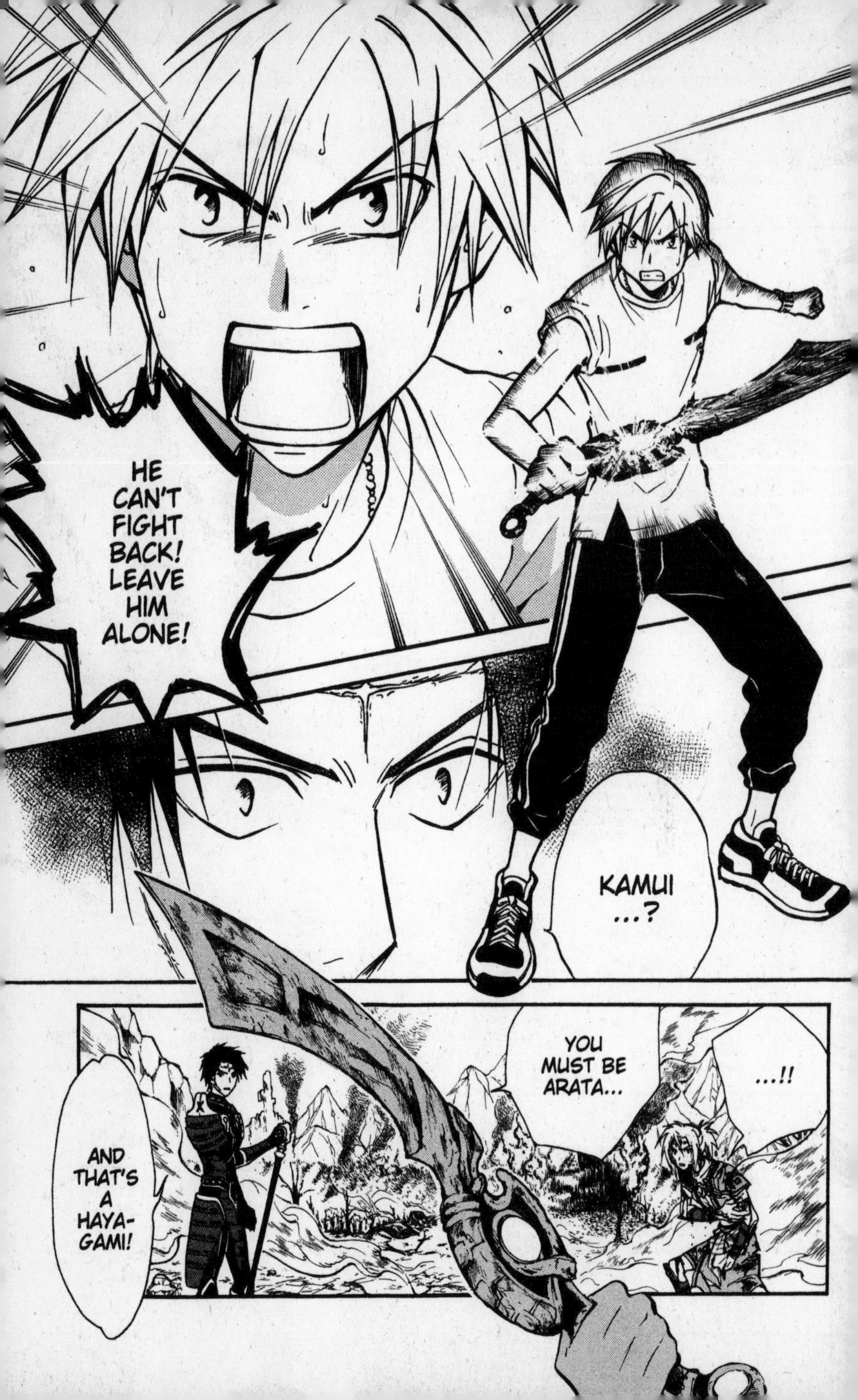
HE CAN'T FIGHT BACK! LEAVE HIM ALONE!
KAMUI ...?
...!!
YOU MUST BE ARATA...
AND THAT'S A HAYA-GAMI!

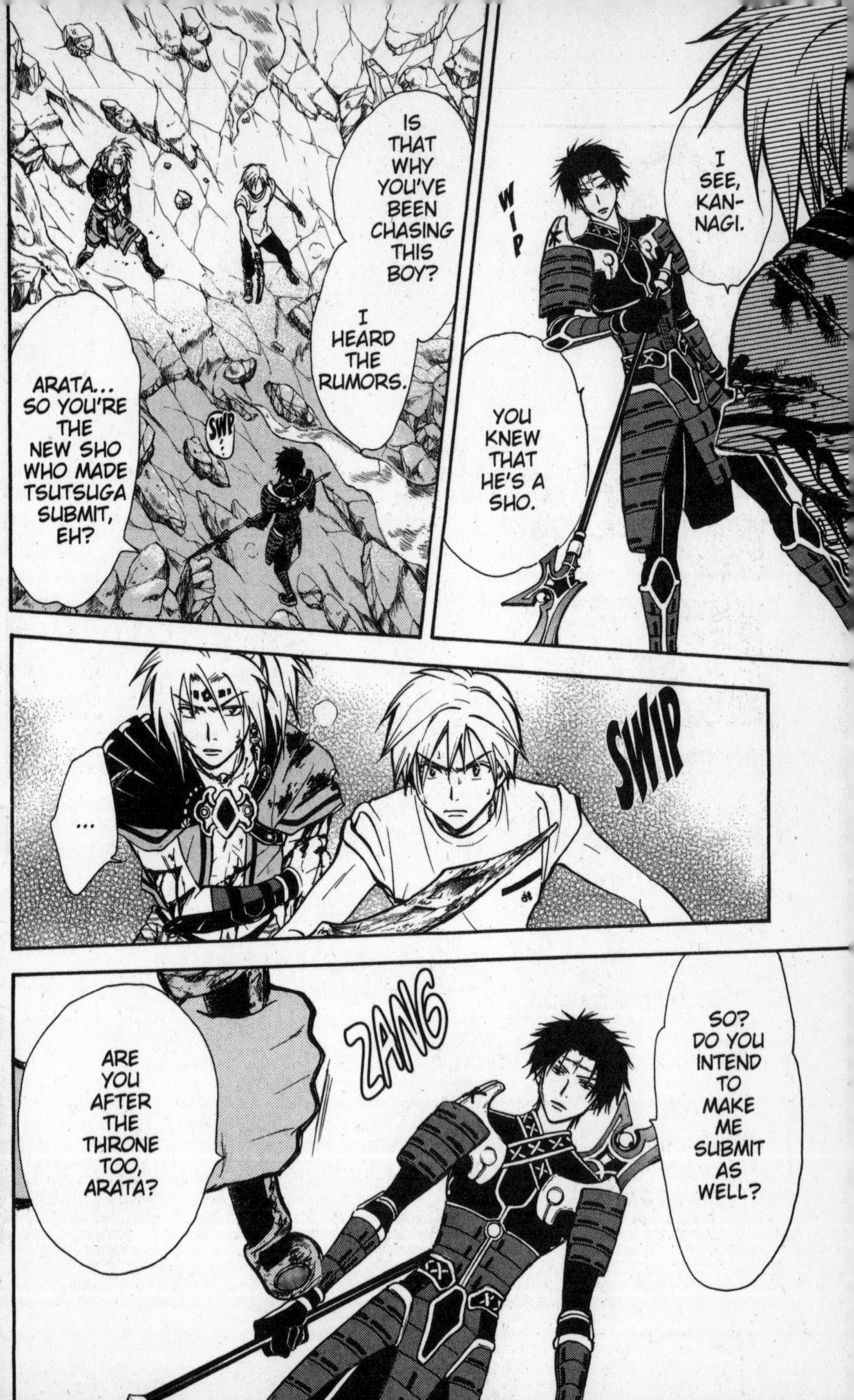
I SEE, KAN-NAGI.
WIP
YOU KNEW THAT HE'S A SHO.
IS THAT WHY YOU'VE BEEN CHASING THIS BOY?
I HEARD THE RUMORS.
ARATA... SO YOU'RE THE NEW SHO WHO MADE TSUTSUGA SUBMIT, EH?
SWP
SWIP
...
SO? DO YOU INTEND TO MAKE ME SUBMIT AS WELL?
ZANG
ARE YOU AFTER THE THRONE TOO, ARATA?

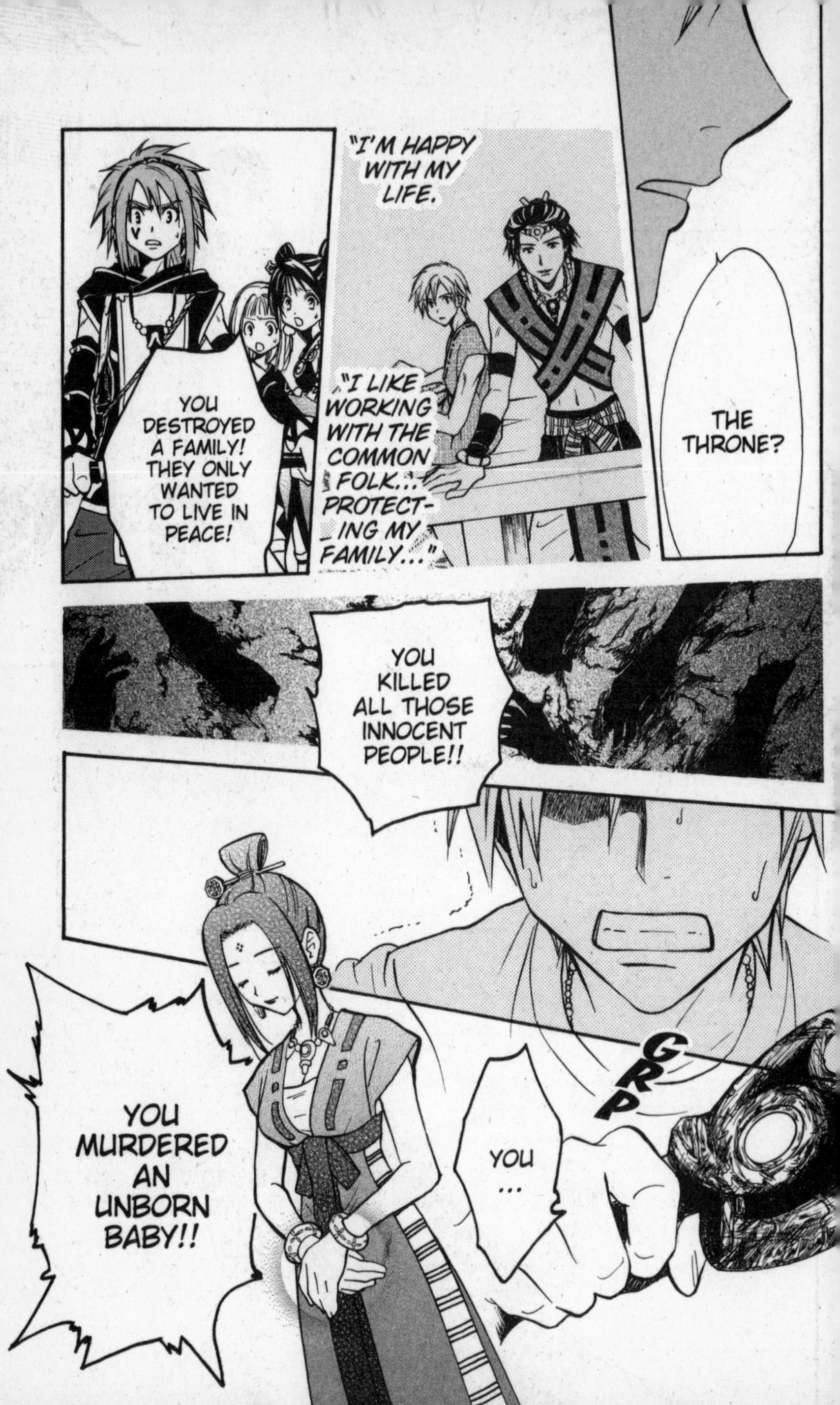
THE THRONE?
"I'M HAPPY WITH MY LIFE.
"I LIKE WORKING WITH THE COMMON FOLK... PROTECT-ING MY FAMILY..."
YOU DESTROYED A FAMILY! THEY ONLY WANTED TO LIVE IN PEACE!
YOU KILLED ALL THOSE INNOCENT PEOPLE!!
GRP
YOU ...
YOU MURDERED AN UNBORN BABY!!

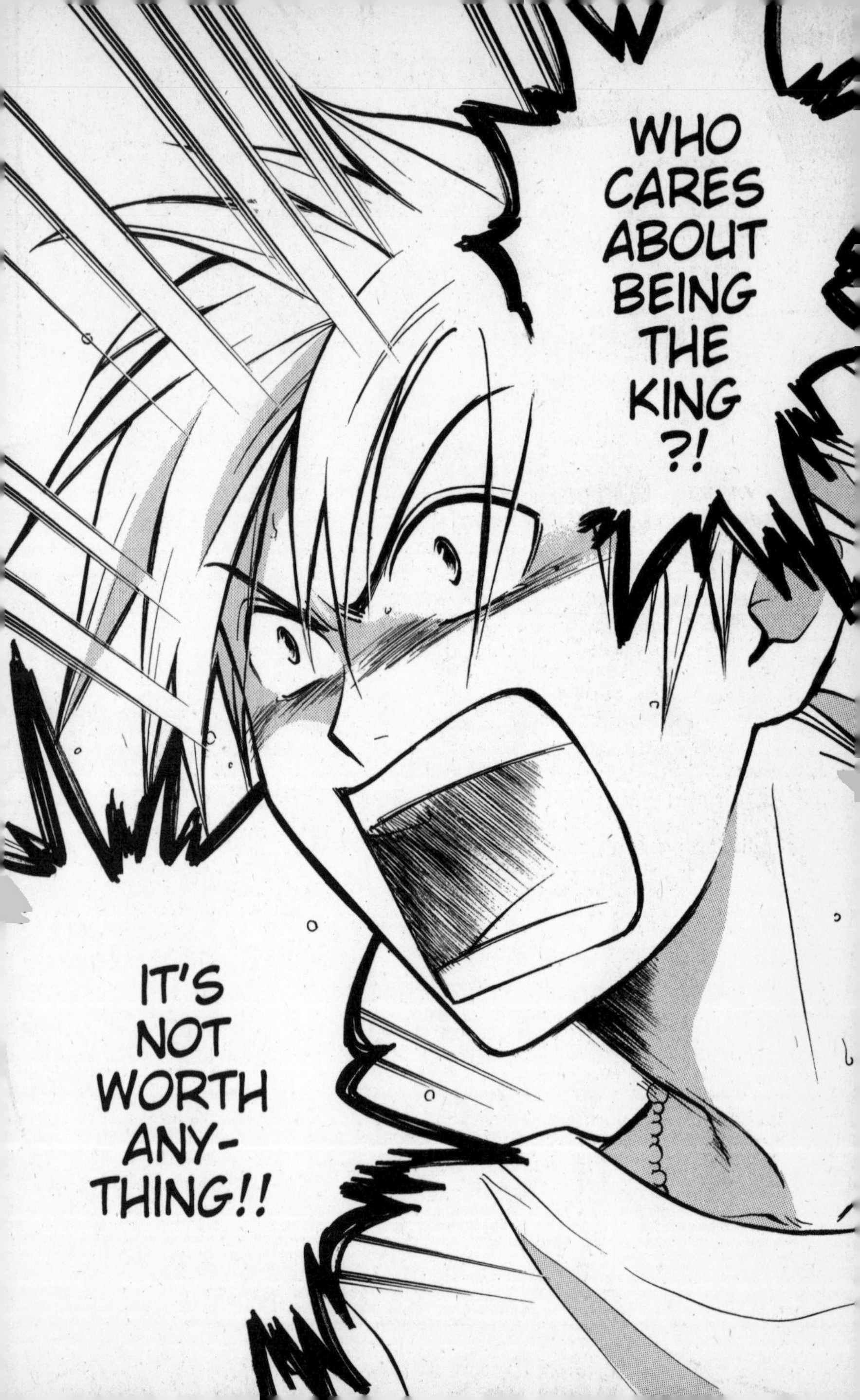
WHO CARES ABOUT BEING THE KING ?!
IT'S NOT WORTH ANY-THING!!

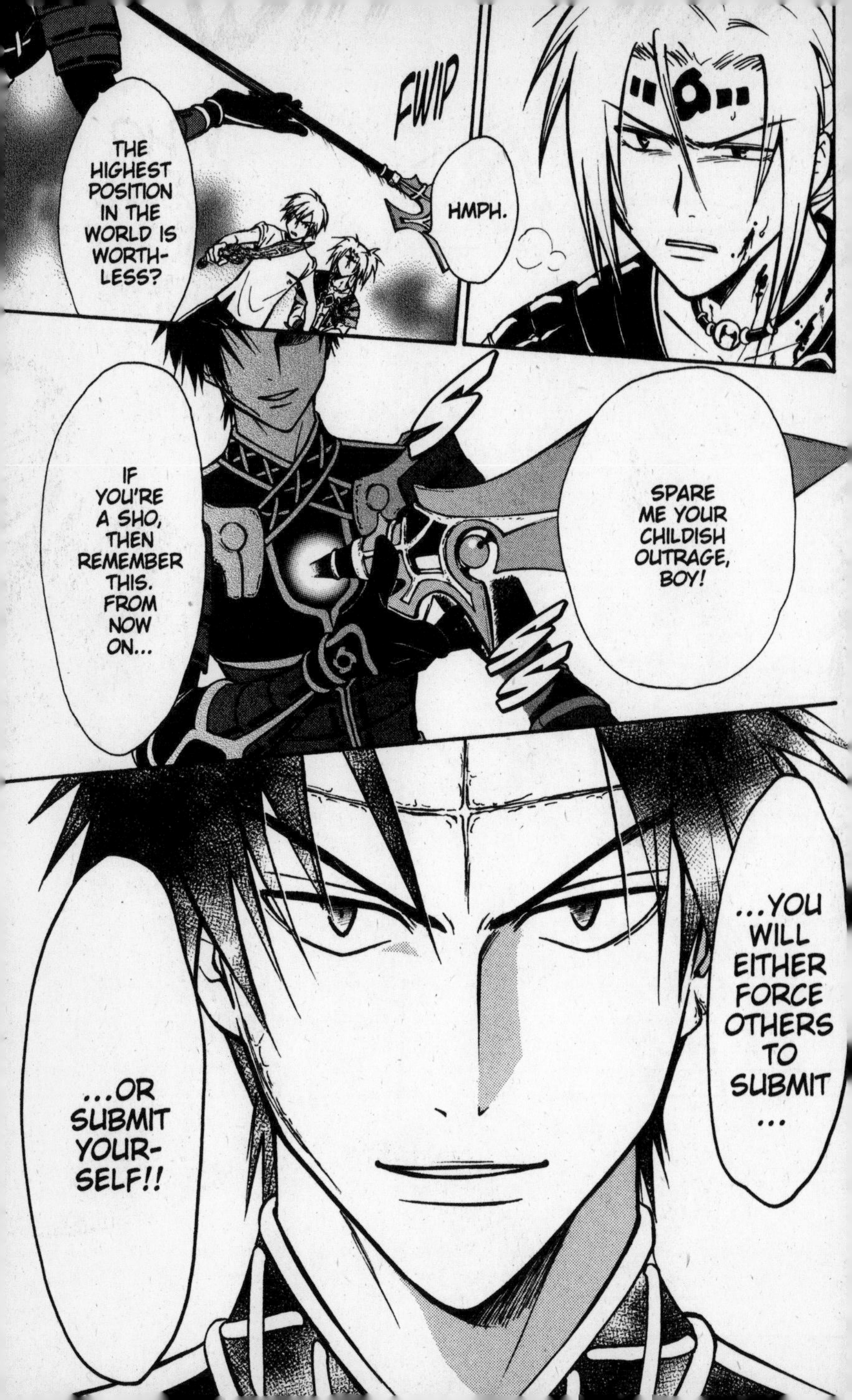
HMPH.
FWIP
THE HIGHEST POSITION IN THE WORLD IS WORTH-LESS?
SPARE ME YOUR CHILDISH OUTRAGE, BOY!
IF YOU'RE A SHO, THEN REMEMBER THIS. FROM NOW ON...
...YOU WILL EITHER FORCE OTHERS TO SUBMIT ...
...OR SUBMIT YOUR-SELF!!

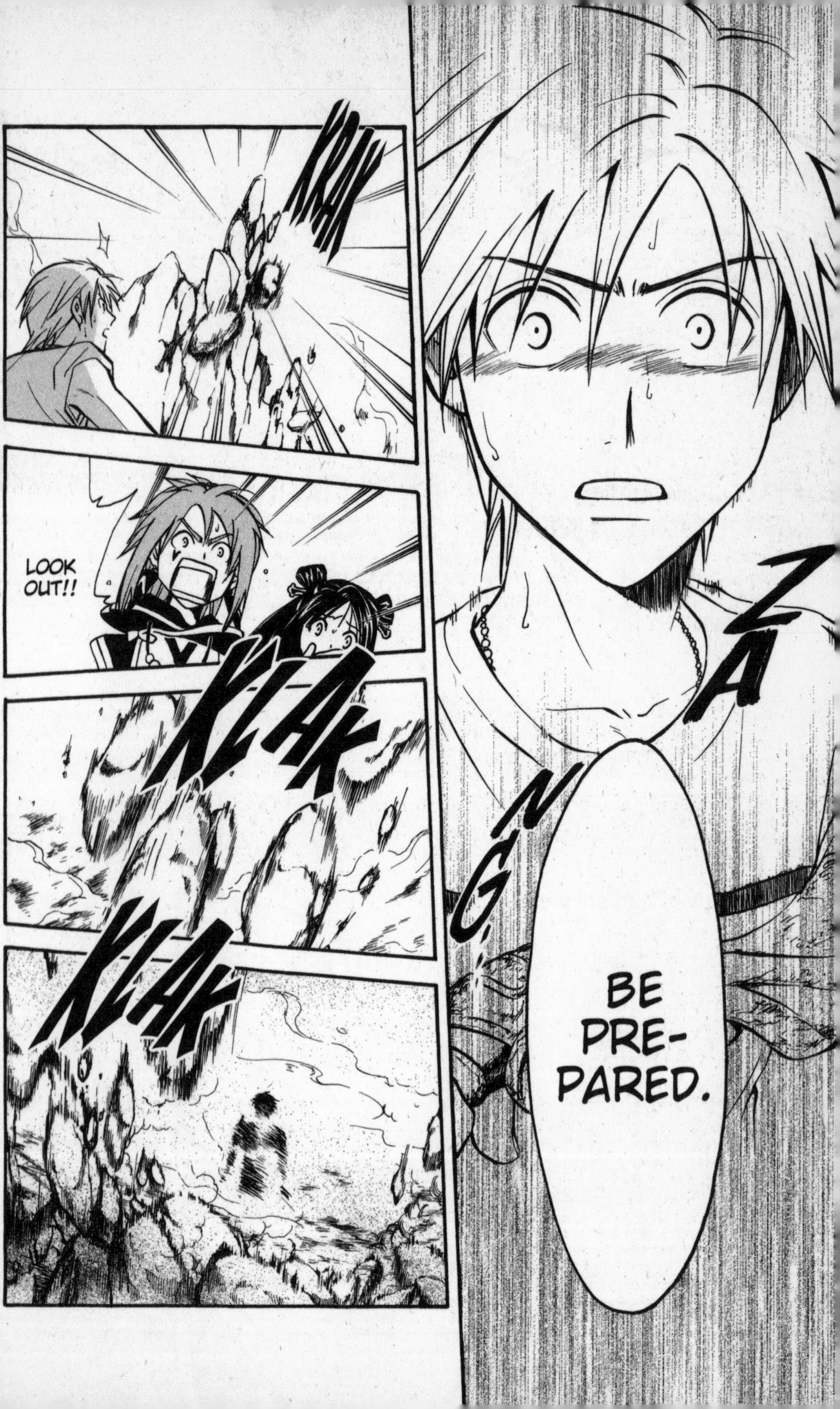
ZANG.
BE PRE- PARED.
KRAK
LOOK OUT!!
KLAK
KLAK

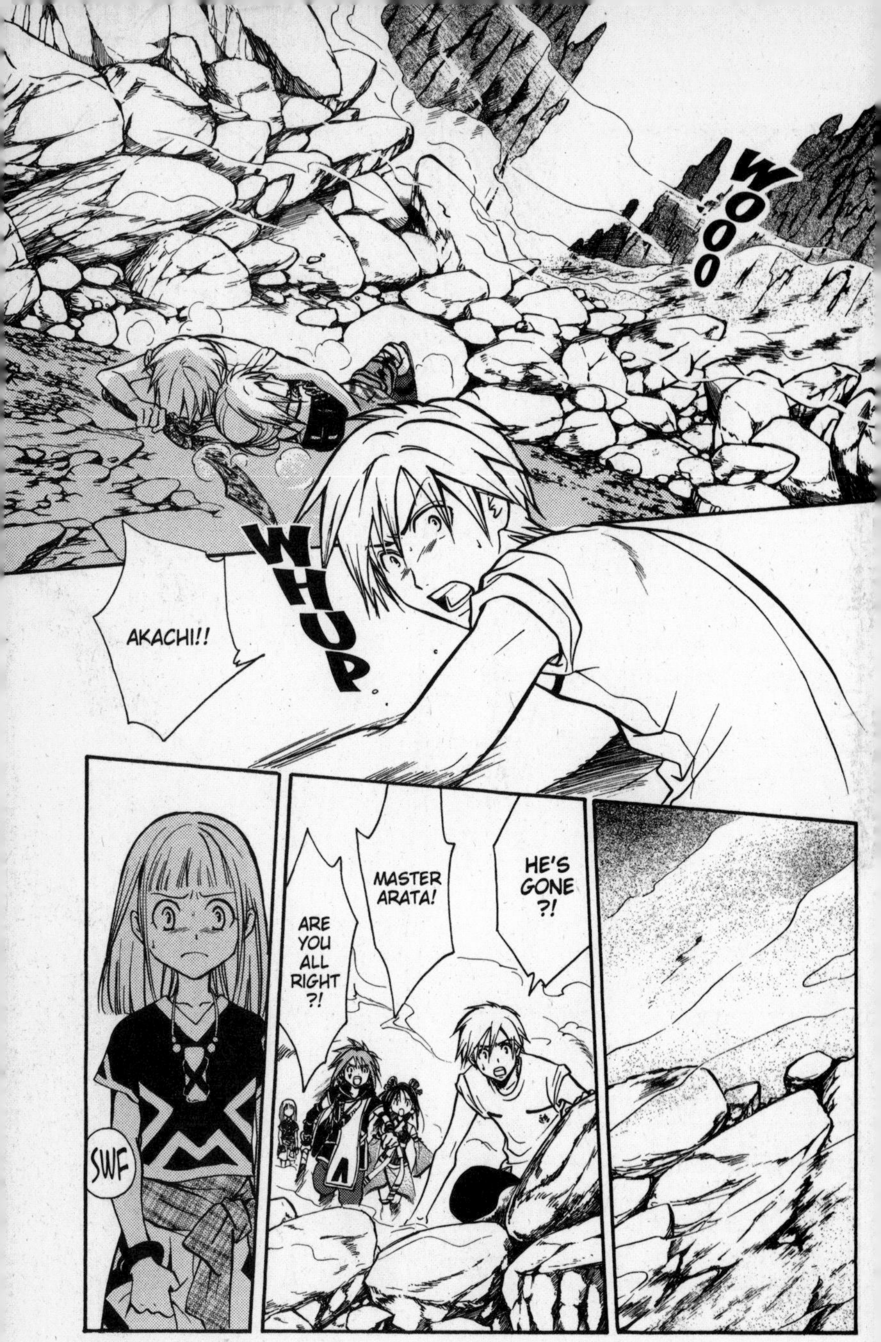
WOOOO
WHUP
AKACHI!!
HE'S GONE?!
MASTER ARATA!
ARE YOU ALL RIGHT?!
SWF

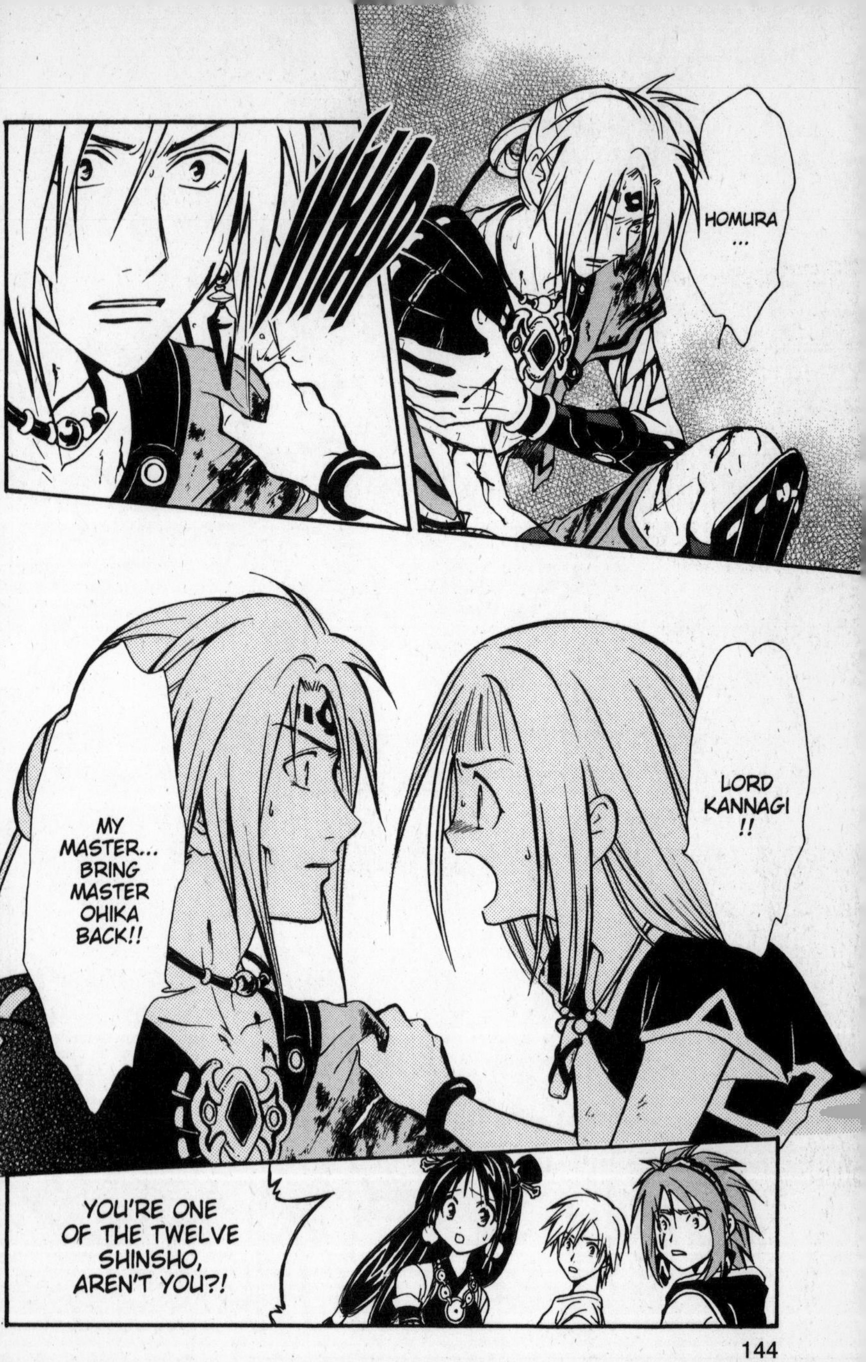
HOMURA ...
LORD KANNAGI !!
MY MASTER... BRING MASTER OHIKA BACK!!
YOU'RE ONE OF THE TWELVE SHINSHO, AREN'T YOU?!

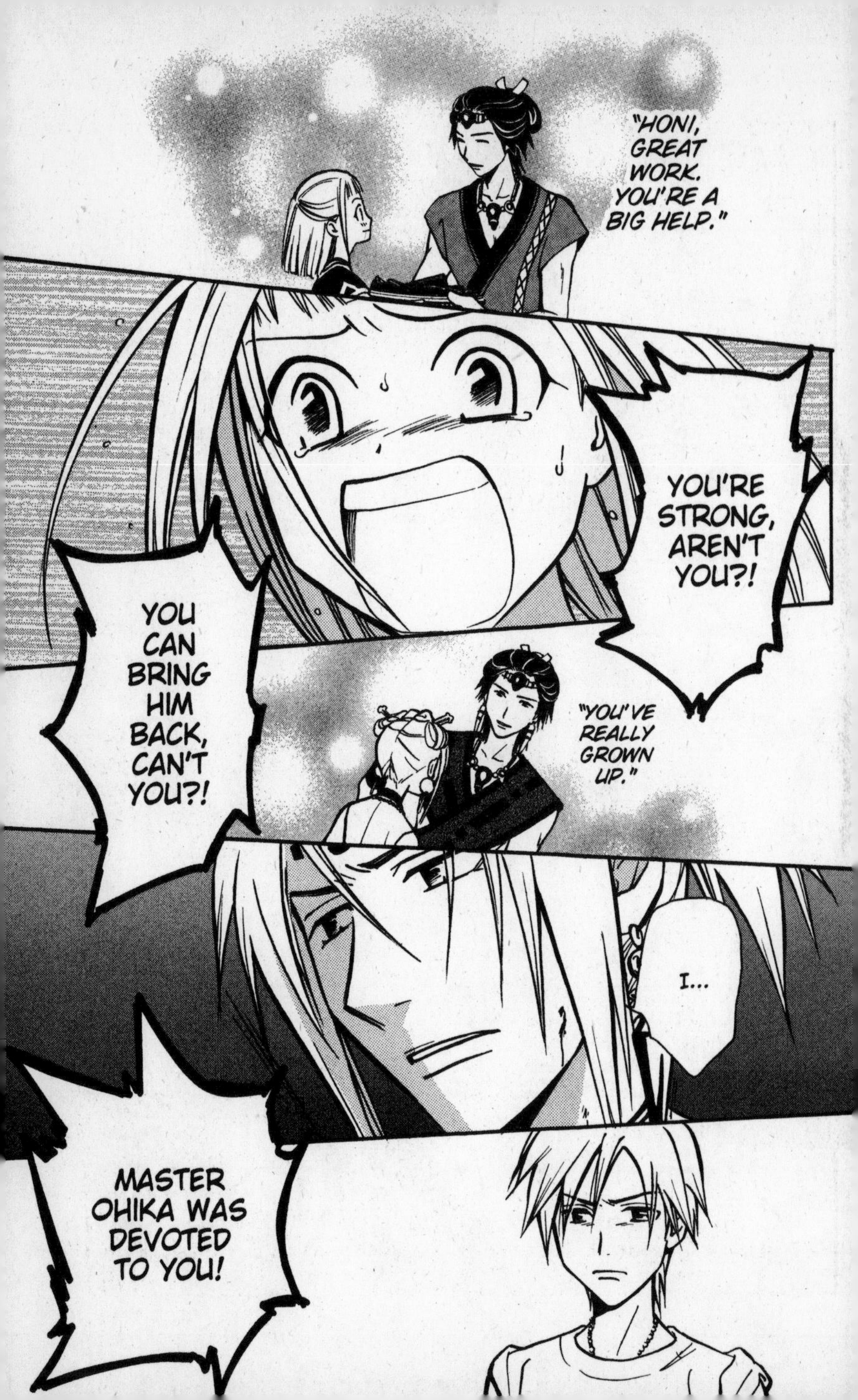
"HONI, GREAT WORK. YOU'RE A BIG HELP."
YOU'RE STRONG, AREN'T YOU?!
YOU CAN BRING HIM BACK, CAN'T YOU?!
"YOU'VE REALLY GROWN UP."
I...
MASTER OHIKA WAS DEVOTED TO YOU!

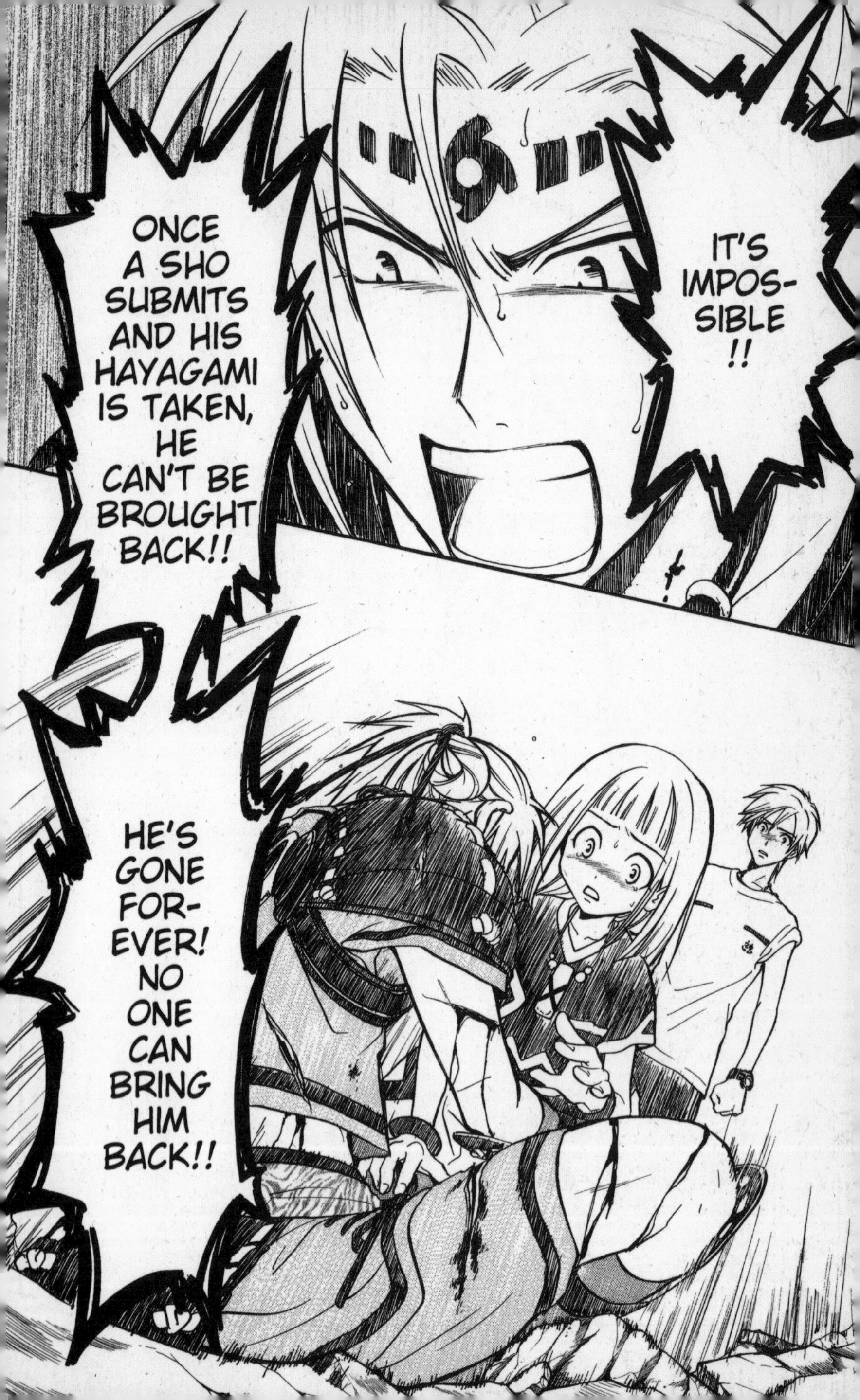
IT'S IMPOSSIBLE!!
ONCE A SHO SUBMITS AND HIS HAYAGAMI IS TAKEN, HE CAN'T BE BROUGHT BACK!!
HE'S GONE FOREVER! NO ONE CAN BRING HIM BACK!!

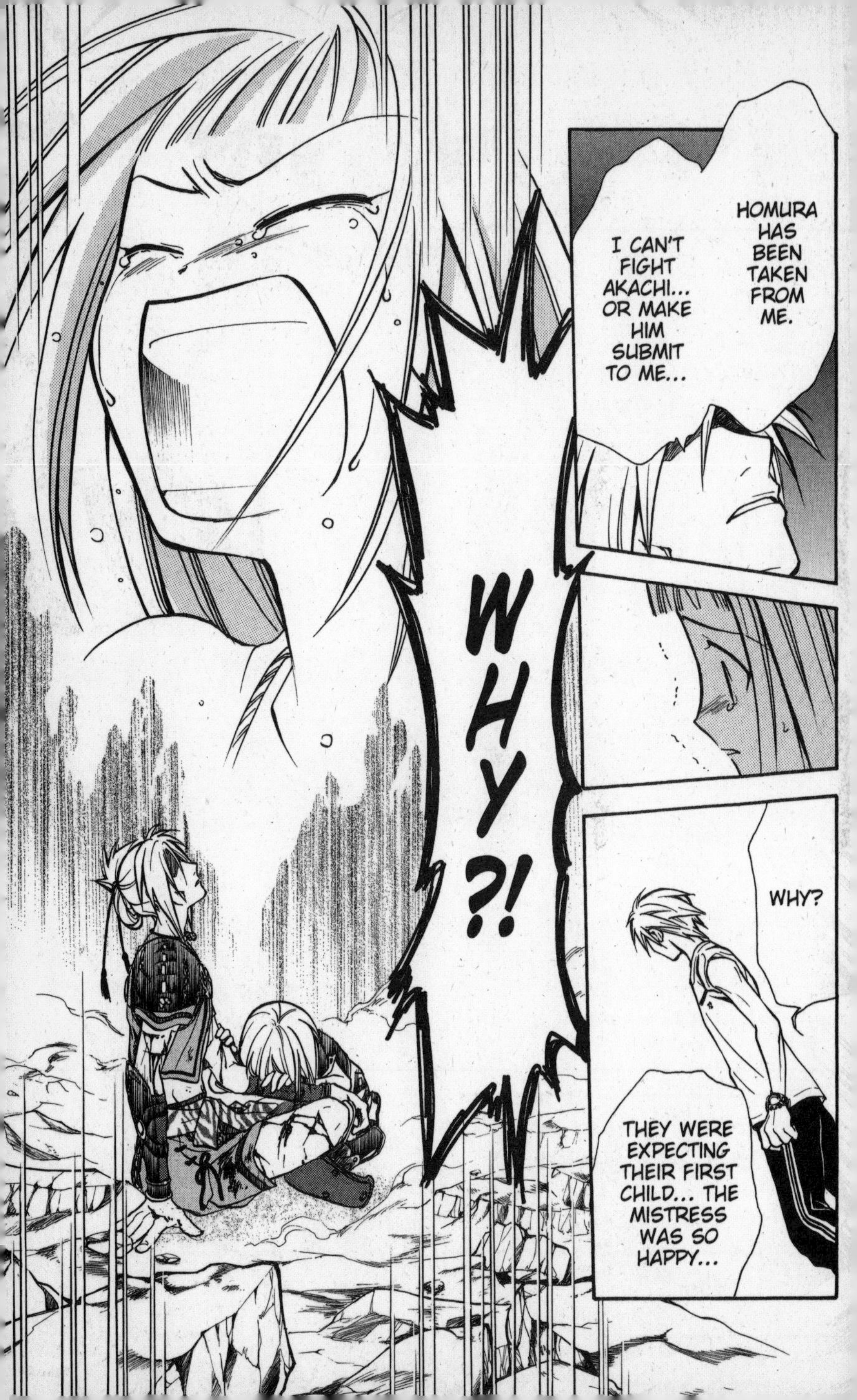
HOMURA HAS BEEN TAKEN FROM ME.
I CAN'T FIGHT AKACHI... OR MAKE HIM SUBMIT TO ME...
WHY?
THEY WERE EXPECTING THEIR FIRST CHILD... THE MISTRESS WAS SO HAPPY...
WHY?!

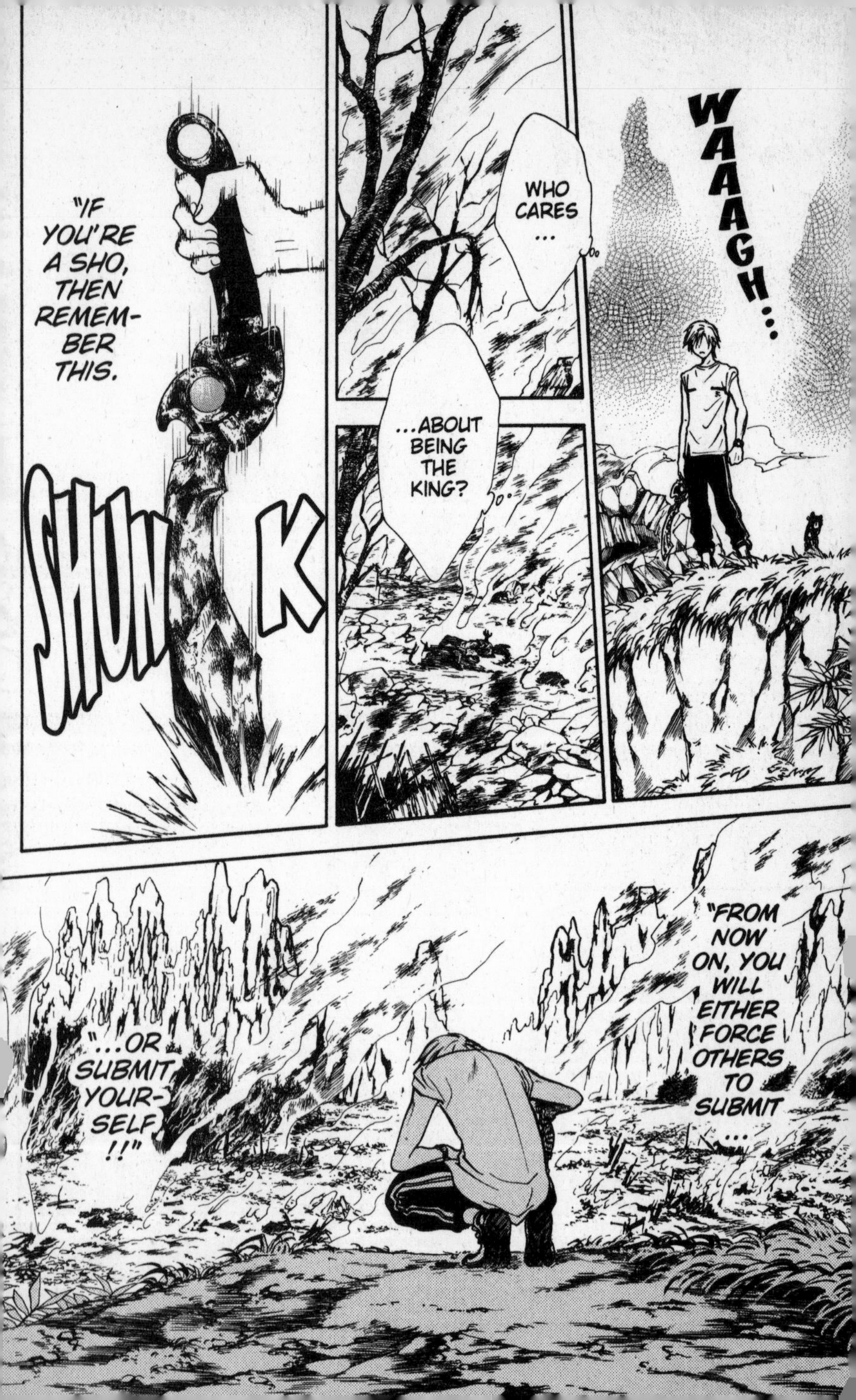
WAAAGH...
WHO CARES ...
...ABOUT BEING THE KING?
"IF YOU'RE A SHO, THEN REMEMBER THIS.
SHUNK
"FROM NOW ON, YOU WILL EITHER FORCE OTHERS TO SUBMIT ...
"...OR SUBMIT YOURSELF!!"

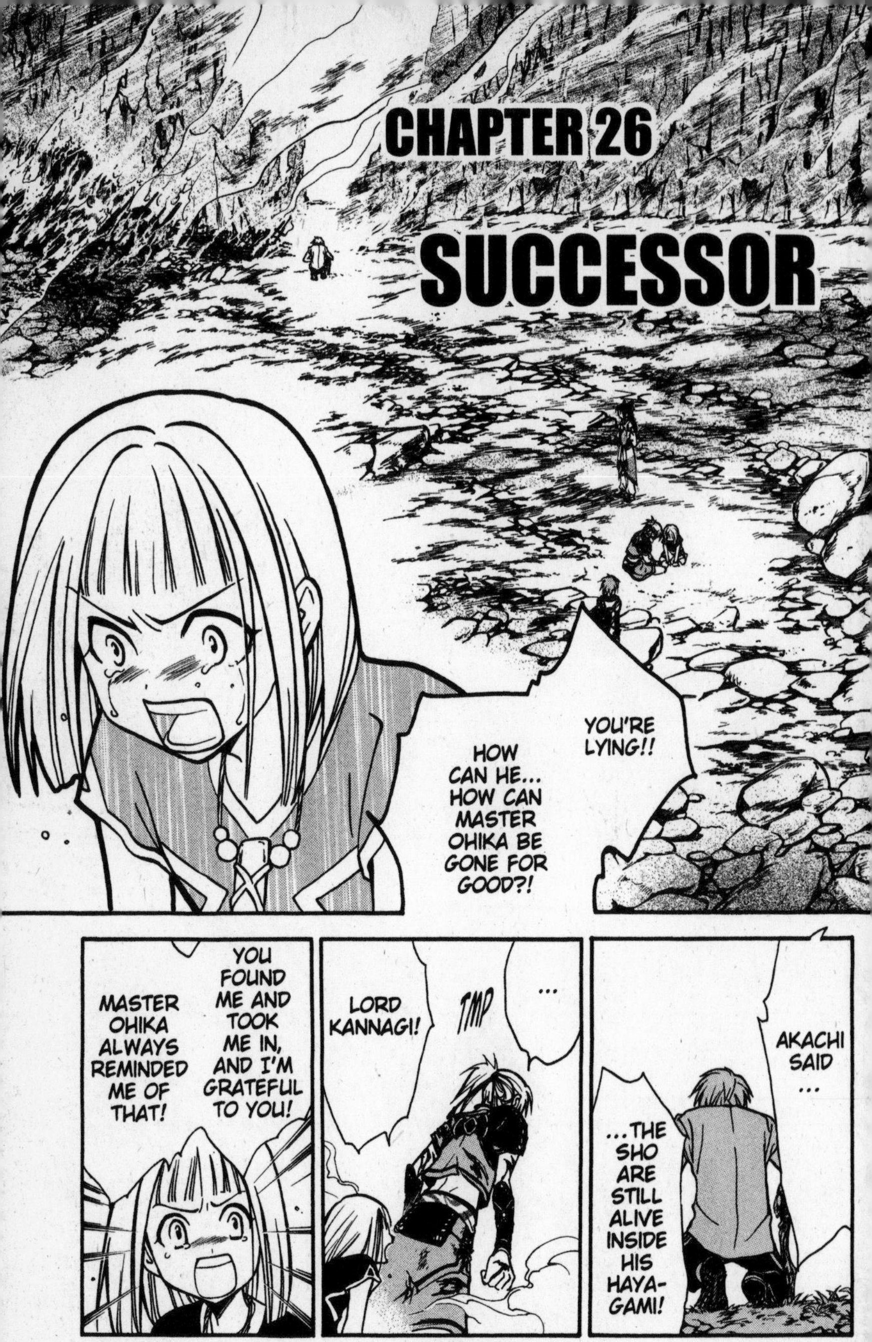
CHAPTER 26
SUCCESSOR
YOU'RE LYING!!
HOW CAN HE... HOW CAN MASTER OHIKA BE GONE FOR GOOD?!
AKACHI SAID ...
...THE SHO ARE STILL ALIVE INSIDE HIS HAYA-GAMI!
...
TMP
LORD KANNAGI!
YOU FOUND ME AND TOOK ME IN, AND I'M GRATEFUL TO YOU!
MASTER OHIKA ALWAYS REMINDED ME OF THAT!

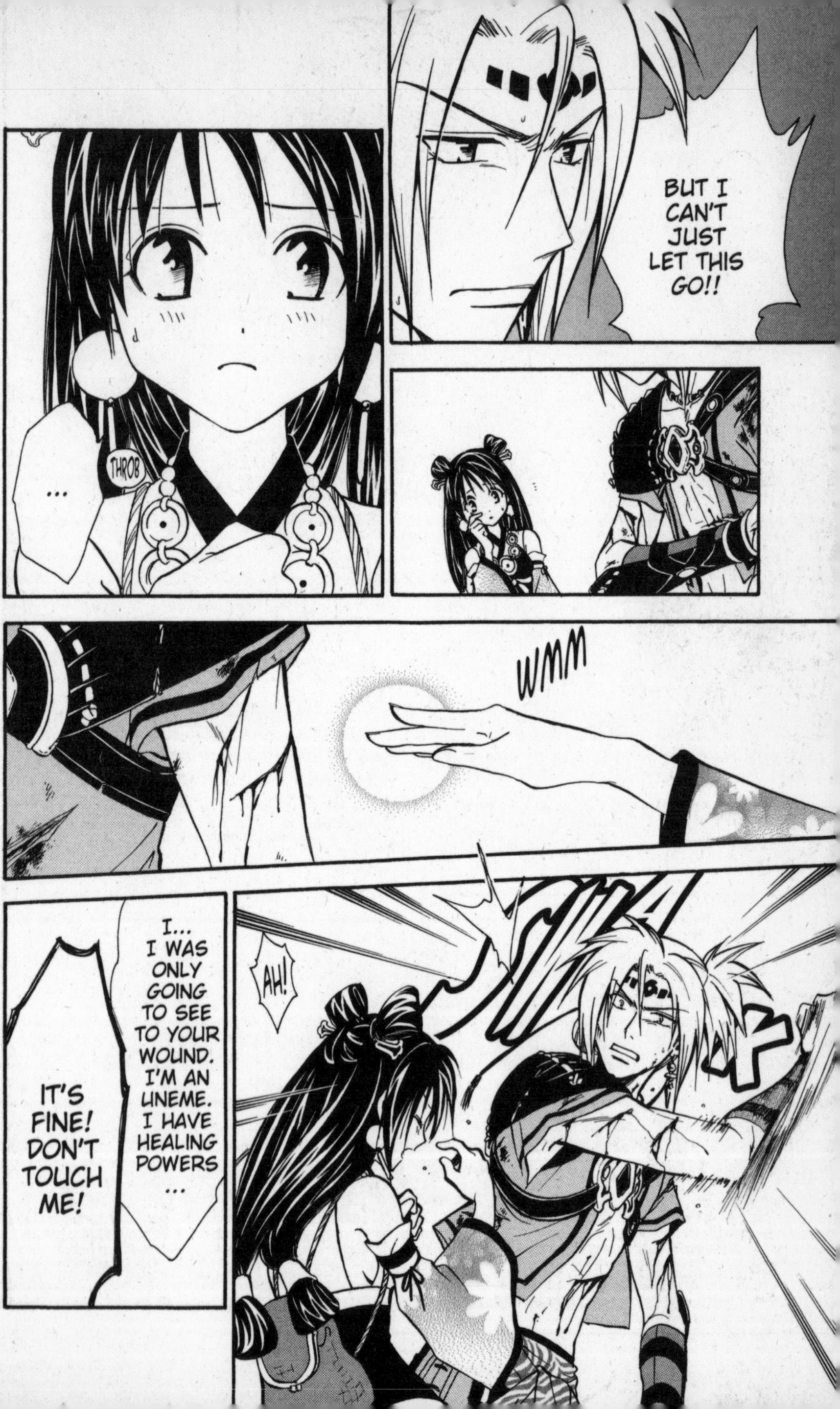
BUT I CAN'T JUST LET THIS GO!!
THROB
...
WMM
AH!
I... I WAS ONLY GOING TO SEE TO YOUR WOUND. I'M AN UNEME. I HAVE HEALING POWERS ...
IT'S FINE! DON'T TOUCH ME!

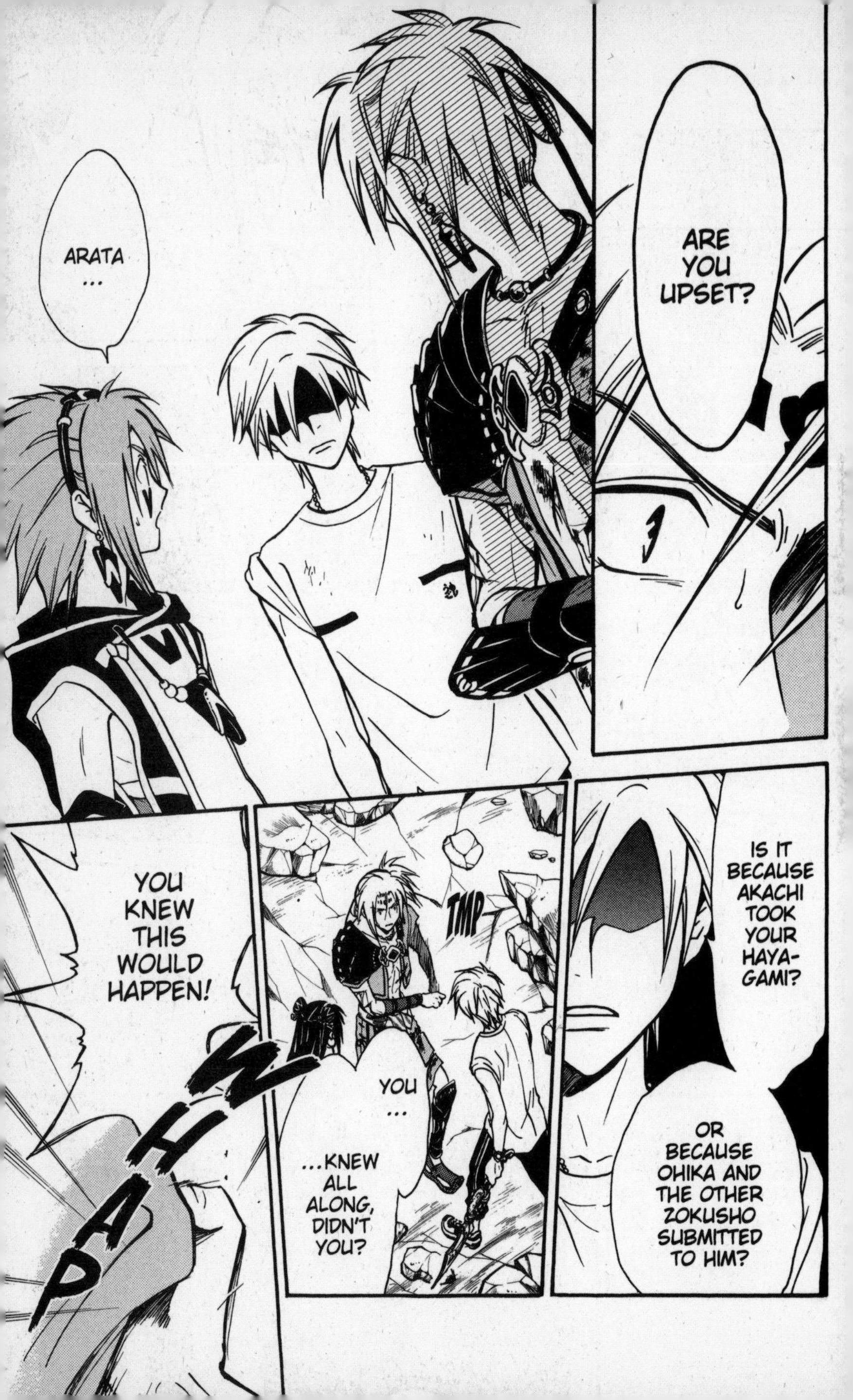
ARE YOU UPSET?
ARATA ...
IS IT BECAUSE AKACHI TOOK YOUR HAYA-GAMI?
OR BECAUSE OHIKA AND THE OTHER ZOKUSHO SUBMITTED TO HIM?
TMP
YOU ...
...KNEW ALL ALONG, DIDN'T YOU?
YOU KNEW THIS WOULD HAPPEN!
WHAP

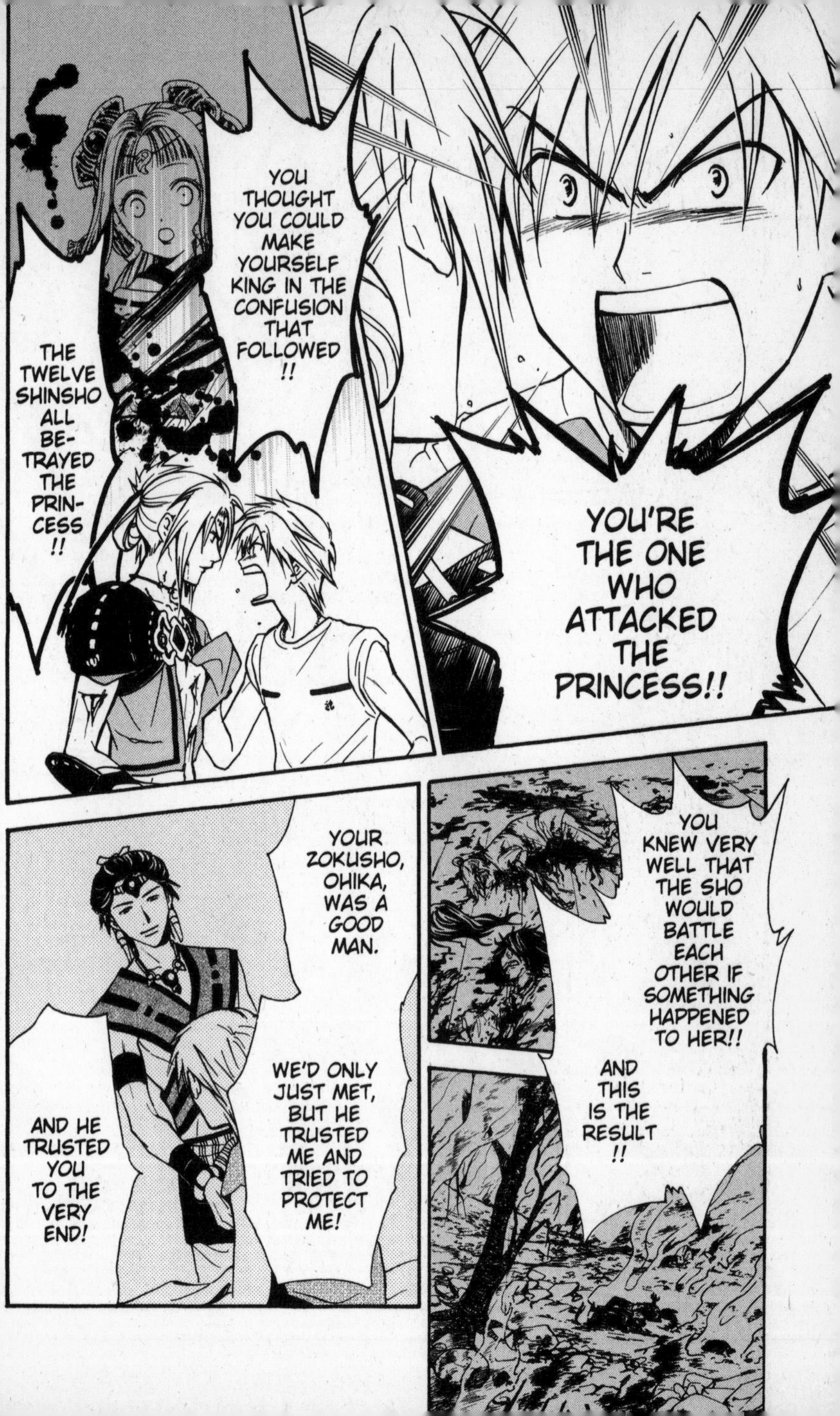
YOU'RE THE ONE WHO ATTACKED THE PRINCESS!!
YOU THOUGHT YOU COULD MAKE YOURSELF KING IN THE CONFUSION THAT FOLLOWED!!
THE TWELVE SHINSHO ALL BE-TRAYED THE PRIN-CESS!!
YOU KNEW VERY WELL THAT THE SHO WOULD BATTLE EACH OTHER IF SOMETHING HAPPENED TO HER!!
AND THIS IS THE RESULT!!
YOUR ZOKUSHO, OHIKA, WAS A GOOD MAN.
WE'D ONLY JUST MET, BUT HE TRUSTED ME AND TRIED TO PROTECT ME!
AND HE TRUSTED YOU TO THE VERY END!

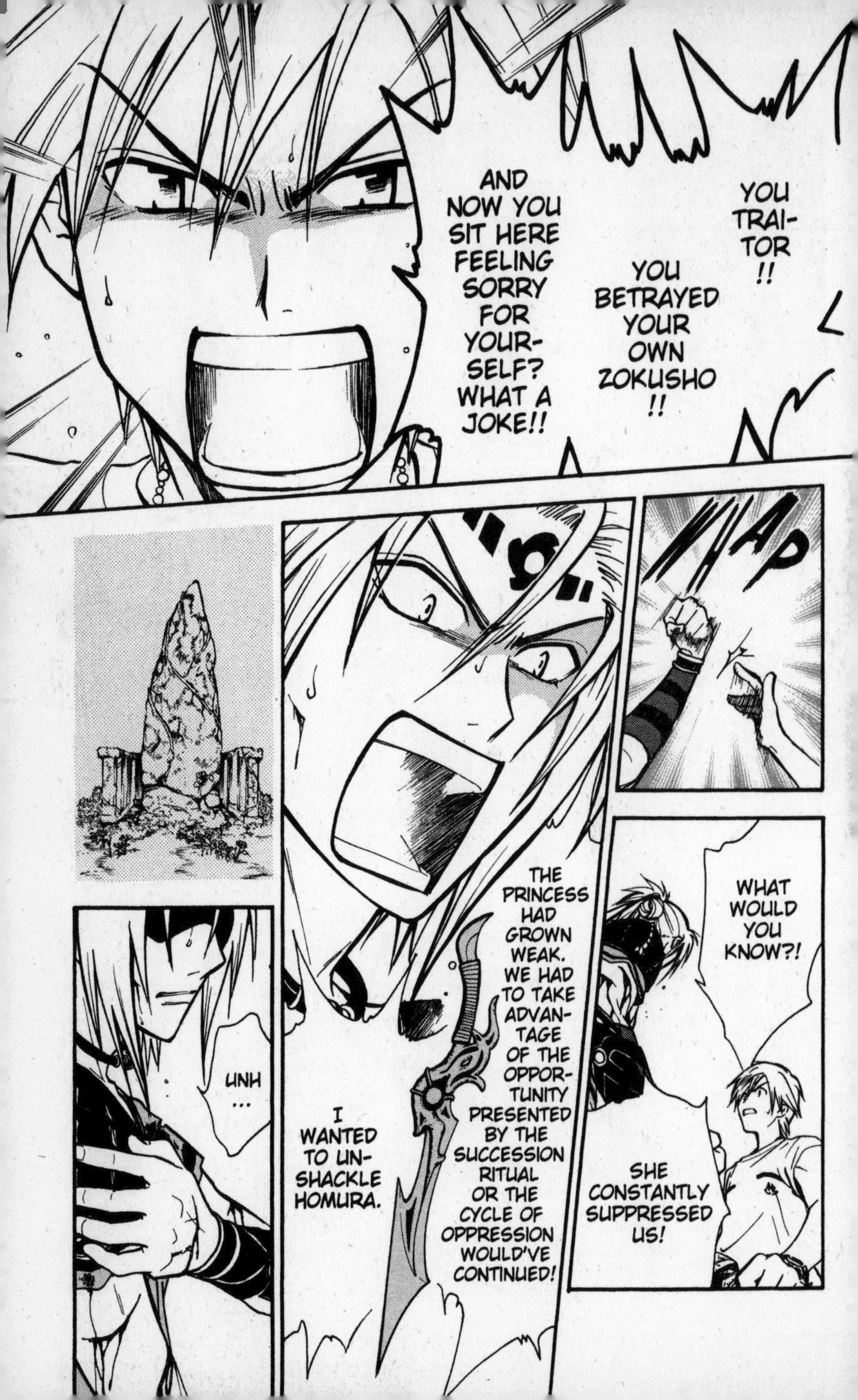
YOU TRAITOR!!
YOU BETRAYED YOUR OWN ZOKUSHO!!
AND NOW YOU SIT HERE FEELING SORRY FOR YOURSELF? WHAT A JOKE!!
WHAP
WHAT WOULD YOU KNOW?!
SHE CONSTANTLY SUPPRESSED US!
THE PRINCESS HAD GROWN WEAK. WE HAD TO TAKE ADVANTAGE OF THE OPPORTUNITY PRESENTED BY THE SUCCESSION RITUAL OR THE CYCLE OF OPPRESSION WOULD'VE CONTINUED!
I WANTED TO UNSHACKLE HOMURA.
UNH...

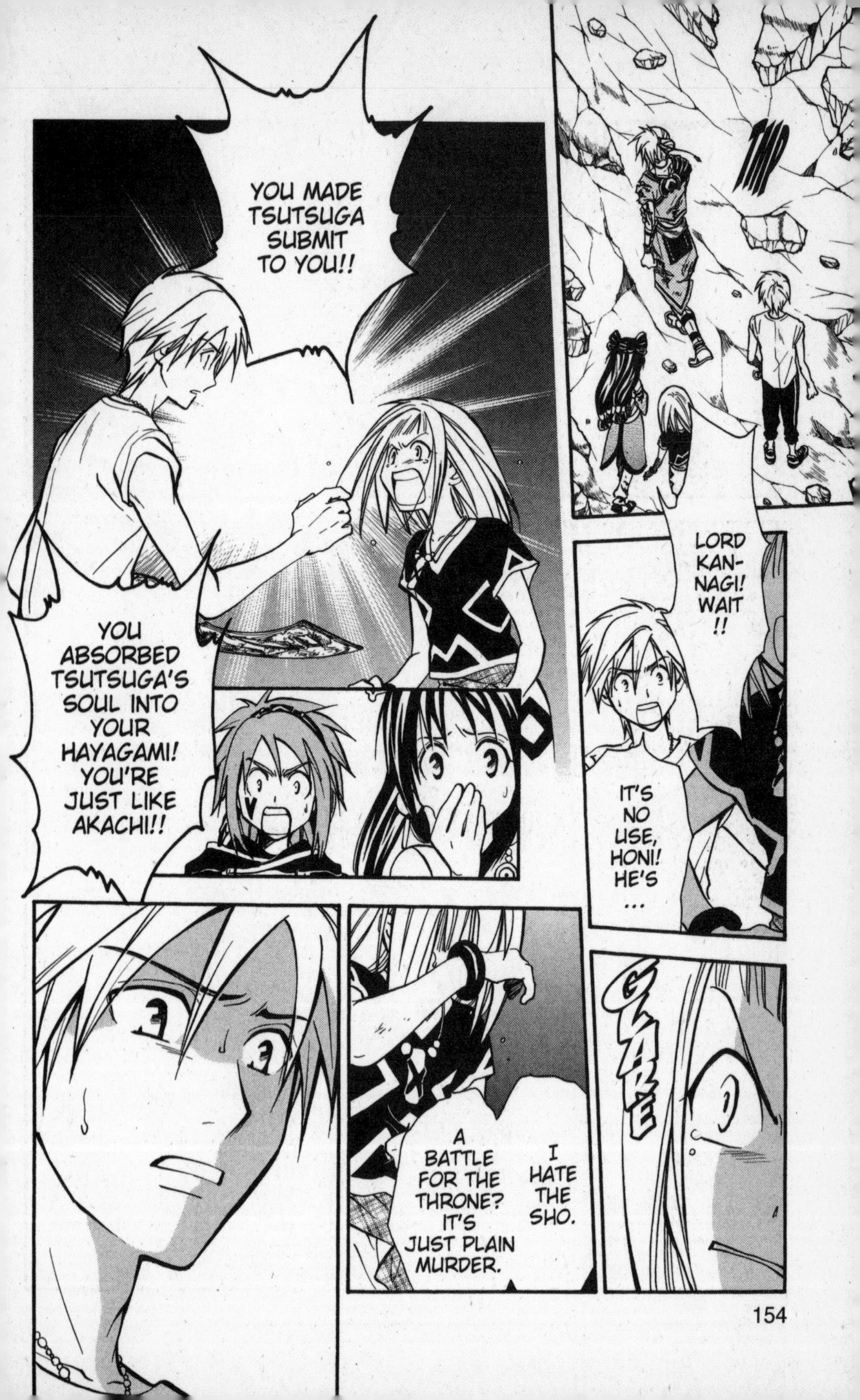
LORD KAN-NAGI! WAIT!!
IT'S NO USE, HONI! HE'S ...
YOU MADE TSUTSUGA SUBMIT TO YOU!!
YOU ABSORBED TSUTSUGA'S SOUL INTO YOUR HAYAGAMI! YOU'RE JUST LIKE AKACHI!!
GLARE
I HATE THE SHO.
A BATTLE FOR THE THRONE? IT'S JUST PLAIN MURDER.

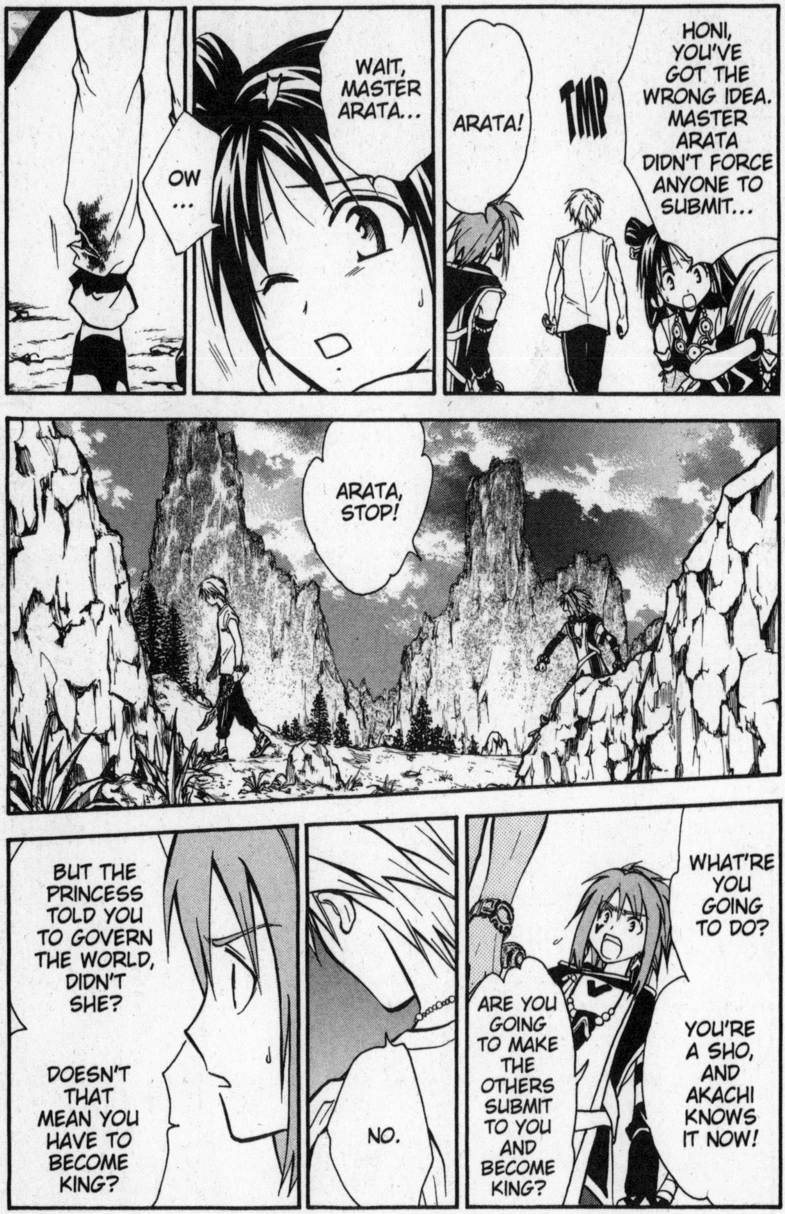
HONI, YOU'VE GOT THE WRONG IDEA. MASTER ARATA DIDN'T FORCE ANYONE TO SUBMIT...
TMP
ARATA!
WAIT, MASTER ARATA...
OW ...
ARATA, STOP!
WHAT'RE YOU GOING TO DO?
YOU'RE A SHO, AND AKACHI KNOWS IT NOW!
ARE YOU GOING TO MAKE THE OTHERS SUBMIT TO YOU AND BECOME KING?
NO.
BUT THE PRINCESS TOLD YOU TO GOVERN THE WORLD, DIDN'T SHE?
DOESN'T THAT MEAN YOU HAVE TO BECOME KING?

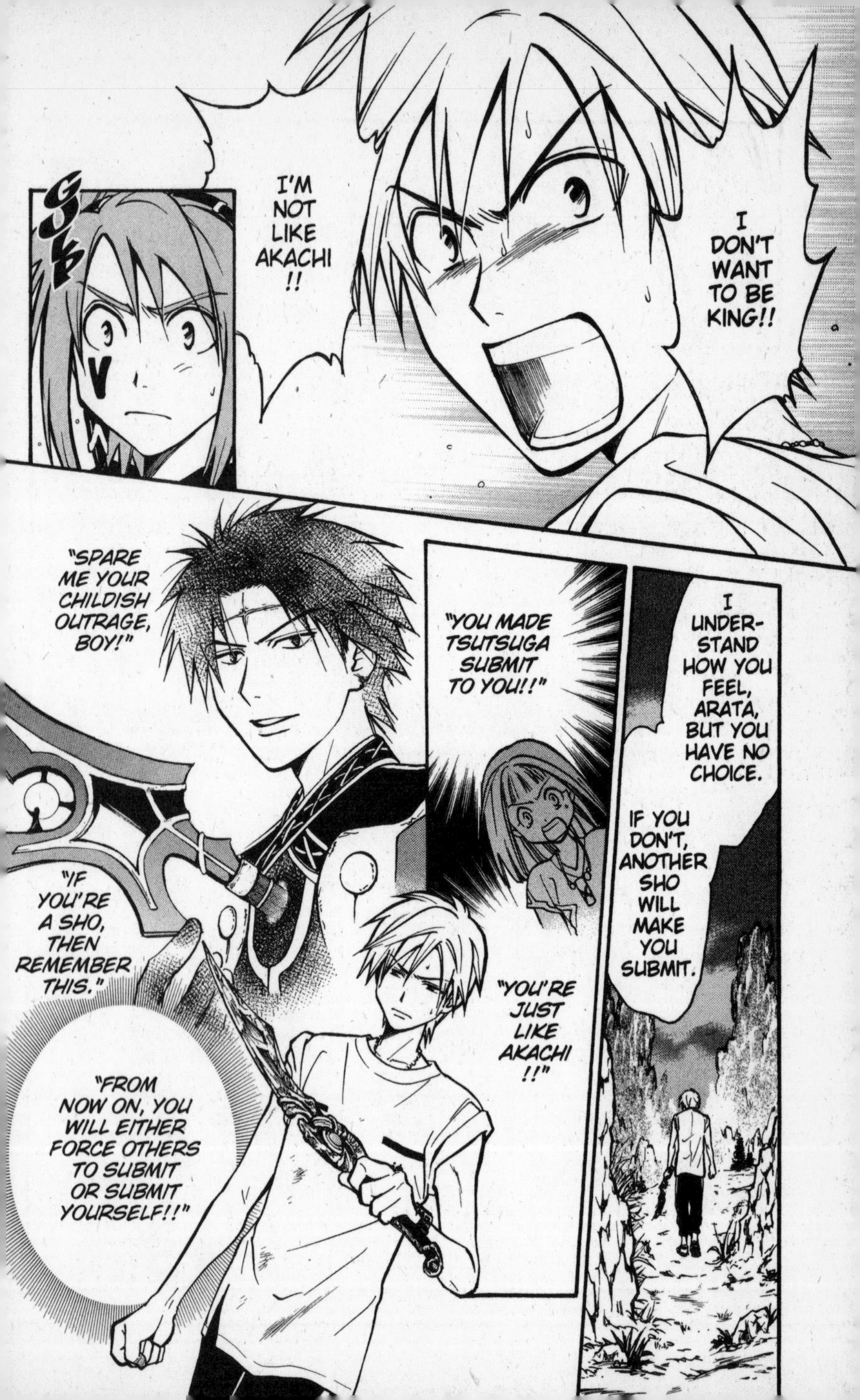

I DON'T WANT TO BE KING!!
I'M NOT LIKE AKACHI!!
GULP
I UNDERSTAND HOW YOU FEEL, ARATA, BUT YOU HAVE NO CHOICE.
IF YOU DON'T, ANOTHER SHO WILL MAKE YOU SUBMIT.
"YOU MADE TSUTSUGA SUBMIT TO YOU!!"
"YOU'RE JUST LIKE AKACHI!!"
"SPARE ME YOUR CHILDISH OUTRAGE, BOY!"
"IF YOU'RE A SHO, THEN REMEMBER THIS."
"FROM NOW ON, YOU WILL EITHER FORCE OTHERS TO SUBMIT OR SUBMIT YOURSELF!!"

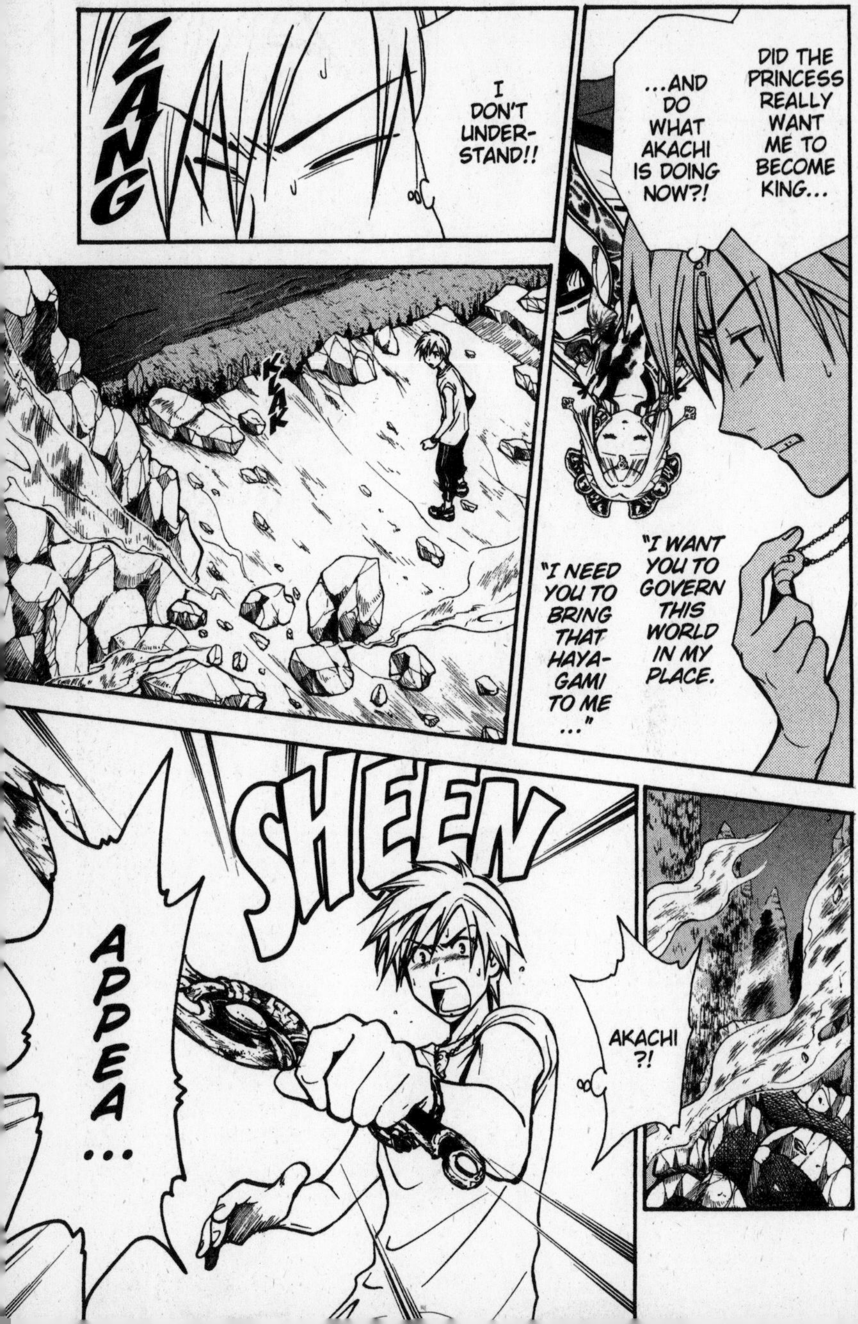
DID THE PRINCESS REALLY WANT ME TO BECOME KING...
...AND DO WHAT AKACHI IS DOING NOW?!
"I WANT YOU TO GOVERN THIS WORLD IN MY PLACE.
"I NEED YOU TO BRING THAT HAYA-GAMI TO ME..."
ZANG
I DON'T UNDER-STAND!!
KRAK
AKACHI?!
SHEEN
APPEA...

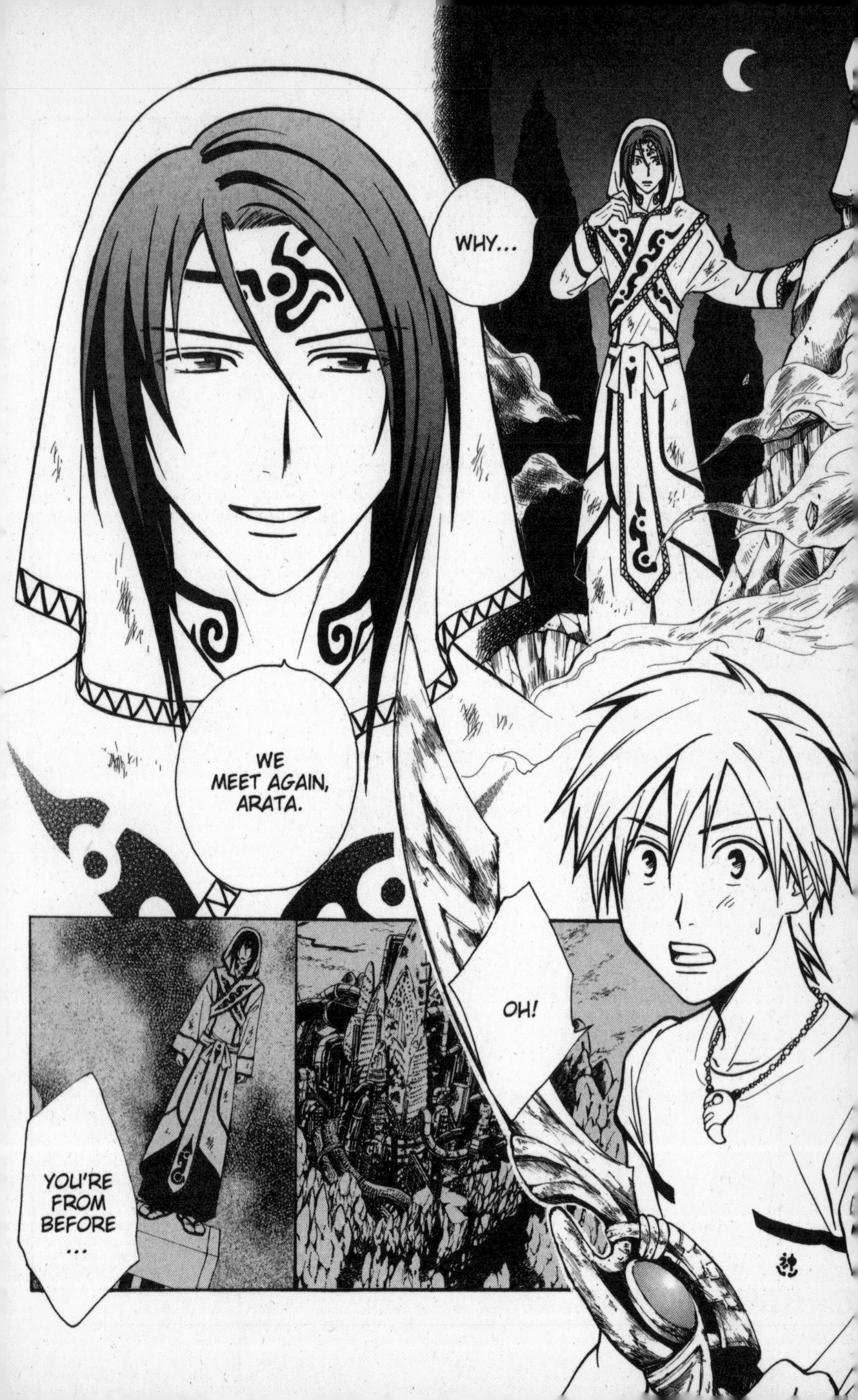
WHY...
WE MEET AGAIN, ARATA.
OH!
YOU'RE FROM BEFORE ...

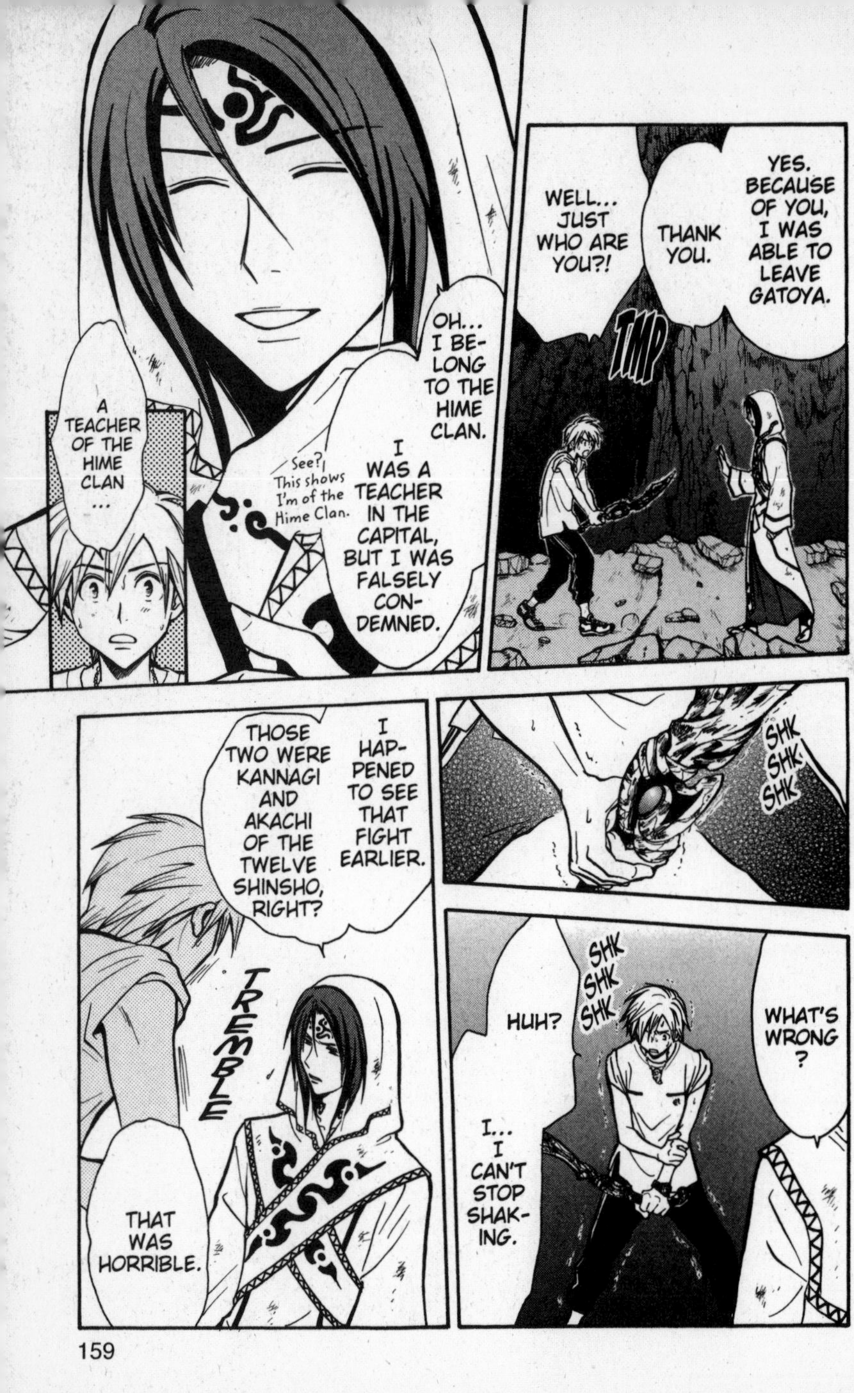
YES. BECAUSE OF YOU, I WAS ABLE TO LEAVE GATOYA.
THANK YOU.
WELL... JUST WHO ARE YOU?!
TMP
OH... I BE-LONG TO THE HIME CLAN.
I WAS A TEACHER IN THE CAPITAL, BUT I WAS FALSELY CON-DEMNED.
See? This shows I'm of the Hime Clan.
A TEACHER OF THE HIME CLAN ...
SHK SHK SHK
WHAT'S WRONG ?
SHK SHK SHK
HUH?
I... I CAN'T STOP SHAK-ING.
I HAP-PENED TO SEE THAT FIGHT EARLIER.
THOSE TWO WERE KANNAGI AND AKACHI OF THE TWELVE SHINSHO, RIGHT?
TREMBLE
THAT WAS HORRIBLE.

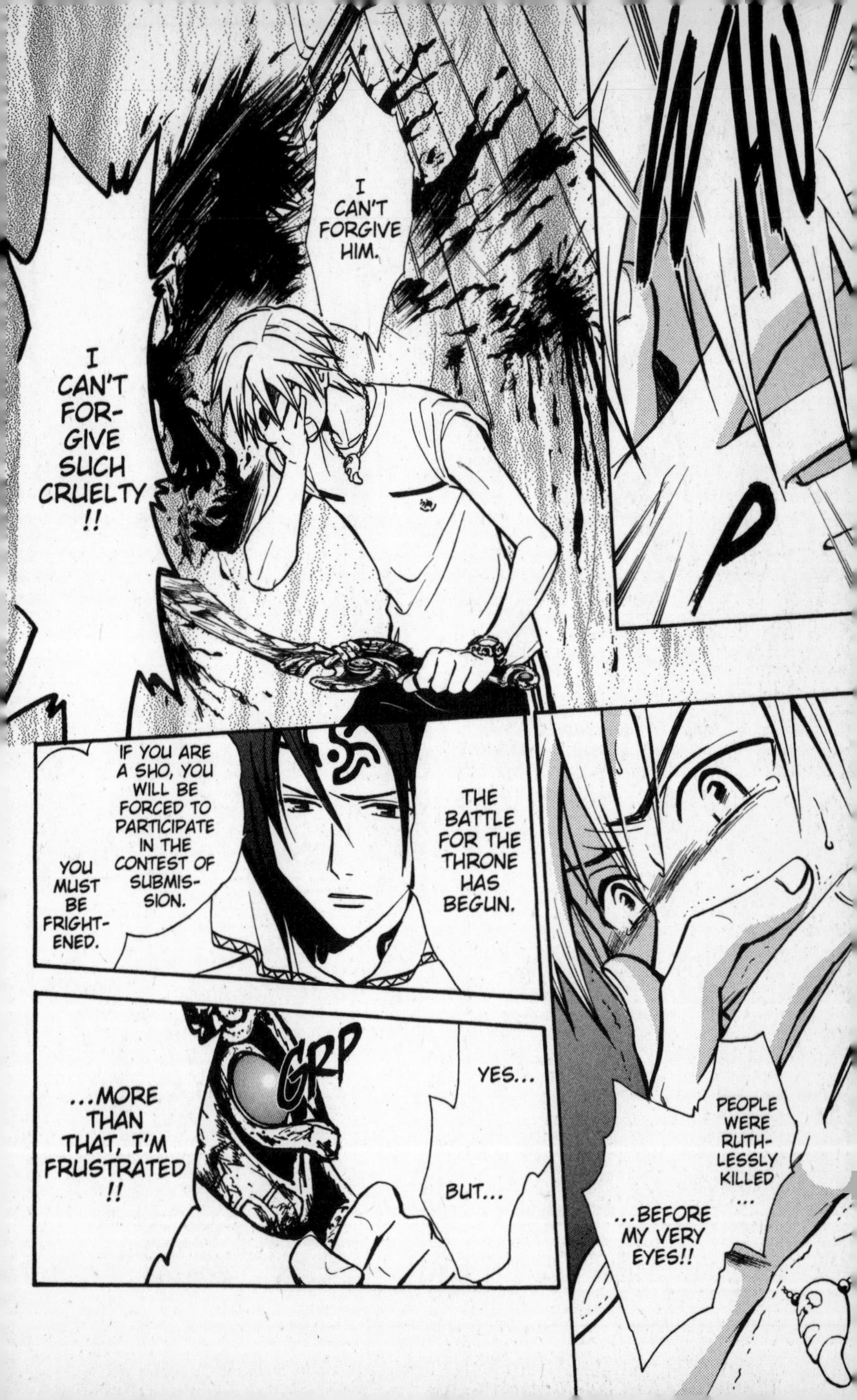
I CAN'T FORGIVE HIM.
I CAN'T FORGIVE SUCH CRUELTY!!
PEOPLE WERE RUTHLESSLY KILLED...
...BEFORE MY VERY EYES!!
THE BATTLE FOR THE THRONE HAS BEGUN.
IF YOU ARE A SHO, YOU WILL BE FORCED TO PARTICIPATE IN THE CONTEST OF SUBMISSION.
YOU MUST BE FRIGHTENED.
YES...
BUT...
GRP
...MORE THAN THAT, I'M FRUSTRATED!!

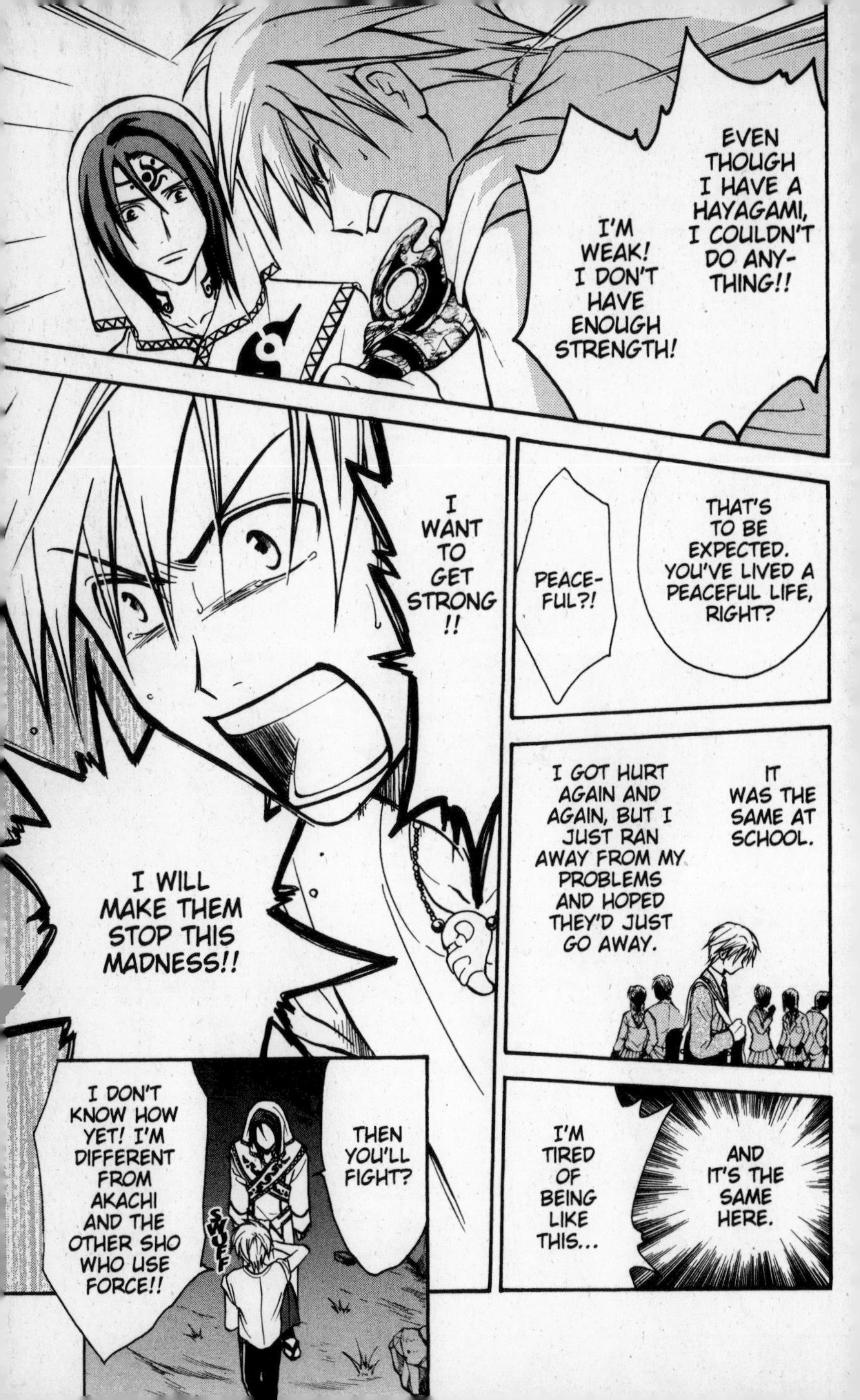
EVEN THOUGH I HAVE A HAYAGAMI, I COULDN'T DO ANYTHING!!
I'M WEAK! I DON'T HAVE ENOUGH STRENGTH!
THAT'S TO BE EXPECTED. YOU'VE LIVED A PEACEFUL LIFE, RIGHT?
PEACE-FUL?!
IT WAS THE SAME AT SCHOOL.
I GOT HURT AGAIN AND AGAIN, BUT I JUST RAN AWAY FROM MY PROBLEMS AND HOPED THEY'D JUST GO AWAY.
AND IT'S THE SAME HERE.
I'M TIRED OF BEING LIKE THIS...
I WANT TO GET STRONG!!
I WILL MAKE THEM STOP THIS MADNESS!!
THEN YOU'LL FIGHT?
I DON'T KNOW HOW YET! I'M DIFFERENT FROM AKACHI AND THE OTHER SHO WHO USE FORCE!!
SWUFF

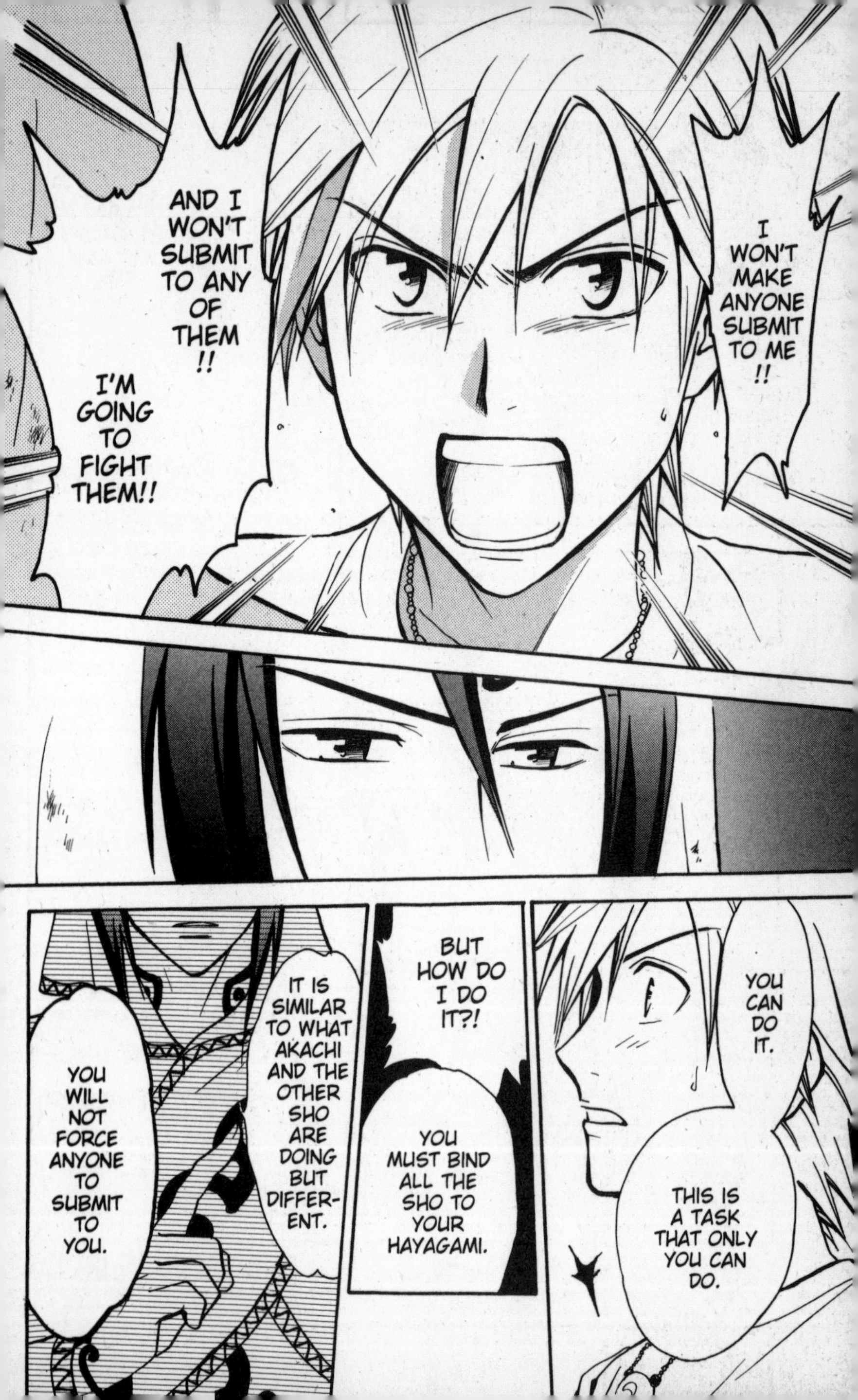
I WON'T MAKE ANYONE SUBMIT TO ME!!
AND I WON'T SUBMIT TO ANY OF THEM!!
I'M GOING TO FIGHT THEM!!
YOU CAN DO IT.
THIS IS A TASK THAT ONLY YOU CAN DO.
BUT HOW DO I DO IT?!
YOU MUST BIND ALL THE SHO TO YOUR HAYAGAMI.
IT IS SIMILAR TO WHAT AKACHI AND THE OTHER SHO ARE DOING BUT DIFFER-ENT.
YOU WILL NOT FORCE ANYONE TO SUBMIT TO YOU.

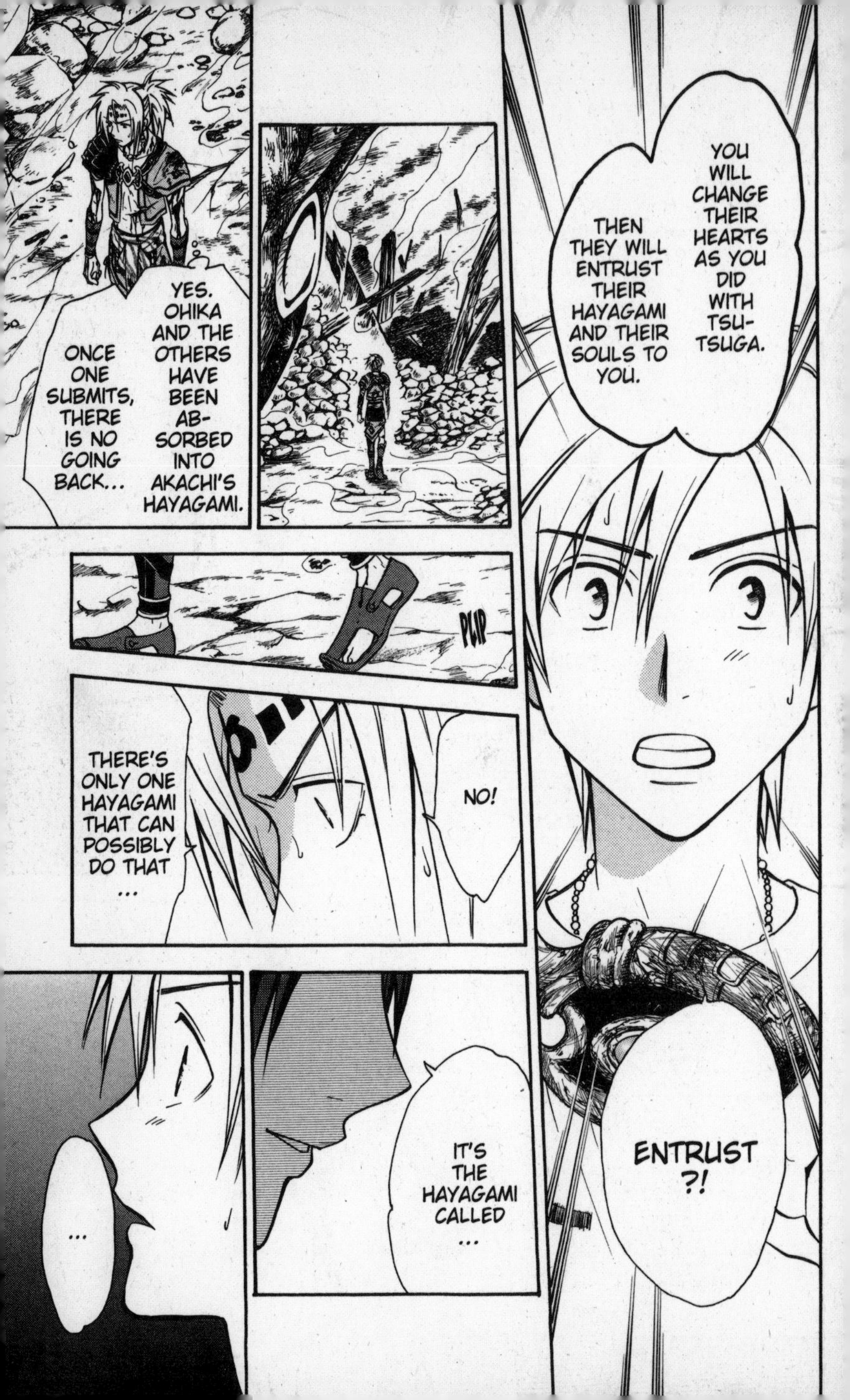
YOU WILL CHANGE THEIR HEARTS AS YOU DID WITH TSU-TSUGA.
THEN THEY WILL ENTRUST THEIR HAYAGAMI AND THEIR SOULS TO YOU.
ENTRUST ?!
YES. OHIKA AND THE OTHERS HAVE BEEN AB-SORBED INTO AKACHI'S HAYAGAMI.
ONCE ONE SUBMITS, THERE IS NO GOING BACK...
PLIP
NO!
THERE'S ONLY ONE HAYAGAMI THAT CAN POSSIBLY DO THAT ...
IT'S THE HAYAGAMI CALLED ...
...

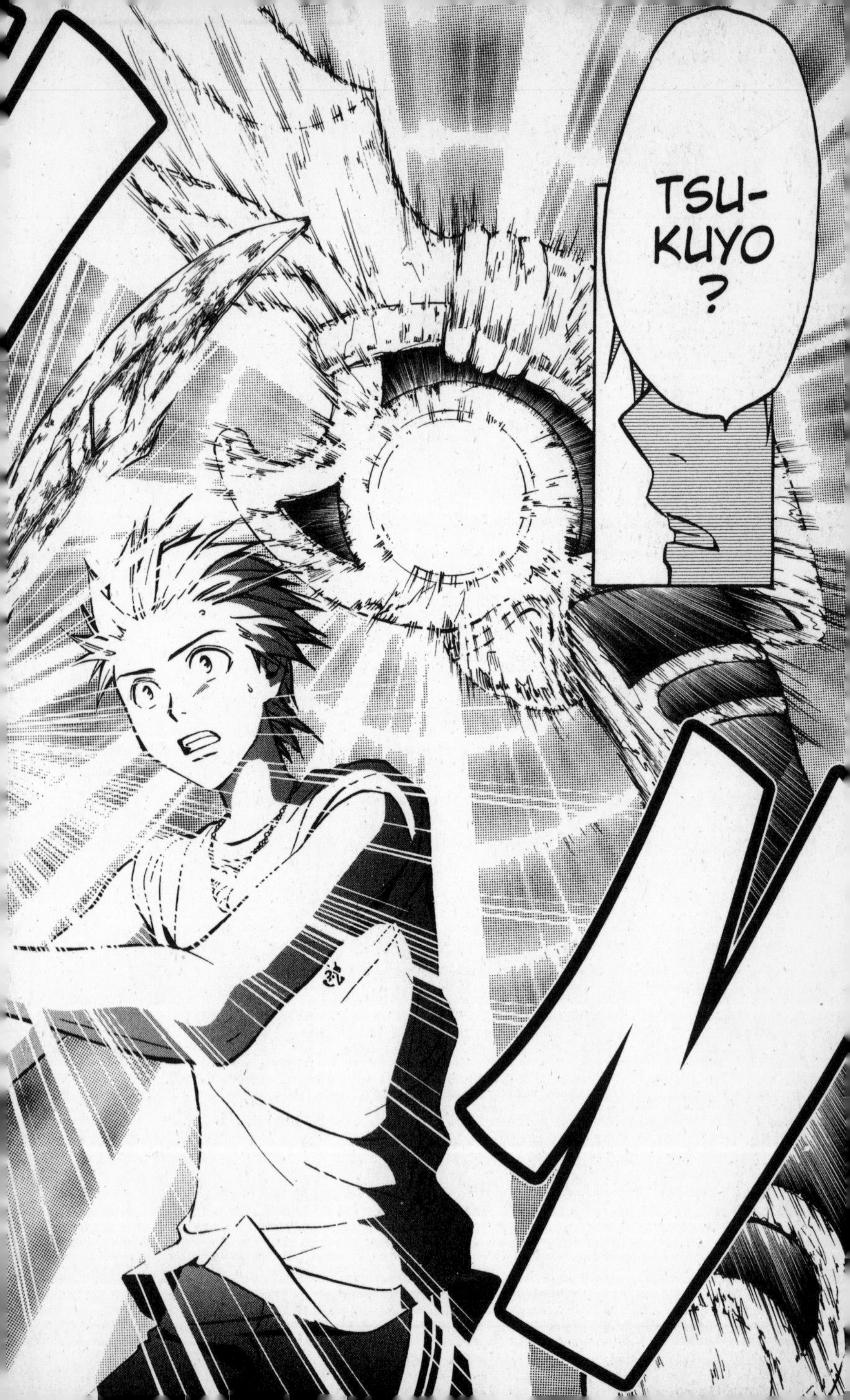
TSU-
KUYO
?

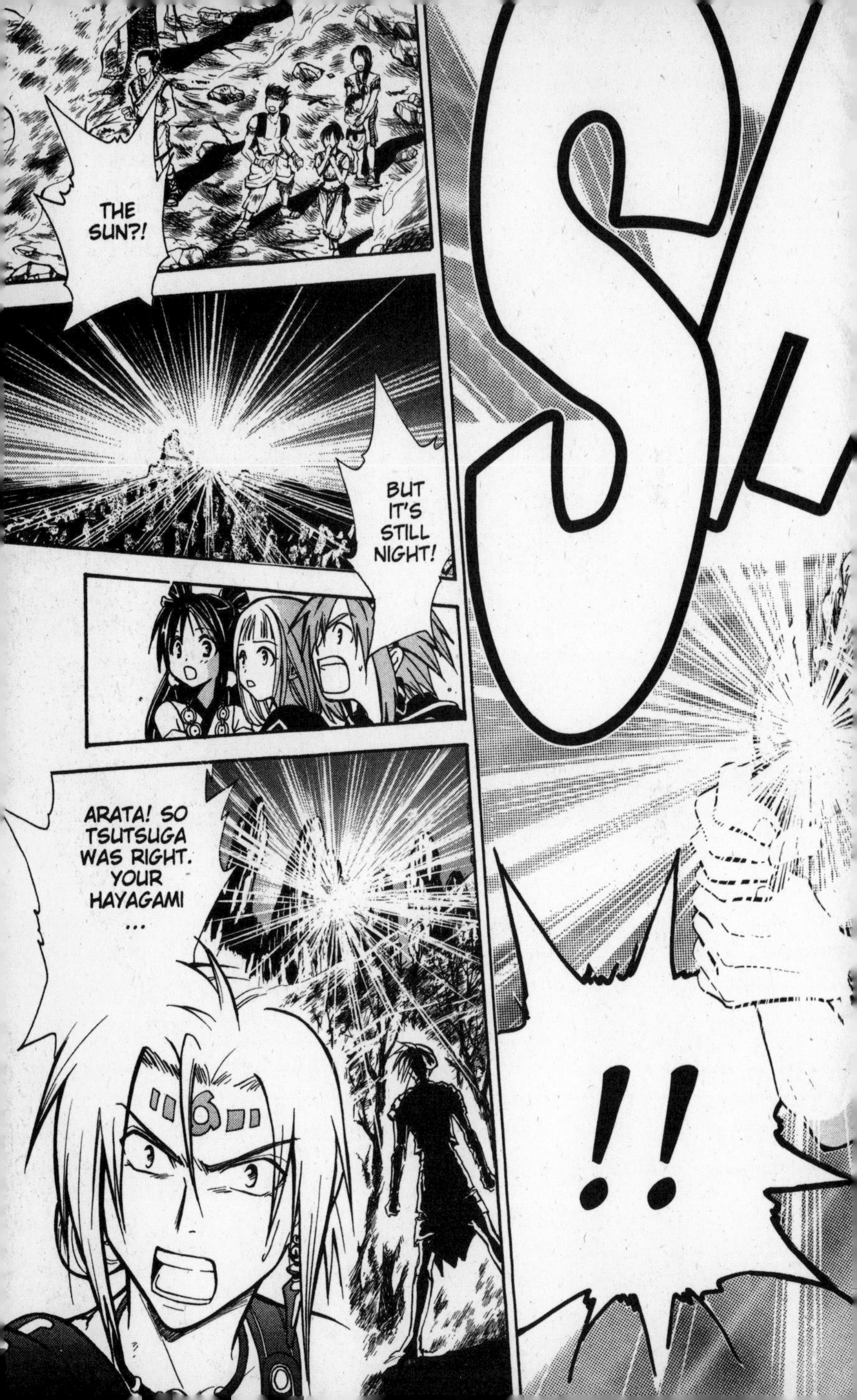
THE SUN?!
BUT IT'S STILL NIGHT!
ARATA! SO TSUTSUGA WAS RIGHT. YOUR HAYAGAMI ...

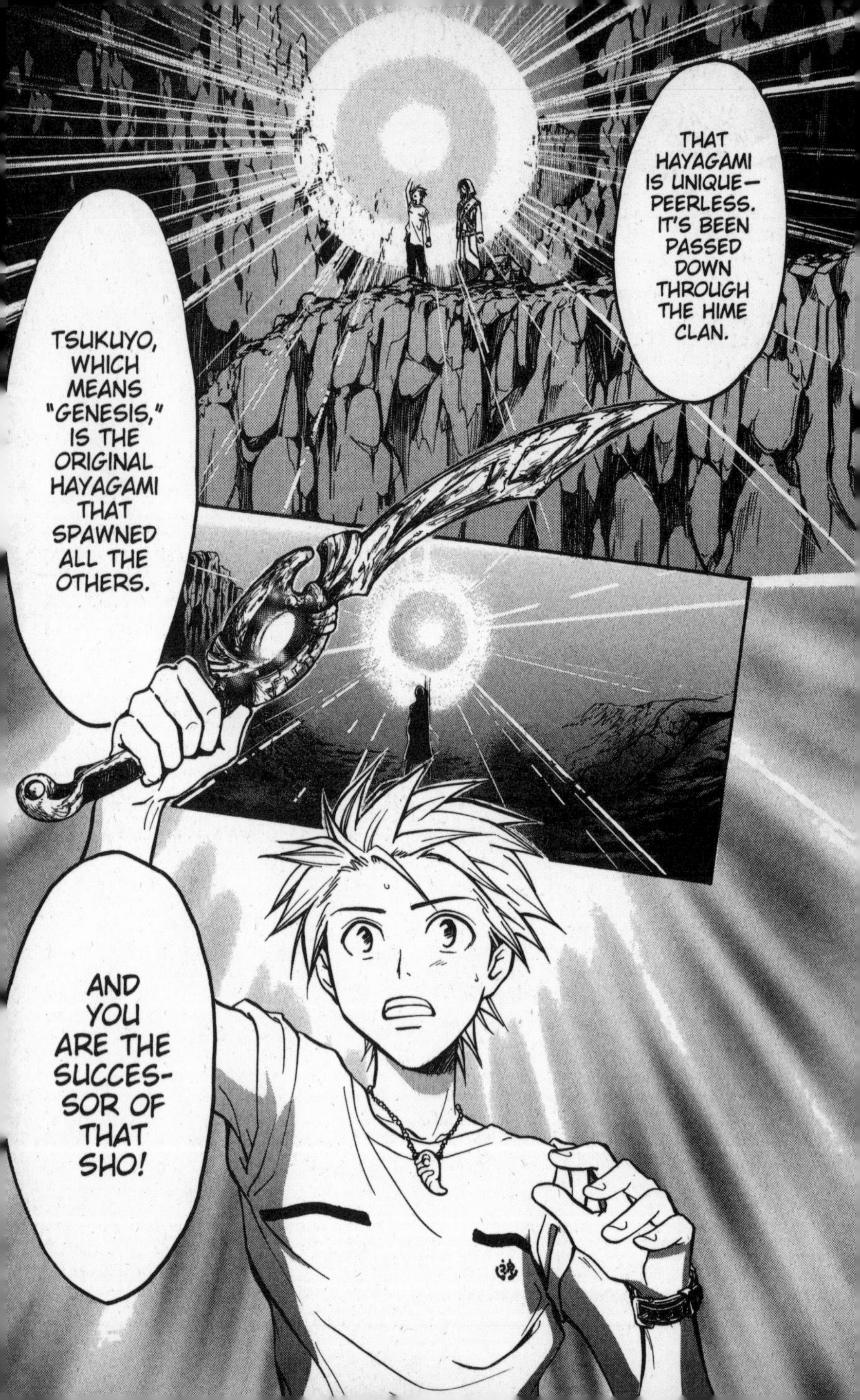
THAT HAYAGAMI IS UNIQUE—PEERLESS. IT'S BEEN PASSED DOWN THROUGH THE HIME CLAN.
TSUKUYO, WHICH MEANS "GENESIS," IS THE ORIGINAL HAYAGAMI THAT SPAWNED ALL THE OTHERS.
AND YOU ARE THE SUCCES-SOR OF THAT SHO!

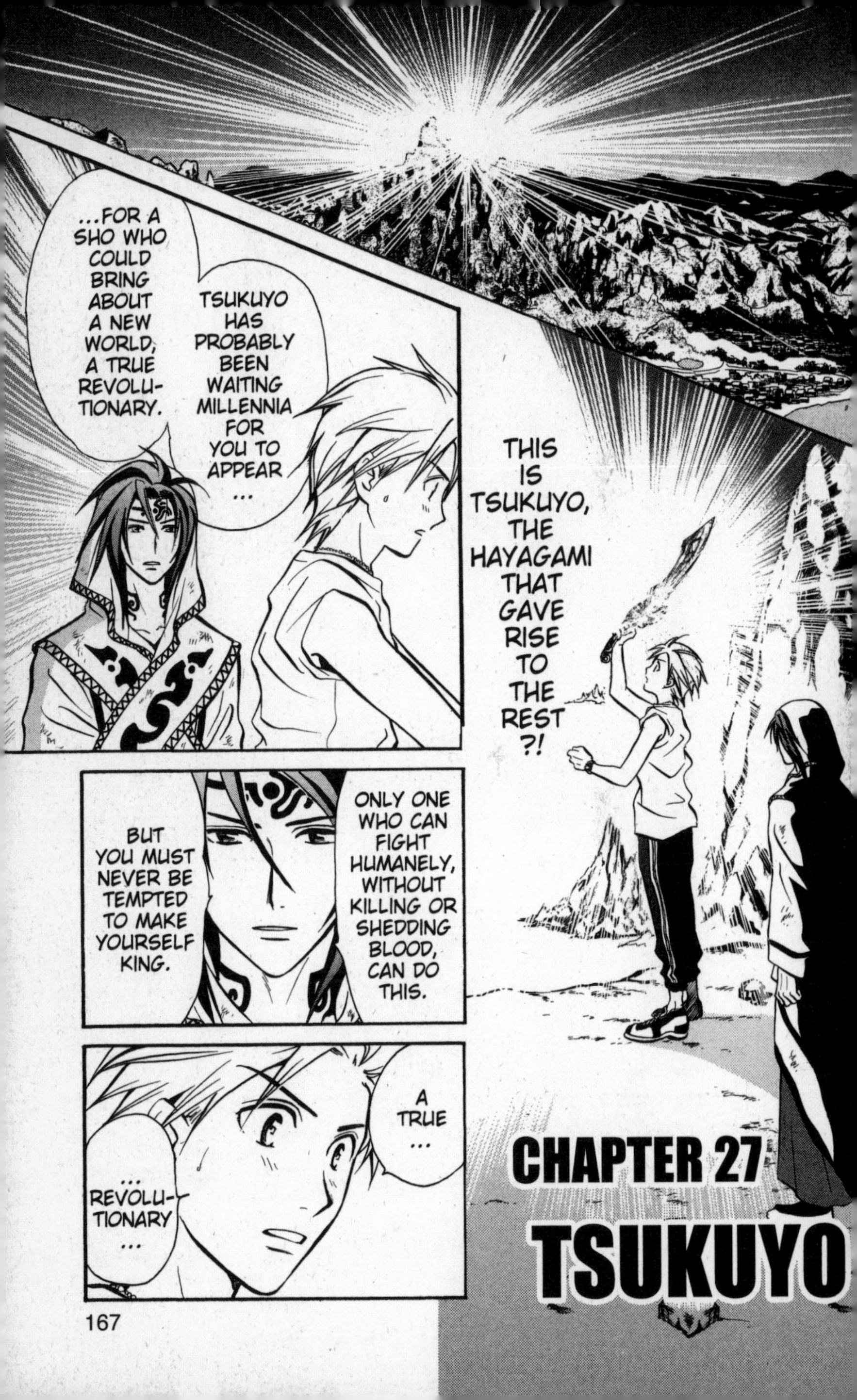
THIS IS TSUKUYO, THE HAYAGAMI THAT GAVE RISE TO THE REST ?!
CHAPTER 27
TSUKUYO
TSUKUYO HAS PROBABLY BEEN WAITING MILLENNIA FOR YOU TO APPEAR ...
...FOR A SHO WHO COULD BRING ABOUT A NEW WORLD, A TRUE REVOLUTIONARY.
ONLY ONE WHO CAN FIGHT HUMANELY, WITHOUT KILLING OR SHEDDING BLOOD, CAN DO THIS.
BUT YOU MUST NEVER BE TEMPTED TO MAKE YOURSELF KING.
A TRUE ...
... REVOLUTIONARY ...

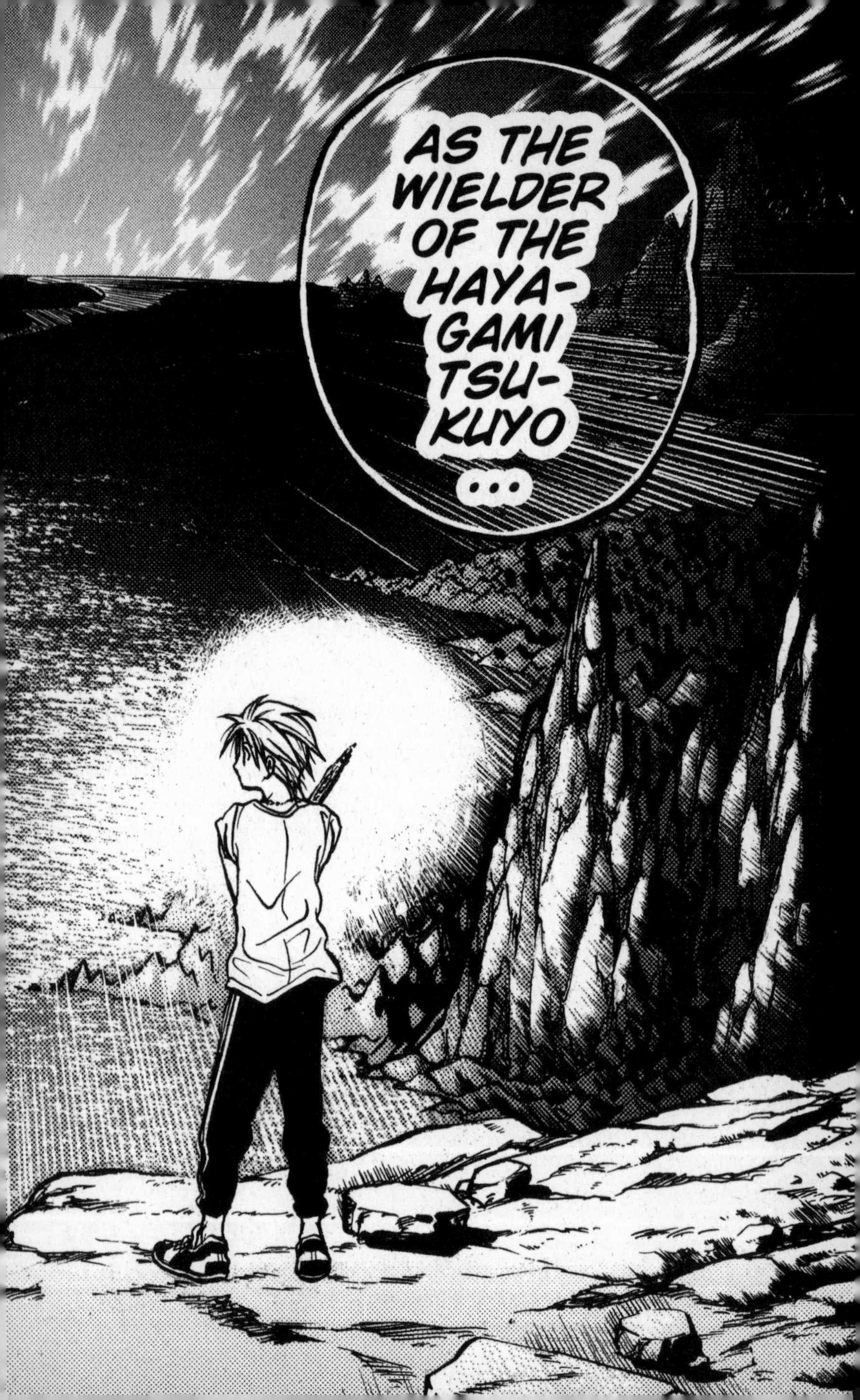
AS THE WIELDER OF THE HAYA-GAMI TSU-KUYO...

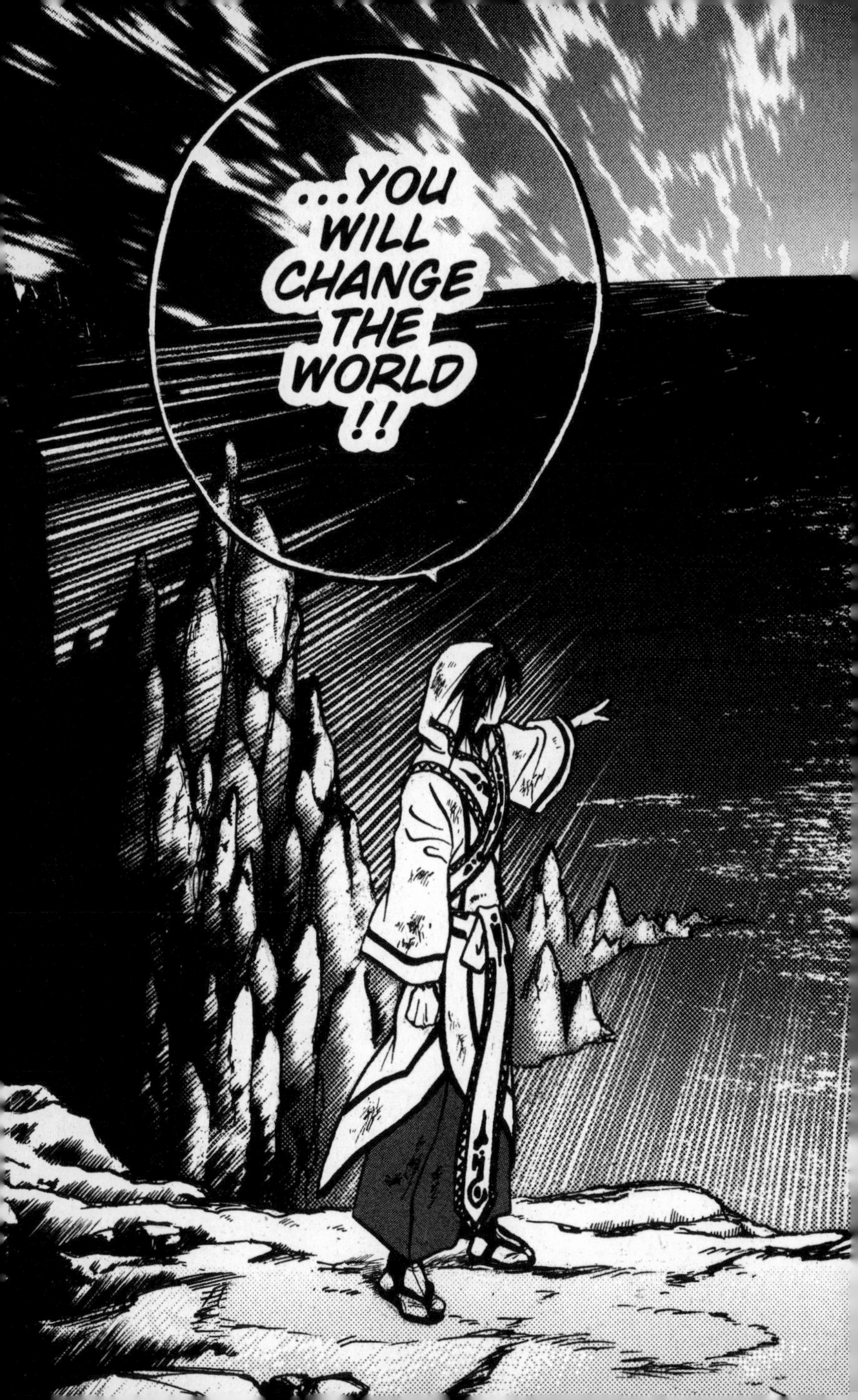
...YOU WILL CHANGE THE WORLD!!

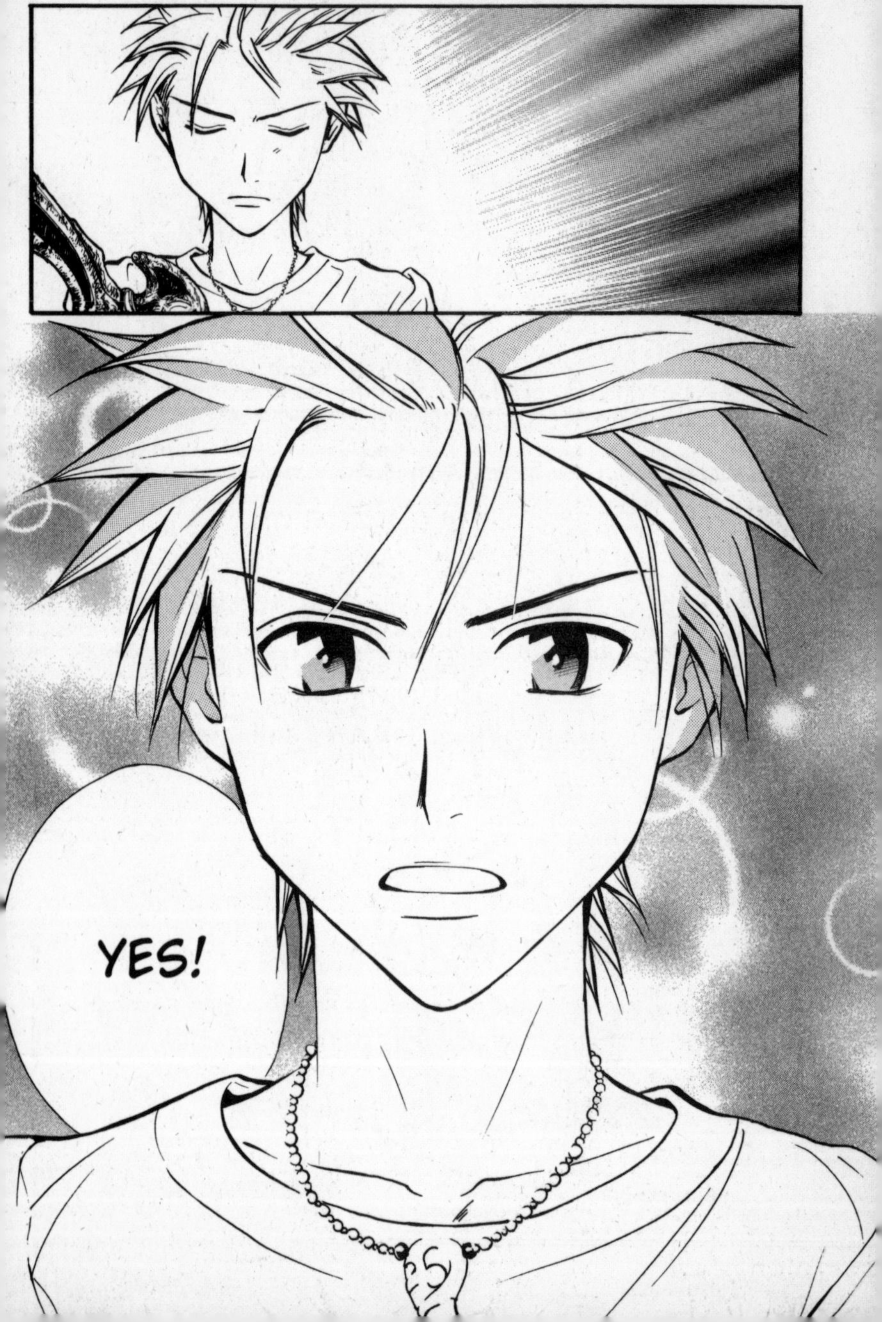
YES!

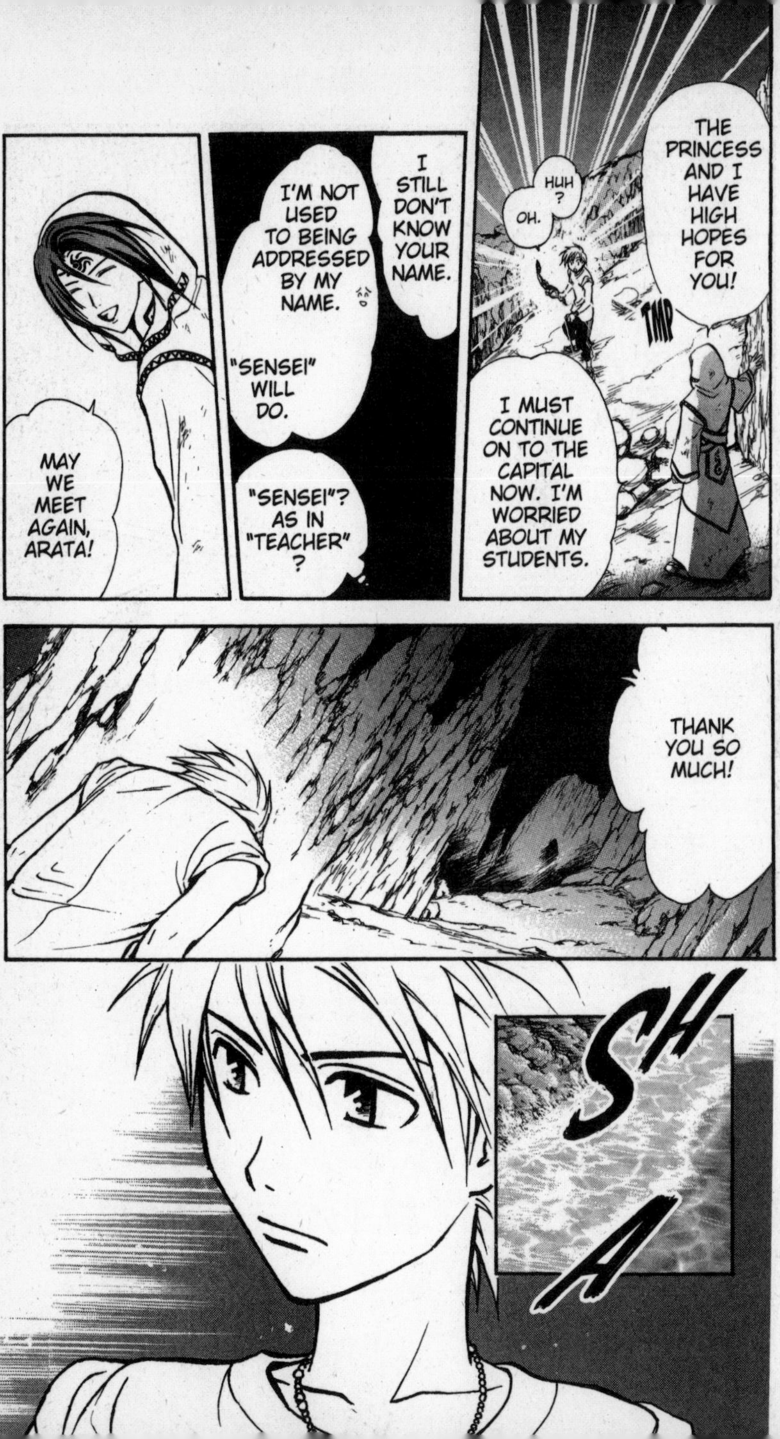
THE PRINCESS AND I HAVE HIGH HOPES FOR YOU!
HUH?
OH.
TMP
I MUST CONTINUE ON TO THE CAPITAL NOW. I'M WORRIED ABOUT MY STUDENTS.
I STILL DON'T KNOW YOUR NAME.
I'M NOT USED TO BEING ADDRESSED BY MY NAME.
"SENSEI" WILL DO.
"SENSEI"? AS IN "TEACHER"?
MAY WE MEET AGAIN, ARATA!
THANK YOU SO MUCH!
SHA

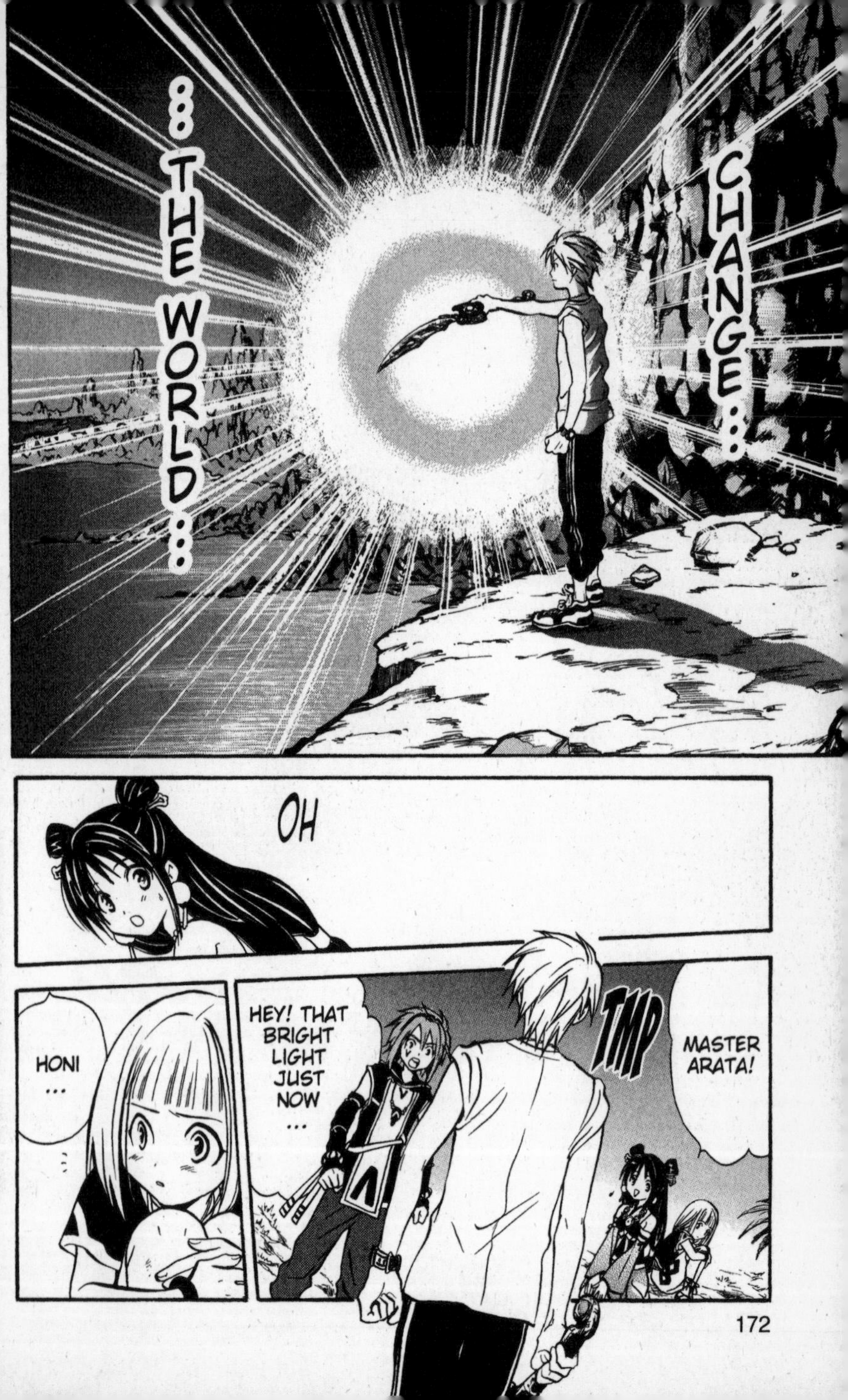
CHANGE...
...THE WORLD...
OH
TMP
MASTER ARATA!
HEY! THAT BRIGHT LIGHT JUST NOW...
HONI...

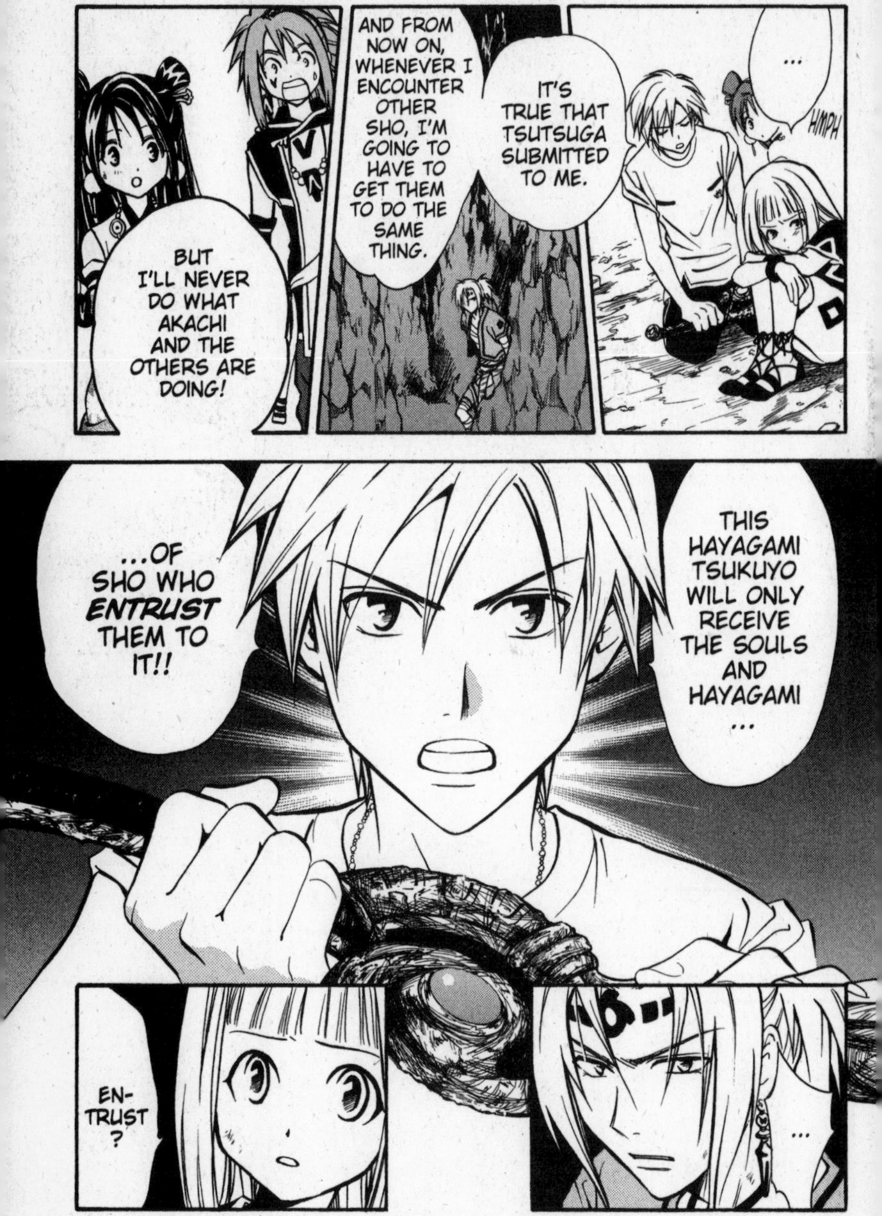
...
HMPH
IT'S TRUE THAT TSUTSUGA SUBMITTED TO ME.
AND FROM NOW ON, WHENEVER I ENCOUNTER OTHER SHO, I'M GOING TO HAVE TO GET THEM TO DO THE SAME THING.
BUT I'LL NEVER DO WHAT AKACHI AND THE OTHERS ARE DOING!
THIS HAYAGAMI TSUKUYO WILL ONLY RECEIVE THE SOULS AND HAYAGAMI...
...OF SHO WHO *ENTRUST* THEM TO IT!!
...
EN-TRUST?

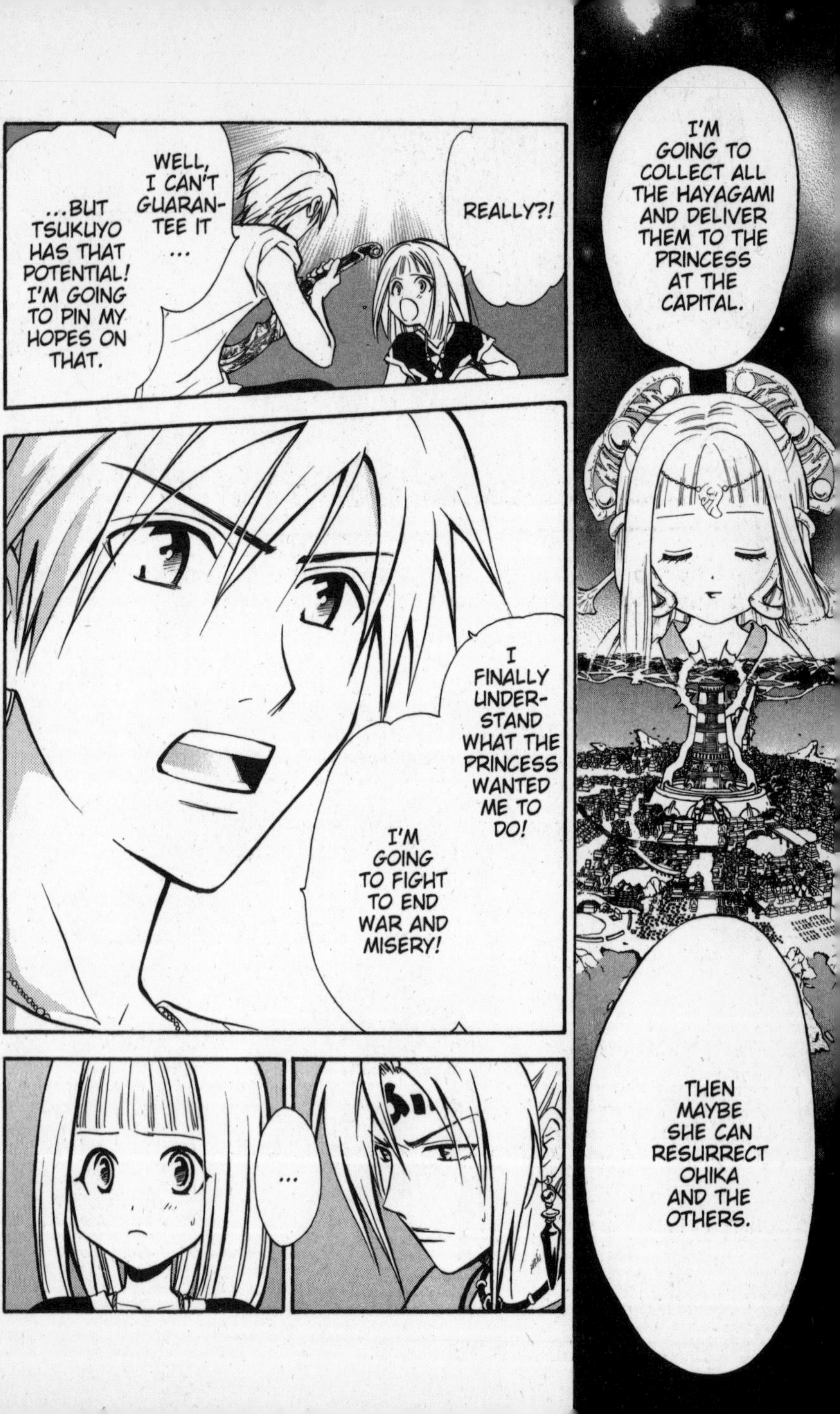
I'M GOING TO COLLECT ALL THE HAYAGAMI AND DELIVER THEM TO THE PRINCESS AT THE CAPITAL.
THEN MAYBE SHE CAN RESURRECT OHIKA AND THE OTHERS.
REALLY?!
WELL, I CAN'T GUARANTEE IT ...
...BUT TSUKUYO HAS THAT POTENTIAL! I'M GOING TO PIN MY HOPES ON THAT.
I FINALLY UNDERSTAND WHAT THE PRINCESS WANTED ME TO DO!
I'M GOING TO FIGHT TO END WAR AND MISERY!
...

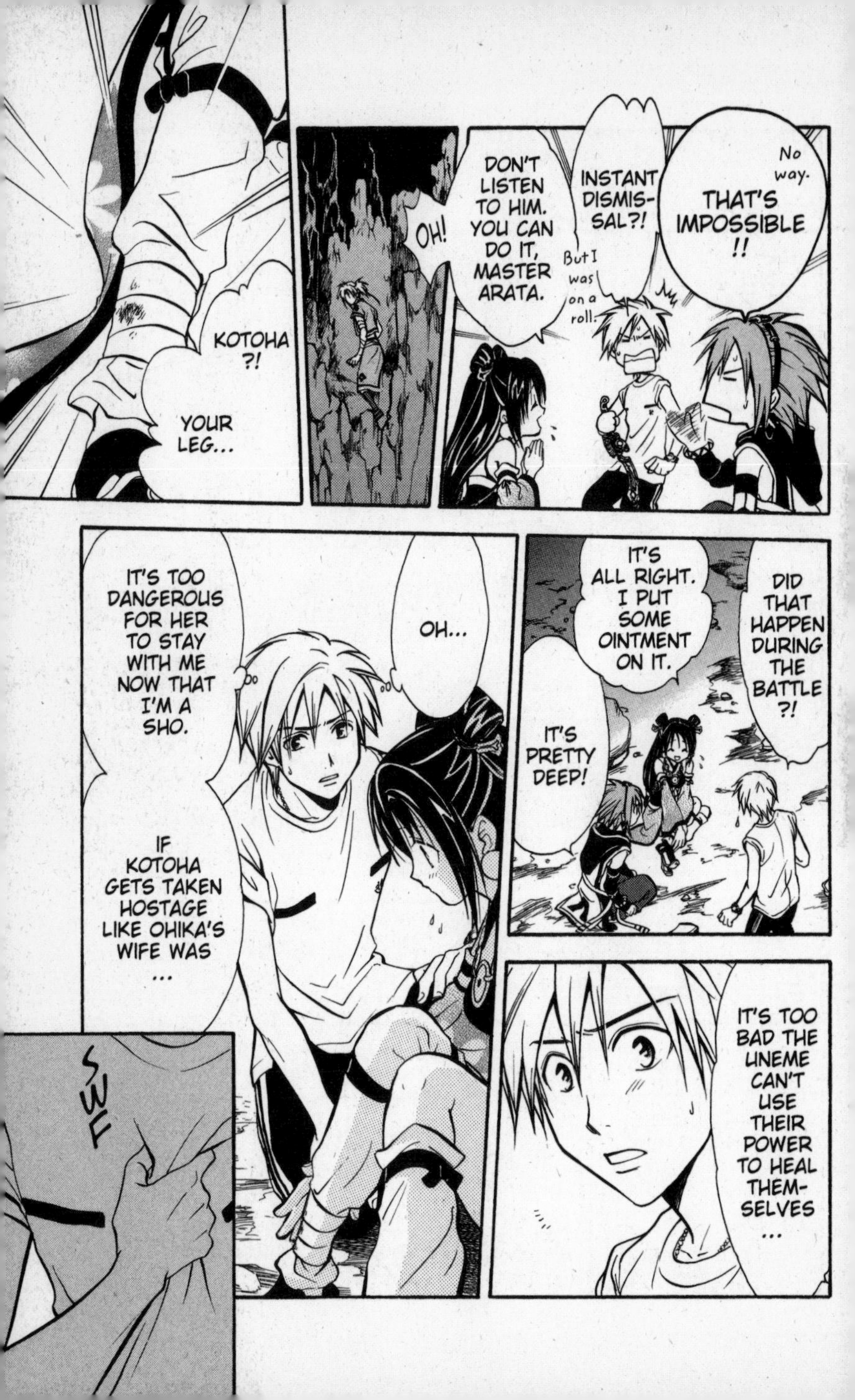
No way.
THAT'S IMPOSSIBLE!!
INSTANT DISMIS-SAL?!
But I was on a roll.
DON'T LISTEN TO HIM. YOU CAN DO IT, MASTER ARATA.
OH!
KOTOHA?!
YOUR LEG...
DID THAT HAPPEN DURING THE BATTLE?!
IT'S ALL RIGHT. I PUT SOME OINTMENT ON IT.
IT'S PRETTY DEEP!
IT'S TOO BAD THE UNEME CAN'T USE THEIR POWER TO HEAL THEM-SELVES...
OH...
IT'S TOO DANGEROUS FOR HER TO STAY WITH ME NOW THAT I'M A SHO.
IF KOTOHA GETS TAKEN HOSTAGE LIKE OHIKA'S WIFE WAS...
SWF

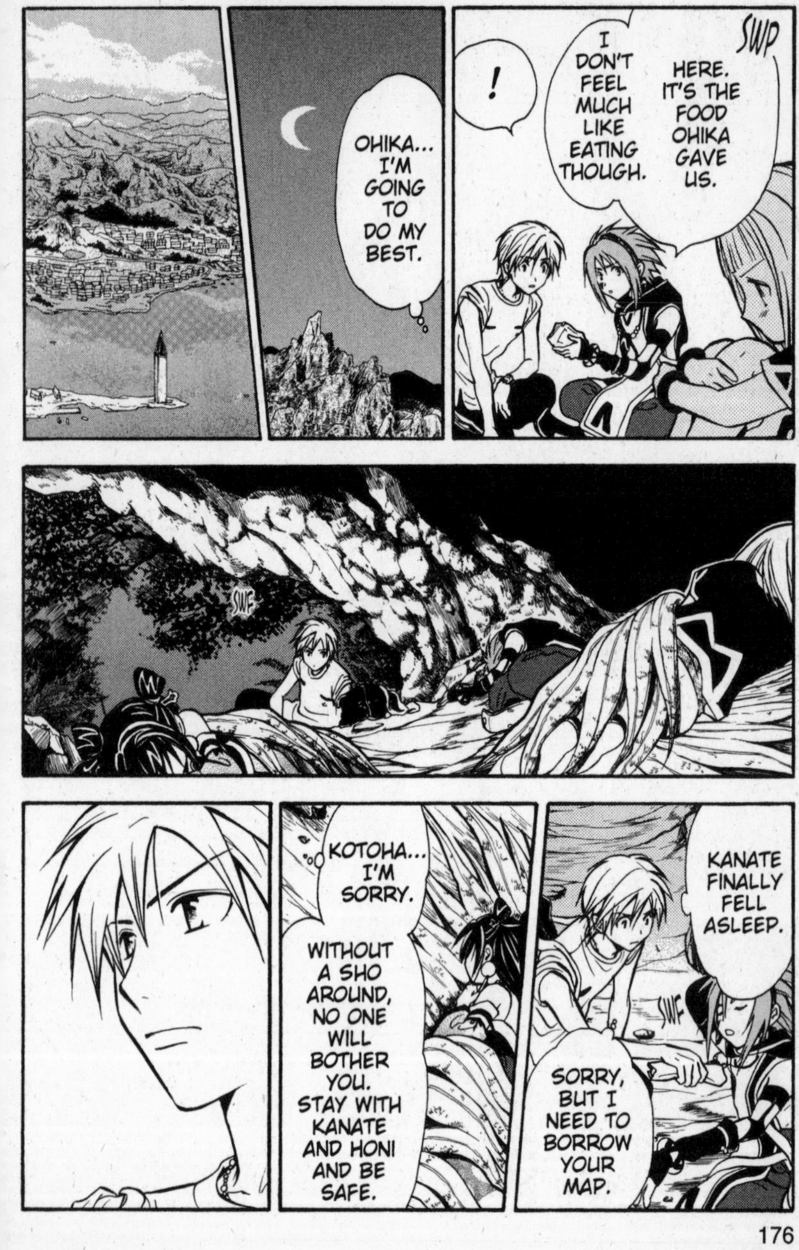
SWP
HERE. IT'S THE FOOD OHIKA GAVE US.
I DON'T FEEL MUCH LIKE EATING THOUGH.
!
OHIKA... I'M GOING TO DO MY BEST.
SWF
KANATE FINALLY FELL ASLEEP.
SWF
SORRY, BUT I NEED TO BORROW YOUR MAP.
KOTOHA... I'M SORRY.
WITHOUT A SHO AROUND, NO ONE WILL BOTHER YOU. STAY WITH KANATE AND HONI AND BE SAFE.

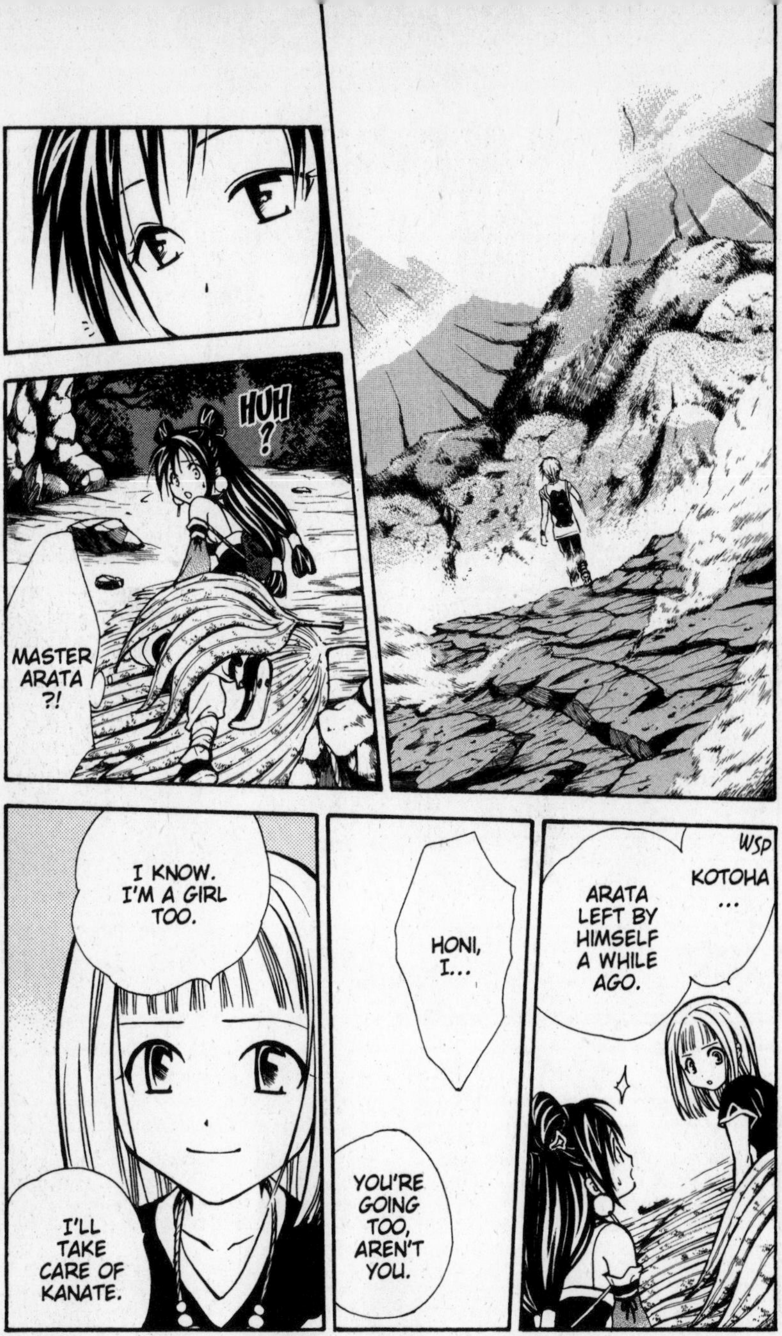
HUH ?
MASTER ARATA ?!
WSP
KOTOHA ...
ARATA LEFT BY HIMSELF A WHILE AGO.
HONI, I...
YOU'RE GOING TOO, AREN'T YOU.
I KNOW. I'M A GIRL TOO.
I'LL TAKE CARE OF KANATE.

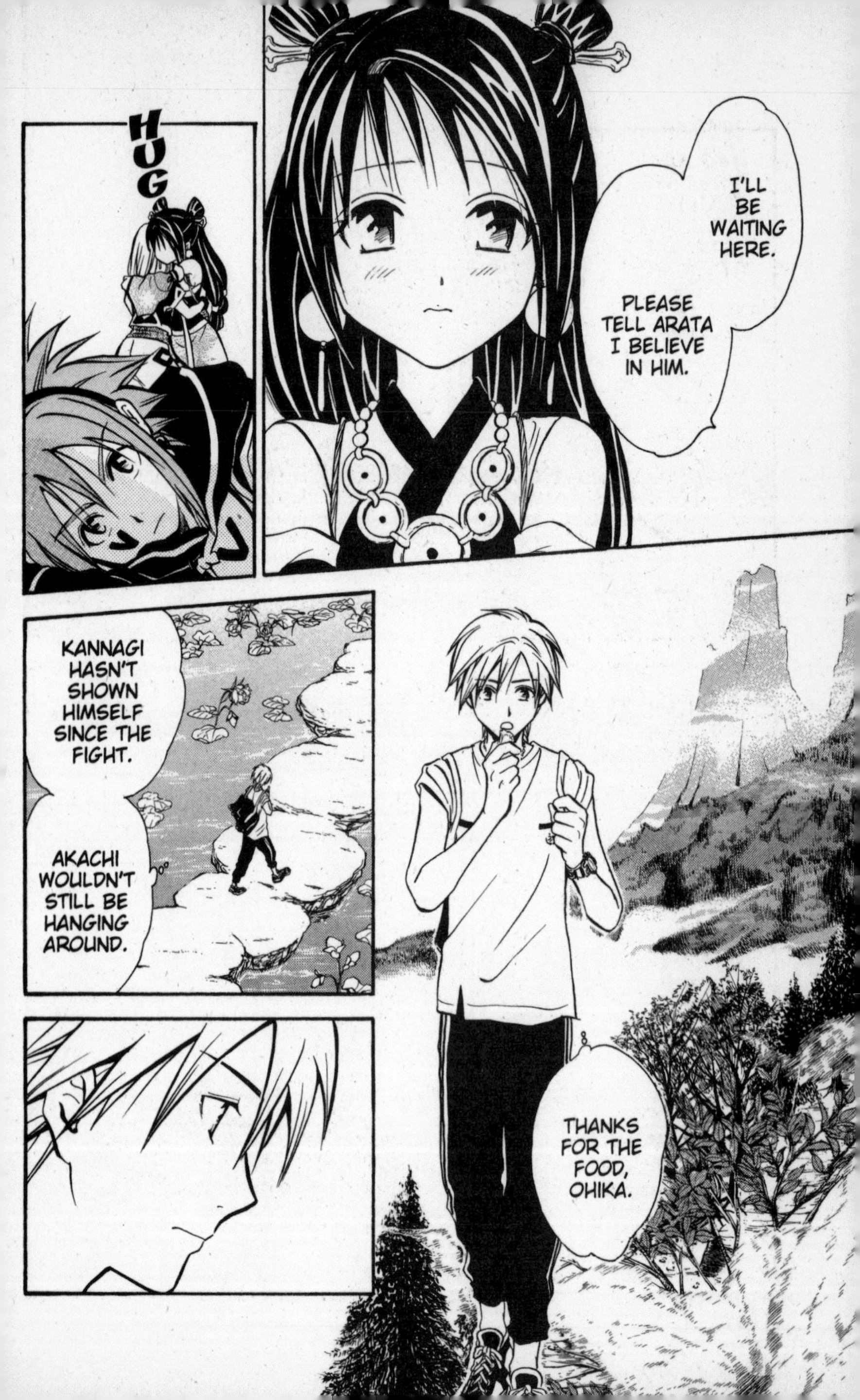
I'LL BE WAITING HERE.
PLEASE TELL ARATA I BELIEVE IN HIM.
HUG
THANKS FOR THE FOOD, OHIKA.
KANNAGI HASN'T SHOWN HIMSELF SINCE THE FIGHT.
AKACHI WOULDN'T STILL BE HANGING AROUND.

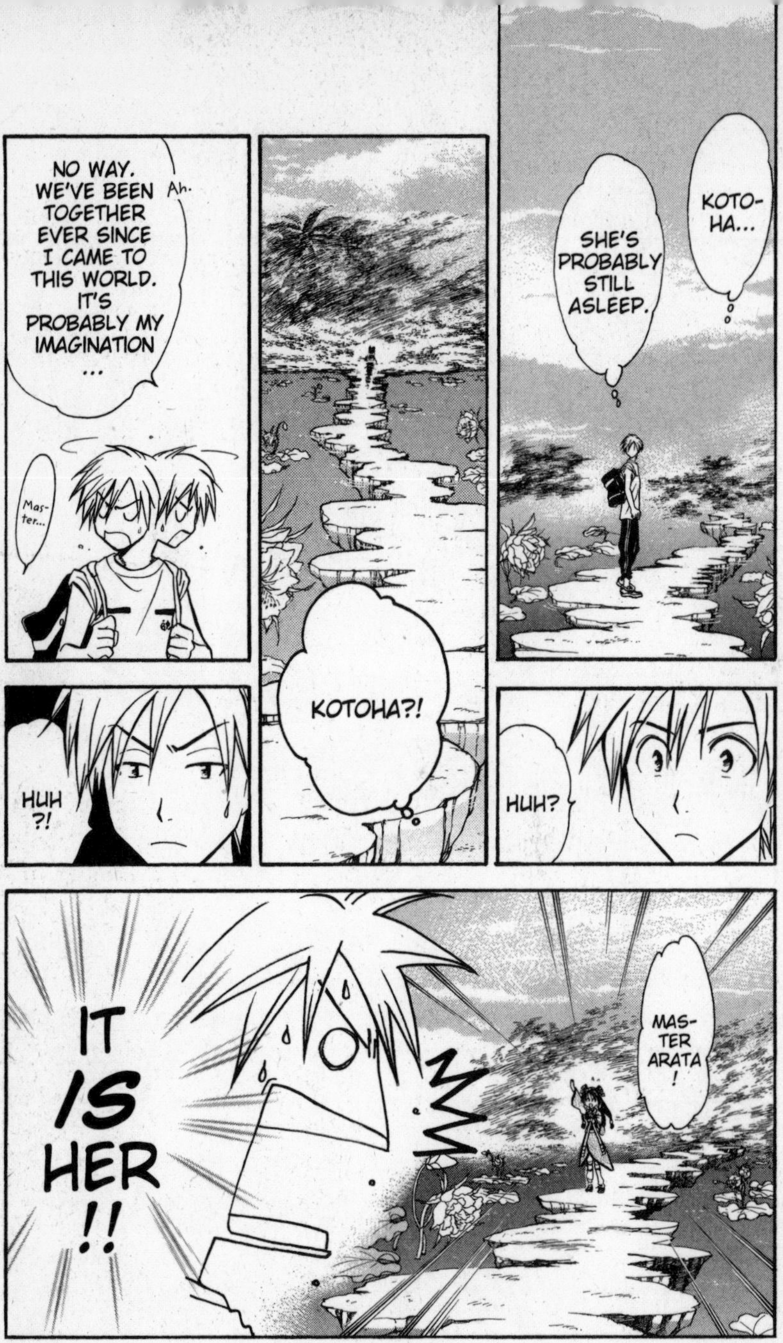
KOTO-HA...
SHE'S PROBABLY STILL ASLEEP.
HUH?
KOTOHA?!
Ah.
NO WAY. WE'VE BEEN TOGETHER EVER SINCE I CAME TO THIS WORLD. IT'S PROBABLY MY IMAGINATION ...
Mas-ter...
HUH ?!
MAS-TER ARATA !
IT IS HER !!

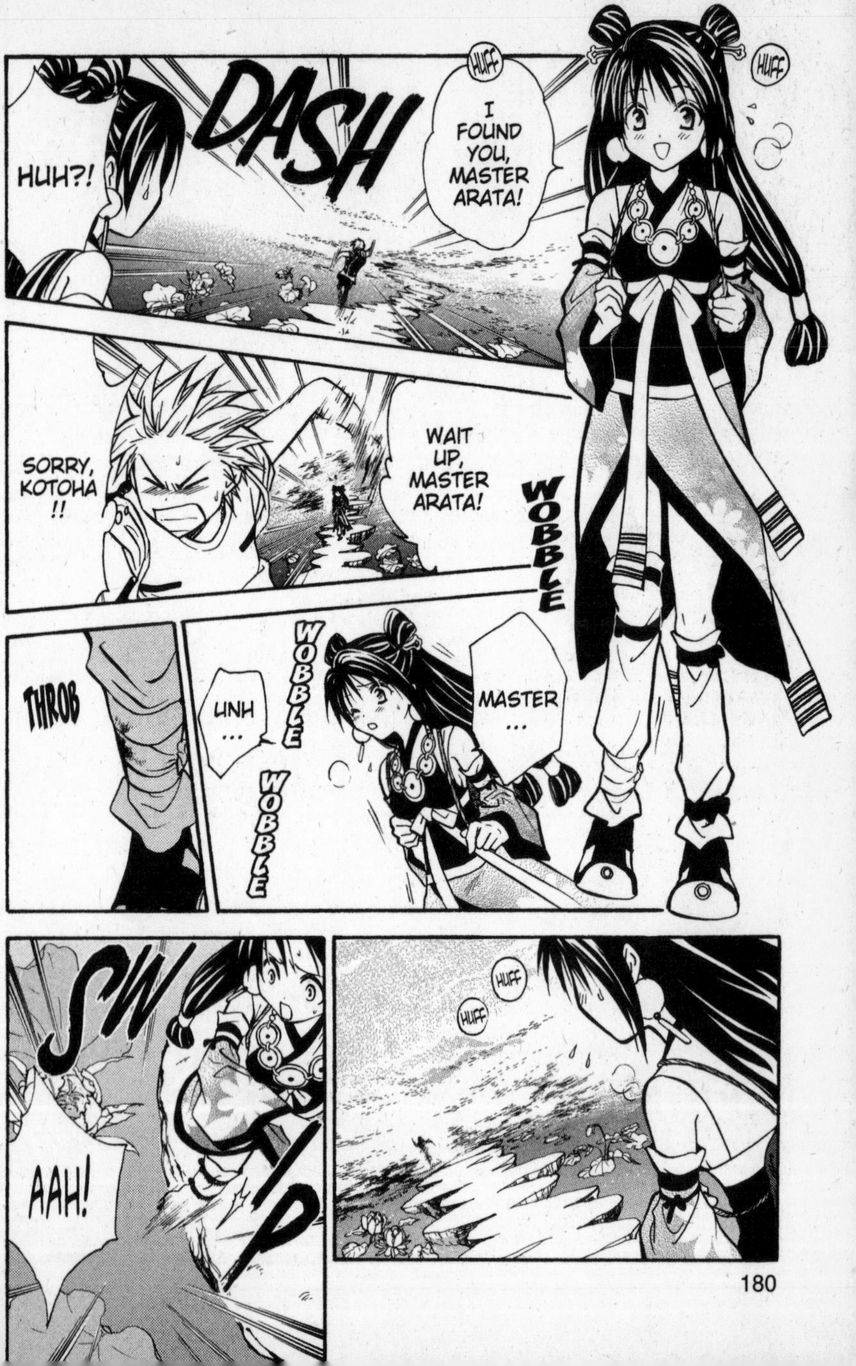
HUFF
I FOUND YOU, MASTER ARATA!
HUFF
DASH
HUH?!
WOBBLE
WAIT UP, MASTER ARATA!
SORRY, KOTOHA!!
MASTER...
WOBBLE
UNH...
WOBBLE
THROB
HUFF
HUFF
SWIP
AAH!

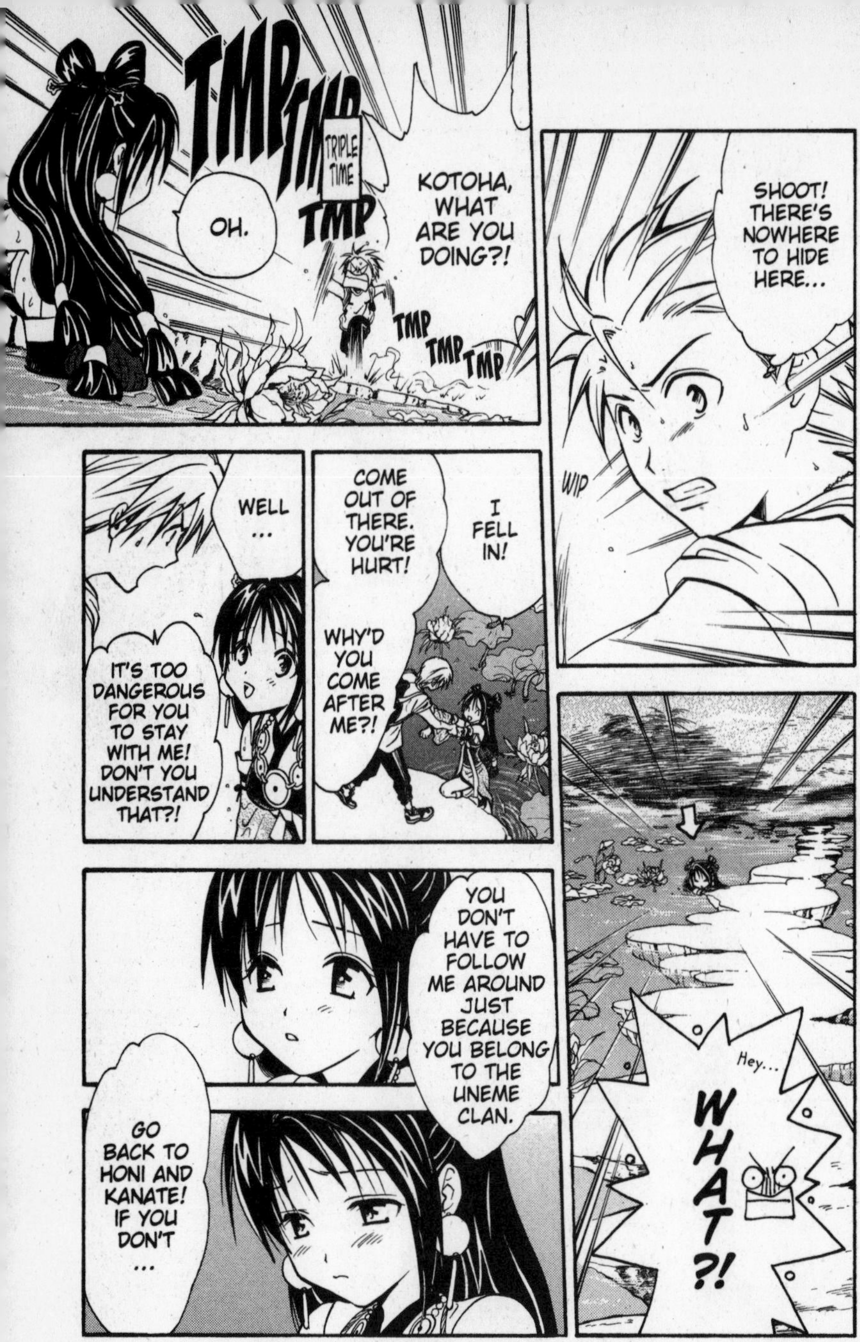
SHOOT! THERE'S NOWHERE TO HIDE HERE...
WIP
Hey...
WHAT?!
KOTOHA, WHAT ARE YOU DOING?!
TMP TMP TMP
TRIPLE TIME
TMP TMP TMP
OH.
I FELL IN!
COME OUT OF THERE. YOU'RE HURT!
WHY'D YOU COME AFTER ME?!
WELL...
IT'S TOO DANGEROUS FOR YOU TO STAY WITH ME! DON'T YOU UNDERSTAND THAT?!
YOU DON'T HAVE TO FOLLOW ME AROUND JUST BECAUSE YOU BELONG TO THE UNEME CLAN.
GO BACK TO HONI AND KANATE! IF YOU DON'T...

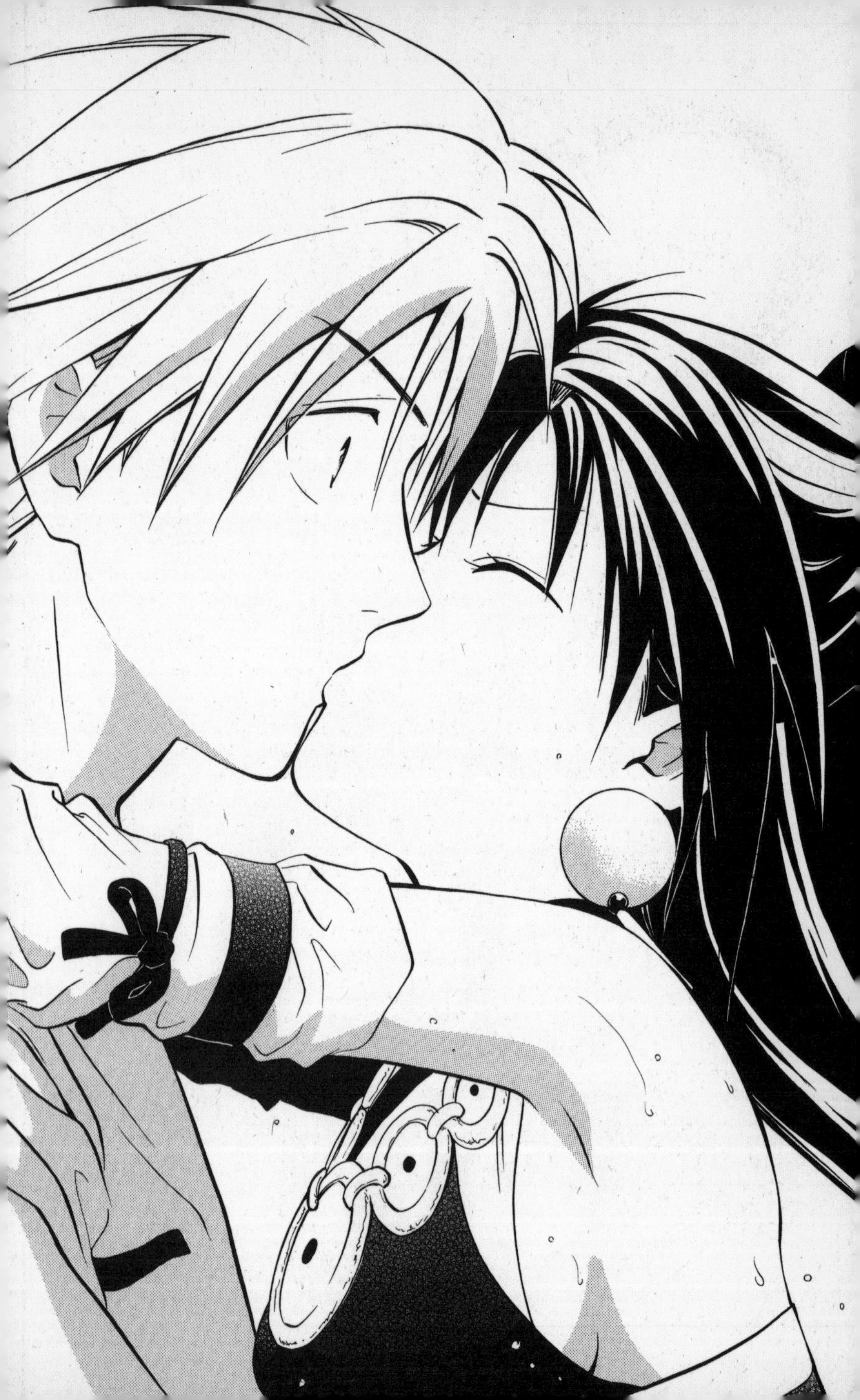

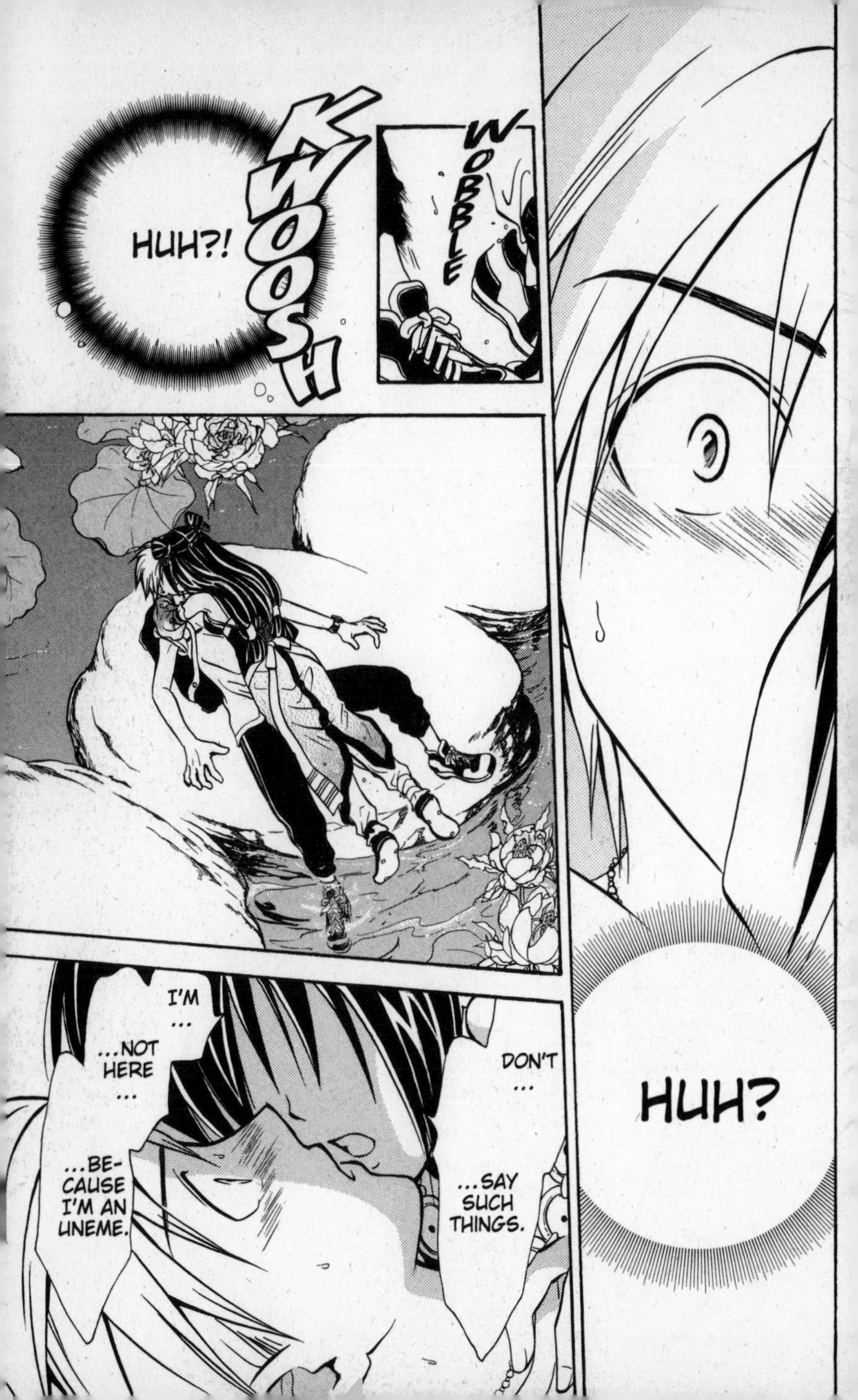
HUH?
WOBBLE
HUH?!
KWOOSH
DON'T ...
...SAY SUCH THINGS.
I'M ...
...NOT HERE ...
...BE-CAUSE I'M AN UNEME.

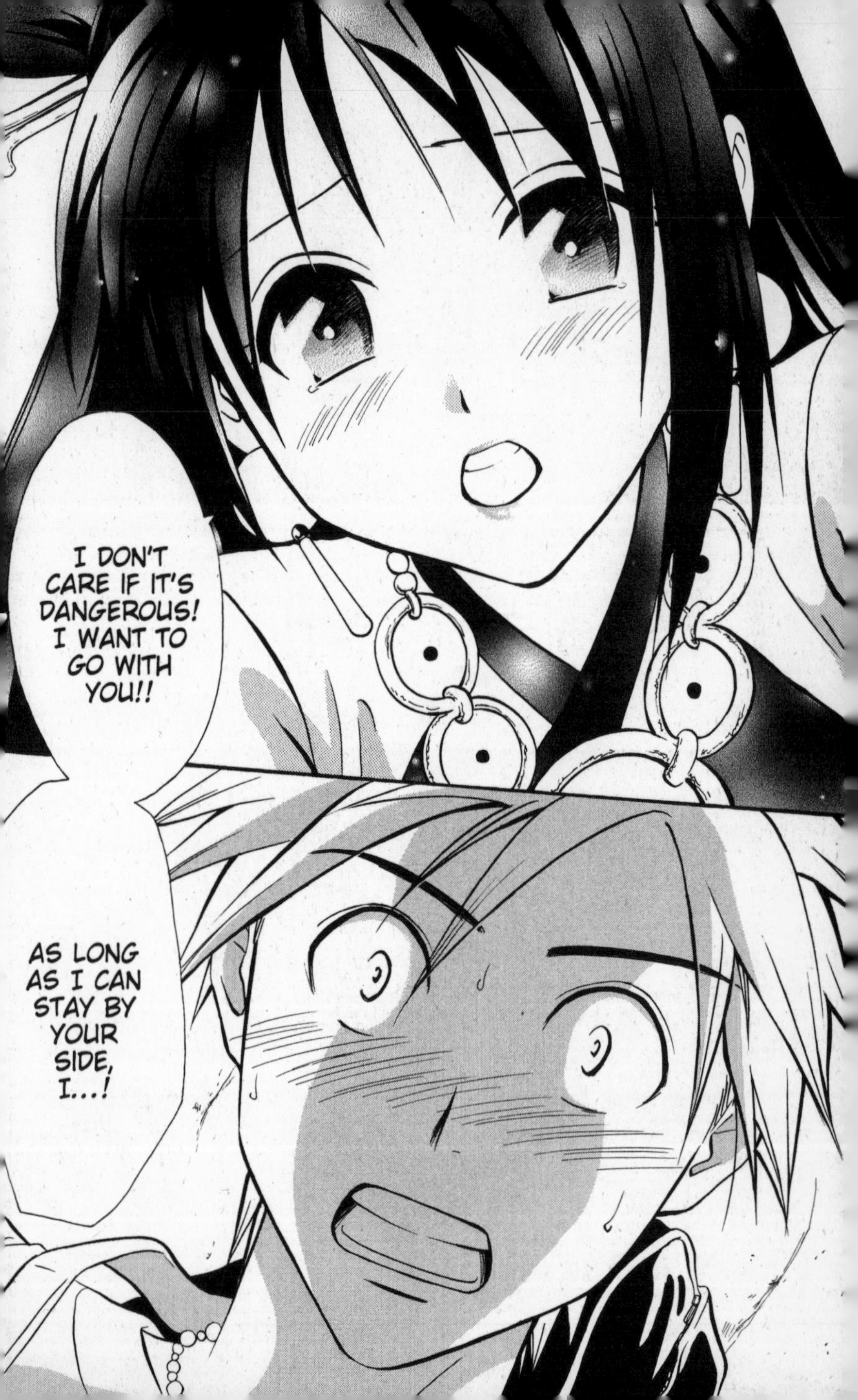
I DON'T CARE IF IT'S DANGEROUS! I WANT TO GO WITH YOU!!
AS LONG AS I CAN STAY BY YOUR SIDE, I...!

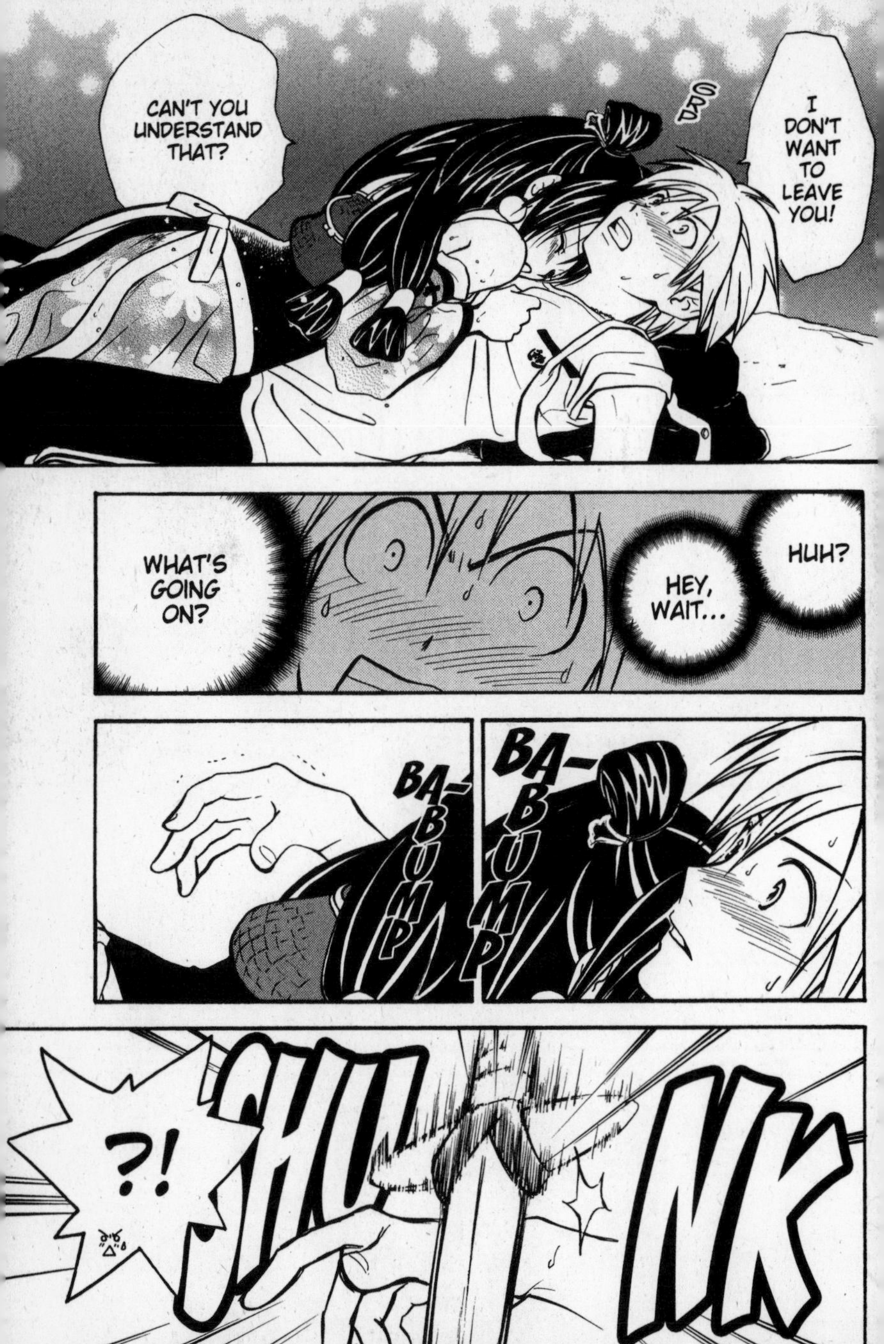

I DON'T WANT TO LEAVE YOU!
GRP
CAN'T YOU UNDERSTAND THAT?
HUH?
HEY, WAIT...
WHAT'S GOING ON?
BA-BUMP
BA-BUMP
CHUNK
?!

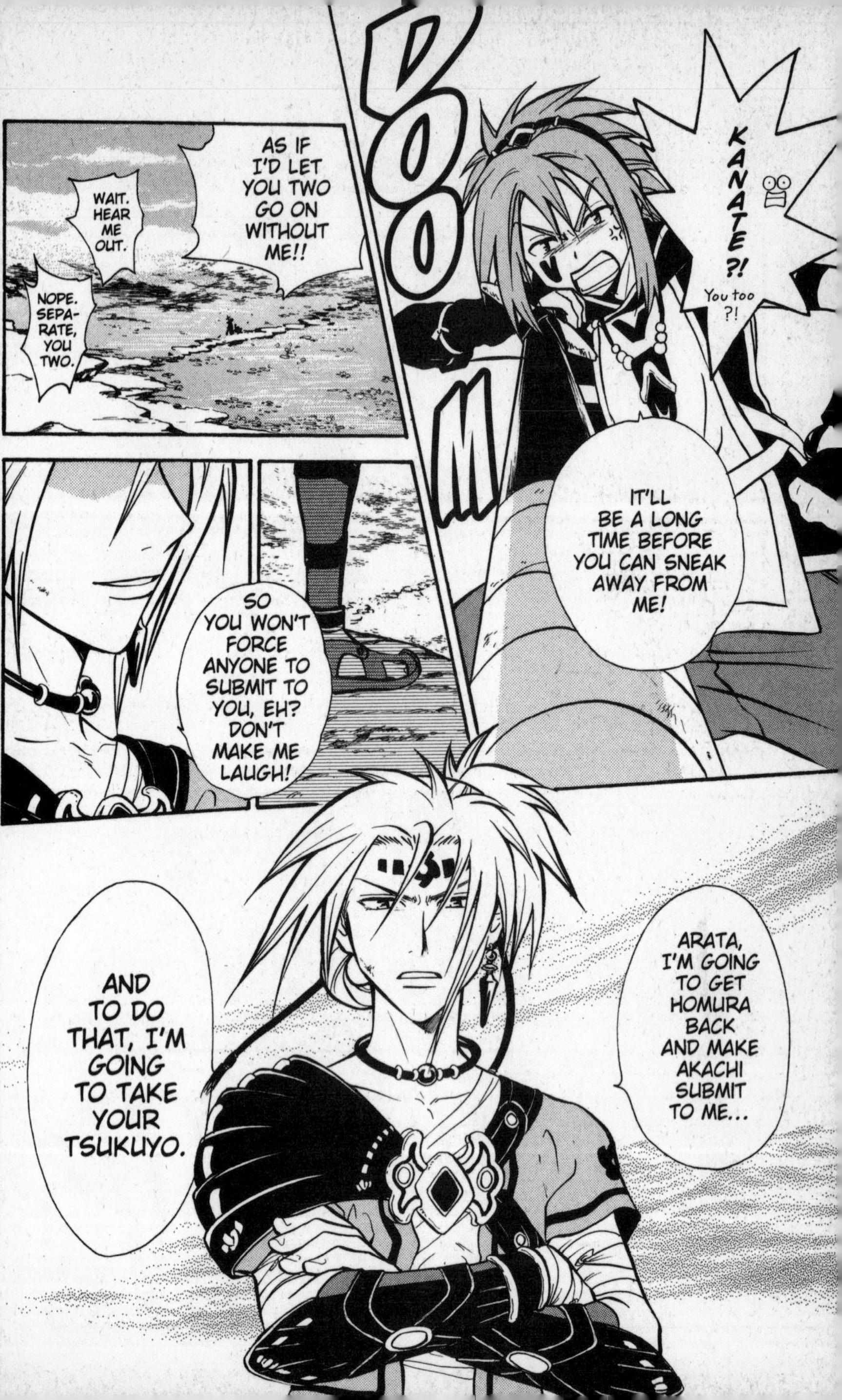
DOOM
KANATE?!
You too ?!
IT'LL BE A LONG TIME BEFORE YOU CAN SNEAK AWAY FROM ME!
AS IF I'D LET YOU TWO GO ON WITHOUT ME!!
WAIT. HEAR ME OUT.
NOPE. SEPA-RATE, YOU TWO.
SO YOU WON'T FORCE ANYONE TO SUBMIT TO YOU, EH? DON'T MAKE ME LAUGH!
ARATA, I'M GOING TO GET HOMURA BACK AND MAKE AKACHI SUBMIT TO ME...
AND TO DO THAT, I'M GOING TO TAKE YOUR TSUKUYO.

MEAT.

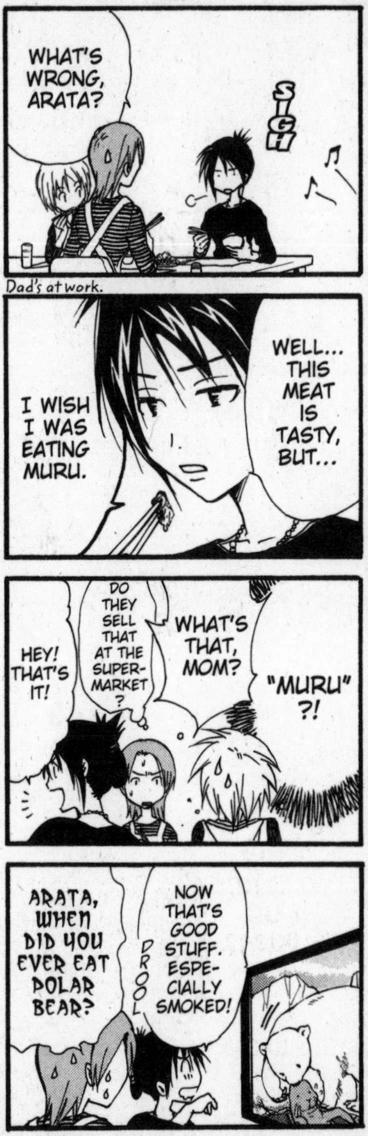
WHAT'S WRONG, ARATA?
SIGH
Dad's at work.
WELL... THIS MEAT IS TASTY, BUT...
I WISH I WAS EATING MURU.
"MURU"?!
WHAT'S THAT, MOM?
DO THEY SELL THAT AT THE SUPER-MARKET?
HEY! THAT'S IT!
NOW THAT'S GOOD STUFF. ESPE-CIALLY SMOKED!
DROOL
ARATA, WHEN DID YOU EVER EAT POLAR BEAR?

AH, THAT MEAT.

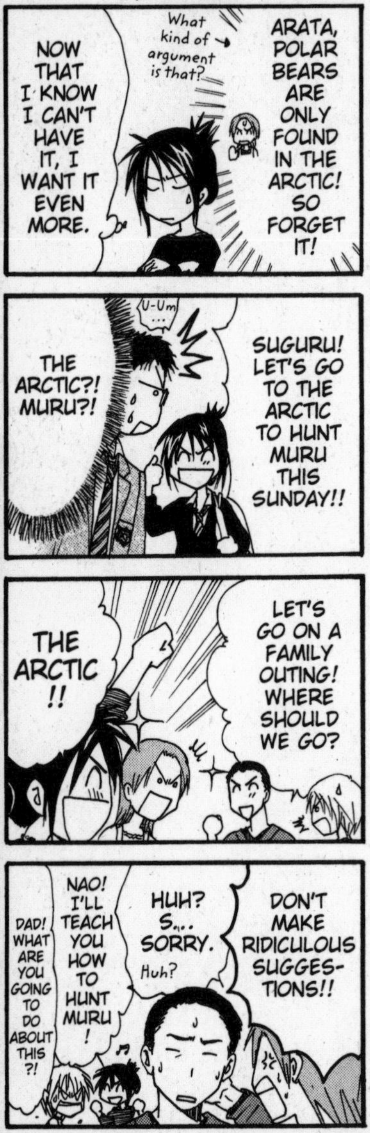
ARATA, POLAR BEARS ARE ONLY FOUND IN THE ARCTIC! SO FORGET IT!
What kind of argument is that?
NOW THAT I KNOW I CAN'T HAVE IT, I WANT IT EVEN MORE.
SUGURU! LET'S GO TO THE ARCTIC TO HUNT MURU THIS SUNDAY!!
U-Um...
THE ARCTIC?! MURU?!
LET'S GO ON A FAMILY OUTING! WHERE SHOULD WE GO?
THE ARCTIC!!
DON'T MAKE RIDICULOUS SUGGES-TIONS!!
HUH? S... SORRY.
Huh?
NAO! I'LL TEACH YOU HOW TO HUNT MURU!
DAD! WHAT ARE YOU GOING TO DO ABOUT THIS?!

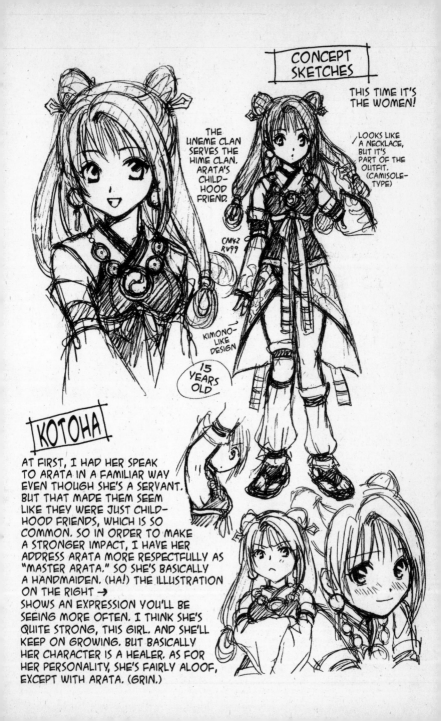

CONCEPT SKETCHES

THIS TIME IT'S THE WOMEN!

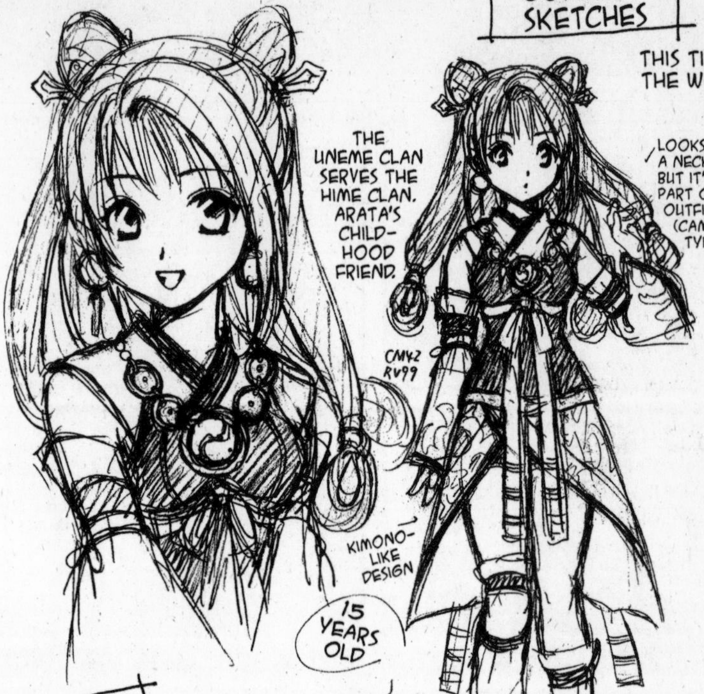

THE UNEME CLAN SERVES THE HIME CLAN. ARATA'S CHILDHOOD FRIEND.
LOOKS LIKE A NECKLACE, BUT IT'S PART OF THE OUTFIT. (CAMISOLE-TYPE)
CM42 RV99
KIMONO-LIKE DESIGN
15 YEARS OLD

KOTOHA

AT FIRST, I HAD HER SPEAK TO ARATA IN A FAMILIAR WAY EVEN THOUGH SHE'S A SERVANT. BUT THAT MADE THEM SEEM LIKE THEY WERE JUST CHILDHOOD FRIENDS, WHICH IS SO COMMON. SO IN ORDER TO MAKE A STRONGER IMPACT, I HAVE HER ADDRESS ARATA MORE RESPECTFULLY AS "MASTER ARATA." SO SHE'S BASICALLY A HANDMAIDEN. (HA!) THE ILLUSTRATION ON THE RIGHT →
SHOWS AN EXPRESSION YOU'LL BE SEEING MORE OFTEN. I THINK SHE'S QUITE STRONG, THIS GIRL. AND SHE'LL KEEP ON GROWING. BUT BASICALLY HER CHARACTER IS A HEALER. AS FOR HER PERSONALITY, SHE'S FAIRLY ALOOF, EXCEPT WITH ARATA. (GRIN.)

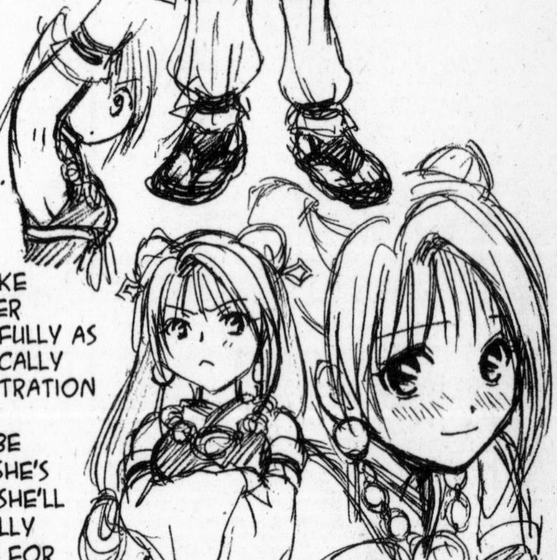

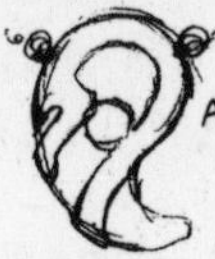

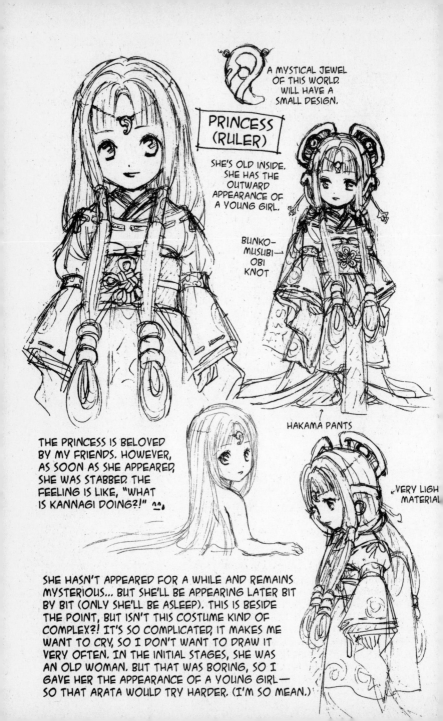

A MYSTICAL JEWEL OF THIS WORLD. WILL HAVE A SMALL DESIGN.

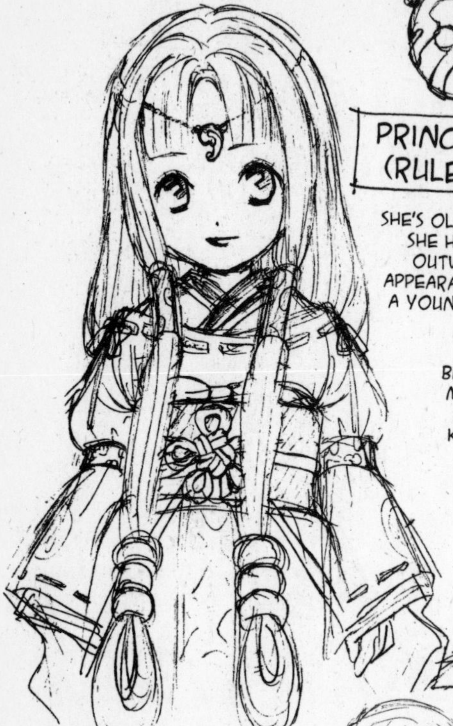

PRINCESS (RULER)

SHE'S OLD INSIDE. SHE HAS THE OUTWARD APPEARANCE OF A YOUNG GIRL.

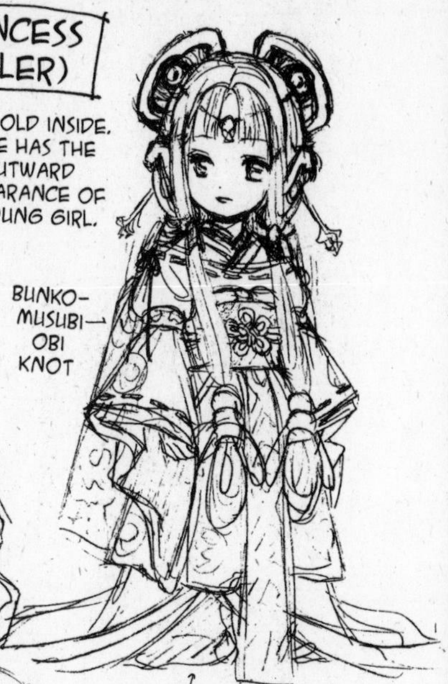

BUNKO-MUSUBI OBI KNOT
HAKAMA PANTS

THE PRINCESS IS BELOVED BY MY FRIENDS. HOWEVER, AS SOON AS SHE APPEARED, SHE WAS STABBED. THE FEELING IS LIKE, "WHAT IS KANNAGI DOING?!" ^^;

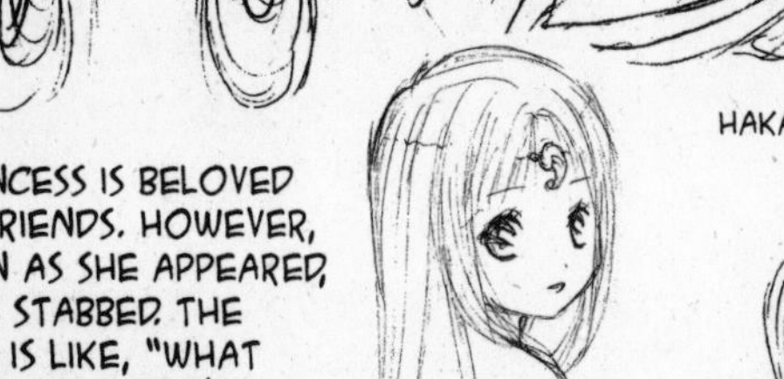

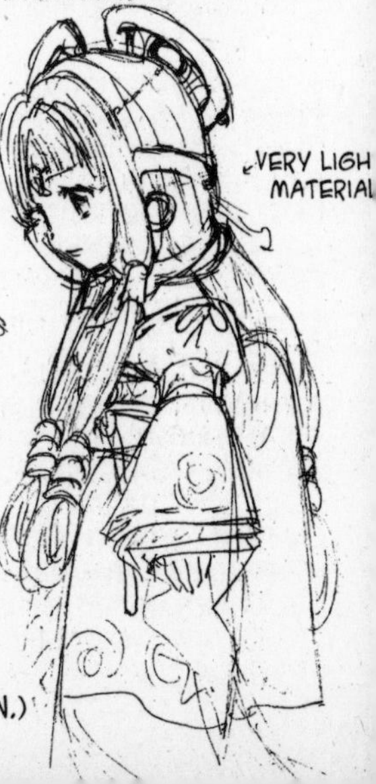

VERY LIGH
MATERIAL

SHE HASN'T APPEARED FOR A WHILE AND REMAINS MYSTERIOUS... BUT SHE'LL BE APPEARING LATER BIT BY BIT (ONLY SHE'LL BE ASLEEP). THIS IS BESIDE THE POINT, BUT ISN'T THIS COSTUME KIND OF COMPLEX?! IT'S SO COMPLICATED, IT MAKES ME WANT TO CRY, SO I DON'T WANT TO DRAW IT VERY OFTEN. IN THE INITIAL STAGES, SHE WAS AN OLD WOMAN. BUT THAT WAS BORING, SO I GAVE HER THE APPEARANCE OF A YOUNG GIRL—SO THAT ARATA WOULD TRY HARDER. (I'M SO MEAN.)

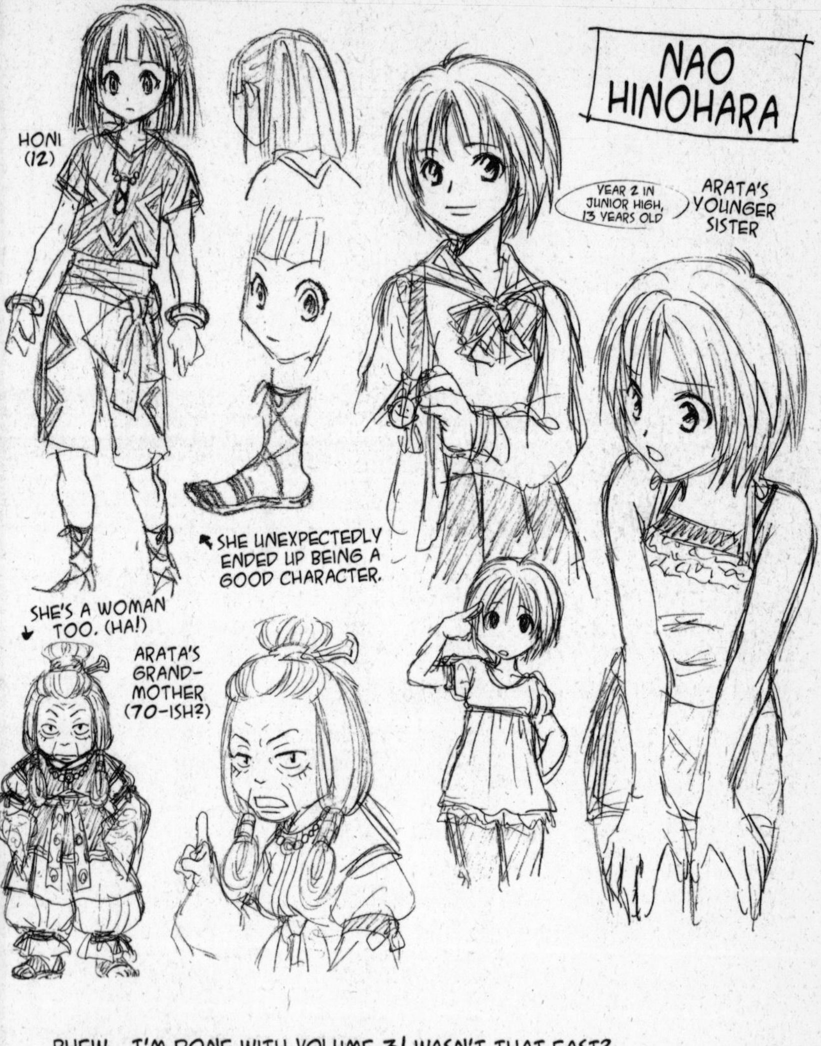
NAO HINOHARA
YEAR 2 IN JUNIOR HIGH, 13 YEARS OLD
ARATA'S YOUNGER SISTER
HONI (12)
SHE UNEXPECTEDLY ENDED UP BEING A GOOD CHARACTER.
SHE'S A WOMAN TOO. (HA!)
ARATA'S GRAND-MOTHER (70-ISH?)

PHEW... I'M DONE WITH VOLUME 3! WASN'T THAT FAST? THINGS HAPPENED SO QUICKLY... THE NAME OF ARATA'S HAYAGAMI IS FINALLY REVEALED. I DIDN'T MAKE IT KNOWN FROM THE START IN ORDER TO REFLECT ARATA'S INNER TRANSFORMATION. I COULDN'T HAVE HIM GOING AROUND WITH "THE LEGENDARY _____" FROM THE BEGINNING, COULD I? HE WAS DEPRESSED TOO... WHAT'S REALLY AMAZING ISN'T THE OBJECT HE WIELDS BUT HIS HUMANITY. BY THE WAY, I HAD A HARD TIME COMING UP WITH THE NAMES. (HEE.) OKAY, SEE YOU IN VOLUME 4!

About *Arata Kangatari*, the Japanese title of this story...

I was determined to have the main character's name be in the title, but at first I couldn't decide on a name. Finally I thought, "What the heck. Just go with *Arata*." (^ ^;) But my assistant said, "That's so weak!" (Ha!) Then I saw the word *kangatari* (god story) in a book, and that got a good response. The majority ruled, and the title was written in katakana to make it look like a spell. It's okay to shorten it to *Arakan* though.

Kangatari can be interpreted as *monogatari* (tale). Titles are always hard to come up with, but when there are three of us, we eventually come up with something good. Thank you, assistants!

–Yuu Watase

AUTHOR BIO

Born March 5 in Osaka, Yuu Watase debuted in the *Shôjo Comic* manga anthology in 1989. She won the 43rd Shogakukan Manga Award with *Ceres: Celestial Legend*. One of her most famous works is *Fushigi Yûgi*, a series that has inspired the prequel *Fushigi Yûgi: Genbu Kaiden*. In 2008, *Arata: The Legend* started serialization in *Shonen Sunday*.

ARATA: THE LEGEND

Volume 3

Shonen Sunday Edition

Story and Art by YUU WATASE

© 2009 Yuu WATASE/Shogakukan

All rights reserved.

Original Japanese edition "ARATAKANGATARI"
published by SHOGAKUKAN Inc.

English Adaptation: Lance Caselman

Translation: JN Productions

Touch-up Art & Lettering: Rina Mapa

Design: Frances O. Liddell

Editor: Amy Yu

Printed in the U.S.A.

Published by VIZ Media, LLC.

P.O. Box 77010

San Francisco, CA 94107

10 9 8 7 6 5 4 3 2 1

First printing, September 2010

www.viz.com

WWW.SHONENSUNDAY.COM